C0-AZG-795

Treasure Under the Sea

Treasure
Under the Sea

N. B. Stirling

LATROBE HIGH SCHOOL LIBRARY

Doubleday & Company, Inc.

Garden City, New York

1957

Library of Congress Catalog Card Number 57–11440

Copyright © 1957 by N. B. Stirling
Copyright 1956 by Fawcett Publications, Inc.
Copyright 1956 by Popular Publications, Inc.
All Rights Reserved
Printed in the United States of America
First Edition

To My Mother

FOREWORD

The assistance of many people was indispensable in the writing of this book. Elsewhere I have named some who helped on individual chapters, but there were a few, notably Hope H. Hollingshead and Beth and Harold Proom, who contributed generously to the whole, and to them go my very special thanks.

I should also like to acknowledge the invaluable service rendered researchers by the New York Public Library, which provides a Typing Room where writers may work directly from out-of-print publications otherwise unobtainable.

My deepest gratitude, however, goes to the man without whom, in a quite literal sense, this book could not have been written. It was the late Waldemar Kaempffert, Science Editor of the New York *Times*, who originally suggested that I do it, and from then on he gave his help and encouragement with the gracious generosity so familiar to all of his friends.

CONTENTS

Treasure Under the Sea

A book about sunken treasure of necessity begins in the sixteenth century. However, in discussing sixteenth-century money it must be remembered that, while we know gold and silver had a value vastly beyond that of today, an exact comparison of these values is almost impossible to arrive at owing to the scarcity of early records and statistics. The most reliable authority seems to be that magnificent historian, William Prescott, on whose books much of this chapter is based, who quoted the peso de oro of 1550 as having a buying power equal to $11.67 in the money of 1850. In its turn the 1850 money had a buying power four times as great as has that of 1957. Therefore one 1550 peso de oro is worth four times $11.67, or $46.68 of our money; and if the reader will thus translate all sums occurring in this chapter (e.g., "One thousand pesos de oro equals $46,680") he will gain a more accurate idea of what the early Spaniards and Portuguese actually found in Peru and Mexico.

Likewise, though money through the centuries has progressively "cheapened," William Phips' seventeenth-century treasure was at least five times greater than it sounds.

I

Treasure on
a Grand Scale

UNTIL THE DISCOVERY of the New World the continent of Europe
was so poor that most of the inhabitants had never owned a piece
of either silver or gold. In actual money there existed less than a
shilling for each of the ninety millions, and even this was largely
gathered into a few royal and aristocratic hands, while much of the
population lived by barter alone—a piece of land for a cow, a week's
wood chopping for a pair of shoes.

This situation had remained unchanged for five or six hundred
years, for although the mines of Europe had been steadily producing a trickle of precious ores, the Rajahs of the Orient had been as
steadily drawing them off, collecting metals and gems like squirrels,
burying them in vaults or turning them into personal adornment.
The churches had attracted much of the rest, gold going into crosses
and shrines, silver into chalices, censers, pyxes, gems into bindings
of psalteries. By the fifteenth century the precious metals had become so scarce, and each nation so jealous of its little store, that
any man found transporting any out of the country was immediately hanged, his body drawn and cut into quarters, and the pieces
displayed at the four corners of the city as a warning.

Then, in the next century, Spain and Portugal overnight became
rich beyond human imagining, and history, which had been jog-
ging along sluggishly for centuries, charged headlong into action.

The direction taken by events was determined largely by the sale of a set of Antwerp tapestries. Christopher Columbus, having been seized with the idea of sailing westward to India rather than by the long eastern route, had taken his project first to the King of Portugal. But that King had recently had his fingers burned in an exploration scheme in Africa, and was fighting shy of men with schemes, so Christopher sent his brother Bartholomew to Henry VII of England. Henry had put aside a certain sum for the decoration of his residence at Hampton Court. England was in a deep depression and this was all he had, and since Antwerp tapestries were a solid investment while this other project was the wildest gamble, he took the wall coverings and let the new route to the Indies go. Columbus then turned to Ferdinand and Isabella; and thus, through the whim of a man without imagination, Spain instead of England became the richest and most powerful nation in Europe.

Columbus, of course, had been seeking not Indian gold but Indian spices, for so monotonous and unappetizing was the food of Europe that anything offering change was almost without price. There was not a potato on the Continent, only two or three kinds of fruit, few vegetables save cabbages, onions, and leeks. Sugar was scarce and prohibitively expensive, while no one had ever seen tea or chocolate or coffee. If meat was not eaten immediately it had to be salted to save it from rot and worms, and since this was not always feasible meals were often eaten with one hand holding a spoon and the other the nose. But spices disguised this taste of putrefaction, and when it was discovered that there might be a shorter way to the rich Spice Islands of the East restlessness began to boil up in every ambitious soul and nothing could hold the fortune seekers at home.

In 1493, Pope Alexander VI had assigned to Spain exploration rights everywhere west of the 60th longitude, with Portugal getting everything to the east, and thus the teeming west coast of South America and all of Mexico and the West Indian Islands became the property of Ferdinand and Isabella, along with a fifth of all revenues therefrom—the "royal fifths." And when the new lands were found to be rich not in pepper and cloves but in silver and gold, the streets of Seville were emptied of young men, for everyone who could crawl was in the New World.

It was the explorer Columbus who brought back to the Old World the first news of these wealthy virgin lands, but it was the conquistadors, following immediately thereafter, who raped them and sent back home their floods of wealth to dislocate European life, unhinge its good sense, and set every country at every other country's throat. Not ten years after Columbus' first landing came Vasco Núñez de Balboa, lighthearted, bold, and proud like most of his compatriots, but, unlike some of them, chivalrous. He had fancied the life of a planter on the rich soil of Hispaniola, but, being a better fighter than farmer, had soon found himself swamped with debts and to escape them had himself sealed into a cask and shipped as wine to Darien on the Isthmus of Panama. There he became the leader of a Spanish colony who had come to spread the rule of Spain and Christendom and to do well for themselves at the same time, among whom was Francisco Pizarro, already near middle age but destined to be the greatest of them all.

To Balboa fell the distinction of being the first white man to learn of the riches to the south. He had led his company of 190 men in many raids against the natives of Panama, but by his conduct had made friends of them instead of enemies. He and his companions were astonished by the lavishness of the golden ornaments the savages wore and by the smiling carelessness with which they gave them away. The Indians in their turn watched in astonishment while Balboa dropped each gleaming piece onto the scales before dividing them up among his friends, and at last the young chieftain Comogre laughed aloud in incredulity.

Knocking the scales aside with the back of his hand, he sent a shower of nuggets and gold dust across the room. "*This* is worth so much to you?" he laughed. "Why, I can tell you of a country where they eat and drink from dishes of this stuff. It is as cheap as"—he pointed to the steel of a pike head—"as cheap as that is with you."

This was the first time any white man had ever heard of the Peruvian gold.

Comogre told Balboa also of a sea beyond the mountains so vast no one had ever seen its farther shore, and this was the first time any white man ever heard of the Pacific.

Since reports ran that the wealthy land lay toward the west and south, Balboa and his men, in heavy quilted doublets under thirty pounds of steel armor, with the tropical sun beating down on their helmets, marched up over the mountainous spine of the Isthmus and down on the other side. And there, on the twenty-ninth day of September, 1513, in the Bay of Panama, Balboa took possession of the Pacific.

Holding high his sword, he strode out into the water. "In the name of St. Iago," he shouted to the wind and the waves, "I do declare that this great South Sea, however far she may reach, and all the lands bordering upon her not already taken by another, together with all the islands within her shores, are now and forever the domain of His Catholic Majesty Ferdinand." There was no one present to dispute his claim, and for several hundred years his successors managed to make a good part of it stick.

Balboa's career was short, and by that the world was the loser. He incurred the jealousy of a man more powerful than he and less decent, and was thrown into prison; under the convenient charge of treason, which like a chameleon could be made to match anything it was laid upon, he was sentenced to death, and four years after his discovery of the Pacific this most humane of the conquistadors lost his head on the block. Had he instead of his lieutenant Pizarro been the conqueror of Peru, the name of the conquistadors would have smelled better down the centuries.

At this same time, history having taken on its uncontrolled burst of speed, violent men were breaking out in many directions. Hernando Cortés, another of the invincibles, landed at Vera Cruz in Mexico in 1519. Shrewd, cruel, and bold, along with his personal greed he cherished a fierce desire to spread the Christian gospel no matter how great the resistance. But his enthusiasm was not always shared by his men; they were, in fact, on the point of backing out as soon as they landed and saw the conditions they faced, so he calmly burned the ships they had come in and left his reluctant cavaliers nothing to do but march forward, steaming and footsore, upon Mexico City.

Mexico at that time was ruled by Montezuma, most famous of the Aztec princes. The Aztecs were a fiery people, constantly at war with the other tribes around them, and Montezuma, brilliant warrior, builder, priest, and engineer, had brought them to the peak of their glory. Cortés, advancing across Mexico, learned of the tribal wars and shrewdly allied himself with the strongest of Montezuma's enemies, marching with them against the city. The Aztecs fought the invaders off fiercely, undismayed, but suddenly, to their bewilderment, their leader gave in without a struggle, routed by nothing more than the color of the Spaniard's skin.

An ancient prophecy had laid it all out beforehand: tradition said that a god with white skin (the Indians were a dark warm bronze) would appear one day from the East and overthrow the present Mexican ruler. Cortés was white and his armor glinted in true godlike fashion, and so, believing himself doomed, Montezuma supinely permitted himself to be taken prisoner and in a few days, from no apparent cause, meekly expired. Cortés became ruler of Mexico.

Under the new Spanish regime the gold mines of Tehuantepec and the silver mines of Zacatecas poured their royal fifths into Ferdinand's Casa de Contratacion at Seville, and after him his successors continued to receive them for a hundred years and more.

The raid initiated by Balboa and carried on by Cortés swept to a glittering climax under Pizarro, Balboa's lieutenant and Cortés' cousin. Coarse, brutal, and ignorant even of reading and writing, Pizarro was handsome in a sinister fashion, with eyes large and dark and calculating, and mustache curved down in a semi-circle over the jutting under lip to mingle with a short pointed beard. He was now fifty years old, but during the next fifteen years, with a body as strong and elastic as a steel spring, he was to survive conditions beyond the endurance of ordinary humans, and through his own courage and self-confidence inspire others to similar feats.

His birth, being illegitimate, went unrecorded, but it was probably at Estremadura in 1471, his parents a colonel of infantry and a certain Francisca Gonzales. The colonel's family was somewhat casually thrown together, one son, Hernando, the legitimate offspring of the colonel and his wife; three other sons, Francisco, Juan, and Gonzalo, by Francisca; and a poor little hanger-on, Martin de Alcantara, Francisca's son by some other man. Francisco left home —or was thrown out—when he was still a child, earning his keep as a swineherd for some years, but by the time he was grown Columbus had returned from his first voyage bringing tales to make a restless young man's eyes pop, and Francisco's destiny was decided. After some preliminary excursions he joined Balboa in Panama.

Following Balboa's execution he spent eight or nine more years in Panama listening to the talk about the country to the south and about El Hombre Dorado, the fabled king who each morning was anointed with aromatic oils and then dusted with particles of gold till he glittered like the sun itself. This country of El Dorado drew men's thoughts like a magnet, but all those who tried to sail there were forced back by the inhospitable sea, and those who tried to march were blocked by the immense Andes. In 1522, however, Pizarro found two men, Diego de Almagro and Hernando de Luque, who were willing to finance an attempt to force a passage.

Inspired by the tales of temples covered with gold and studded with emeralds like birds' eggs, and spurred on by the recent rich victories of Cortés in Mexico, a hundred assorted ruffians joined him in a co-operative venture held together solely by the common appetite for gold and glory. Each man supplied his own equipment, the wealthier bringing a horse and suit of armor in addition to the indispensable helmet, sword and crossbow, and the others, the mere scum, making do with their own feet and a covering of stuffed cotton reaching to the knees.

After two years of preparation the men set out in two small boats, jaunty in their own vast ignorance of what they were attempting. But soon they had a glimpse of their future. Going ashore at an Indian village some miles down the coast, they found that the inhabitants, vanishing at their approach, had left behind many gold ornaments, which was pleasant and reassuring. But they had also left their meal roasting before a fire—human flesh, and the men rushed back to their boats with their stomachs turning over, hastily running down the coast in search of a friendlier shore.

Friendliness was the last thing these shores offered, however, the jungles along their edge repulsing them with an impenetrable density no Spaniard had ever seen before. Laced almost solid by creepers, the trees were matted together overhead in an eternal dusk, and every step forward was an individual adventure, for alligators lay in the swamps, all but their eyes and snouts submerged, and boa constrictors clung like bloated vines along the branches. Indians, vanishing silently at the first sight of the white men, lurked at a distance and cut off any solitary stragglers, Pizarro himself being wounded seven times in these cut-and-run encounters.

The distant scenery was no friendlier than that close at hand. The peaks of the Andes, which ran like a chain parallel with the shore, rose in successive waves ever higher and whiter and were finally lost in the clouds, a solid silver curtain that dropped down out of heaven and merged with earth. Pizarro glared at this barrier resentfully, for behind it lay the cities of gold.

One of his first acts had been to capture a young Indian, who soon learned Castilian and became indispensable as an interpreter, and it was through this Felipillo the invaders learned particulars of the place whither they were going and of the man who ruled it.

The kingdom of Peru lay south of Quito, the country where they had now come ashore to rest and plan. The rulers of the two countries, both sons of the late Emperor, had recently been warring over the succession, and Atahuallpa, having defeated Huascar, was now occupied in consolidating the two kingdoms. Known as the Inca, Atahuallpa was a monarch more absolute than any European ruler had ever been, with power not only of life and death but ownership of every acre, every ounce of goods, and every stick of forest. Handsome and fierce, he was reported to be an invincible leader, cruel in war and merciless in revenge. His official residence was the holy city of Cuzco, but at this moment he was taking the baths in the mountain city of Caxamalca, surrounded by ten thousand picked troops, while the rest of his two hundred thousand warriors were spread the length of Quito and Peru guarding the two kingdoms. It was an awesome prospect for Pizarro and his men.

When Felipillo had described the country to the south, many of the Spaniards were all for turning back, for the voyage had already proved rugged beyond their worst nightmares. Their armor by now was rusted, their clothes were torn from their bodies, and starvation was sapping their strength for, attempting to live off the land, they might eat but an ear or two of corn all day. Accidents had taken many lives, and then malaria, the great killer, had followed on, so that, shivering and sweating, a miserable half of his original force huddled on a damp beach, swearing at Peru and at Pizarro, who had brought them there.

Several times along the way Pizarro had had to send back the ships to Panama to beg more supplies and men; then he would push south again, sharing every hardship and insistently reminding the men of the temples and palaces of gold just ahead. But at last he realized they were near mutiny. Some of them were on the point of seizing the ships and sailing home.

Now, grasping the initiative like a threatening sword, he turned it back upon his adversaries. Pretending to see nothing of the disaffection, he landed the entire company on a desert island. Then selecting the few men he knew he could trust not to desert him, he suddenly ordered these few back to Panama with all the ships, before they sailed even confiscating the letters the others were sending back, for he had no intention that Panama should hear of his failure.

So there the fifty trapped men sat, hating Pizarro for the trick he had played and for his uncrushable optimism, and infuriated that in addition he had sent back the little gold they had found as a bait for further volunteers. Their clothing no longer covered them, and mosquitoes swarmed about in such clouds that many times they were driven to burying themselves up to their faces in the sand. Wild potatoes and coconuts and the crabs that scuttled along the beach were their only sustenance.

Then, after many dreary weeks a ship appeared bringing not volunteers but orders to return to Panama. Though Pizarro had intercepted the packet of letters, one soldier had hidden a note in a ball of cotton and it had reached the Governor's wife. The shocked Governor had sent the ship back for all the men still alive, and most of them were glad of the order, for now they could retreat without losing face.

Confronted, it seemed, with inescapable frustration, Pizarro stood on the beach facing a ring of sullen, resentful men and wondered if he could hold them. On the next few minutes, he knew, depended his whole future and the two things he most desired. Glory was one of them; unlike Christopher Columbus, who had come to the New World sponsored by the King and Queen and thus had a smattering of glory to begin with, Pizarro was on his own. But he knew that the royal eyes at Castile were watching him, and he too dreamed of kneeling in velvet at the court in Cádiz. He might even win a title and a coat of arms (the circumstances of his birth carefully overlooked, of course.)

The other thing he cared about, gold, would buy him the royal favor in exact ratio to the number of royal fifths dispatched. Thus he was eager to begin the dispatch, deducting the fifths even before his own share of the spoils was counted; but first of all he must reach his destination and subdue the golden land, and even his full fifty men were hardly a match for an empire.

Fifty men he did not have, either; how many were with him, if any, he did not know. They stood watching sulkily while he strode across the beach to the water's edge. His quilted doublet was briny with three months' dirt and sweat, his helmet was rusty and dented, and above the matted black beard his cheeks were hollowed out by hunger. But defiance blazed in his eyes as with his sword he slashed a line in the sand parallel with the equator and, straightening up, glared at the ring before him.

"Now choose. On this side of the line"—he flung his arm toward the south—"you will find starvation and nakedness and suffering. If you come with me you will rot in the rains and freeze in the snow, some will be eaten by cannibals, many will never see Castile again." Boldly he stared down their wavering glances. "But the ones who survive will go back richer than any man who ever lived. This is one choice. On the other side"—he waved a contemptuous arm toward the north—"is safety. Back in Panama there will be peace and obscurity and finally death in bed." His eyes ran challengingly along the thin faces. "So choose. For me"—with one stride he placed himself a yard to the south of the line—"there *is* no choice." He waited, his black eyes narrow.

Bartholomew Ruiz, the man who had piloted their ship through many a storm, stepped across. He was followed by Pedro de Candia. Eleven others crossed the line, and then there was a pause. With Pizarro the company stood at fourteen.

This was the force that undertook to conquer an empire of eight million people.

When the deserters had sailed away, the rest settled down on a small island to spend more months in waiting. Pizarro had sent back a message to Luque and Almagro demanding supplies and volunteers with stouter hearts, and for seven interminable months he and the thirteen others waited for them. At last they arrived, but even that was not the end of the delays. Not only did Pizarro have to sail farther down the coast to get the lay of the land, he even had to expend many months on a trip all the way back to Spain, where he finally won from Charles V a royal charter to explore, on the strength of which he acquired a force of 180 men, including his four brothers, and twenty-seven horses. Then with this support he sailed back to the New World and down the west coast to Peru.

This present one was his third expedition. Eight years had passed since he had first set out so jauntily, and he was now over sixty, but a man still of steel on whom wounds, heat and cold, thirst and starvation seemed to have no effect. Having explored the coast line and through Felipillo learned details of his goal, he made his final plans.

Throughout his career Pizarro followed a pattern originated by Cortés and then time after time elaborated and improved on his predecessor: Cortés, sensing defeatism among his men, had burned his ships to cut off their retreat; Pizarro twice removed his from the reach of possible deserters. Cortés, entering Mexico with a small band of men, demanded a correctness of conduct from them that disarmed the unsuspecting natives; Pizarro likewise cautioned his men against showing too greedy an interest in the gold, and himself maintained the air of one who could take it or leave it alone. Cortés, finding Mexico split by internal wars, drove the gap still wider and by dividing conquered; Pizarro found Peru torn by a war between the brother kings and, since there was no common front, was able to strike directly at the soft, unguarded heart. Cortés came proclaiming the reign of the Church and the Holy Vicar of God, with that of Charles V a close second, and at the same time hardly mentioned the gold. Pizarro used the same words (though in his case the piety wore thin very soon and the avarice was presently showing through all over).

In one instance, however, Pizarro had to diverge from Cortés' pattern. Cortés had gone straight to Mexico City, the capital. But Atahuallpa was not at his capital now, and since Pizarro had advanced down the coast proclaiming everywhere that he was on his way to meet the Inca; since he knew that a corps of Indian runners was always carrying news swiftly from one end of the kingdom to the other, and that if he seemed to avoid a head-on encounter word would go out that the white man was afraid, he saw that Caxamalca, where the Inca was, must be his goal, despite the fact that Cuzco, the capital, with its famous Temple of the Sun rich in solid gold ornaments, was the more attractive mark.

His plans made, in September 1532 he left fifty men in a little colony, San Miguel, on the coast, and struck inland. With him was a pack of fighting dogs and 177 men, of whom sixty-seven were cavalry and a few were crossbowmen and arquebusiers. The country round about was a paradise of plenty; though rain almost never fell, the Indians had diverted the mountain streams into an artful irrigation system, and the wide variety of new vegetables and fruits and grains took their breath away. And since the odds of eight million to 178 left them no choice but to be polite, the Indians were soon accepting them as friends and offering them gifts with lavish generosity.

But one day a less friendly note was struck when an Indian from the far side of the Andes was caught hanging about the Spanish camp. Dragged before Hernando Pizarro, he refused at first to answer questions about the Inca, but a little judicious torture brought out the fact that Atahuallpa was awaiting the Spaniards in the valley beyond with fifty thousand soldiers.

Some leaders might have suddenly remembered business elsewhere, but Francisco Pizarro loved danger. He stood before the kneeling Indian, legs apart, hands on hips, and looked calmly down at him.

"I will let you go now," he said, his white teeth gleaming in a smile that was almost benevolent. "Tell your King I am delighted to hear that I shall see him so soon. Tell him I think it gracious of him to come to meet me. And"—his smile grew broader, more reassuring—"tell him he has nothing to fear from me. He must have heard how kindly I have treated his people all along the way."

The Indian bowed and backed out.

Pizarro turned to his men, now urgent and intense. In a pinch they were always most responsive to a religious tone, and so now he said to them, "Take heart. God fights for His own. Through you He is going to humble these heathens and bring them to the true faith." It was just the right note, and the men shouted their eagerness for the holy crusade.

Now they set out on the final stage of the invasion, the crossing of the Andes. Accustomed for eight years to the humid heat of the coast, now within a few days they had to climb two miles into the air where, exactly on the equator though it was, the snow never melted. The rarefied atmosphere made every step double the effort and the cold nearly paralyzed them. Those men who had horses were forced to dismount to keep from freezing in their saddles, and the entire company trudged single file along narrow ledges chipped out of the sides of the mountains. Icy winds, whistling through the slits between the peaks, all but blew them into the depths below; but at last, after several days of constant tension, the trail opened onto a flat plain and they spread their tents thankfully and relaxed.

Soon a messenger arrived bringing an assortment of gifts from the Inca, two stone fountains in the shape of fortresses, some lengths of wool embroidered with gold and silver, and a jar of dried goose flesh to be used as perfume. The man told Pizarro that his Emperor, the greatest and wealthiest ruler in the world, with the most invincible army, sent greetings, that he and his army were camped not far from Caxamalca, and that the city itself had been emptied to make room for the guests.

Since Pizarro's principle was never to show surprise at anything, he calmly nodded and thanked the messenger for the Emperor's hospitality. "However," he said, "I must make one correction. The Inca is undoubtedly very powerful, but no king on earth is as powerful as the white king I serve. All white people are supremely powerful. This is shown by the ease with which I and my men have overrun every country we have passed through. However, you can tell your King that he has no cause for alarm provided he does nothing to provoke me." He smiled blandly into the wide, expressionless eyes of the Indian, who withdrew noiselessly.

Two days Pizarro and his men marched across the top of the Andes and then, after five more days of descent, suddenly emerged from a mountain pass and looked down on the valley of Caxamalca. A wide bowl lay before them, thirty miles long and carpeted with green meadows and brown farms. At the bottom sat a little city,

its neat white houses shining in the sun. They stared, for this was
no primitive village like the ones they were used to encountering.
Clean, orderly, civilized people lived here. Then they raised their
eyes to the opposite slope of the valley.

The Inca's army, a white cloud of tents, covered the green fields
like a snowfall for miles. Pizarro and his 177 men paused just a
second; then, with heads up, banners streaming and panoplies
glistening in the sunlight, they marched down the hill into the city.

Not a soul came to meet them; in eerie silence the men marched
through the deserted streets. Here was an example of the devotion
of the Indians to their rulers, for he had decreed that the city be
emptied and not one of its ten thousand inhabitants had disobeyed.

The men looked the city over as they rode through. There was
a huge square in the middle surrounded by a stone wall, and at
one end the convent of the Virgins of the Sun. Felipillo had described these convents; their inmates were of the highest rank and
strictest virtue, and though they were shut away from the world the
Inca often chose a wife or two from among them for the sake of
their exceptional beauty.

Pizarro's men eyed the convent with interest, eager to learn
whether they had been included in the evacuation, but Pizarro was
edgily intent on the main business. He sent his brother Hernando
and Hernando de Soto with forty-five horsemen to call on the Inca.

When they arrived Atahuallpa was sitting motionless in an open
courtyard. Tall, about thirty, and exceptionally strong, with a grave
calm expression, he would have been handsome but for his blood-
shot fiery eyes. Surrounded by nobles dressed in richly embroidered
robes, he himself was in plain white; on his head he wore the royal
borla, a crimson circlet of woolen fringe that hung down almost
to his eyes. Silent, he sat and waited. The Spanish cavalcade, armor clanging and trumpets blasting, thundered down upon him,
and though no Indian had ever seen a horse till that day Atahuallpa's face remained a blank, not a muscle twitching.

Hernando Pizarro reined in with a clatter of steel and, without
dismounting, bowed. "I bring compliments from my brother, the
commander of the white army, who wishes me to announce our
arrival. We come as ambassadors of a mighty prince in a distant
country, the mightiest in the world. We have heard of the glorious

LATROBE HIGH SCHOOL LIBRARY

victories of Your Majesty in the recent war, and now offer our help in arms."

There was a silence while Atahuallpa merely looked at him.

Pizarro went on, "My brother also offers his services in helping you to renounce your heathen faith and learn the true one. And he invites you to come and visit him tomorrow in his quarters in the city."

Felipillo was interpreting briskly, but the Inca gave no sign that he understood. At last one of his courtiers said, "It is well," and there was another silence.

De Soto, with a vague feeling that the interview was beginning to drag, suddenly drove his spurs deep into his mount's side. The shocked horse with a snort catapulted across to the far end of the courtyard, where De Soto, showing off the animal's fierce grace and his own matchless horsemanship, wheeled and returned to pull up sharply right at the Inca's feet. Still the Indian's face remained a blank, but a few of his nobles did so far forget themselves as to draw back a little. (They were, the Spaniards learned later, executed that evening for their timidity.)

Atahuallpa finally spoke. "Tell your captain that I am keeping a fast. It will end tomorrow morning, and I will then visit him with my chiefs." Enormous golden vases of wine were offered the Spaniards by ten beautiful girls from the Inca's harem, and the men rode away, their heads in the air to the last.

Back at Pizarro's camp, however, they broke into confusion, appalled by the Inca's power and the size of his army. Many were for hurrying to Cuzco, making a quick haul, and getting out. But their leader acted typically; each time his men were shrinking from one danger he offered them another twice as great, and this time his proposal was so spectacular, so outrageous, that they were hypnotized into agreement.

His plan would, he knew, have been useless against a different kind of enemy, but he had learned enough of the Peruvians to know that, bizarre as it was, it might succeed.

These Peruvians were a peculiar people, eight million peaceful and happy bodies with a single head. Every smallest fact of their lives was based on the one supreme fact that the sun was God and that their Inca was the embodiment of this God. According to ancient legend, many centuries ago the inhabitants of the land had been so wicked that the sun had sent two of his own children to earth to redeem them from their sins. This brother and sister had married, and the present line of kings were their descendants. In order to keep the royal line pure the Incas continued to marry their sisters, but since they had many other wives as well, the royal family was multiplied hundreds of times each generation. When the Spaniards landed there were thousands of these Incas, who married only among themselves and constituted a powerful aristocracy quite distinct from the rest of the population.

The chief Inca was the direct descendant of the sun, which made him God. He was also head priest and as such officiated at the sun-worshiping ceremonies. He made all laws, was commander-in-chief of the armies, and actively led the forays against the neighbor countries. And he owned everything in the kingdom.

Since he was God, any insubordination or disobedience was an act of blasphemy punishable by instant execution, and since all lands and property belonged to him, there could be no buying or selling, which resulted in the condition most astonishing to the invaders, the complete absence of any money or medium of exchange, the gold and silver being used solely for ornamental purposes.

Crimes against the Inca's property being crimes against the Inca, theft was so rare that when a man left his house he placed a small stick across the threshold, not to keep thieves out but as a polite warning that visitors would find no one at home. What crimes there were, such as an occasional adultery or murder, were punished immediately by death, as were offenses against the public good like destroying a bridge or diverting a stream from a neighbor's lands to one's own. Every moment of a Peruvian's life was ordered for him; his wife was chosen by the local authority and he married her on the one annual wedding day, receiving a piece of land and a house which were enlarged as the family enlarged. This land the man worked but never owned, and each did, besides the particular task assigned to him according to his age and ability, enough to keep him busy but never enough to wear him out. He paid his taxes in man-hours of work, and the state saw that he had every living comfort. There was no such thing as poverty in Peru, no famine, no unemployment.

Since the Peruvians had never invented an alphabet or other means of writing save the *quipu*, a bunch of colored knotted strings with which they performed mathematical miracles, the Inca received no written reports on his country's conditions, but regularly he made journeys the length of the land, traveling over thousands of miles of magnificent roads to see that his people were well cared for and content.

And contented everyone appeared to be, placid, obedient, and friendly. Festivals were common among them and dancing was their chief recreation except drinking, of which everyone did a great deal. Eight million children with a rich and generous father, they were gentle and considerate, never taking advantage of each other's good nature and incapable of suspicion. When the invaders arrived they were almost eerily ripe for them.

Knowing this, Pizarro proposed his plan to his followers with such irresistible confidence that they hesitated no longer and made ready to put it into action.

Saturday, November 16, 1532, the day after the two horsemen's visit to the Inca's camp, dawned clear. Fortified with an extra-hearty breakfast, their arms polished and the breastplates of the sixty-seven horses garnished with clanging bells, the men received Mass with great solemnity, invoking success from the God whom they believed themselves to be serving. Then they took their appointed places and set themselves to wait for the Inca.

The central square of Caxamalca was surrounded on three sides by low buildings with wide halls; in two of these halls Pizarro stationed his cavalry and in the third the infantry, while a few foot soldiers and the artillery—two small cannon—were secreted in a fortress on the fourth side of the square. After five or six hours of waiting almost unbearable to the keyed-up Spaniards the Inca's retinue was seen starting from his hillside camp—thirty thousand men, Pizarro's secretary estimated, while another witness swore later it was fifty thousand.

To Pizarro, watching this fighting strength approach, they must have looked like a hundred thousand, and perhaps for a moment he wondered if he had been a fool. But then an extraordinary stroke of luck dispelled all possible doubt, for the Inca, whose reputation for craftiness and ferocity had met the invaders all along the way, now sent word that he was leaving the greater part of his force in camp and would come with only a few courtiers, and, moreover, would come unarmed. This childlike trust was proof positive to Pizarro that God was on his side.

Shortly before sunset the procession began to enter the city gates, several hundred servants first, singing and sweeping the royal path, and then various ranks of courtiers, some dressed in large red-and-white checks and some in pure white, while the guards were in blue glittering with silver and gold ornaments. Then came Atahuallpa, wearing the imperial *borla* and a collar of enormous emeralds. His massive throne of pure gold was borne high above the crowd, and as the procession entered the square the marchers, five thousand in number, divided and left a space in the center for him. Not a Spaniard was in sight and the monarch finally asked, "Where are the strangers?"

Now Fray Vicente de Valverde, Pizarro's chaplain, came forward, Bible in one hand and crucifix in the other, and while the Inca listened in growing amazement, Felipillo translated. The Friar began by explaining the Trinity, from the creation of man, his fall and redemption, to the crucifixion and ascension. The Apostle Peter was next introduced as the first Pope, followed by Alexander VI, who, Valverde said, had given the King of Spain a franchise to conquer and convert the heathen. The King, in turn, had given his franchise to Francisco Pizarro, and thus the Inca was exhorted to reject his own faith forthwith and adopt Christianity. If he did, King Charles would be glad to receive him as his subject.

Atahuallpa stared, incredulous. Felipillo himself was a little hazy on some of the fine points—the Trinity, for example, came out as an arrangement of three gods and one god, which made four gods —but he did manage to communicate the main idea. Atahuallpa's eyes were blazing now as he demanded by whose authority Valverde made such insolent proposals.

The Friar pointed to the Bible in hand; Atahuallpa took it, glared at it for a moment, and then dashed it angrily to the ground.

This was all the Spaniards needed, and now, watching from inside, Pizarro waved a white scarf. One of the cannon boomed and at the same moment the captain and 176 men, shouting together "St. Iago and at them!", poured from all sides into the square.

Suddenly the hollow structure was a mélange of noises, the rattling fire of a hundred muskets, the quivering boom of the cannon reverberating from wall to wall, the clatter of armor, the clanging of the bells which Pizarro had affixed to the horses' harness for just this purpose. The Indians, stunned by the confusion of sounds, their lungs filled with the sulphurous smoke from the gunpowder, unarmed and helpless, looked around wildly for security somewhere and in a wave of panic made for the one exit.

In the next few moments so many rushed for the single archway that one stumbled over another and both fell on those beneath, piling up until the opening was clogged with smashed and suffocating Indians. More pushed against them from behind, pressing in such numbers against the adjacent walls that a mass burst through the masonry and fell screaming to the ground outside. Still more came on, blind with terror, and meanwhile the Spanish cavalry thundered close behind, hoofs pounding and swords swinging.

At the same time the maelstrom of massacre was centering around the Inca, who, true to his promise, had come completely unarmed. His bearers were now struggling to hold up his throne out of reach of the Spaniards, while his courtiers formed a protective ring around him. Some of the invaders worked their way through the milling mob and raised their swords for a quick dispatch, but Pizarro shouted:

"Don't strike. Take him alive!"

In putting out his hand to shield the Indian he came by accident in contact with the sword of one of his own men. This was the only wound received by any Spaniard that day.

As the struggle around the Inca increased, the throne rocked ever more wildly, at length capsizing and spilling him into the arms of those below, and the imperial *borla* was snatched by a foot soldier as he fell. His badge of divinely appointed invincibility now a mere souvenir in the hand of an alien, the captive Atahuallpa was pinioned and dragged struggling to one of the great halls.

At that moment the hearts of the Peruvians died, for this King, this high priest, this leader and lawgiver, had been their god and the mind that thought for them, and when he fell it was God falling from the sky. Complete panic took hold of the ones remaining in the square, scattering them in such noisy terror out into the fields that the troops stationed at a distance, hearing the pandemonium, rushed away themselves before the oncoming horsemen.

Night finally dropped with the suddenness of the tropics and put an end to the butchery. Ten thousand Indians had been killed and many more wounded, and when it was over the power of the Emperor had been smashed and the Spaniards were the country's new rulers. The gates to the Western treasure had been thrown rudely open.

The whole time consumed was a little more than half an hour.

After a contented night's sleep the conquerors, who forty-eight hours earlier had never seen the city they now owned, went about the task of mopping it up, while Pizarro, reasoning that Atahuallpa alive and able to give orders to his subjects would be more useful than Atahuallpa dead, installed him in an apartment with all the comforts of royalty except freedom. Servants and his favorite wives and concubines were sent for and he was allowed to wear the imperial *borla* and a robe of bats' wings soft and sleek as velvet; a tremendous supply of gold and silver dishes was brought from his camp, since any garment or utensil used by him had to be thereafter promptly destroyed; and he was permitted a sort of court, receiving courtiers who brought him gifts and offered their wistful condolences. Though the Spaniards kept watch against sabotage, they need not have bothered, for the sight of their god in captivity had so unnerved the Indians that they were incapable of resistance.

Pizarro's first move was to send to the Emperor's residence for his gold and silver and gems, the bodies of the dead likewise being stripped of their valuables, and everything was put in one pile in the great hall.

Atahuallpa watched with heavy brooding eyes as Pizarro divided the spoils out into shares and the soldiers, their hands shaking with excitement, marched past to receive their allotments. The Inca noticed also that, despite the protestations of Pizarro and Fray Valverde that his conversion to the one true faith was their only interest, their hearts appeared to be elsewhere. So several weeks after the division of his property he requested his captor to join him for a game of chess, a game he had learned from the white man and now played brilliantly.

While their hands hovered casually about over the chessmen, Atahuallpa in a voice equally casual began speaking of the gold in his domain. "The gold you have seen here," he remarked smoothly, "is only a fraction of all the gold in this country."

Slowly and carefully Pizarro set down the pawn he had been moving. He scarcely breathed, his eyes searching the Indian's face.

The Indian went on in a level voice, "All of the gold in my kingdom belongs to me, is my individual property. If you will give me my freedom, you shall have enough of it to cover the entire floor of this room."

Pizarro stared, first at the Indian and then around the room. It was seventeen feet wide and twenty-two feet long. His eyes met those of the other two Spaniards present and they smiled together at the foolishness of such talk.

Laughed at for the first time in his life, the Inca with a terrible frown jumped to his feet and strode proudly across the room, where, stretching to his full height, he touched a spot on the wall. "You do not believe I can do it?" While the others watched, openmouthed, he pointed to the spot on the wall. "Not only will I cover the floor, I will fill this room solidly, up to this point." Now they laughed outright.

Then they checked themselves, for although the idea was incredible what they had already seen was incredible too, and their eyes met in a common thought—what harm in trying, he is still our prisoner. Pizarro called for a notary to write out the contract.

A red line was drawn around the walls at the height Atahuallpa had indicated and it was agreed that the enclosed space, 3,366 cubic feet, was to be filled with gold, the Inca stipulating only that the objects remain in their original form. An adjoining room somewhat smaller was to be filled entirely twice over with silver. He was to have two months to fulfill the contract.

Now messengers went out all over the kingdom bearing the edict that every palace, temple, and public building was to be stripped and its gold brought to Caxamalca. Soon the porters began arriving, day after day stumbling in with packs of gold and silver on their backs, thirty thousand, forty, fifty thousand pesos de oro in a day. The floor of the room was covered, then in the far end a pile began to accumulate, statues, vessels, dishes, cups, temple altars, and dozens and dozens of flat plates that had lined the walls of the temples from floor to ceiling.

At first the Spaniards were genuinely incredulous and almost out of their minds with excitement, but very soon they began to take the windfall for granted, scanning each day's returns with critical eyes and after a month becoming impatient and irritated. The Inca, they complained, was taking too long; he was perhaps even holding up delivery and meanwhile spreading orders for an insurrection. Utterly changed men, they fretted and scolded with anxiety, for, bold and careless and cheerful in poverty, now with riches they were ridden with fear, hardly sleeping at night in dread of attack from beyond the mountains. All they could think about was escaping.

Pressure to move on was likewise coming from another quarter, for Almagro, Pizarro's old partner, had arrived with a group of new men as reinforcements, and these late-comers, ineligible to share in the spoils already taken, wanted to hurry on to fresh pastures. Cuzco, they had heard, was stiff and creaking with gold, and not a white man had laid a finger on it.

Although the ransom was still pouring in daily, Pizarro shrugged and agreed. First, however, must come the computation and division of the accumulated returns, and for this a whole month was consumed merely in melting the gold into ingots. After this was accomplished, the whole must be weighed—1,300,000 pesos de oro —besides nearly enough silver to fill the two rooms.

Dividing it, Pizarro first set aside the royal fifth, then he deducted his share, 57,222 pesos de oro, 2,350 marks of silver, and the Inca's great gold throne worth over twenty-five thousand pesos. The shares of Hernando Pizarro and De Soto were a third less, and in a declining scale came the cavalry, foot soldiers, and menials. At last they were ready to move.

One embarrassing question, the disposal of the Inca, remained for resolution. They could take him along, of course, or they could leave him behind, but either alternative presented certain difficulties, for the first would call for a continuing guard about him and the second would constitute a constant temptation to the Indians to revolt. A third alternative was suggested and, the obviously sensible answer, it met with almost universal approval.

On August 29, 1533, a court was set up, with Francisco Pizarro and Don Almagro as judges and an attorney for the crown appointed to prefer a number of charges against the Indian. He was accused of (a) idolatry; (b) squandering the public revenues since the conquest of his country and of lavishing them on his own family; (c) usurping the crown of his brother Huascar; (d) adultery; and, (e) attempting to incite an insurrection against the Spaniards. There was considerable solemn talk about the immorality of the Inca's past behavior, and after a short consideration the long-faced judges pronounced him guilty as charged and sentenced him to be burned alive that same evening.

A few men, among them Hernando de Soto, were revolted by the proceedings and signed a paper to say so, but they were outvoted ten to one and the plans for the Inca's execution went forward briskly.

When he was told of his fate Atahuallpa turned to Pizarro with tears in his eyes, the eyes so fiery a few months before. "I cannot understand," he said. "You have met with nothing but friendship from my people, and I have shared my treasures with you. Why do you do this to me?"

Pizarro turned away without answering.

Atahuallpa made one other appeal, "Be kind to my little children. See that they come to no harm." Pizarro had already made Atahuallpa's grown daughter his mistress, but perhaps the Indian thought the younger ones might fare better. It was his last request.

At sunset the soldiery poured into the square to watch the Emperor being led forth into the center of the open plaza, chains on his hands and feet. At his side trotted Fray Valverde pouring out a last-minute offer—let the Indian renounce his faith and be baptized a Christian, and he would be spared death at the stake. Atahuallpa looked at the pole standing starkly in the middle of the square, the fagots piled high around it, and at the executioner waiting with his torch. Slowly he bowed his head and received the new name of Juan de Atahuallpa.

So now he was a Christian, and the Spaniards, true to their promise, did not burn him. A rope was placed around his neck with a stick thrust through it at the back, and at a signal the stick was twisted and twisted and twisted, and thus, by the garrote instead, died the Inca of Peru.

Pizarro immediately went into mourning.

The death of their ruler brought a strange kind of freedom to the Indians, a freedom that left them utterly at a loss. For centuries they had existed in a state of total slavery, the bonds of which, however, had been so light and painless, like the strands of a spider's web, that they had hardly known they were there. All of them obedient together to one omnipotent god and father who had their comfort and safety in his hand, they had lived and worked in order and comely harmony.

Now, suddenly, there was no one to tell them what to do, and thrown upon the necessity for thinking for themselves, the entire population went, as it were, into a nervous breakdown. All the laws they had lived by, based on the Inca's omnipotence, were now obliterated, and drunkenness, always a weakness, became a universal vice. Thievery replaced honesty, licentiousness replaced order, and now that their conquerors had taught them greed for gold, they became as avaricious as the rest. The news of the Inca's assassination having torn like a hurricane across the land, porters trudging towards Caxamalca stopped dead in the mountain passes; everywhere porters stopped dead and turned aside, and the treasure they hid in the jungles of Peru was ten times greater than that which ever reached Caxamalca.

But Pizarro's men, distrustful of their luck here any longer, were feverishly eager to get on to Cuzco and the search for El Dorado, that fabled creature everywhere heard of and nowhere seen. The men loaded their gold and silver and their favorite Indian women on the backs of llamas and made for the capital city.

Cuzco, a beautiful metropolis of half a million people, they entered without resistance, for the bewildered Indian population had scattered meekly before them and they stripped its temples and public buildings, even to the Inca mummies, at their leisure, adding thus a third more to the previous spoils.

A wealth of beautiful women was also discovered in the convents, six thousand virgins attended by fifteen or twenty women each, and here was a windfall indeed for the starved soldiers, who lost no time in putting them to a practical use. A population of *mestizos*, half white and half brown, was suddenly on its way.

The rest of Peru being quickly overrun and gathered into the Spanish fold, Pizarro set up a hit-or-miss government and founded the city of Lima. But he never left off pursuit of his main objective, and he found that all the gold previously mined was scarcely a sample of that still remaining untouched, in the mines of Carabaya and in the streams dashing down the Andes' slopes. All they had to do was pick it up. And one day a few years later an Indian, pulling a bush out of the ground at Potosí, noticed a few small white globules clinging to the fibers, and so now here was silver too, so abundant that when the Spaniards' horses lost their iron shoes they shod them with the more plentiful silver.

For the business of getting the stuff mined, thousands of bewildered Indians were herded into chain gangs and driven up the mountains, where they spent the rest of their lives digging the ore and carrying it out on their backs. If by chance one of them worked up enough spirit to strike an overseer, ten hostages were burned alive for each Spaniard hurt, and so for the most part they labored meekly until death overtook them. Hundreds fell dead in their chains from overwork, the guards saving themselves the bother of unfastening the chains around their necks by more expeditiously lopping off their heads. The hundreds of the dead swelled into thousands and at last into millions, and finally the extermination was so great that in two hundred years the Peruvian population was reduced from eight million to one.

Meanwhile the gold and silver and jewels were pouring back across the Atlantic, one fifth into the royal treasury, and the conquistadors were national heroes. The King fulfilled Pizarro's old dream by creating him a Marquess and at the same time confirming him as Governor of Peru, and many others were similarly honored by the royal hand. All of them were known to be rich beyond belief.

It was inevitable that other fortune hunters should rush across the Atlantic to share in these good things, and soon Pizarro was being harassed not only by the newcomers but by rivals for the leadership within his own ranks. He and his partner Don Almagro quarreled and made up, quarreled and did not make up, and finally there was full-scale civil war between the two factions, which ended with Pizarro taking the Don prisoner. As in the case of Atahuallpa, a noose was put around the neck of the kneeling man, a stick was slipped through it and twisted, and, as formerly, the brothers Pizarro immediately went into mourning.

Then came the turn of Francisco Pizarro himself, and since in these bloody times hardly a conquistador but died by public execution or private murder, the Marquess' end was appropriate in manner.

Pizarro well knew that the group who had been followers of the garroted Don were hungry for revenge, and with caution would have gone about with a bodyguard; but caution was foreign to his soul, and so on a Sunday morning in May 1541 his murders caught up with him.

Members of his own faction had heard rumors of a conspiracy; indeed, the young city was bubbling with rumors. His friends argued that if he would not carry a bodyguard he might at least stay home from Mass that one Sunday morning, and to humor them he did. So the conspirators had a vain wait at the church, after which they dashed across the square towards his palace.

On the way one of the warriors stepped aside to avoid a puddle of water, and another jeered at him, "What, afraid of wetting your feet when you are so soon to be wading knee-deep in blood?"

Francisco Pizarro, surrounded by his brothers and friends, was sitting at noonday dinner when the conspirators rushed up the stairs shouting "Death to the tyrant!" His brother Alcantara held them off while Pizarro sprang for his armor, but, unable in the excitement to buckle his cuirass on, he threw it away and, without protection other than the cloak wrapped around his left arm, grasped his sword and rushed into the fight.

Nearly seventy years old, a machine compounded of steel and fury, he battled like the angel of death. More than his share of the conspirators fell to his sword, but while his steel was deep in the chest of one man that of another ran him through the throat. Sinking to the floor, he traced a cross in the blood from his own veins and bent to kiss it. At that moment another sword entered his heart.

At once the city was in an uproar. Almagro's friends went about the streets shouting "The tyrant is dead! Long live the Emperor!" and crowds swarmed through the Marquess' house, destroying the furnishings and looting his enormous cache of gold and silver. The dead bodies lay for hours soaking up their own blood, forgotten, until a group of the conspirators seized on the idea of dragging

Pizarro's to the market place to exhibit on the end of a pole. But the corpse was saved from this indignity by four faithful attendants who, in the darkness of the night, wrapped it in a cotton cloth and scuttled through back streets to the cathedral. A grave was dug in an obscure corner, services were mumbled, and Pizarro was dropped into the earth.

Thus came to an end one of the bravest and most merciless men in history. "And there was none," said the secretary who chronicled his career, "to say, 'God forgive him.'"

Like water the warring elements closed over Francisco Pizarro's head, continuing their struggles for the rich earth he had left. Though Atahuallpa's daughter had borne him two children he had had no legitimate offspring. Even the son he did have died in childhood, and while his daughter married his own brother and might have given him an heir thick with Pizarro blood, Hernando was ninety at the time and, though he lived to be a hundred, failed in this respect. Thus Francisco Pizarro left no descendants to carry on his bizarre career.

In a sense, however, all those who followed were the heirs of his genius, for during the next hundred years the conquistadors made a mark peculiarly their own. Cruel, greedy and, until the decline set in, brave beyond praise, they dedicated their lives to making themselves and their monarch rich. Up and down the coast of South America they spread, across the continent and into Brazil, while the followers of Cortés continued to press the goodness out of Mexico.

During the last half of the sixteenth century five times as much gold and silver swept across the Atlantic as had ever been seen there until the galleons started running, and by the year 1600 the Casa de Contratacion had received eighty million pesos de oro.

Twice yearly the treasures arrived at the ports of Spain and Portugal, transported in great silver fleets across the Atlantic. One, named the Galleones, under command of a general, brought the treasure of the Incas from the Andes, gold from Maracaibo and Peru, silver from Potosí, pearls and emeralds from Margarita and Guayaquil; the other, the Flota under an admiral, bore home the Mexican hoard. At Havana the two fleets met and mingled and then, under the eyes of escort frigates, made in company for Hispaniola, the island later divided into Haiti and the Dominican Republic. Then the long dash began. Northeast they had to go, threading their way through the three thousand rocky islands and cays of the Bahamas, and at last struck the open sea.

Handsome and imposing these galleons were, with fighting towers and high poops painted vermilion and gold, sculptured figureheads and sails decorated with the cross of St. Iago, patron saint of soldiers. But the truth is that they were designed more for looks than efficiency. Too tall and too square, so that they plunged and tossed in a heavy sea, their luxurious appearance belied the homely facts. Vermin and rats abounded under living conditions which, for them, were ideal, but which put the humans' hardihood to test. As long as live pigs and cattle held out the voyagers ate fresh meat, but after that salted meat and fish had to serve, and the end of any long voyage found a good proportion of those on board suffering from scurvy, with teeth dropping out, flesh blue and bleeding, and bodies denatured and exhausted. Many more would be dead.

Fresh water was carried in jars, and on the long Atlantic passages was rationed stringently. In a mid-ocean calm the horses were the first to suffer, and many a good animal, crazed with thirst, had to be pushed overboard in these "horse latitudes." But still the treasure must be delivered and each year, despite pirates and privation and gales, the Silver Fleets gathered.

In the autumn of 1643 one of the richest ever assembled lay in a bay on the north side of Hispaniola facing the ocean, the flagships of the Admiral and the Vice-Admiral, twelve other galleons, and two frigates as convoys. Their combined cargoes equaled well over a million pesos de oro, gold nuggets large as apples and cauliflowers, gold and silver coins, silver in bars and sows and pigs, ecclesiastical vessels, sacks full of gems of all sorts, and an unestimated quantity of a whitish metal used for ornamental stripping alone. False silver the Spaniards called it; later it came to be called platinum.

The combined crews numbered some hundreds, including one particular Spanish cabin boy.

Through the first night out the Silver Fleet made routine time till a few miles north of Hispaniola there was only one obstacle left between them and safe open sea. The Abroxes were a group of tiny islands with, scattered about among them, a mélange of jagged rocks and coral reefs hidden by the water but still so close to the surface that the seas boiled up over them in green and white foam. These Boilers were well known, and every pilot heeded them respectfully.

The flotilla was approaching confidently before a fair southwest breeze, making for Cádiz. Then the wind died and the morning blue of the sky turned to cold gray. The wind rose again, but too sharply and from the wrong quarter, and now the ships were scudding nervously before a horizontal rain. Suddenly, with a clap, the hurricane struck, and the tall ungainly galleons heeled over, the men skidding across their decks. Nothing built by hands could withstand the force of the gale, and the sixteen ships were driven helplessly toward the Boilers and, like a handful of gravel flung against a wall, dashed themselves onto the reef.

Some of them, impaled on sharp points of rock, hung for a moment and then, shaken loose by the wind, went down. Others scraped across the reef; bottoms torn out and entrails spilling, they drove through the waves onto the next mass of rock before they sank. One, the flagship of the Vice-Admiral, was carried by the gale right across the reef. There, a great hole smashed in her side amidship, she jammed between two tall rocks and settled on the bottom, one of the rocks, of a soft disintegrating substance, sticking its head above the water like a gravestone.

Of the sixteen vessels only two survived, a frigate and the Admiral's ship, and when the Admiral himself returned to Cádiz he was court-martialed as a matter of routine. The hurricane, however, was adjudged an act of God for which he could not be held responsible, and he was acquitted.

So died the great 1643 Silver Fleet.

Out of the hundreds of men aboard the sunken ships miraculously a few escaped. Even in that panicky moment the treasure was uppermost in their minds, and so, dropping a few chests of silver into a small boat, they made, half driven and half paddling, back through the subsiding storm to Porto Plata.

Among the survivors was the cabin boy. He knew that the Vice-Admiral's cargo was, next to the Admiral's, the richest in the fleet, he had seen the ship go down and had marked the rock that stood over her grave. He never forgot.

After this spectacular catastrophe treasure hunters swarmed like fruit flies over a dish of rotting melons. The survivors had several times tried to return to the wreck to dive for more silver, to be driven back each time by storms, but in time others farther away heard of it, and soon honest men and pirates alike, from adjacent islands and from the far coast of North America, came hurrying with baskets and grapnels and a wild light in their eyes. Indeed, Sir Thomas Lynch, Governor of Jamaica, sailing about the Bahamas, reported disgustedly to the English King that the islands were barren of anyone save straggling thieves who had come not to settle and plant like honest colonists, but to snatch silver off the bottom.

A group of islands somewhat to the north, on which a Spaniard named Juan de Bermúdez had been shipwrecked with a cargo of hogs, had later acquired a small colony of respectable Englishmen; most of these, it now seemed, had come south *en masse*. One of them made a living renting out a contrivance he had invented, a wine cask with lead weights around its open lower end, inside which a diver could stay under water three quarters of an hour, and with this diving tub English and Spanish adventurers forced Indian slaves captured in Florida to strip the few ships that had sunk in shallow water. But the wreck of the Vice-Admiral's flagship, which held a large proportion of the fortune of the fleet, was not found.

Still she was the grand prize, sought by all, and the cabin boy, who made a small living selling his recollections of the one great day in his life, distinctly recalled a tall rock marking the spot, and so insisted to all and sundry. But no such tall rock was visible, and thus mystery was added to her other charms, spreading the fame of the fabled ship everywhere that people had a mind to get rich fast.

This was a get-rich-quick period all over Europe, a sort of fever burning the hitherto cool and calm. Charles II of England reasoned that what Ferdinand and Charles and Philip of Spain had done so easily, he should be able to emulate. First of all, of course, footholds in the New World were needed; Spain had pre-empted the richest islands, but there were others, Bermudas and Bahamas, not so well endowed but at least conveniently situated, and these Charles claimed for the crown. Then came a series of treasure-trove laws.

By their provisions, all treasure found on English territory or in English waters belonged to the King. He could at his discretion grant treasure-hunting licenses covering specific areas and specific lengths of time, which gave the licensees ownership of everything they found and could be abrogated only if someone else could present indisputable proof of ownership. The King, as original owner, retained a share of all proceeds, usually a tenth, and his interests were protected by a supervisor who recorded every ounce of treasure as it was recovered and by an armed guard which convoyed it home.

These were the laws, and no unlicensed scavengers were to be tolerated. Nevertheless, hundreds of untenanted islands of the Caribbean were hard to police, and all throughout them furtive groups of men were diving without permission. When word came back to England, the local Governors were ordered to increase their vigilance.

Sir Hendor Molesworth, looking out for the King's interests, wrote from Jamaica enclosing a deposition from one Thomas Smith, a seaman, to the effect that while he was on a cruise on the northeast side of Hispaniola his ship had come on a reef on which had been seen several ingots of silver and one of gold and within forty feet of it the hull of a ship wedged upright between two rocks. The wind having freshened, they had been unable to stand by, but the witness believed that he could find the spot again.

Smith believed it so firmly, indeed, that he was willing to stake his life on his conviction. The King being interested in hearing more, Smith made a bargain with the Governor whereby he was to pilot a ship to the wreck, receiving, in return for his good offices, one fifth of everything recovered. If he could not find it, he was to be hanged. (Later Molesworth, apparently having a softening of the heart, moderated the penalty to a flogging and seven years' servitude without pay, and promised a hundred-pound bonus for success.)

Acting for the King, Molesworth then dispatched Captain Edward Stanley in the *Bonito* to the reef under Smith's direction, secretly suggesting to Stanley that if the expedition failed he might tactfully look the other way and give Smith a chance to escape. In addition to Smith, Stanley had for guide much seaport gossip and, especially valued, certain latitudes and longitudes given him by a Spaniard, middle-aged by now; all in all, he seemed well fortified.

Nevertheless, as week after week the *Bonito* sailed about the area no tall rock showed, no reef, no wreck, and at last the captain released the seaman from the terms of his bargain and dismally sailed back home. But like so many other men, he had got the flagship into his blood and, begging more backing, returned for another try the following year, equally well documented and equally fruitless.

That was the end for a time. The flagship was not to give up, for a little while longer.

The seventeenth century was a time of adventurers everywhere. From England, France, and Holland as well as Spain and Portugal men were spreading their sails to see the world outside and lay hold on whatever part of it looked promising. These adventures were not for the soft, and the men who colonized the shores of the Atlantic had to be sharp-witted and tough and impervious to hardship.

James Phips was one of these, a man who, leaving England at eighteen, had hacked a farm out of the forest near the Kennebec River in Maine, and with his wife, Mary, a woman with a stamina at least equal to his own, produced twenty-one sons. (Later Mary, having survived Phips, married his partner, John White, and went right on producing, this time turning to girls and adding five to the population of Maine.) The Phips' twenty-first son, William, was born in 1651, eight years after the event in the Abroxes which was to give his life its meaning.

The boy grew up in the Maine woods and there acquired a useful knowledge of woodworking, while his father saw that he learned all about guns. He was then apprenticed for four years to a ship carpenter in Boston, and there learned all about ships. Reading and writing came later, as an afterthought.

At this time Boston, like all other seaports in the colonies, was a haven for rough folk, many of its leading citizens having come up in very queer ways indeed, of which privateering was one of the more respectable and piracy the most amusing. Into this atmosphere William Phips slipped like a foot into a shoe.

Tall, muscular, with round cheeks and a small determined mouth, he swaggered through Boston's narrow streets, pushing aside any who interfered, bragging hard, fighting hard, forever on the lookout for a chance to forward himself, and finding this chance most romantically. Mary Hull, nee Spencer, was a widow of some means, and though she was four years older than Phips he promptly fell in love with her and all that she possessed. Through her he picked up a smattering of education and a smattering of grace; through her he also acquired a ship and went into the West Indies trade, carrying lumber south and bringing rum back north. He had his bad times as well as his good, but, up or down, he never lost his self-assurance.

"One day," he told her, "I shall command a king's ship and buy you a brick house in the best part of town. I don't yet know how it will be done, but I shall find a way." On his voyages south he picked up a hot scent.

All through the West Indies the talk was of the flagship that had gone down thirty-odd years before. It was said she was not as rich as that of Governor Bobadilla, a ship which had carried a fortune including a solid gold table alone worth three hundred thousand pounds, but the Governor's ship was lost irrevocably, while everyone believed the Vice-Admiral's ship could be found. In the meantime, without benefit of government licenses, divers were picking the lesser wrecks as they came across them.

Phips' first treasure hunt was an amateurish attack on a wreck lying close to shore and consequently already stripped all but bare. He did find one silver ingot weighing ninety-three pounds, however, and that was enough for the moment.

He decided he needed to put himself on a firmer basis, with backing, official permits, and ships, and since the Bahamas were a colony of England, who thus controlled their affairs, it was to London he must go. He was aware that Charles II, always desperate for money, had had high hopes of Captain Edward Stanley, but that when Stanley had disappointed him his faith in treasure hunters had been somewhat dampened. However, Phips believed that his silver ingot could do wonders towards rekindling it, and the moment he landed in London he sold his ship and set about getting the King's ear.

Will's Coffee House near Covent Garden was the rendezvous of the young bloods and political bigwigs, and there William Phips repaired, lace and ribbons, high-heeled shoes and huge curled wig replacing the Puritan clothes that had marked him an outsider. Keeping his ears studiously open, he heard talk of a man high in royal favor who still had great faith in West Indian treasure, and unabashedly maneuvered for an introduction.

The man he sought, Christopher, second Duke of Albemarle, was the son of one of England's foremost peers, a boy who had managed to be legitimate only by the skin of his teeth, for his father had married his mistress, daughter of a streetwalker and a blacksmith, literally on her childbed. At sixteen Christopher had in turn married the fourteen-year-old Lady Elizabeth Cavendish, who had lost no time in starting on the career of pathological spending that was to be her husband's lifetime cross. Although the irregularity of his birth was nothing uncommon, the Duke found this to be a second cross, for Samuel Pepys and the rest of scandalmongering society never let the world forget about his mother, and so harassed was he by the weaknesses of his womenfolk that by the time he was nineteen he was a confirmed drunkard. At eighteen, indeed, he and several high-born friends had murdered a man in a street fight, and at twenty he made the acquaintance of another drunkard who had murdered not one man but hundreds.

This Sir Henry Morgan, tremendously wealthy, cruel, debauched, had for some years been the most successful of all the West Indian pirates who flourished just outside the law with the connivance of local officials, but in 1672 he had been recalled to England. Most of his victims had been Spanish; England and Spain were technically at peace, so, to satisfy the Spaniards, Morgan had to be reprimanded. He had operated in a mutually profitable partnership with the Governor of Jamaica, Sir Thomas Modyford. Modyford was a cousin of the Duke of Albemarle, so when Morgan was brought to London for a public reprimand Albemarle was behind the scenes making things easy.

For the next three years, while tempers cooled and Spain forgot her grievance, Morgan and Albemarle's son, the young Christopher, tore London apart. The youth, already satiated with conventional excitements, reveled in Morgan's tales of Spanish galleons ravished of their gold, of tropical cities burned and looted, and through his influence Morgan was not only exonerated but returned to Jamaica as Lieutenant Governor with a knighthood and a diamond-studded snuffbox from the King. He and Christopher corresponded regularly, and one part of the young Duke's heart was forever in the Caribbean.

Thus when Phips let his plans be known around Will's Coffee House, word of them got to Christopher, now twenty-nine and the second Duke, and before long they were putting their heads together over charts and maps. The Duke promised to introduce Phips to the King, from whom any license to fish must be obtained, but it was nearly a year before he did so, and in the meantime Phips was driven to living frugally on the proceeds from the sale of his ship.

This waiting was made easier by an astrologer's prophecy which promised that in the thirty-seventh year of his life he would find a great treasure and in the forty-first year his King would employ him in a great trust beyond the sea. Phips threw the letter in a trunk, where years later it was found by his wife.

Albemarle finally made good his promise. Since, like all royalty, the King lived in a house almost literally made of glass and any day of the year any citizen could wander through to watch him being shaved and dressed, Albemarle had merely to walk his friend into the King's sitting room and present him. Charles was impressed by the silver ingot and charmed by Phips' self-confidence. For a quarter of the proceeds, terms Phips was in no position to protest, he agreed to lend him a ship.

Albemarle would, of course, privately get a part of Phips' share. The treasure-hunting ship was a 160-ton frigate mounting eighteen guns which had recently been seized from its Algerian owners and renamed the *Algier Rose*. Neither the King nor Albemarle offered to pay the crew's wages and Phips had no such funds, so the ninety-five men were signed on as partners, furnishing their own food and small arms and ammunition. Shares in the proceeds were

to be allotted according to the rank the men held. Phips was to receive one share for his person and another for his commission and
one as refund for the diving equipment he provided. Each sailor
got a smaller share and each boy one half that, while the doctor
rated a share plus twopence monthly from each man for medical
supplies. The cook, the only one to receive regular wages, was ex-
empted from furnishing the usual hundred-pound bond.

This arrangement absolved Phips of responsibility for his crew's
wages, but it also deprived him of all discipline, and he soon found
the men to be corrupt, unmanageable, and given to stealing, brawling, and bizarre sexual excesses. Stopping at Limerick for last supplies, they stripped a farmer's land of its sheep and poultry and
raped another farmer's wife, and when they finally fetched up at
Boston they all but tore the town to pieces.

Phips maintained his hold on his men aboard ship only by always
siding with them ashore; indeed, he joined in their Boston rioting
so heartily that the whole crowd was brought before Governor
Bradstreet and stayed out of jail only because Phips arrogantly declared he was on personal business for the King and thus immune
from ordinary discipline.

So long as the prospect of wealth held the men together Phips
retained command, but when they reached the West Indies his
troubles began. His directions for finding the wreck they sought
proved to be erroneous; they did find one, to be sure, but when
the Indian divers investigated it developed that it was not a Silver
Fleet vessel at all. Furthermore, she had already been stripped.

This disappointment destroyed the crew's confidence in their
captain and during the following months, while they sailed about
looking for another wreck, they became so disgusted with honest
treasure seeking that they declared their intention of going on the
account. Phips acknowledged that piracy might pay better but he
refused to countenance it anyway, and his size and strength came
in handy in a fist fight so tremendous that for a while there was
no more talk of piracy or rebellion.

But they were still too difficult to handle, and at last he set sail
for the roaring town of Port Royal in Jamaica, the resort of privateers and pirates and the center of shipping activities, and there
calmly set ashore all but a few and then signed on a new crew.

Among those he retained was his second mate, Francis Rogers, a man invaluable later on; Abram Atherley, who was to come to such a tragic end; and Henry Covell and William Davis. With these and his four Indian divers, but recently recovered from smallpox, he sailed for Hispaniola.

At Porto Plata he found the Spaniard who had seen the flagship go down and listened to his directions, "Look for a North Reef, (that which they call the Abroxes or Ambrosia Bank) and a South Reef, like two horns of a crescent moon, and between them a tall rock jutting up out of the Boilers." He paid him and checked his own bearings.

Once more they sailed; around and about among the hundreds of small rocky islands they poked, but nothing showed itself, and as the weeks went on this crew, like the other, became restive. At last Phips took stock.

The *Rose* was leaking badly at many seams; food was running low; the grapnels, chains, and nets were obviously too fragile for his requirements, and Phips finally concluded that trying any longer under present conditions would be futile. The only sensible course was to go back to England and start over.

When they got as far as Bermuda they were greeted by the bad news that Charles II had died and his brother the Duke of York was now James II. James, who had been Lord High Admiral, was known to be tough-minded where his Navy was concerned, and the battered ship Phips was bringing back was hardly the *Algier Rose* he had borrowed two years before. He slunk into harbor sheepishly, fearing the worst.

He had reason for trepidation, moreover, for not only was he ordered to turn in the *Rose* without more ado but a five-hundred-pound charge was slapped on him for repairs. As for ever getting another ship—he would have to present his case before Samuel Pepys, Secretary of the Admiralty, and this gentleman was notoriously cold to treasure hunters.

His old friend the Duke, glad though he would have been to be of assistance, could do nothing in this case, for the scandal-loving Pepys never let people forget the Duke's ancestry and Albemarle could not bring himself to ask favors of such a man. Phips must look out for himself.

He presented himself to the Lords of the Admiralty with his credentials all marshaled—the old Spaniard who had seen the flagship go down and simply had to be right, a new diving bell he had perfected which would make diving so easy, the Indians who could stay under water nearly two minutes at a time, his expert calculations on all points. Samuel Pepys shook his head; England's relations with her neighbors were too touchy, he said, to waste a ship on such a wild-goose chase.

Faced with this setback, the Duke, whose wife was spending him into a fever, went directly to the King and begged for a license for himself; he would get the expedition financed privately. James was delighted by the prospect of getting a royal tenth without risking a ship and complied with alacrity.

This license gave Albemarle rights to "all flotsam, jetsam, lagan, bullion, plate, gold, silver, bars, coin, pigs of silver, ingots of gold, merchandise and other goods shipwrecked and lost before July 16, 1689, on the North side of Hispaniola in the Bahamas on the Gulf of Florida." That date gave him three years' leeway.

He now gathered about him a group of wealthy and titled friends who banded together under the name of the Gentleman Adventurers. This syndicate was to furnish vessels, supplies, victuals, and wages for the crew (Phips was going to have no more undisciplined partnership ventures). The ships were to carry a cargo to trade with, both as a hedge against failure and to serve as a blind for the real purpose of the trip, and in return for their investment the Gentleman Adventurers were to receive, after deduction of the King's tenth and costs, one eighth each, except Albemarle, who rated one quarter, and Phips, who had to be content with one sixteenth, not being a gentleman.

Two vessels were bought, one of them, the *Bridgewater*, burden 200 tons and mounting 22 guns, being renamed the *James and Mary* after the King and Queen. These names gave Phips private satisfaction, for they were also the names of his own father and mother, and somehow that seemed a good omen. The *Henry of London*, a frigate, burden 50 tons with 10 guns, was put in command of the faithful Francis Rogers. Each ship carried a pinnace, a longboat, and a canoe.

A cargo of eye-catching trifles was laid in, painted mugs, stockings, knives, hats, scissors, serge, buttons, bottled brandy, pictures, powder, and spirits—all told, about five-hundred pounds' worth. The latest fishing equipment, heavy grapnels, chains, Phips' patent diving bell, hooks, nets, crowbars, and buckets were stored below, while live animals and fresh water to last two months filled every possible corner. The Gentleman Adventurers had sunk 3,212 pounds in the expedition.

Phips bound himself to keep accounts and write a journal of his trip, and though he furnished a bond to insure performance of his obligations, the Duke sent along a former page, Charles Kelly, just to make sure.

On September 12, 1686, the *James and Mary*, with the *Henry of London* in company, weighed anchor at the Downs. There were seventy men besides the four divers on whom the whole expedition depended.

This crossing had a dignity in keeping with its noble auspices—no rebellions, no thefts, no rapes—and two months and 3,430 miles later they put in neatly at Carlisle Bay in Barbados. Fresh water, firewood, and food were quickly laid in and then the two ships moved on, losing sight of each other in the storms but fetching up simultaneously on November 28 in the small sandy bay of Samaná on the north side of Hispaniola. Immediately Phips sent a longboat to seek a place to careen, for leaks must be caulked and the ships' bottoms scraped of barnacles before being tallowed to make them slip easily through the water. But before a suitable spot was found the men in the longboat, peering over the side, gave a yelp of excitement.

Eighteen feet below in the clear blue water, her outline dulled by an overgrowth of coral, lay the skeleton of a ship. Back they hurried to the *James and Mary*, yelling ahead for one of the divers, and watched eagerly as the brown figure cut down through his own bubbles to the hulk. But the wreck was too close to the surface and too close to shore, and it had already been stripped. It yielded only three or four broken bits of plate.

However Phips grinned: "At least we know we are in galleon country."

Towards the middle of December the *James and Mary* came to anchorage at Porto Plata in Hispaniola, where the survivors of the flagship had landed with their silver forty-three years before. It was a little community now, Spaniards mostly, occupied with hunting and trade, and on entering, Phips fired a three-gun salute and sent a present to the Governor with elaborate compliments and expressions of his desire for peaceful trade. Nothing was said about treasure hunting and, indeed, he hung about trading for a month instead of hurrying off to the Ambrosia Bank in order to show what an ardent trader he was.

At the same time, careful preparations were going forward quietly. Mindful of the Boilers, whose submerged peaks endangered any boat but that of the shallowest draft, the Maine woodsman went into the forest and cut down a tall tree. Out of it he fashioned a pirogue, the long shallow craft with which the West Indians customarily went skimming over the water. At last, on January 13, he loaded it and the diving equipment onto the *Henry* and sent her off with Rogers, Covell, and the divers to find the Ambrosia Bank, the reef the Spaniard had described. The *James and Mary* he kept in Porto Plata, in plain view of the Spanish traders.

For the next three weeks Phips had nothing to record in his log but the purchase of a bundle of hides at a satisfactorily low price. Otherwise the waiting was empty and tense. At last he began to grow worried; he gave the *Henry* until February 9, and if she had not returned by then he would go to Jamaica, the prearranged rendezvous in case of trouble.

The weather was consistently bad—wet and boisterous—and the visibility through the rain almost at zero. But on the first of February the *Henry* could be seen dimly in the distance struggling against a contrary gale. For a solid week she beat back and forth and Phips had to bite his nails and wait, but on the seventh the winds died and she approached.

The longboat brought Rogers to the captain's ship, where he climbed aboard with a long and serious face. To Phips' eager questions he replied in an apologetic tone, albeit defensively:

"We did our best. We had only two or three days of fair weather and no man could have done more. The last night before we left we were in the canoe and got caught in the Boilers. Nothing but God's grace saved us."

Phips had steeled himself for disappointment, and now he could nod slowly, resignedly. His Puritan training came out as he replied, "We will wait on God and not give up hope."

Rogers, his face still long and grave, said he was sorry not to bring better news, and went back to the *Henry*, suggesting, however, that the captain be sure to visit his ship the next day to speak to the men.

The following morning Phips paid his call and was invited below to the main cabin. Standing about the table were Covell and the divers. They all sat down solemnly and again the defense began. He listened; he watched their faces gloomily, asked a few questions. And then his eyes noted that the tension in their manner belied their disheartened words.

"What are you doing?" he cried. "Is there something more than you are telling me?"

At this their faces broke with laughter. He jumped to his feet, and in the excitement stumbled against a lump lying on the floor beneath the table.

It was shapeless, encrusted with coral, the size of a watermelon. He had seen such things before, for anything brought up from a long stay in the depths was covered with coral, and now, seizing an iron adz, he brought it down on the lump. Like a piece of ore, it split apart and laid bare a solid mass of silver.

Now, while he stared, the men's laughter grew, and after a gaping moment he raised his arms to heaven, shouting, "Thank God. Now we are all made."

Next, talking all together, they had to show him the rest of the treasure they had hidden behind the door, great bars of silver in various sizes and shapes, and two-thousand-odd Spanish dollars. If the men had expected the big hulking captain to break excitedly into a hornpipe they did not know him. He merely sat grinning broadly at the pile on the floor and listened to their account of the past four weeks.

The *Henry* had sailed from Porto Plata along the trail of the Silver Fleet, four days later hitting Cape Cabirone, the last sight of Hispaniola, and from thence started fifty-one miles due north for the Ambrosia Bank. In two more days they found the area they sought, two reefs stretching out in a curve towards each other. They passed the South Reef first. Beyond this the Boilers bubbled up over their submerged rocks and beyond them lay the North Reef, the Ambrosia Bank.

Everywhere they had looked for a single tall jutting rock, and seeing none had felt a chill of disappointment. Nevertheless, after anchoring a mile away in deep, safe water, they had dropped the boats and paddled all day along the north side of Ambrosia Bank, peering down through the strangely clear blue water.

The sand at the bottom was perfectly white, reflecting the sunlight back onto anything in the water above. Rocks in every imaginable shape covered with seaweed led them many times to suppose they were over the wreck, but each time when Franko the diver went down he came back shaking his head.

At first, Covell told Phips, the divers had been reluctant to go down, for moray eels, the most vicious things underseas, poked their ugly round faces out of crevices in the rocks, and sharks—hammerhead, basking and blue—could be seen cutting curves through the water. Barracudas shot past with predatory eyes, and when one of the men by accident lost his white shirt over the side a big specimen turned and struck at it viciously. Soon it was observed, however, that dark objects attracted less attention than white ones, so the Indians inside their naked brown skins began to relax.

Over and over that first day the men had dived, forty, fifty, sixty feet, with no results. The north side of the Bank was adjudged a failure. The next day they tried the south side, Covell taking the canoe with two divers and Rogers the boat with one. All along the edge of the reef they paddled, eyes on the bottom. Nothing could be seen but vividly colored fish darting about, jellyfish like enormous umbrellas trailing behind them undulating frills thirty feet long, green vegetation, and pink and white coral shaped like pear trees, candelabra, and fans twenty feet tall.

Sometimes the beauty below momentarily detached their minds from their main quest while they stopped to admire, and this was fortunate, Rogers said, smiling, for towards the end of the second day, when no wreck had been discerned, the vivid beauty of a bright red coral branch was the turning point in their lives.

Hope had nearly been given up; if there had still been hope of treasure no one would have taken time for picking submarine flowers. But as a sort of consolation, seeing the red sea feather beckoning up from the bottom, they reached out to beauty when wealth eluded them. Franko, the Indian in the boat with Rogers, sprang over the side. Forty feet below they could still see him clearly, stretching out his hand to the coral branch to break it off. Then he stopped in mid-gesture. Here and there he darted, peering like a fish at the dark mass from which the sea feather sprouted. Then he gave the line around his waist a sharp jerk and Rogers pulled him to the surface.

His eyes were popping when he broke the water. "Guns!" he gasped. "Guns!"

"Mr. Covell!" Rogers shouted across the water. "Guns!"

The canoe was beside them in a moment, and another of the divers went over the side and brought up a lump of coral. It was long and oblong and clumsy, and when they hit it with a metal rake it fell apart and showed silvery white inside. Now another Indian went down, and soon a sow of silver and a bar lay in the bottom of the canoe.

They had arrived, it appeared, right over the waist of the midship hold. The wood had rotted and fallen away from the galleon's ribs and her precious entrails had spilled out onto the sand. Their task was so easy it was almost laughable.

Then they realized why so many before them had failed. The tall jutting rock was nowhere to be seen, but beneath the surface it was plainly visible. Of a soft disintegrating substance, it had been worn away by the waves and only the stump remained, like a broken tooth. Directly at its base lay the ship, wedged forty-five feet down between it and another stump of rock. Broken open by the point on which she had impaled herself and by the ceaseless tearing of the water, seemingly a part of the rocks she lay among and altogether overgrown with coral, she and her guns and her chests and bags had become one with the underwater scenery and nothing less than the red sea feather could have disclosed her identity.

Yet, once found, she gave them no more trouble, and by nightfall of the first day they had picked up two sows of silver from the sea floor, fifty-one pieces of eight, and some broken plate, and in the next three days eighty-two sows and bars of silver and two thousand pieces and half pieces of eight.

There had been, all told, but two or three days of good weather, and on the twenty-second it blew so hard that they left a buoy over the wreck and scurried back to tell Phips. He listened and at once began making plans.

For the next week all was muffled excitement and preparation, while, preserving their casual air for the benefit of their neighbors in harbor, they again cleaned and tallowed their ships and bought wild hogs and a cow under the supervision of the Spanish hunters, learning how to bone them and dry the meat in the sun. They laid in water and fruit and salt, and on February 17 weighed out of Porto Plata. Then for the first time Phips' log carried the bold heading, "On board the *James and Mary* bound for the wreck."

The equipment provided by the Gentleman Adventurers had stopped short of luxuries and the log book was one already used; Phips kept account of his treasure hunt on the backs of pages devoted to a trading voyage around the world.

Five days out of Porto Plata they arrived at the Ambrosia Bank, where, sailing around the reefs for Phips to have a good look, they finally came to anchor four miles off in deep water. But Covell, unable to wait until morning in his eagerness, took the pinnace with Strong and two divers to the wreck and as evening shut down returned with eighty-nine whole pieces of eight and fifty-one half pieces. A careful count was made by Thomas Waddington, Phips' servant, and a cross check by Charles Kelly.

The next day the captain himself went to the wreck. (He had abandoned his fashionable wig and was going about, shamelessly, in his own hair; furthermore, being out of sight of land, he and Rogers and Covell had thrown off their woolen coats. They kept their white skins carefully covered against the sun, but the Indians went stark-naked save for their knife belts.) Now in a small boat he and Covell and a diver moored over the wreck in the narrow channel between the two stumps.

Phips watched Franko slip a bit of oily sponge into his mouth, grasp a big stone under his left arm, lift his chest in four deep practice breaths, and after a long soft whistle of exhalation take the deepest breath of all and dive over the side. Weighted by the stone, the shining body streaked down to the white floor of sand and shells, where, dropping his stone and chewing vigorously to check the impulse to breathe, the Indian struggled for nearly two minutes with a lump of coral, finally loosing it from its bed. He jerked the line at his belt, grasped the lump in one arm and the stone in the other, and was drawn swiftly to the surface. Gasping for breath but grinning, too, he lifted the lump and Phips took it from his hands.

He said nothing for a moment; it was a smallish piece of coral, far from impressive, but this act of reaching over the side of his own canoe and taking the wet lump of bullion into his own hands was perhaps the highest moment of this ambitious man's life. The treasure was found and the treasure was his.

The *Henry*, anchored nearer the wreck than the *James and Mary* because of her shallower draft, had sent her longboat with men and divers, and now they too were going down. Unlike the crews, the divers were working on shares—ten pieces of eight for each thousand they brought up and the same proportion for other articles—and were as keen as Phips himself. They dived, sent up the lighter pieces in buckets and nets, tied chains about the heavier, rested, dived again, far into the dusk. That night 989 half pieces of eight and one bar were recorded by Waddington and Kelly and stored in the *James and Mary*.

Next morning at daybreak they were out again, and that day there were 2,639 pieces of eight and 1,177 half pieces in calcified sacks to be stowed away. The next, being Sunday, they rested. The weather that day was unusually fine and some of the men had suggested working anyway, but Phips, a mixture of tawdry and genuine, had put his foot down hard. Callous to the point of dishonesty—he had left unpaid bills behind in every port—he was yet sincere enough Puritan to sacrifice a good day's fishing for his faith, and instead of work he led the men in a service of prayer and thanksgiving. (Many years later the eminent New England divine Cotton Mather noted the incident approvingly in his history of his friend, Sir William Phips, Governor General of Massachusetts.)

Monday a disturbing incident occurred, when, far to windward, two sails were seen bearing down. Phips had such uncomfortable visions of pirates that, annoyed as he was at the intrusion, he felt only relief when the ships came closer and he recognized old friends, a sloop in command of William Davis of Bermuda and a shallop mastered by Abram Atherley of Jamaica. Having been with him on his previous trip, they had come now to fish themselves.

Phips' license from the King would have privileged him to send them packing, but that would have meant backing up his orders with threats and the threats with force, and so instead he took them into partnership, allowing them half of whatever treasure they found in return for use of the sloop and their divers.

On the very next day he had reason to be glad he had done so, for the weather was tempestuous, with a wind from the east, and the pirogue disappeared into the troughs of the waves like a flea in the wrinkles of a blanket. The morning was half gone before the boats reached their goal, and when they did cast anchor the waves so tossed them about that on the first dive the line of the Indian fouled the anchor line. When he struggled to the surface his face was dark with rage.

"We'll use no anchor," he said firmly.

Here on the wreck the divers had the final word, so from now on the men had to paddle furiously against the currents simply to stay in one place. Let one stop for food or rest and the dancing chip of wood went scurrying over the waves.

Below conditions were no better, for the fiercely running current tore the divers from their footing and, like moths fighting a high wind, they expended most of their strength and time struggling with the water itself, forced up for air before they had more than got their hands on their quarry. Phips, suddenly grateful for William Davis and his sloop, suggested the diving bell.

This, like the wine cask the Bermudian had rented out years before, like the tubs of Taisnier and other inventors in Europe, operated on a simple principle which Phips had first seen illustrated with a drinking glass and a pail of water. The glass, turned down onto the surface of the water and pressed to the bottom, retained air inside itself. In a more elaborate demonstration he even saw a bit of candle remain alight in the glass under water.

In quiet inland waters Phips had made his own experiments. A large wooden bell, heavily weighted about its lower rim and with three legs on which to stand, had been slung from a derrick by a cable and winch. Inside it he had had himself lowered to the bottom of a lake, where the bell stood comfortably upright high enough to allow him to swim out from under it. So long as he remained inside only his legs got wet and the breathing space contained enough air for forty-five minutes' submersion.

He had planned to operate it from the deck of the *Henry*, the men descending to the wreck, darting out for their work, and returning to it for more air, and thus saving the strength and time lost in diving from the surface. But the Boilers had prevented the *Henry* from approaching the reef.

Now, however, the lighter sloop was anchored fore and aft over the wreck and from the derrick the bell was lowered to the water's surface. Franko ducked inside and, drawn down by the lead weights around its edge, it sank.

Phips was aware that the bell must descend on the pure perpendicular; once or twice he himself had tipped it accidentally, thus spilling some of the air and sharply reducing the breathing space within. But he had worked in quiet waters where it could go down straight and stand evenly on the bottom, and now the waves pounded it on its windward side and swung it aside like a bit of fluttering ribbon.

More lead plummets were fastened to the rim. Finally it sank with only a slight list and hit the ocean floor forty-five feet below. The men on the winch, feeling the sudden release of weight and slackening of the line, expected Franko to swim out between the tripod legs and make for the wreck. But what had seemed a flat white floor from above was in reality like a plowed field, with furrows ever shifting under the worrying of the current. The bell kept tipping over. For the rest of the day they raised and lowered it trying to find a level spot, and at evening, swearing, Phips and his men returned to the *James and Mary*. The divers had been suspicious of this unknown device from the beginning, and now they shook their heads with more conviction. But Phips would not give up yet.

"We'll use it another way," he suggested. "Let it down onto the wreck itself. Surely we can find a level place." But it always tipped. When he hung it beside the hulk just short of the bottom the current caught it and banged it against the timbers.

The divers were getting impatient and irritated. "Let us do it the way we know," Franko begged.

But Phips had spent a lot of money on the bell. "We'll try it one more way," he insisted.

This time it was allowed to dangle well above the hulk, a little bubble of air halfway to the surface. There seemed nothing wrong with this idea, and Franko grudgingly admitted that with a supply of air nearby he should be able to penetrate farther into the interior of the hulk. Fifteen feet above the bottom he left the bell and swam down.

The ship lay on her side, her planking fallen away but the huge oak beams still curving up like the ribs of a skeleton. The timbers of her decks had partially collapsed across each other, the mast had toppled sideways, and everything was overgrown with seaweed and coral. Between the broken shards Franko slid, the light from above glancing through the interstices as through the branches of a forest.

Almost buried among the timbers lay a gun. He knew it by its shape, fuzzy with pink coral though it was. A chain with a hook dangled from the sloop above ready for use, and now he caught it and began securing it around the barrel.

Thirty seconds he worked, sixty seconds, ninety. With lungs squeezed to half their size by the weight of the surrounding water and fast losing oxygen as carbon dioxide accumulated, with eyes smarting and vision blurred, chewing and swallowing regularly, he grappled with the chain while the current dragged him this way and that. Grunting and straining and pulling, he felt his lungs begin to warn that they were near the bursting point but, conscious of the supply of air close overhead, he stayed to give the chain a final twist. Then he turned to the bell—and found that it was gone.

Long streamers of vegetation rippled on the current, a grouper with black and white stripes hung over his shoulder watching in openmouthed concentration and grunting in his ear, purple sea fans waved rhythmically. A school of tiny bright fish like a shower of sequins flashed past the diver, enclosing him in a moving cloud of light, while, blinded and suffocating, he gave a frantic tug to the line he had not expected to use. He was still inside the hulk and it caught on one of the overhead timbers. There was no response.

Now, bursting and panic-stricken, he tugged again. With oxygen gone, he expelled the poisonous gases from his lungs in a great burst of bubbles and on his last strength pulled clear of the wreckage. A third time he tugged. This time the jerk went home, and the men on deck, who had seen the current sweeping the bell out of his reach and been helpless to drag it back, grabbed the line and pulled.

By the time Franko reached the surface he was unconscious, the surrounding water was brown, and when they lifted him up, blood was pouring from his nose and mouth and ears.

Though the Indian recovered, the sight of him lying groaning with his head in a wash of blood had had a chilling effect on his companions and now they flatly rejected this dangerous device. If there were silver and gold to be had it would have to come up in the conventional way. The bell was put aside, written off as a total failure in the log.

The next fine day the sloop went back to the wreck. Phips had given Franko a rest, but the others, relieved of newfangled experiments, returned to their familiar tools and began a straight six weeks of diving, twenty dives an hour for eight or nine hours a day.

On March 3 the brass gun was brought up, along with 4,900 silver pieces of eight in chests and some broken silver vessels. On March 5 2,399 pounds' weight of coins was added, on March 8, 1,958 pounds of silver, a twenty-six-pound bar, a sixty-one-pound sow, a 177-pound sow, a bar of gold, and some small sacks of uncut gems. Even on a day when the divers were not feeling well 3,931 in whole pieces of eight and 1,500 half pieces went into Waddington's and Kelly's books.

Inevitably the divers were suffering from the strain of wrenching free heavy lumps of limestone, fighting tides which made a wrestling match out of a task like securing a chain around a gun, holding their breath until they nearly burst. They were fast ruining their health, and all of them now came up with blood in their mouths; longer and longer they lay gasping on the deck, and gradually the twenty dives were reduced to fifteen, then to ten, finally to five.

Although Phips was by no means a brute, impatience tortured him, for time was against them. The only interlopers so far had been Davis and Atherley, but how long he could remain undisturbed was anyone's guess, and in a crosscurrent of emotions he alternately counseled his divers to rest and urged them on to one more effort. So, in spite of illness, in spite of the March storms that rolled them onto their beam ends, the work went on and the tally grew.

Week by week, reading over the log, Phips himself was hardly able to believe the figures. At the same time his anxiety grew, for food was running low. He knew that the crews, working on straight salary, had not the feverish interest he and the divers felt in the size of the haul and could not be expected to endure the same privations and dangers. So he took a calculated risk. The unsold trading goods, the painted mugs and what not, he moved into the sloop from the *James and Mary*, and on March 29 sent the sloop with Charles Kelly to Samaná Bay. There Kelly was to trade the stuff and return with food and water. Meanwhile the fishing continued.

On April 14 the wreck's midship hold had been cleaned out. At once they looked for a new cache, the men weaving in and out through the rotting timbers till the coral formations began to take on meaningful shapes, and that day the prize was small but notable, a massive gold cup. The next day the flow of silver began again, seemingly inexhaustible. And yet within four days the ships were gone.

Phips, measuring the grain and salt meat and water in the hold, saw they were all but exhausted, and, turning in desperation to the horizon, saw no sign of the sloop either. Kelly himself, he reasoned, was not one to betray their good fortune, for he was the King's own man, but how could he be sure that the crew, surrounded by Spaniards and French privateers, would be so discreet? Perhaps the sloop had even been captured and the men put to torture. If word got around, he and his treasure were not worth a spit in the sea.

Pacing the deck in a torment of uncertainty—should he stay and clean out the wreck or get away with what he had?—he finally fixed on a sort of compromise. The *James and Mary* and the *Henry*, heavy with silver, should go to the isolated Turk Islands and hide, while Atherley stayed in the shallop to continue fishing and wait for the sloop. If Kelly and the sloop had not returned in a week Atherley was to give up and hurry to the Islands.

On her way through the uncharted cays the *James and Mary* nearly ran aground on an unseen reef, but Phips' expert navigation brought her to harbor at Cotton Cay three days later. Soon the

Henry arrived, and soon after that Atherley in the shallop to deliver the proceeds of his six days' work, a ton and a half of silver. "And there was no end in sight," he reported ruefully.

Kelly and the sloop were never heard from. She might have sunk in a gale, but the alternate possibility that she had been seized by French pirates and her men forced to talk made Phips wish to get home as fast as winds could carry him. But before the ships separated he called every man of the enterprise together and solemnly swore them in the sight of their Maker never to reveal the location of the wreck, for he planned to return and finish off the job and could only pray that no one else would get there before him.

Out of Cotton Cay the *James and Mary*, with the entire treasure in her hold, soon lost the *Henry* and had to continue nervously alone. Heavy and clumsy and inadequately armed, she was unequipped to cope with pirates. Phips could only maintain a twenty-four-hour watch and keep out of shipping lanes. He dared not even stop at Bermuda for food and supplies for fear word had got abroad about his cargo, and so the long voyage was made by a half-starved crew.

Mutiny was an ever-present danger; the men seemed loyal enough, but on the lonely wastes of the Atlantic it would be easy to kill him and make off with the ship, so as insurance he promised each man a bonus, undertaking to pay it from his own share if the Gentleman Adventurers refused to make good.

The possibility of hurricanes, fortunately slight at this time of year, he handled in the only way he knew, by prayer. As in previous crises, he now turned wholeheartedly to his God, and vowed that if he came safely across the Atlantic he would devote his future life to the service of Jesus Christ and the welfare of his country. Later he had the grace to try to fulfill his pledge.

At three o'clock in the morning of June 10, 1687, Christopher, Duke of Albemarle, was sleeping soundly in his heavily curtained bed in London when a thunderous knock and shout awakened him. Though the Duke's regular rising time was not till five his servants knew he would not want to wait today.

"Your Grace," they cried, "Your Grace's man William Phips is anchored in the Thames. They say he is the richest man in England."

Out of bed the Duke tumbled and, hardly dressed, drove wildly with Sir James Hayes down the river to Gravesend. The news had already penetrated to the Admiralty and a guard had been placed about the *James and Mary's* dock, only authorized persons being permitted to pass through. But certainly the Duke had that right, and he greeted Phips with a roar, demanding details of the adventure and an itemization of the score. Solemnly Phips handed over the tally.

When the Duke was able to speak he expressed his joy in a manner typical of his tastes, ordering every man and boy on board to drink his health. Phips he carried off to Newcastle House to present him to a group of fluttering peers and peeresses, and the New England sailor was suddenly the lion of London.

For the next three months adulation swirled about his head like a strong hot wind. And without a doubt the King and many others had reason to be pleased with him, for immediately on his arrival the warden, the master worker and the comptroller of the royal mint, along with the veteran goldsmith Charles Dunscombe, had gone to meet the *James and Mary* in the King's ship, transferring the treasure to the *Rising Sun*, where it was weighed and divided into shares. Of pieces of eight there were 37,538 pounds troy; of bars and other measures of silver bullion 27,556 pounds, four ounces; of silver plate 347 pounds; of gold ingots twenty-five pounds, seven ounces; plus jewels and oddments. The total value was over three hundred thousand pounds.

Thirty thousand pounds of this came to the King, which made him Phips' firm friend, while Albemarle's share, in excess of fifty thousand, put him in such a fine glow that he built a furnace in the garden of his mansion to melt down his metal and, overcome by enthusiasm, nearly fired his own house and person as well. The Gentleman Adventurers, flushed with their shares ranging from eight to twenty thousand pounds, voted to make good Phips' promise to the crew, and consequently the mate, bosun, and carpenter received a thousand pounds each and the seamen from twenty to sixty, according to their rating. Phips' share was but sixteen thousand pounds net. This was augmented, however, by a job lot of copper guns, stirrups, candlesticks, silver cups and saucers, broken gold buttons and beads, part of a gold chain, a gold hatband and a few uncut gems, while the Duke kindly took cognizance of the patient wife at home by sending the golden cup valued at nearly a thousand pounds. Mary's patience was beginning to pay off.

The furor over the treasure hunter filtered down from the fashionable world to the crowds in the street and outward through broadsides and letters to America and the Continent. Daniel Defoe wrote scathing pamphlets on the mania that had seized the people, but his scorn could not prick the bubble of excitement. The Duke proudly presented Phips at Windsor Castle, where the great ruddy-faced sailor knelt on a velvet cushion and received the sword of knighthood on his shoulder, and at the same time he was offered a place among the commissioners of the Navy, or whatever else he desired.

Phips stopped and considered this offer. Now, it seemed, was the moment when he could begin keeping the vow made on the high seas. The Massachusetts Bay Colony had lost its charter and without a fair jury system was at the mercy of the Governor's whims, so instead of a favor for himself Phips asked that the charter be restored. The King's generosity did not extend quite this far, but he compromised on the post of Provost Marshal General, or High Sheriff, of New England (for which position Phips eventually found himself paying some hundred guineas, so the King's generosity had a sting in its tail after all).

The colony of Massachusetts Bay having been absorbed into the dominion of New England under a royal governor, this position gave Phips some power and authority in the community, and so the moment the news crossed the ocean Mary Phips, her patience suddenly exhausted, rushed out and bought land for that fine house in Greene Street without waiting for her husband to get home. She was Lady Phips now, and she was not going to lose a moment of the fun.

The celebrations in London continued, the Gentleman Adventurers giving Phips a tremendous banquet at the Swan Tavern, where he was presented with a gold medal and chain and the sailors with silver ones, all adorned with pictures of the King and Queen.

But ever more frequently an underlying thought kept popping into the conversation—there was still a tremendous treasure in the wreck. Phips was eager to get back, and Albemarle's interest in the tropics was stronger than ever, for his friend Sir Henry Morgan had been writing him. The erstwhile pirate was rapidly drinking himself to death, but he still had a vigorous love for treasure and had sent Albemarle tempting hints about the wrecks still to be investigated. So, the incumbent Governor of Jamaica having conveniently died, the Duke staggered fashionable London by announcing his acceptance of the governorship. While the island was hot and primitive compared with London, the jaundiced Duke and his unbalanced wife enjoyed the prospect of a life of unbridled spending in the company of their amusing friend.

This time backers for the treasure-diving venture were easy to find, even though the King was now demanding not a tenth but a full half. Phips, master of the new *Goodluck and a Boy,* was in charge of the expedition and Rogers captained the *Princess,* while the *James and Mary* and the *Henry* were relegated to lesser commanders. Sir John Narborough's *Foresight* was convoy, and with him was that same pathetic Captain Stanley who had earlier failed to find the Vice-Admiral's ship himself.

The Albemarles were to have accompanied them in the royal frigate, but the Duke, dying slowly and unattractively, caused some delay and it was December before the two parties rendezvoused in Samaná Bay.

When at last they arrived at Ambrosia Bank, which was already beginning to be called the Silver Shoals, they were dismayed to find no less than twenty-five sails dotted about the reef, sloops, brigantines, shallops—all busily fishing for silver and gold. The English flotilla, armed with an exclusive license from the new Governor of Jamaica, rushed about among the interlopers, driving them off, and then in a state of shock assembled for a conclave.

Hurriedly a canoe with divers was dispatched to their own special wreck to learn the worst, and at nightfall the waiting Sir John Narborough and Sir William Phips guessed the news from the droop of the men's bodies as they approached. The wreck had been discovered and ransacked.

It was inevitable, of course, that the furor over Phips' adventure should have attracted other treasure hunters to the Ambrosia Bank, and while depending on the crews' oath of secrecy to protect the flagship, he had been prepared to find a few strangers poaching on his preserves. But here were men from all over Western Europe, from New England, New York, and the other Atlantic colonies; in Bermuda, it was said, all the able-bodied young men had gone off to the wrecks and left not even enough to tend the homes and farms, and every one of them seemed to have landed on his reef.

He soon learned the sad explanation: after he had sailed away in the spring Abram Atherley had stayed on in the vicinity with his shallop enjoying his new wealth; he had faithfully discharged his own oath of silence, but he could not prevent one of the shallop's boys from taking other employment when his vessel was laid up, nor foresee that the new captain would torture the boy till he told where the flagship lay. Indeed, so distraught was the conscientious Atherley when the news of its discovery came that worry and remorse unhinged his mind and after a season of running about demented he fell sick and died.

The entire expedition was a wretched anticlimax, so poorly rewarded that when one day they brought up a gold enameled case containing a small lump of ambergris they thought this worth recording. Later they found four great copper guns and some smaller ones, but week after week there was nothing more than a small pile of broken silver plate to lift their spirits, which were already damaged by scurvy, dysentery, and smallpox, and in the spring everybody realized it would be nonsense to continue. The trifling results of five months' fishing were divided after deduction of James II's share, and on May 8, 1688, Phips said good-by to his patron. The Duke, gazing at him fondly through the alcoholic haze to which he would succumb within the year, patted him and adjured him to hurry back, and he set sail for Boston, having been gone five years.

The unpleasant memory of his early brawls having been obliterated by the more recent news of his knighthood and his request to the King for restoration of the New England charter, Boston was ready to welcome him as a friend. Lady Phips, listening gravely to a public lecture when the news of his arrival broke, nearly fainted with excitement, and rushed out to meet him with a good portion of the town following; though he was returning as their rich new High Sheriff, it was the world's most successful treasure hunter they went out to see.

That was what the world remembered, too. While both parts of the astrologer's promise came true—in his thirty-seventh year he did find a great treasure and in his forty-first the King did employ him in a great position—the later achievement was always overshadowed by the earlier. He became a military leader of an expedition against the French in Canada; winning favor from a third English King, William III, he obtained for his native colony the charter he had so long sought, and he was finally appointed first Royal Governor of the Massachusetts Bay Colony. But it was as a man who had fulfilled a dream almost all men dream in their hearts that the people loved him.

Recognizing this fact, Lady Phips paid deference to it at the end. Her husband having died while on a visit to London, she had the task of ordering a tomb for him in St. Mary Woolnoth in Lombard Street, and reviewing the important events of his life, commissioned a suitable monument.

All of marble, it displayed several carven cupids looking down on a carven ship and a little boat surrounded by swimming men, the whole scene surveyed by one large eye equipped with wings, presumably that of God. The inscription told the story:

"Near to this place is interred the body of Sir William Phips, Knight, who, in the year 1687, by his great industry discovered among the rocks near the banks of Bahama, on the north side of Hispaniola, a Spanish plate-ship, which had been under water 44 years, out of which he took in gold and silver to the value of 300,000 pounds sterling; and with a fidelity equal to his conduct, brought it all to London, where it was divided between himself and the rest of the adventurers. For which service he was knighted by his then Majesty, King James the 2nd; and afterwards by the command of his present Majesty, and at the request of the principal inhabitants of New England, he accepted the government of Massachusetts, in which he continued to the time of his death, and discharged his trust with that zeal for the interest of his country, and with so little regard to his own private advantage, that he gained the good esteem and affection of the greatest and best part of the inhabitants of the colony. He died on the 18th of February, 1694."

The thing he started, however, the idea, never died. He was the first known salvor of sunken treasure, the first heir of the wealth lost by the conquistadors, and he proved that the most outrageous dreams could come true. Hot on his heels, therefore, came a host of other treasure fishermen. A few achieved success openly, men with government licenses who found anything from a single silver bar to a fortune in six figures, who reported their finds and were duly taxed thereon. Altogether these men paid taxes to William Constable, agent of the King, on nearly a quarter of a million pounds.

But of the others, the ones who did not report, no one knows the tally. Furtively for three hundred years men in craft of all sizes have slipped into secluded bays to unload their cargoes in the night, and no one can estimate their total. Still, it is certain that, of the enormous Portuguese and Spanish losses, the hundreds of ships lost to the Caribbean gales, only a fraction have been salvaged. The wood of the sunken galleons has rotted and been shaken apart by the waves, but the gold and silver and gems are as good as ever, still lying encased in their two-inch coat of coral waiting for another William Phips.

It is well known that of all adventurers treasure hunters are the most secretive. There are obvious reasons: first, that the treasure-trove laws of most countries claim ownership for their governments of any treasure found, with the consequence that successful hunters generally find themselves in long and unhappy lawsuits; second, that acquisition of some types of treasure render the owner liable to United States income tax. The result is that many good treasure stories never reach a typewriter.

The following account of such a hunt required many months of detective work on my part. I found the original clues in the book, They Found Gold, by A. Hyatt Verrill. After that came interviews with Dr. Jose Vicente Trujillo, Ecuadorian Ambassador to the United Nations; Mr. Ralph Atwater, former president of the Schultz Dredging Co.; Mr. Andres Salvador-Zaldumbide of Guayaquil, Ecuador; Mr. Nathaniel Mann, formerly of Ecuador, now of New York; Mr. Henry Gruntphal, Curator of the American Numismatic Society, and Mr. Robert I. Nesmith, member of the Society's Council; Mr. Jorge Vela, now First Secretary of the Ecuadorian Embassy in Venezuela, and Mr. Gustavo Ycaza of the Ecuadorian Consulate General in New York, to all of whom I am deeply indebted. I also obtained invaluable information from friends and relatives of the man whose story this is, but at the same time was forced to agree that, for obvious reasons, his identity would not be revealed. Consequently I have changed his name and profession and a few other details, without altering the essential facts as I found them.

There is no secret about where I found Drake's own story. He and his chaplain, Fletcher, and several Spaniards he met and robbed wrote accounts of his exploits, and these books, though difficult to obtain, can be read in any large public library.

II
Drake's Forty-five
Tons of Silver

Two MEN SAT in the window of the University Club looking out at the apple sellers on Fifth Avenue. Thaddeus Wilkie, who was a scientist and too poor to belong to the club, was the luncheon guest of E. G. Duane, a college classmate, who was a magazine publisher and did belong.

The apple seller on the corner, shivering in a coat too small for him, depressed them both, and Thaddeus Wilkie, a kindly man, burst out angrily, "It's all a matter of faulty distribution. It isn't that there is no food and clothing, there's plenty, there's too much. The producers are starving as badly as that man out there. I tell you . . ."

As he went on the publisher nodded absently; in December 1932 everybody was talking about faulty distribution, and the little mineralogist's fulminations skidded over the top of his mind unnoticed until suddenly a phrase caught his ear, "—billions of dollars lying around unclaimed——"

He jerked back to attention. "What's that?"

"I said that if we could just bring up all the gold and silver that's gone to the bottom of the ocean and distribute *that*, we'd——"

The publisher pounced like a hunting dog on a scent. "You mean sunken treasure? What do you know about sunken treasures?"

"Well, I've run across a good bit about them in the course of my regular job."

"You have? You mean dates, names, amounts, that sort of thing?"

The little man with the close-cropped white hair, his eyes gleaming, climbed onto his hobbyhorse and cantered off briskly, "The pay ship of the Armada sunk in Tobermory Bay, 1588, with thirty million in gold in a secret cell; H.M.S. *Grosvenor*, sunk off East Africa in 1782 with $4,800,000 in currency; the *Hussar*, sunk two hundred feet from Manhattan Island in 1856 with four million in gold; eleven Spanish galleons sunk in Vigo Bay in 1702 with eighty million on board; Sir Francis Drake's forty-five tons of silver thrown overboard in——"

Duane waited for no more. "Can you write an article for me? About all this stuff just waiting to be discovered?" His eyes shone happily. "With this depression on, and everybody so frantic for money, we ought to sell an extra hundred thousand copies."

So the following February, when all the banks in America were about to close, a two-thousand-word article appeared in Duane's weekly describing the enormous treasures lost in the waters of the world and never found again. The editor had asked for five thousand words, but Wilkie had protested that preparation for a forthcoming trip left him no time to write more. However, the magazine achieved something tolerably splashy anyway, with a full-page painting in four colors of Sir Francis Drake and his pirate crew tipping a chestful of silver coins over the side of a ship. It was garish and highly unscientific and Wilkie hoped none of his academic friends read mass-circulation periodicals, but he was nonetheless glad of the fee, for like others he was finding money scarce. His wife's long illness and death had drained his bank account, mining companies had not been sending out mineralogists to look for new deposits as freely as in the lavish twenties, and now that one for whom he had formerly worked had made him an offer he had lost no time in accepting. By publication date he was on a ship bound for Ecuador.

For the rest of that year the depression and his loneliness were forgotten in the job he loved, as, in company with a geologist and a native crew, he beat through the jungles and mountains of Ecuador, Peru, and Bolivia. The work was no sinecure, sometimes requiring revolvers as protection against the uncivilized Indians of the interior, but for all the hardships and for all his fifty-nine years he returned to Lima to file his report full of health and glowing spirits.

The glowing spirits, however, did not long survive civilization, for after two days a cable came back from the Chicago office, "Company's operations suspended see agent Lima fare home sorry."

He surveyed his situation. He was no longer young; the depression was as deep as ever; there was, he supposed, some salary deposited in his New York bank, but since his next job was of uncertain date he would need to conserve that. No one was waiting for him now, either; so he decided to hitchhike home. After picking up his fare at the agent's office and taking leave of his colleague, he boarded a *motorvelero* carrying miscellaneous local cargo to Trujillo and there made contact with an Englishman taking a cargo of sugar farther up the coast to Manta.

When he went aboard the run-down vessel and met his shipmates he found that, in a company of seven, five races were represented. Cyril Harrow, the owner, had the cadaverous cheeks and decayed teeth that bespoke an undernourished English childhood, while his wife's bland flat face proclaimed her Chinese parentage; Estevan, the fireman, and Jose, one of the deck hands, were as copper-colored and broad-cheeked as any Indian on the coast, while the engineer, Rafael, was unmistakably Spanish. The other deck hand, Charlie Jockel, was an American whose educated accent and sleazy gentility, strikingly out of place in these surroundings, set Wilkie puzzling until a whiff of alcoholic breath told him all he needed to know.

He expected to spend at most two nights on the *Bridlington*. His host had said, "I'll be glad to have someone to talk to besides Charlie for a change. I'm getting sick of Mr. Know-it-all." Wilkie paid down his seventy-five *soles* passage money and slung his luggage aboard with no premonitory prickle of excitement.

Cyril Harrow was indeed eager for conversation, or at least for an audience, and during the next twenty-four hours Wilkie somewhat unwillingly listened to a steady stream of reminiscences covering Harrow's years from nativity to date. As a boy he had eked out the family income wandering about the harbor of the Yorkshire resort of Bridlington scraping periwinkles off the rocks and selling them to a local lodging-house keeper. Later he went into mussels, which were larger and paid better, but for those you had to wade out into the icy waters of the North Sea. By his eighteenth year he had developed a deep loathing of cold weather, which was not much alleviated by four years on a mine sweeper on the Archangel run, and when peace came in 1918 his bones were so full of cold that he hastened to the tropics and never strayed more than ten degrees north or south of the equator again.

After a period as a steward on a coastwise steamer plying between Georgetown, British Guiana, and Pernambuco, Brazil, he wearied of seasick passengers and jumped ship, making his way by easy stages past Puerto Cabello, past Cartagena, across the Isthmus, down the west coast, finally bringing up at Manta, a roadstead for shipping in Ecuador, where he got a job with the Chinese owner of a battered tugboat and derrick lighter. This Chinaman was almost as old and battered-looking as his craft, but his daughter was considerably younger and sprightlier than either, and her Harrow married. All three lived comfortably enough on the tugboat till one evening the old gentleman, full of native *puro*, fell backwards overboard and Harrow found himself the owner of a little lightering business. He changed the tug's name from *Szechwan* to *Bridlington* and the lighter's from *Mukden* to *Goole*, the name of his birthplace; he displayed a Union Jack on state occasions, and gradually the *Bridlington's* galley became a kind of clubhouse for sailors touching Manta.

Between these visits Harrow depended for conversation on his tall and weedy deck hand, who claimed proficiency in half a dozen professions, including medicine and the law, but who handled the cargoes of the *Goole* with a loftiness bordering on total repudiation. Jockel wore a shirt with a raw neckband and a greenish-black bowler which he never removed during the day for any cause whatsoever, and since he insisted on sleeping in a cabin alone he was never seen to remove it at night either.

Though Harrow's reminiscences had filled all conversational gaps on the first night out, on the second Jockel managed to get in a few impressive references to golf, the stock exchange, Harvard Law School, and Brooks Brothers, all obviously aimed at Wilkie.

The three were sitting in the galley eating Dolly's Chinese-Spanish cooking, while Estevan in the boiler room, Rafael at the engine, and Jose aloft at the wheel kept the *Bridlington* wallowing north through the night. Suddenly Harrow put his head out of a porthole and shouted up at the pilothouse, "Jose, don't forget . . . Light on Plata." Returning to his stool, he grunted, "Idiot never remembers that lighthouse."

Wilkie had looked up in interest. "Was that La Plata Island you were talking about?"

"Yes. Why?"

He smiled a little sheepishly. "Are you passing close by? I'd like to have a look at it. There's a famous treasure dumped somewhere there, Sir Francis Drake's silver. I'd be curious to see the actual place."

Harrow's mouth had dropped slightly ajar and he asked in a hushed voice, "What do you know about that silver?"

"Well, only that Drake jettisoned about forty-five tons of it before he crossed the Pacific in 1580. Why, have you been looking for it?"

"No," breathed Harrow, "but I've read about it and I've been trying ever since to find out where it was." An American freighter had passed through Manta some months before, and going aboard for a drink, he had been given some discarded American magazines, in one of which he had read about the world's unrecovered treasures. He had rushed about Manta and even gone to Guayaquil seeking more information, but though many people had heard of it vaguely, no one could give him any particulars. "I asked a man in a bank if anybody's ever raised any and he said no, he was sure they hadn't, because he knew a man in the Casa de Cultura—that's the government place where they look after those things—and he had said they hadn't. Why *not*, God only knows, except that everybody's so bloody lazy here. And then of course there's the sharks."

"Sharks never attack human beings," Jockel remarked loftily. "That's an exploded theory."

"You just try telling these natives that," Harrow sniffed.

Wilkie, enjoying the sensation he was about to cause, leaned back and said with elaborate calm, "That article you read, I guess that's one I wrote."

Harrow and Jockel gaped for a moment and then crowded around him. "Then you know where the silver is—the actual spot?"

"Well, no," he replied, retreating instinctively into the scientist's guarded accuracy. "I've read Drake's own accounts of his voyages, and Ringrose's narrative, and the depositions of several Spanish eyewitnesses; I know what happened leading up to the dumping and about where it took place; but I have no idea whether any of it's still there."

The galley was silent save for the thumping of the wheezy steam engine. Jockel eyed Harrow and Harrow eyed Wilkie, while Dolly, impressed by the stillness of the men, stood with a coffeepot in her hand staring at all of them. At last Harrow spoke softly. "Fifty-fifty. I'll go fifty-fifty with you."

Wilkie found himself swept along on a wave that allowed him no time to set his feet on solid earth. His fumbling objections were swept aside: Did he have any imperative reason for hurrying on to New York? What had he to lose? Couldn't he use—how much was forty-five tons troy weight at sixty-five cents an ounce—God in heaven, $702,000! How could he refuse? All he had to do was tell them what he knew and they would do the rest.

The man on whom their putative fortunes rested had died over three hundred years before. But the roots of his reckless act reached back even further, through Francis Drake's personal feud with certain Spaniards in the New World, through his Queen's personal feud with her brother-in-law Philip of Spain, back to the feud between a weak and impoverished England and her blustering *nouveau riche* neighbor to the south. All of these sixteenth-century feuds in their turn dated back to the fact that the fifteenth-century explorations of the Italian mariner Christopher Columbus had been financed by Spain, and that as a consequence the vast wealth of the New World belonged to the Spanish crown.

Since 1521 the conquerors of Mexico and Peru had been sending back to Spain and her sister Portugal yearly shipments of such treasure as no one in Europe had even known existed, and as Spain's New World wealth increased, so had her power. By the middle of the sixteenth century Charles was not only Emperor of that country and the Netherlands but overlord of Germany and

Italy, with only France and England standing him off. And the expansion continued, until the inevitable explosion occurred. But that was not yet, nor for a long time yet.

While Spain was expanding, England was going through a depression and was too weak to interfere. But France's King, who was always quarreling with the Spanish Kings anyway, took immediate steps. In 1523, only two years after the shipments of treasure began, François I commissioned a sea captain, Jean Ango, to hold up one of the treasure fleets off the coast of Mexico, and from then on privateers operating under a royal license diverted considerable Spanish wealth to the French King's treasury.

But these privateers soon discovered that robbing the King's enemies under the King's orders had certain disadvantages—they were restricted to those certain enemies' ships, and they got only a small share of the spoils, while operating on their own, and against *any* country's ships, was extremely profitable. So piracy came to the New World.

Meantime England, too poor to be rude to either power, kept a nervous peace with both and rushed to pile up a navy. But for ships one needed money, and for money trade with one's neighbors. France had no need of the wool cloths which were her chief product, but Spain liked the stuffs, and so England had to keep smiling politely at the southern neighbor daily getting richer and more dangerous. And on the proceeds of that trade she built ships with which to destroy her.

Spain watched the shipbuilding with increasing anxiety. But at the same time she needed these busy little watchdogs that kept the English Channel open, for without them swarms of pirates would take over and then how could she keep in touch with her Netherlands dominions? She too watched her neighbor and smiled politely.

Soon after Columbus discovered the New World, Henry VIII came to his throne. Twenty-five years later, when Cortés and Pizarro had begun their shipments and the race for power was on, Henry had the start of a nice little navy. But then England fell behind, for after his death the boy king Edward VI and then Queen Mary, Bloody Mary, contributed little but corruption and stupidity. (Mary, strongly partisan in the Catholic-Protestant struggles of the time, muddied the situation even more by marrying the Spanish

Philip II in order to make him King of England and bind the two countries together under the Pope. But the scheme never worked; England and Spain were oil and vinegar, which, shaken together, might emulsify for a time but inevitably must fall apart again.)

After Mary came her brilliant, cynical, twenty-five-year-old sister. Elizabeth was always polite to her dead sister's husband; when her sea captains chased Philip's ships she was astonished and apologetic. The shipbuilding went on, nevertheless, and the sailors increased in numbers and efficiency, and finally there came a time when she could drop her bland innocence and thumb her nose. But that was not yet, not for a long time yet.

When she became Queen in 1558 the country was paralyzed with poverty and corruption. The citizenry were starving and the soldiery disorganized while the nobles were wasting extravagant sums on luxuries. With weakness inside her borders and enemies without, the Queen stood in need of strong and daring men. And the need called them forth. Breathing in the fresh air of a new age, they strode to the far corners of the earth and inscribed her name on stone and tablet for all who followed to wonder at.

They were not fastidious men, these Elizabethans. England wanted three things, customers for her products, churches independent of foreign jurisdiction, and strength equal to her neighbors'. These, the Queen told herself, were legitimate aims, therefore anything done to achieve them must be legitimate. If English merchants wished to trade in a certain area and another power claimed a monopoly there, they must simply trade anyway; if stealing an enemy's gold weakened that enemy, stealing was legitimate. Men to carry out this policy had to be brave and cheeky, and the men that came forward were.

The traders went out first. An expedition to Morocco was organized with the help of two Moors of royal blood who happened to be in London; it carried cloth, hardware, firearms, and Old Testaments for the Jewish merchants who controlled the trade, and brought back sugar, molasses, dates, and almonds. The transaction was a huge success, and soon English ships were scurrying all up and down the African coast, exchanging cloth and hardware for gold and ivory and pepper.

According to English views, this was all quite legitimate. According to Portuguese, it was offensive in the extreme. In 1493, Pope Alexander VI had issued his famous bull dividing up the new lands, whereby Spain was given all the New World except Brazil, Portugal receiving that part of South America and, for good measure, that part of Africa not already settled by Moors, Egyptians, and the like. So now the English were poaching on Portuguese preserves, and the King protested loudly to the Queen.

Elizabeth replied politely that she never allowed her ships to trade where they had no right. But, she added with gentle innocence, wasn't it possible that the Pope had had no right to give away all that land in the first place? And even if he had, didn't you really have to *occupy* a place and put in some form of government before it could be considered yours? Everyone knew there were almost no Portuguese living in Africa. Surely the King didn't wish to be a dog in the manger.

The English went right on trading, and since the King had no desire for open warfare at this time he could only fume and look the other way. Profits were enormous. Gold, ivory, and fresh vegetables brought such prices in England that even if two ships out of three never reached home everyone profited.

Everyone, that is, except the sailors, for scurvy and fever carried off a large proportion of them. Most were in their teens and early twenties, since few lived beyond that age, but the lot of the people on the land was so wretched that the wages of six or seven shillings a month at sea kept the vessels manned.

Actually there was another incentive besides profit. The vastness of the world had just struck England in full force, and her curiosity was nearly as strong as her avarice. As soon as the African coast was an old story the merchant sailors began to listen to the tales Spanish and Portuguese travelers brought back from the New World.

The early Spanish conquerors having killed off the Indian populations of the West Indies and the Spanish Mainland by overwork and brutality, now there were none to work the fields and mines. But across the South Atlantic a supply of black people, immune to sunstroke and helpless against firearms, was waiting to be captured, and this slave trade was flourishing, the newest way to get rich quickly. True, Philip had given his own concessionaires a monopoly on this most lucrative of trades, but this monopoly kept the prices high, and the local planters welcomed foreign traders so long as the trading was done *sub rosa*.

News of all this came to a certain English merchant sailor and he determined to see for himself. John Hawkins was a good mariner as well as a man of charm and education. On his first voyage down the African coast he picked up four hundred Negroes and disposed of them in the West Indies at a tidy profit. To protect the Spaniards he made a big display of firearms so that they could report home that they had traded under compulsion, overpowered by the unholy *luteranos* (all Protestants were Lutherans), after which they all sat down together to a pleasant banquet.

Hawkins went out again the following year, this time his chief backer the Queen herself, who, as the manager of the large business concern called *England*, chipped in the *Jesus of Lubeck*, an ancient 700-ton four-master, and a year later received a sixty per cent profit on her investment. To show her pleasure she granted him a coat of arms with an appropriate crest, the head of a Negro bound with a cord.

In spite of the planters' caution Philip got wind of Hawkins' activities and made such a noise that Elizabeth, for the sake of peace, withdrew further support for the moment. Thus it came about that the first voyage to the Indies of young Francis Drake was not under the aegis of the lady he was to serve so well and so long.

Francis Drake was born around 1541, at the depth of the depression, in Tavistock near Plymouth. His father, a farmer, was a Protestant when that was a daring thing to be. He had twelve sons (the daughters and wife went unrecorded) and during a religious fracas Edmund Drake took them all to Kent, where he settled in an old ship on the bank of a river. In this leaky hulk Francis, the eldest, spent his boyhood, learning to read and write from his parents and to take care of himself from the forces of nature. At fourteen he was apprenticed to the elderly owner of a coastwise bark, and by the age of nineteen had so won his confidence that, dying, he left the young man his decrepit little ship.

Shortish and stocky, with curling hair, round gray eyes that danced with humor, and eyebrows that could pull down in a thunderous bad temper or rise in relish of an impudent adventure, Francis Drake was the sort of man other men liked. He had one aristocratic connection, his godfather, Sir Francis Russell. Through this gentleman he was appointed page to the Duchess of Feria, maid of honor to Mary Tudor and wife of the Spanish Ambassador in London. Here he had a glimpse of the London court. And when the young Duchess took her retinue to Toledo for a visit to the court, there he acquired a smattering of Spanish which was to stand him in priceless stead later on.

Though his courtly bearing was acquired, his genius for leadership was his own. All through life he was harsh in discipline, but exacted nothing he was not willing to give. Fiery without being cruel, he tolerated in his men neither gambling nor filthiness. He confided his life to a God in whom he believed implicitly, and this faith was a bulwark against panic and defeat.

His real career began at twenty-four. Finding life at court as cramping as that on a coastwise vessel, he sold his bark and signed on with John Lovell for the West Indies. Hawkins was the real owner, but Queen Elizabeth had advised him to keep his face out of the Indies for the moment, so Lovell was delivering the cargo of Negroes for him. Drake, second-in-command, learned much about the West Indian Islands, the Spanish Main, that coast line stretching from Panama to Guiana, and the Spaniards themselves. He forgot nothing, least of all the galling experience on the Main which was the opening shot in a feud that lasted his lifetime.

Lovell, a simple soul with little talent for bargaining, had been cheated by the Treasurer of Rio de la Hacha in a transaction concerning ninety Negroes, and Drake, a party to the deal, was party also to the humiliation. His capacity for hatred was bottomless, and the minute he returned to England he consulted a chaplain, who assured him that, theologically speaking, revenge was not only a right but an obligation, so his path was set, and thereafter he never wavered from it.

Nothing could have pleased him more, then, than the news that John Hawkins was planning another voyage. This time Elizabeth was taking a considered risk, allowing Hawkins the *Jesus of Lubeck* again, and with it the equally old and battered 250-ton *Minion*, on condition that no provocative acts be committed against Philip's subjects. The *William and John*, 150 tons, the *Swallow*, 100 tons, the 50-ton *Judith*, which Drake was soon commanding, and the *Angel*, 32 tons, completed the fleet.

They made for Africa, where 150 men went ashore at Sierra Leone to capture Negroes. A number were struck by arrows; weeks afterwards, when the wounds had apparently healed, the men were seized with a curious lockjaw and slowly starved to death. Hawkins was one of the wounded, but he applied a clove of garlic to the wound and so saved himself. Drake escaped altogether.

Landing on the Spanish Main with five hundred pieces of flesh, they disposed of half at Domenica, Margarita, and other coast towns. Then they came to Rio de la Hacha, scene of his early humiliation.

Drake had a flypaper memory and now, despite the Queen's admonitions, he took the *Angel* and the spunky little *Judith* on a private expedition. Right into the harbor, right under the nose of the Treasurer, he steered his cockleshells and sat there, so to speak, sneering. The trigger-tempered Spaniards fired a couple of shots. Drake fired a couple back, managing to get one smack through the roof of the Treasurer's house, and then drew out of range and sat sneering four days longer. This time, when the rest of the fleet arrived, the farce of enforced trading was acted out in good earnest; Hawkins took the town; the inhabitants fled six miles into the woods, and the Englishmen followed and did their trading with the help of pistols. Drake, having lost the first round in his battle with Spain, had won the second.

Of course, such an affair was not going to look well on paper, so another version was prepared for the Queen, all full of the Treasurer's inhuman refusal to allow them drinking water for their slaves and their consequent necessity to take the town in self-defense. It read well if not examined too closely.

Next town along the Main was San Juan de Ulúa, and while in time Drake's bitterness over Rio de la Hacha might have wobbled, this encounter confirmed and fixed it forever.

They had not planned to go there at all, for it was a new place to them and they had nothing to trade. But the old flagship was leaking near to foundering and before starting home they needed to rest and repair in quiet waters. Inquiries along the coast brought the information that San Juan, a settlement protected by twelve mounted guns and situated on a small flat island four hundred yards offshore, was the nearest harbor. It was also the port where Mexico's treasures were loaded into galleons for Spain, and twelve glutted ships were at anchor now awaiting their convoy.

Though the ships were unarmed, Hawkins hesitated to enter. But a gale was blowing outside, the *Jesus* was leaking, and they needed food; so with the royal standard whipping aloft the six small ships sailed toward the mouth of the bay. The flag's lions rampant and fleur-de-lis were faded quite beyond recognition; thus as the ships approached, the Spanish officials ashore mistook them for the expected convoy and put out to meet them in an imposing galleon, only too late seeing their mistake. Hawkins with a grin signaled them to draw alongside. The sheepish officials, one ship to the stranger's six, had no choice but to comply, and thus they and Hawkins entered the harbor apparently hand in hand. This was a signal for the shore garrison to fire a respectful salute. Then they too realized their mistake and, panic-stricken, deserted their guns and ran like the wind that was sweeping the harbor. Hawkins, without intending anything so dramatic, had taken the town without a shot.

Delgadello, the captain of the island, nervously inquired his intentions.

He spread his empty hands, smiling and wide-eyed. "Why," he answered through Robert Barrett the interpreter, "I wish only peace. I am under orders from my Queen to respect all things Spanish, your lives, your property."

Delgadello relaxed and managed a smile.

"Of course," Hawkins went on, still bland and ingenuous, "it is true that I am in a strange position—a simple English trader suddenly master of a port full of treasure ships. Some men, I imagine, might be tempted to help themselves to that two-hundred-thousand-pound cargo. But my Queen has nothing but love for her brother-in-law your King, so I have nothing but love for his people." For emphasis he dispatched two messengers up the coast to reassure the Vera Cruz officials.

In a relaxed atmosphere the Englishmen went about their business. The *Jesus*, full of gold, pearls, hides, sugar, molasses, and silver, was unrigged in preparation for careening, caulking, and refitting, while those men not at work drank comfortably with the Spanish. Drake alone did not fraternize; he had no fondness to waste on Spaniards, even civilians.

Two days later, while the *Jesus* was, so to speak, *en deshabille*, Hawkins descried far at sea thirteen large sail—warships come to escort the treasure home. Quickly he took counsel with his captains. The Englishmen felt at ease under present conditions, but thirteen warships altered the balance of power, and so to guard against surprises Hawkins removed the Spaniards' guns from the island to his ships and mounted his own towards the harbor mouth. Thus, if he wished, he could hold the entrance against the newcomers.

It would take considerable self-discipline to let them come in, for his six small ships, one of them out of commission, were no match for those approaching, but he dared not flout the Queen's orders, since the fleet was bringing Don Martin Enriquez to Mexico as the new Viceroy, and to obstruct his entrance would be an act of war. As an alternative he sent word to the Spanish commander that while the harbor was technically in his hands and he could if he chose block their entrance, leaving them to the mercy of the gale outside, peace was his only interest, and so he would be glad to make the fleet welcome upon receipt of a pledge of nonaggression and an exchange of high-ranking hostages.

The Spanish blood boiled. Don Martin, an aristocrat with a very white face, a very black pointed beard, and eyes that slanted calculatingly, muttered, "Lutherans!" and spat. That the terms for entering his own domain should be dictated by one of these insects was an insult calling for bloodshed. He was all for running the blockade with guns. But cooler heads took the gauge of the other's battery and called instead for a conclave in the great cabin of the flagship.

They decided to agree to every demand, including that of ten hostages of high rank. Actually real noblemen would not be sent, for the heretics would undoubtedly murder them on arrival; instead common sailors could go, masquerading in velvet and plumes. But these expendables showed little enthusiasm, and Don Martin, realizing that under torture they might reveal the rest of the strategy, had to ask for volunteers from among the passengers. At the

same time a boat was dispatched to Vera Cruz demanding reinforcements.

In the morning ten queazy gentlemen in borrowed finery left
for the *Jesus* carrying Don Martin's pleasant letter agreeing to Hawkins' demands. Hawkins immediately sent back ten of his own best
men. He watched the thirteen vessels crowded with a thousand-
odd men dip the cross of St. Iago and enter the harbor.

The galleons scattered among the English ships to anchor, and a
great hulk settled down right next to the *Jesus*. But Hawkins and
Drake did not worry. Hostages had been exchanged and pledges
given, and they spent the next three days storing food, water, and
livestock and repairing the ship.

Early in the morning of September 23, Spanish actions became
suspicious. Two of the smaller and older of the galleons were
struggling upwind to the opposite shore for no apparent reason,
and guns were being removed from some of the farther ships and
planted onshore, all, curiously enough, pointing in the same
direction.

Hawkins, eating breakfast in the *Jesus'* cabin, heard strange
sounds inside the adjacent hulk, the movement of many men and
of sawing wood. He saw that holes were being cut in her side. He
sent Barrett to the Viceroy for an explanation, but before the interpreter could return—he had been taken prisoner and never did
return—a trumpet sounded. Hawkins jumped to his feet. One of
the hostages in the cabin made a move with his dagger and, shouting to a sailor, "Throw him in irons," Hawkins rushed on deck.
Someone was waving a white flag from the Viceroy's poop deck.

Don Martin's elaborate plans exploded into action all together.
Armed soldiers rushed from the moored ships to shore, spreading
along the water front and cutting off any Englishmen on land, and
then fanned out through the countryside, killing stragglers at their
leisure. A few who had drifted over to the island for a friendly drink
with the English drew hidden daggers and fell to with a will. Meanwhile the soldiers from Vera Cruz, secreted below decks, poured
out of the vessels and rushed the shore batteries, turning the guns
back onto the English.

Now from the hulk next to the *Jesus* swarmed soldiers across her
decks and onto the *Minion* beyond, and soon both were a battle-

ground. The fortunes were at first to the English. Bellowing "God and St. George! Kill those traitors!" Hawkins jumped from the *Jesus* onto a Spaniard on the *Minion*, stabbing as he landed. He cut the head cables of the *Jesus* and the *Minion*, and as they swung clear opened fire on the Spanish ships. Two of these, crushed by the guns at close range, caught fire and burned to the water. Many others were silenced, their crews fleeing ashore, and Don Martin was left alone beneath the flag he proudly refused to strike.

Hawkins glared about him. "We are in command. Let not a single traitor live. Samuel!" he called to his page. "Bring me a cup of beer to drink to our victory."

No sooner had he set the silver cup down than a demi-culverin shot struck it away. He laughed. "See how God looks after me. He will take the same care of all of you."

But the Spaniards were not finished. During the early afternoon the island guns began smashing cannonballs onto the *Jesus'* decks. Old and rotten, the wood crumbled under the battering and she began to list. Hawkins saw that the Queen's old ship was doomed, so, shouting to Drake to bring the *Judith* closer, he ordered the food, the bullion, and the trading goods moved onto the *Minion* and the *Judith*. Drake hastily took in his share, but before the bullion could be transferred he turned and saw that the two galleons upwind had been set afire and were now flaming down upon them like torches.

Hastily he stood away. The crippled *Jesus* lay dead in the way of the oncoming fire, and her men leaped to the *Minion's* decks. The little ship rolled under the impact but, trimming her quickly, they ran out to sea with gunfire following. There were two hundred men aboard, her own and the *Jesus'*, and enough food to last normally two weeks.

At Hawkins' orders Drake anchored outside the harbor, and from his poop deck watched the end of the little fleet. The *Angel* had caught fire and burned to the water's edge. The *Swallow*, her masts shot away and her side stove in, listed heavily and went down with a sigh. The last Drake saw of the *Jesus*, Spaniards were swarming over her decks.

"God," he whispered, shaking his fist, "God, God, let me have revenge!"

The Spaniards had bought their victory at the cost of five hundred men killed and four vessels sunk. But there were plenty of both left, and in sole possession of the *Jesus* they poured down her companionways to assess their spoils. It was a rich prize: fifty-seven Negroes Hawkins had been taking to England as souvenirs; a silver dinner service; and the entire proceeds of the trading voyage. Don Martin congratulated his companions; the strategy had been handsomely carried out and the enemy was scattered forever. He was proud of the report that would go back to the King.

Scattered the English certainly were, and only two ships remained to them. The storm had raged all night across the Gulf, and the next morning Drake found himself alone on the open sea. He did not know that the *Minion* was sheltering nearby under the lee of an island and, supposing her lost, did what he thought Hawkins would have wanted. He made for home.

When the storm abated, Hawkins emerged and looked for Drake in vain. The *Minion* was packed with men and already short of food; many were for giving up there and then and so the company split, a hundred disembarking to look for food and shelter onshore while the other hundred proceeded to England.

No more than a fraction of either party survived. Fifteen reached Plymouth with Hawkins; of those left in Mexico the tally was hardly greater. They fell into Spanish hands and in company with the English hostages were turned over to the authorities. One was stripped, tied to a horse, and driven through the streets of Mexico while two hundred stripes of the lash were laid across his back. Another was sentenced to three hundred lashes and ten years in the galleys. A third was hung up by his hands till the blood spurted from his finger ends. The rest fared according to their guilt, which in no instance was inconsiderable.

The new Viceroy of Mexico relaxed, confident that he had heard the last of the English marauders. But before he died he was to weary of hearing of them, for the man with the flypaper memory and the gift for hatred had got his scent and had found it even more objectionable than that of the Treasurer of Rio de la Hacha. To Drake all Spaniards were an offense to the nostrils and nothing could clear the atmosphere short of exterminating them.

When he arrived in Plymouth he was bedraggled and hungry, a

sorry-looking captain for a ship of the Queen, but rage gave the stocky figure a certain grandeur. He stamped off to London to report the Spanish treachery and demand reprisals, and after five days was followed by Hawkins in a condition even worse than his own. The two poured out their indignities to the Queen's Council, and Elizabeth, hearing of it, was privately sympathetic, for she had lost her ships along with the anticipated profits. But until her Navy was stronger she could do nothing overt against her brother-in-law and she hesitated to act.

Drake hung about for the Queen to make up her mind, meanwhile joining the Navy and, on July 4, 1569, marrying an obscure girl named Mary Newman, neither of which events circumscribed his freedom in the least. Finally, since the Queen was still hesitating, he took action himself.

Of all the bizarre sights of his voyage the twelve Spanish ships lying heavy with treasure and virtually unprotected had made the strongest impression. If he had not hated Spaniards so deeply he might have let it go at that, but with his itch for revenge and his chaplain's carte blanche approval, his brain was whirling with schemes. He persuaded Hawkins to lend him two small vessels, the *Dragon* and the *Swan*, and off he went on an unpublicized expedition.

These treasure fleets, he knew, followed a prescribed course. The wealth from Peru was brought on muleback across the Isthmus to Nombre de Dios on the Gulf, where the ships received it. From thence they had to scurry along the coast of the Main, past Cartagena the capital, past Rio de la Hacha of unhallowed memory, and on to Porto Plata and the open Atlantic. That coast line was indented with many sheltered bays, and Drake wished to know more of them. Six or eight months he puttered about, very unobtrusive and harmless, and when he came back said little to anyone. In 1571 he set out again with a single vessel, the *Swan*.

On the coast of Darien he found a small harbor between two protecting arms of land. Smothered in tall jungles and stocked with fish, pheasants, fresh water, and fruit, this "Port Pheasant" gave him a safe base for forays. All along the coast he went poking and sniffing, and even, disguised as a Spaniard and fortified with the bit of Spanish picked up in Toledo, stuck his nose right into Nombre de Dios itself.

Fifty years earlier Diego de Nizeuza had landed here. "On this spot," he had said, "we will found a settlement in the name of God," and Name of God it was called. Its one excuse for existing was that, fifty-five miles directly across the Isthmus from Panama, it served as east coast terminal for the treasure trains. Drake found it a wretched settlement of about sixty houses. Once a year, when the ships came in, it sprang into distracted life; merchants and soldiers swarmed then, and the poorest room cost a thousand crowns rent.

With its church bells ringing, men shouting, harness jingling, cows bellowing, guns firing salutes, it was a steamy torchlit bedlam where fever and leprosy raged and every ship entering lost one third of its crew in death. Then suddenly, when the fleets weighed anchor, another kind of death took over. Hardly thirty people remained through this "dead season."

Standing on its water front like David taking the gauge of Goliath, Drake studied the tall lumbering galleons, their strong points and weak. The high poop forced the mounted guns to direct their fire straight outwards; if a ship, he mused, were small enough to slip in underneath these guns would be helpless to retaliate. He nodded to himself; one thing he had was small ships. Many other interesting details he noted too, then sailed back to Port Pheasant and home, leaving behind a cache of supplies and a crew member who wished to trade on the Main.

Near the coast he captured several Spanish ships, stripping them of valuables and taking their personnel prisoner. This, to Drake, was legitimate privateering. True, privateers operated only on orders from the monarch and only in wartime. True, too, that England and Spain were technically at peace. But he knew the heart of his Queen; and, more important, *he* was in fact at war, a private war that legalized every attack or retaliation. One piratical measure he stopped short of—he never killed his prisoners but always released them with enough provisions to see them to safety.

In Plymouth, Drake began preparations for the adventure ahead. This time he was on his own; he had raised the money himself and

bought the *Swan* and the 70-ton *Pasha*. They were provisioned for
a year and the separate parts of three slim pinnaces were stowed
away for later assembling. His crews were no press-gang malcon-
tents or down-and-outers; all seventy-three were volunteers, eager
for excitement and, except for a single man, all under thirty. He
himself was thirty-one and his brothers John and Joseph several
years younger.

They left Plymouth on May 24, 1572, his first act as captain of
his own fleet being a call to prayer. The crews soon became accustomed to praying; there were services before dinner and supper
and, on special occasions, sermons and psalm singing running to
glorious lengths. Drake's religion, according to his own lights, was
deep and sincere, and his faith in his personal providence invincible.

On July 12 they landed at Port Pheasant and he immediately
built an enclosed harbor for his dainty pinnaces. Drake had an
affection for these versatile little vessels that could be sailed in a
wind or rowed in a calm, could hold as many as ten men, and yet
were light enough to be portaged. In the attack he planned on
Nombre de Dios he would need their speed and maneuverability.

Leaving the ships at Port Pheasant, Drake ordered his boys into
the pinnaces. For arms some carried the conventional swords and
pikes, while others were equipped with ingenious fire weapons—
nails carrying tufts of flaming tow, to be thrown at houses or ships
to set them ablaze, pikes and arrows specially treated for night fighting with a paste of powder, oil, pitch, sulphur, camphor, and spirits
stuck onto their points and set alight just before attack, balls of
hemp soaked in paste and studded with nails for setting fire to a
field of hay or a thatched roof. Some of the men carried muskets
and culverins. Four went to war armed with trumpets and drums.

They made their way towards the Isthmus, where in the jungle
dwelt a tribe of Cimaroons. Many years before these mixed Negroes
and Indians had fled the brutalities of their Spanish owners and
ever since had carried on a ceaseless war with them. At times groups
had been taken captive and dropped onto islands offshore (it was
done so often the practice took their name, "maroon"), and on his
way to Nombre de Dios, Drake ran into such a group. With his
instinct for appropriate action he rowed them back to the mainland

and set them free, after which their gratitude made them his firm allies, and very useful they were, too, for they knew every yard of the forest about the town and were delighted to join in any expedition against the common enemy.

On his previous visit Drake had made note of two gates on opposite sides of the town and also of the Governor's house, where the treasure was stored, in the central market place. He knew also that during the night the harbor armed battery was manned by a single gunner.

At sunset of July 28 the pinnaces, crowded with seventy-three excited boys, approached the town and as dawn broke slid round the point of land and made for the landing place, where Drake left twelve men in the boats and with the rest clambered up the redoubt. The solitary guard saw their shining helmets and fled towards the town, bellowing an alarm, with his pursuers hot behind him. Before the town wall Drake divided his forces, nineteen under John Drake and John Oxenham going to the east gate, he and the remaining forty to the west.

The great church bell was already banging out its warning and frightened citizens were rushing about in the dark, but, led by a trumpet and drum, Drake and thirty-eight men advanced behind a barrage of burning arrows. Some of the Spaniards sent a volley of musket shot. The trumpeter fell dead and certain other damage was done which went unnoticed at the time, but the English pushed on to the market place and there met the enemy head on.

Now into the confusion rushed twenty English from the east, closing the pincers. The surprise of the attack, the clatter of drums and trumpets, and the glare of flying fire threw the Spaniards into panic. They fled through the east gate, leaving the English in control of the town.

Everyone made for the Governor's house and rushed down to the cellar, and there, in the light of torches, English eyes saw for the first time one of the fabled Spanish treasures. Silver bars weighing forty pounds each stood stacked in a pile twelve feet high, seventy feet long, and ten feet thick. The silver was not shining and it was not beautiful, it was only overwhelming. Drake had had no experience in computing such quantities, but he reckoned deliriously that there must be at least a million pounds' worth.

The tantalizing part was that the treasure was no good to them, for they could not carry it away there and then, and they knew the Spaniards would soon return with reinforcements. But they guessed there must be stores of gold and gems elsewhere, so Drake sent his brother and John Oxenham to break into the treasury, and he himself was just stepping forward when without a word he dropped unconscious. No one had noticed the bloodstains on his leg; perhaps he did not notice them himself at the time or know that the same fusillade that killed the trumpeter had made a deep wound in his thigh. Suddenly for his men treasure hunting had no more charm. They bound up his leg with his own scarf, poured spirits down his throat and, though he stormed and ordered them back to the attack, picked him up and carried him away.

This was the end of the expedition, for Drake's leg was two weeks in healing. But still they had had a good adventure, they had given the Spaniards a scare, and above all they had set them to watching seaward.

This was important, for the next attack was to come by land. Drake had abruptly changed his tactics. Schooled by the careful Hawkins, he had tried careful planning, but after this fiasco he began a career of high-spirited improvization. His basic purpose never deviated—to rob, cheat, harry, frustrate, undermine, tease, and humiliate Spaniards wherever and however he could—but the means he left to the inspiration of the moment. Drake already knew that the mule trains crossed the Isthmus between Panama and Nombre de Dios, and he intended to intercept one on its way, so now he took stock and decided he had a ship too many. Having started with but seventy-three men and lost four since, he lacked enough to man the three trusty pinnaces and the two ships as well, so the *Swan* would have to go. But he knew his brother John, who had command of her, would never acquiesce, so he took aside Thomas Moone, a gunner, and gave him a secret order.

In the second watch of the night, while all others were asleep, Moone went below and bored three holes in the *Swan's* bottom. Next morning she was low in the water, and by afternoon, in spite of pumping by all hands, she was down to her gunwales, obviously doomed. With a consoling pat Drake promised his brother the command of the *Pasha* and the combined crews instead, so John, whose remaining days were few, was happy for a while.

Now the *Pasha* with her satellites made for the Gulf of Darien, southeast of Nombre de Dios, and there pitched tents onshore. Since Drake's projected raid depended largely on the co-operation of the Cimaroons, he spent the months of the rainy season cementing their friendship, and meantime made the Spaniards miserable by a series of needle-thrust raids, darting in here and there and leaving them with small annoying wounds and a vast exasperation.

It was on one of these raids that John met his death. And some weeks later, New Year's, 1573, an epidemic of yellow fever broke out, which within a short time carried off twenty-six more, Joseph Drake among them. In the hope that a post-mortem might suggest a remedy, Drake ordered an autopsy. And with a born leader's willingness to shoulder the worst of the burden, he chose his brother's body for this degradation.

Nothing helpful having been uncovered, the doctor, who had concocted a potion and needed a guinea pig for it, followed his leader's example and gulped it down himself, but unfortunately his medical skill was not equal to his heroism and he died of his own cure, horribly. Twenty-eight were now gone.

But Drake had not come these thousands of miles to give up, and when the rains stopped and the treasure trains began moving again he gathered his striking force of eighteen English and thirty devoted Cimaroons. The *Pasha* and the pinnaces and the sick he left hidden in a bay, and the rest started across the mountainous spine of the Isthmus to meet the caravan halfway. On the coast their clothes, foul with heat and damp, had clung stickily to their skin under the metal helmets and cuirasses, but now as they ascended the air became clean and dry, and they could breathe again. Whereas below none moved in the daytime, but slept the hot hours away and worked and played by night, here they could turn in like normal folk after assembling in the dark to kneel for the Lord's Prayer.

On the eleventh of February they topped the ridge where Pedro, an Indian with a sense of the dramatic, led Drake to a tall tree. Into its trunk were cut ladder-like steps and in the branches was built a lookout platform. Drake followed Pedro up and looked where he pointed. Back over the path he had covered he looked northwards and saw the great Atlantic. Then Pedro, smiling, turned him about towards the south.

Exactly sixty years before Vasco Núñez de Balboa had stood on that very spot and seen the same sight. To his eyes the great South Sea was a further extension of the domain of His Majesty of Castile and Leon, but to Drake's eyes it looked equally like an English ocean, and he knelt in his perch and prayed God to let him sail it in the name of Queen Elizabeth. Further possibilities sprang to his mind, colonies of English settlers building cities and extending the wealth and power of his sovereign indefinitely, but the immediate first step was the capture of the treasure train.

Shortly a Cimaroon scout brought news of a rich train just leaving Panama, the Treasurer of Lima himself and his daughter at the head of sixty mules. Planning to encounter them in dead of night, Drake ordered his men to wear their white shirts outside their jerkins to distinguish them in the dark, and after a fine supper and an extra dram of brandy, stationed them along the route.

Silence was the order, but one Robert Pike, too full of brandy and excitement, accidentally let out a nervous titter, which warned the approaching train and they turned back and saved themselves.

Drake nearly killed Pike, but once his anger was spent he cheerfully began planning the next try. Since the Spaniard now had had warning of him by land he would have to direct his gaze back to the sea again. And since his numbers had been nearly halved he was willing to accept an ally.

Having met a French ship whose company was dying from starvation and thirst, he slaked their need and took them with him on a raid, stressing only that though there were but eighteen English against thirty Cimaroons and twenty Frenchmen, he was to have sole authority. The two ships were left hidden on the coast while the men transferred to the three small boats. At the mouth of the Rio Francisco twenty miles from Nombre de Dios they consolidated again and rowed in two pinnaces as far upstream as the depth of water permitted. There Drake sent the boats back downstream with orders to return four days hence.

The raiding party was made up of disparate elements held together solely by Drake's magnetism, for Captain Tetu and his

Frenchmen distrusted the Cimaroons and the Cimaroons despised the French. Only the Englishman's laughter and infectious daring held them together. And indeed the plan required daring—to intercept the quarry not halfway across the Isthmus but right at the Nombre de Dios gate, where the train drivers would have relaxed their precautions.

Led by the Cimaroons, they crept close to the road where the ambush was to be sprung. The heat of the night was intense, the smell of rotting underbrush steaming about them as, encased in steel, they waited for the bells of the mule trains, while from the town the noise of hammering, sawing, shouting, and cursing could be heard through the trees. Then just before dawn Cimaroon scouts reported that the mules were near. This train, they said, dwarfed that of the Lima Treasurer, no less than 190 animals loaded with gold and silver and gems. The muleteers, relieved to be approaching their destination, could be heard shouting back and forth.

Drake had deployed his men in a long line on either side of the trail and now, holding his signal till the head mule was abreast of the first man, he blew his whistle and from both sides at once English, French, and Indians sprang upon the full length of the train. One man seized the first mule's head and another the last, whereupon the 188 animals in between, thinking this another routine halt, methodically lay down. Drake had ordered that no unarmed persons be hurt, but the sight of Spaniards was like red pepper thrown in the eyes of Cimaroons, and they fell on them with such an abandon of blood lust that the terror-struck men dropped everything and fled.

Only two raiders were injured: a Cimaroon killed and the captain wounded in the stomach. Everyone else fell upon the heavily burdened mules and tore open their panniers.

At last Francis Drake had caught up with the will-o'-the-wisp he had been chasing. Once before, in the Governor's house at Nombre de Dios, he had glimpsed it; but now it was in his hands. The first fifty mules carried silver, bar upon bar of the whitish stuff in such endless repetition that soon boredom set in as the men pulled open the sacks. Then came the gold, bags of fine dust, nuggets, delicately worked ornaments, dishes, drinking vessels. Since this was Peruvian gold, the one thing missing was coins.

Each man stuffed as many small pieces in his clothing as it would accommodate, and then seized a basket from a mule's back and piled larger ones into that. Before they had even begun on the silver the baskets were full.

Now dawn was breaking, and since without doubt the muleteers had given the alarm and soldiers would be returning soon, they realized they would have to leave the silver and come back for it later. Hastily they buried the bars in the bed of a stream, down the holes of land crabs, under tree roots, and in rotten trunks. But before all of the fifteen tons could be stowed away horses were heard in the distance and the marauders staggered away under their loads. Three Frenchmen remained to care for the captain with the hole in his stomach.

The raid had taken two days. The return journey, through a tropical storm, took two more. But when they arrived at their trysting place on schedule and looked about for the pinnaces nothing was there. Far away at the river's mouth could be seen a ship, a galleon, and all but Drake gave a groan, counting themselves lost, for doubtless this ship had captured their friends and by torture learned of their present whereabouts.

Now did Drake's high spirits serve them well, saving them from panic. As they stood on the riverbank, soaked, hungry, their ship lost, cut off from deliverance, before them a stream clotted with trees uprooted by the storm and behind them pursuing Spaniards, his confidence hardly quivered. God was on his side, the chaplain had said so, and how could he worry?

Where others saw a wall he saw a door. "Look." He pointed at the trees floating down the river and laughed. "God has sent us a raft."

Immediately everyone's spirits bounced back, and in two hours one tree had been hacked into lengths for a raft, another formed a mast, four more paddles, and there was even a sapling rudder, while the biscuit sack served not too badly for a sail. Since the raft could hold only four men Drake took the rudder, and an English boy and two Frenchmen, chosen because they could swim, were the crew. When they stepped aboard the raft they sank waist-deep in water, but, undismayed, Drake waved good-by and swore by his God to come back for the rest.

Downstream the four men floated, on an invisible raft. When they reached the sea the galleon had passed on, but the elements were enemy enough, for a scorching sun had emerged after the storm and under it they continued to paddle without food or water, up to their waists in the waves. After twelve hours of struggling against a strong south-easter they saw the two pinnaces on the darkening horizon. Drake waved the dirty biscuit sack, but without responding they disappeared behind a point of land. Now he maneuvered the raft inshore and, scrambling off it, made across the intervening hills.

The four men in the pinnaces hastened to explain their defection. "We tried to come back for you, but we could not paddle upstream against the gale that was blowing out to sea." Drake nodded understandingly, and they relaxed, for his rages could be terrible.

"And your news?" they asked. "Did the raid go well?"

With an expressionless face he nodded. "Well enough."

This was his way when things were at their worst. Three times they had failed. They sighed.

There was a long sad silence, then with a bored look he put his hand into his doublet, drew forth a round yellow thing shaped like an onion and tossed it to them. They looked, first at it and then at him, with startled eyes, and he nodded. "The voyage is made," he said. "Thank God."

Anything following this, no matter how important, could not but be anti-climactic. The rest of the raiding party was fetched back to the *Pasha,* and the lost four, and the buried silver, were also sought. But the unfortunate four had been found by the Spaniards and torn neatly into quarters, while the ground where the silver was buried had been dug up for a square mile and all but fifteen bars discovered. This part of the story was a little sad, but the expedition, all told, had been vastly successful, and now nothing remained but the long voyage home.

On the way they had to pass Cartagena. Considering the strained relations, Drake might have elected to slip past at night, but instead he piled on all sail and every conspicuous flag and pennant and in a burst of gunfire, but just out of range of their guns, swept past with his five fingers waggling at his nose. Twenty days later they entered Plymouth.

This return was very different from the previous humiliating retreat. Drake had been away fifteen months, he had brought back over a hundred thousand pesos de oro, divided between his party and the French, and still he was only thirty-two: the best of his life lay ahead.

England took him to its heart, for no matter what the official position might be the man in the street hated Spain and loved Spain's enemies. Freebooting, though perhaps not sanctioned in the Bible, was a peccadillo like gambling or drinking, with a certain rakish splendor, and Francis Drake was the most glorious, the most willful, wild, adorable freebooter that had ever been seen.

Elizabeth privately agreed, but her position was more complicated since at the moment efforts were being made to negotiate a pact with Philip of Spain, and this English raid on Spanish property might well muddy up the whole affair. She protested to the Spanish Ambassador that she had had nothing to do with Drake, did not even know where he was now. And to make the last statement true he was sent off to Ireland to lose himself in fighting a local rebellion.

After a year and a half the negotiations broke down when Philip was discovered establishing a naval base on the Scilly Islands directly athwart the English Channel, and was also suspected of having been mixed up in the Irish trouble. After that how could she trust her brother-in-law, pact or no pact? So the belligerent little sea dog was recalled.

In Ireland, Drake had formed a friendship that was to cause him much embarrassment, but at the time Thomas Doughty, lawyer, man of elegance, scholar, and friend of very special people at court, promised to be most helpful, for Drake had told him of the plans he had been evolving and Doughty had offered his assistance.

The plans were impressive. Ever since Drake had knelt in the lookout tree he had dreamed of sailing an English ship on the great South Sea, that sea Magellan had named the Pacific. The Portuguese explorer had entered it via the Southern Strait fifty-seven years before, and since then Spain had pre-empted the ocean for her own private property, but now Drake proposed to violate that privacy. He would pass through the Strait, sail quietly up the west coast, and surprise the unsuspecting ships that ferried the gold to the storehouses at Panama. On that long coast line he would also look for places for Englishmen to settle, for it was ridiculous that Spain should own this rich new world just because of some technicality about prior claims.

This view and these plans, however many men in high places might privately approve them, were contrary to official policies and not to be expressed in the wrong places. But his friend Doughty picked his place carefully, and took Drake to Walsingham, Secretary of State and a close friend of the Earl of Leicester, who was more than a close friend of the Queen.

Walsingham received the stocky little soldier formally. Then, after studying him, the tall man with the scraggly beard dropped his guard. "I have heard a great deal of you," he said. "Indeed, I am interested in your plans. You have proved that you know how to fight Spaniards."

Drake smiled. "I have only started, if God be willing."

Walsingham nodded, pleased. "I do not think God likes Spain. And privately I can tell you that the Queen does not either. She has received many injuries from them, and she wants revenge. We have discussed a variety of ways to—annoy the King of Spain, and"—he paused to give Drake time to take in his words—"we have discussed you."

Drake's eyes glistened, but he said nothing, and Walsingham went on. "However, the Queen must be politic, and she will consult her councilors." He smiled quizzically. "She may even listen to them. But, at any rate, they must be won over before she will care to sanction such an expedition as you propose."

Drake asked, "Do you think they can be persuaded?"

"Some of them, yes, some no. And there is one—I am speaking very plainly, but you will not dare to repeat it, I believe . . ."

"You can be sure I will not," murmured Drake.

"There is one whom it would not be wise to tell at all. He is a very honest, very earnest man, but at times he does not guard his tongue well enough and King Philip's spies have already learned of several plans not for his ear."

"May I know who that is?"

"My Lord Burghley."

Drake sighed. "Without the Lord Treasurer how could one hope to outfit an expedition?"

Walsingham smiled. "There might be expeditions the Treasurer would approve. If you first won his co-operation, then, later, when you got out on the high seas . . ." His voice died away significantly.

Drake grinned, and would have slapped the other's back except that he was so elderly and grand, but he hitched himself forward on his chair and prepared for a long talk. Walsingham pressed his finger tips thoughtfully together. "First I want a letter from you, outlining your whole plan, which I will present to the Queen. When she has given me her approval we can then——" Drake had stirred uncomfortably and Walsingham glanced at him. "What is the matter?"

"You mean my real plans? The plan to invade Philip's territory and raid his ships?"

"Only for her own eyes, privately, of course."

Drake sat looking down thoughtfully. "I beg Your Lordship's indulgence," he murmured. "This is a touchy business. Unfortunately our sovereign is mortal. If I were to write a letter describing my plans—and it were to be mislaid—and the Queen, God forbid it, should die—and the next sovereign should not dislike Spain as she does . . ." He raised his eyes to Walsingham's and smiled. "You see my dilemma."

Before he had finished, Walsingham was nodding. "Then I will take you to her and you can say these things directly into her ear."

This was an honor Drake had secretly yearned for. A number of men he knew had talked with her and at least one, the Earl of Leicester, had done even more. He knew her eyes were sharp and she was not insensible to male appearance, so he prepared for the interview with care, and at eight on the appointed morning he studied himself critically as he waited for the Secretary in a hall of Windsor Castle. He had ordered a new green velvet cloak and a purple doublet with leg o' mutton sleeves and a belly stuffed out with cow tails into the shape of a seven-month pregnancy, which, with the stuffing in his breeches, made sitting difficult. It was fortunate, he reflected, that audiences with royalty required standing throughout, and besides, standing made him look more than his five foot three, as did the tall plumes in his stuffed hat. (All the cows in England were going tailless these days.) He straightened the freshly starched ruff and twisted the heavy finger rings so lately worn by Spanish conquistadors, and when Walsingham joined him strutted along the stone corridors towards the Queen's chamber with every appearance of self-confidence.

At last a page opened a door and they walked into a large room where an eight-foot log blazed and tapestries flapped in the drafts whistling along the walls. The Queen, erect in a high-backed chair, nodded as the two men entered.

Lord Walsingham presented the visitor and then stepped aside to let him do his own talking. Elizabeth waited, long fingers scratching thoughtfully in her crinkled red hair, lashless eyes studying him. "Well, Drake, what do you wish to say?"

Francis Drake bowed, his mind racing; this woman was notoriously impatient, and anyone seeking her help would have to catch her interest in the first five minutes or not at all. "If the Queen's Majesty will permit me . . ." He spread out his maps of Spanish America, the gold coast of Chile and Peru and Quito, the Isthmus of Panama with its ports for the Silver Fleets, the slave port of Cartagena and the pearl port of Margarita and the silver port of Hispaniola. He read aloud each name redolent of treasure and then stood silent.

"Well, well, what is all this?" snapped the Queen.

"This, Madam," Drake sighed gently, "is the property of the King of Spain."

Bent low, he could see from the corner of his eye the angry jerk of her body. If she took this as a taunt it might be the end of him, for men had lost their heads for less audacity, and he breathed shallowly, in trepidation, while Walsingham breathed hardly at all. But he had not misjudged his woman. In a moment she made a sound like a hiss, "'S blood, it is true. And by what right? By what divine right does it all belong to him?"

Drake and Walsingham watched tensely while she glared at the maps. "Drake," she said suddenly, "the King of Spain has used me mighty ill. I want revenge. Get me revenge."

After that it was clear sailing; he had come at the psychological moment, for though his proposal was not new there had always before been some reason for hesitation. Now the time was ripe. As they talked, the project assumed even greater magnitude. Besides piracy (but they did not name it that), Drake was to do some exploring for the glory of England, find that northern passage to the East similar to the southern one Magellan had found, or perhaps, if that was not feasible, follow Magellan around the world, exhibiting to all pagan lands the glory and might of England. Without doubt there would be other lands as rich as those Spain had occupied and Drake should be Governor of this New Albion. Meanwhile he could reimburse himself from the booty for the injuries received at San Juan, and anything beyond this would go into the Queen's vaults in the Tower of London.

Elizabeth broke off spinning her plans to look at Walsingham. "The Council will take years to see the sense of this proposal," she said grumpily. "If they ever do."

Walsingham nodded. "But there *are* proposals they would entertain."

She was plainly thinking the same thing. "Terra Australis. That is a part of the world they all wish explored. Philip may claim it but he has not occupied it, and even the most timid councilor should not object to taking unoccupied land." She scowled. "But Burghley must not know of it." She meditated for a minute and then nodded with decision. "Offer them the Terra Australis plan. But do not tell Burghley. By my crown, I will behead anyone who tells Burghley."

Thus it came about that when Drake outfitted his ships the expedition was like a Chinese puzzle egg. At the core was the actual plan, piracy on the west coast of America, followed by exploration and annexation of Pacific lands. Not a soul but Drake and Elizabeth and Walsingham knew this one. Next layer was the Terra Australis plan, approved by the Queen's Council and an inner circle who guarded it against anyone who might let it slip.

This plan had been projected by many men before Drake. Since the beginning of the sixteenth century the Portuguese had been carrying on trade with the Far East around the south of Africa and Spain had opened up a way to the West via the Strait of Magellan. England alone had never sent a ship to the East, and the fact was irking her.

Explorers were not above using their imaginations in making

maps of their voyages, and one copied another in showing the bottom of the world filled by a great continent. Magellan, they said, must have found the one strip of water that linked the Atlantic to the Pacific; all else was land, clean across from Patagonia to Africa, rich, fertile, inviting . . . Terra Australis.

In 1570 some of Elizabeth's councilors had considered sending men to settle an empire there, the object to be increase of shipping, sale of manufactured goods, work for the unemployed, discovery of wealth, and propagation of the faith. Indeed, letters of patent had been drawn up, but each time Elizabeth, fearful of provoking Spain into a premature war, had withheld her consent. This time, however, the moment seemed auspicious.

Drake was presented to other members of the Council, heads were put together, and the next weeks were exciting ones, for, besides Walsingham, Lord Leicester was in favor of the expedition; Christopher Hatton, Gentleman of the Privy Chamber, offered a thousand pounds' backing and Thomas Doughty twelve hundred. Even Lord Burghley, who was always so careful of Spain's sensibilities, saw nothing against this exploration.

The contract as finally drawn up stipulated that Captain Francis Drake, General of the Fleet, was to proceed southwest across the Atlantic to the 52nd parallel, through the Strait of Magellan and northwest along the Terra Australis coast to the 30th parallel, all the time prospecting for treasure, making friends with the lords of those countries and bestowing on them presents up to the value of fifty pounds. After five months he was to return by the way he had come, having consumed in all thirteen months. The contract was signed by Leicester; Walsingham; Hatton; Lincoln, the Lord Admiral; William Winter, the Surveyor of the Navy; George Winter, Clerk of the Queen's Ships; and John Hawkins, Drake's old friend.

As General of the Fleet, Drake was to keep a diary, make maps of the countries and waters explored and turn them over later to the Council. Backing was raised principally among the scions of noble families, several of whom contributed not only money but their persons. Though the Queen's name was carefully omitted from the contract, she was represented *sub rosa* both by ships and a thousand pounds in cash. And privately she gave Drake a paper to wave in the face of anyone challenging his commission.

This was the project as announced to the court circles—the second layer in the egg. But even this was too delicate a matter for common ears and was hidden inside a third, in consequence of which the prospectus advertising for mariners named the expedition's destination as the Levant; Drake was going there to trade with the Turks.

Thus many surprises were in store for the common sailors, and at least one for everyone but Drake.

The articles were signed the summer of 1577, and by autumn everything was assembled. The vessels were five in number: the *Pelican*, 100 tons, known as the Admiral of the Fleet, the flagship of Captain-General Francis Drake; the 80-ton *Elizabeth*, the Vice-Admiral, captained by John Winter, Gentleman; the *Marigold*, 30 tons, under John Thomas, Gentleman; the *Swan*, 50 tons, under John Chester, Gentleman; and the *Benedict*, 15 tons, under Thomas Moone, Mariner. Also carried were the parts of four pinnaces, to be set up as needed. The *Pelican*, which had an inner and outer sheathing, carried eighteen guns in sight as well as pikes, swords, and firearms below decks. The *Elizabeth* had sixteen guns and the others even fewer, while the pinnaces were like rabbits, defenseless but fast.

Drake's flagship was the last word in style, with a cabin of carved oak, a silver dinner service, and kitchen utensils engraved with his insignia. There were bunting and flags and pennants for special occasions, four violinists to play at mealtimes, and Diego the Indian to serve as his body servant. Caulkers, carpenters, coopers—every artisan needed to keep a fleet in repair was included among the crew, and for company Drake brought his fourteen-year-old cousin John, who stood behind his chair at meals and at night joined him in painting maps and sketches of the places they had passed. The only luxury Drake did not permit was a gambling device; cards and dice were forbidden and severe penalties were imposed for infraction of the rule.

The company of 164 was divided sharply into two groups: the hard-bitten sailors who could neither read nor write but could bring a ship into port in the hardest gale and received ten shillings a month plus victuals, and the gentlemen. Captains of the ships, leaders of the fighting, underwriters of the venture, they were the sons of rich families who had never hauled a line nor reefed a sail, and whose names suggested their aristocratic origin, Cary, Chester, Elyot, Ffortescu, Thomas, Winter, Hord, Hawkins, two Doughtys —ten in all, as well as Francis Fletcher the chaplain and a brace of Drakes. These men were richly furnished with helmets, cuirasses, swords, daggers, and pistols. And, being in the confidence of the general and the Queen's Council, they knew the real destination of the expedition—or thought they did.

Just before sailing, Drake had a last audience with the Queen, to receive her blessing. Holding out her sword, she said, "Use this in your own defense, as if defending me, for I account him who strikes you to be striking me. Here too is a keepsake from your Queen." It was a gold-embroidered cap and scarf, the ends of the scarf worked by the Queen's maid of honor with the motto, "The Lord guide and preserve thee till the end."

"And the Lord will preserve you, Drake," she said, "for you are about His work. His Grace Bishop Fuller has assured me that to exact reprisals from the Spaniards is most pleasing in the sight of God."

At five in the afternoon of November 15, 1577, the fleet sailed out of Plymouth harbor, but it ran almost at once into a storm which battered the *Pelican* so badly it was four weeks before they actually left England.

When they did get under way the sailors received their first surprise as they came abreast of Gibraltar. They should have turned east for the Mediterranean but Drake blandly ordered them straight south for Morocco, and then dawned on them the explanation of all the gentlemen's knowing and mysterious looks. Soon after, more of the real purpose became apparent, when, near the Cape Verde Islands off the African coast, they sighted a Portuguese vessel bound for Brazil and Drake gave chase. Attacking Portuguese vessels had not been in the articles the gentlemen had signed, and one or two protested. But the mood of the times was such that to protest chasing ships of an unfriendly nation was like teetotaling in a company of drinkers; the few who did were jeered out of countenance, and very soon even they said no more, for the Portuguese carried a cargo of wine, and drinkables were always at a premium.

Also aboard was a Portuguese pilot, sixty-year-old Nuño da Silva, with a squat body and a long black beard, who was well acquainted with the Brazilian coast. Drake took over the pilot and the ship, and after provisioning his own *Benedict* with a butt of wine, victuals, and clothing, he turned the Portuguese passengers loose in it.

On February 1 they struck out from the coast of Africa across the Atlantic. And here disturbing things began to happen. Weather unfamiliar to these North Atlantic seamen, doldrums and sudden gales, bewildered the most experienced. And Thomas Doughty acted as queerly as the weather. The five ships, while under the loose leadership of Drake, were captained by men operating more like partners than subordinates, but Doughty was none of these five and this began to irk him. He complained to Drake that his investment and his connections with the powers at home entitled him to a position of command, so Drake put him over the Portuguese prize ship, since renamed the *Christopher*, but even this did not satisfy him.

Word began seeping back to the *Pelican* of speeches Doughty had been making, offers of money if the men would shift their allegiance to him; promises of better rank and accommodations; claims to have been the real inspiration for the voyage and of exerting influence with the Queen's Council. Drake also learned that he had helped himself to some of the property on the prize ship, an inexcusable liberty in privateering circles, but when taxed with it he accused Drake's own brother Thomas. The gossip and disaffection that racketed back and forth between the ships were enough to shake the confidence of any leader.

After fifty-four miserable days they sighted the coast of Brazil, but even then things got no better. The natives onshore were hostile and barbaric, the ships were forever losing each other, sometimes, most mysteriously, in clear weather. Doughty continued his insinuations about the General's morals, about his ethics, about his abilities as a leader, and halfway to the Strait, Drake was told that Doughty's brother had boasted that Doughty had the powers of a witch and could conjure up the devil in the shape of a bear or a man as quick as you please.

This was the most disquieting of all, for every sailor knew one had to be alert lest the devil come aboard. Indeed, he seemed to be already there, for something supernatural had to be responsible for the abominable weather and the attacks of the natives, for the quarreling and division, gentleman against sailor and ship against ship. And the worst of the voyage was still ahead and the worst of the winter's weather. These evil influences must be exorcised.

Just north of the Strait, with an icy wind tearing the sails and whipping the waves into mountains of foam, Drake ordered the entire company ashore to pitch tents on a barren island. When all were settled he chose a jury of forty men, among them the lawyer and several of Doughty's best friends, and called a trial of Thomas Doughty for sedition and inciting to mutiny.

Even after the trial started, Drake was not completely convinced of his guilt. But when he let slip that he had told Lord Burghley of the secret mission of the voyage, hoping thus to keep in the good graces of the Lord Treasurer in case the expedition failed, he doubted no longer. The various men who had witnessed the accused's efforts to undermine the General's authority and replace it with his own were called to testify. And in the end the jury, friend and foe alike, voted him guilty and the sentence death.

Drake, still with a sneaking liking for the fellow, offered to put him ashore to take his chances of survival, but Doughty chose instead to die among his friends, for they would at least bury him in hallowed ground. Then Drake offered to shoot him personally, that he might die by the hand of an equal. But Doughty, something of a snob, elected the traditional death of kings and princes, beheading.

For two days he prayed and on the third asked Drake to take communion with him, after which they moved to the captain's table, where they ate dinner with the company, chatting cheerfully of this and that and drinking to each other. Just before the execution, at Doughty's request, they retired for a moment's private conversation, and though Drake never repeated the talk, his manner suggested that Doughty had confessed.

Now the solemn procession moved to the execution block, where, kneeling, Doughty prayed for the Queen and the success of the voyage. He laid his neck across the low wooden block, wryly apologizing that it was too short for a perfect fit, and the sword fell. The severed head was held aloft as a warning to all traitors.

The scene of the trial Drake named the Island of True Justice and Judgment.

Now that the gangrenous spot had been cut out the expedition needed time for its wound to heal. It was July, midwinter, and the Strait could not be attempted anyway, so Drake turned the time to advantage by remodeling the structure of the group. Hitherto command in such fleets had been held by a council rather than a single person, and the various classes of men kept apart, even in emergencies, with the common sailors doing the work and the young gentlemen nothing. Hatreds were mutual and violent.

After a month Drake summoned the company to his tent. One side was laid back, the better for all to see, and he stood up. Diego laid on a table his *Lives of the Saints*, and Chaplain Fletcher, thinking a service was expected, stepped forward. Drake shook his head. "No, Mr. Fletcher, this day I shall preach myself, poor at it though I be."

"Is everyone here?" he called. There was a murmured "Yes." "Then," he said, "my masters, I am a very bad orator. But remember what I say now, for I will answer for every word before Her Majesty.

"My masters, we are very far from home and friends. No man's life is cheap here, for we could not buy another if we had ten thousand pounds. Therefore these mutinies and discords must cease, for by the life of God they drive me mad. Here is such controversy among gentleman and gentleman, among gentleman and sailor, as I will not have. The gentleman must haul and draw with the sailor, and the sailor with the gentleman. Gentlemen are necessary for the government of the ship, and neither can we do without sailors, so let us throw ourselves all together and not give our enemy occasion to rejoice at our decay. But if there are any here who wish to return home let me know them now. I will give them the *Marigold* and furnish her with what I can afford. But only one thing—let them go straight to England, for if I find them going in my direction I will surely sink them. Who will go?"

Not a hand was raised.

He nodded, and pressed his advantage. "Now, that we may all

understand that there are not many leaders but only one, I hereby relieve all my officers from their command, so that everyone, gentlemen and sailors, stand equal together." They stared, shocked, but he went on, suddenly soft and winning, "My masters, let us consider what responsibility we have taken on. We have stirred up the Kings of Portugal and Spain against our sovereign the Queen, and if this voyage should fail we should not only be a laughingstock to our enemies but a stumbling block to our country, for no one else would attempt such a thing again." There was a long silence. Drake looked around, reassured by their faces. "Now," he said, "let us all forget it. Let every officer of you get back to his post, with Francis Drake your General. And thus we will sail, a company strong in heart."

On this day was born the English Navy as it grew to greatness, one clean-cut command responsible for a combination of lesser commands.

While they waited for good weather Drake stripped for action. His ambitious fleet having proved top-heavy, now he trimmed it down by scuttling the *Christopher* and the Portuguese ship. The *Pelican* he rechristened; Sir Christopher Hatton, a friend of the Queen, was one of the expedition's more influential sponsors, and now Drake renamed her the *Golden Hind*, after the symbol on Hatton's crest. Thus, on August 20, 1578, the *Golden Hind*, the *Elizabeth*, and the *Marigold* sailed south towards the Strait. The winds were high and cold, and to their right was a long series of rocky cliffs, uninviting and gray, against which the waves crashed with a constant roar. Towards afternoon they sighted Cape Virgin Mary, four leagues ahead at the 52nd parallel. This, according to Magellan's maps, was the spot, the very spot, where their real adventure would begin.

Sure enough, as they rounded the jutting point of land, there, instead of more rocks, was open water running west.

Drake ordered his musicians on deck; the drummer stood at attention, and as the *Golden Hind* turned towards the Pacific the topsails were struck in honor of the Queen. Diego produced the *Lives of the Saints* and a prayer cushion, and Drake preached a stirring sermon on true obedience, rededicating himself and the

company to Queen Elizabeth and the Council, the common welfare and the Church of God.

The winds being fair, they made the passage in sixteen days,
twenty-one fewer than had Magellan himself, and Drake was planning to celebrate this accomplishment by setting up an engraved
monument. But the moment the ships debouched into the Pacific
all the furies of hell were let loose upon them, rain, thunder and
lightning, an eclipse of the moon, and screaming gales that ripped
their canvas and drove the ships off their course, one back down the
throat of the passage and one off into the unknown, never to be
heard from again. Doughty might be dead, but there were still ma-
levolent spirits abroad.

For a month the ships fought the gales, the *Elizabeth* being
driven so far back into the Strait that she was never able to re-
emerge. Four weeks her captain, John Winter, waited for a sight
of Drake, and then gave up and went home. The *Golden Hind*,
caught by a differing wind, had been driven south and then east,
and as a consequence, quite unintentionally, Drake performed one
of the most useful acts of his life.

South of the Strait, Drake should have run on Terra Australis,
the continent covering the bottom of the world; and, driven south
and ever farther south, he did indeed find land, a continuous string
of islands. But then at the 57th parallel, as he looked ahead, his
jaw dropped. The land had stopped, and beyond was nothing but
water. Terra Australis did not exist.

Now, having made a discovery that would change the future
maps of the world, Drake had to celebrate. Despite the tempest he
ran his ship into a cove on the southern shore of the most southerly
island and he and the chaplain disembarked with a bag of tools.
Striking a heroic pose, he shouted to the land on which he stood,
"I do christen thee and thy sister islands after the Queen's Majesty
—the Elizabethides." Compass in hand, he strode to the extreme
tip of the land and, casting himself flat, stretched his hands into
the sea, the first man ever to reach so far to the south. Next, while
he superintended, Fletcher set up a great stone and chiseled
thereon the Queen's name and the momentous date.

At that precise moment the gale, which for fifty-six days had
driven them on without mercy, suddenly ceased, as if satisfied with

its work. The scurvy-ridden men crawled ashore to lie gasping with exhaustion, slowly over several days recovering their strength on a diet of fresh penguin and fresh herbs and clean fresh water. And when they were ready to go on, the wind took them north again.

Now the great events of his life were about to begin; behind was the warming up, the feints and dodgings by which he took the measure of his adversary; ahead was the duel. He never knew in advance what he was going to do, knowing only that all his life long he would do anything that would give him and the Queen satisfaction and the King of Spain distress.

It was a pleasant spring day, October 31, when he turned north to look for his companion ships. He had lost all but eighty men and all vessels but the *Golden Hind*. The surgeon was gone with the *Elizabeth* and so were good men like John Winter and John Thomas. But before entering the Strait he had set the next rendezvous on the coast of Chile where it intersected the 30th parallel, and if the other ships had come through the storms he would find them there.

Having no English maps to follow, he was compelled somewhat shamefacedly to rely on Spanish ones, and now off the coast of Chile he looked for an island named, on account of its size, Mucho. Coming to anchor, Drake and a few men rowed to land, where several Indians were watching them approach.

"Now do not forget," he told his men, "these Indians know no white men but Spaniards. If they have been treated the same here as Spaniards treat Indians elsewhere they will hate them all. Therefore be friendly in manner. And, above all, use no Spanish words, for we do not wish to be confused with their enemies."

The Indians, to their surprise, met them with bows and salutes of the hand. And when the English brought out knives and beads and cups they gave them in trade fat sheep and chickens and maize. Even more important was fresh water, however, and Thomas Brewer made signs of drinking, but the Indians looked puzzled. Then Thomas Moone, losing his temper and his head, shouted crossly, "Aqua, you fools, aqua."

The Indians started and stared. Drake swore softly, but when after a moment the Indians were smiling again and nodding their comprehension, Drake drew a sigh of relief. The Indians made signs towards the sun, indicating that at dawn next morning they would lead them to a spring.

That night the intoxicating smell of roast fresh mutton floated through the *Golden Hind*, and come morning every man begged to go ashore to forage for himself. Drake chose John Brewer and his brother Tom, Martin, Flood, the huge Dane Nele and a small Fleming by the same name, Gripe, Mariner, Rayment and the brown Diego, who went everywhere with him. Being laden with empty water barrels, they carried no arms but swords, and rowed briskly up the creek to a knot of waiting Indians. Brewer and Flood jumped out onto the beach. While Brewer set down his barrel Flood pulled in the boat, and when its keel scraped bottom dropped the rope.

Immediately the tall rushes fringing the creek were alive with Indians rising to their feet. One seized the rope while others caught Flood and Brewer and pinioned their arms. No fewer than five hundred rushed to the water's edge and let fly darts and arrows like a swarm of gnats, and Drake and his men, jammed together in the little boat, with no weapons but swords, had to sit like toads and take them in the face. So thick were the arrows that not a man but stopped a couple; some came off with ten and one had twenty-one in his hide. Francis Drake took one that went through the cheek and on almost to the brain, and none would have escaped alive had not someone cut the rope with his sword and freed the boat.

As soon as the wounded men regained the ship a fresh crew returned to rescue Brewer and Flood, but when they came near they stopped dead, nauseated. Two thousand Indians armed with spears, pikes, and arrows all silver-tipped and shining in the sun were dancing in a great double circle. In the center lay the two white men, bound hand and foot and screaming while four bizarrely painted Indians capered around, waving long knives, and from time to time bent and cut off hunks of flesh, which they tossed into the air. The rest, without breaking the rhythm of their dance, caught the chunks on the fly and devoured them laughing. The four with knives worked from the extremities in, so that life of a sort remained till the bodies were hardly more than bare exposed bone. Sickly the boatload of Englishmen turned and rowed away.

The *Golden Hind's* men were all for turning the ship's great guns on shore, but Drake showed one of his flashes of something above the ordinary. "These Indians have only acted according to the nature of Indians. They think we are Spaniards"—he shook his fist at Thomas Moone—"and it is natural they should hate us. Let them alone." So they coasted north from Mucho, leaving behind Brewer and Flood and—dead of their wounds because there was none but an unskilled boy for surgeon—brown Diego and Nele the Dane.

This bloody introduction to the west coast dampened their spirits temporarily. "See how great their hate for the Spaniards is," Drake sighed, shaking his head. "We shall be in a bad way if they have all been spoiled in this way." Doubly relieved were they then to find on the next encounter an Indian as gentle and friendly as any of themselves. There being no good watering place nearby, he offered to show Nuño da Silva the way to Valparaiso, where, he innocently informed Drake, was not only good water but a ship laded with gold from Valdivia, the finest mine in Chile.

Now at last the trail was becoming warm. And when on December 5 they reached Valparaiso, sure enough the *Grand Captain of the South*, her sails peacefully furled, beat a tattoo of welcome across the water.

Drake grinned. "They do not expect English ships in these waters."

Eight of the men rowed towards the great ship. Drake's armor, a plate-mail cuirass and comb morion helmet, was indistinguishable from a Spanish warrior's and so were those of the other gentlemen, while the sailors, who did not run to such luxuries, had blackened their blond beards with charcoal and pulled down their fighting caps. As they approached, three Negroes and eight Spaniards leaned over the port gunwale waving cups and shouting words that Drake recognized as "Chile wine." He made signs of pleased anticipation, and when they had drawn alongside they climbed aboard smiling and murmuring sounds that might have been any language.

Drake had planned nothing specific, preferring, as always, to wait for inspiration. But Thomas Moone, the unpredictable, decided for him. Hardly waiting till his friends were all on deck, he let fly with his fist to the nearest face, crying in bad Spanish "Go down, dog," and quickly the rest took their cue. The amazed Spaniards, who had not suspected there was an Englishman within a thousand

miles, fell into a panic and rushed down to the hold—all except
one, who leaped off the stern and swam ashore to spread the alarm.

The *Grand Captain* thus was taken without a murmur, the English battening down the forecastle hatches on the remaining men
and with some interest examining her cargo, which turned out to
be seventeen hundred jars of wine. While this occupied the attention of the sailors, Drake and his council—Elyot, Ffortescu, and
Fletcher—made for the strong room.

Battering down the door with an oak chair, the men walked in.
Four chests nearly filled the room, three of black leather with round
covers and, bound with iron bars, a great broad chest of mail with
a flat cover. Ffortescu smashed the locks with his pistol. Inside was
a hoard of gold and silver—coins, chains, crucifixes, nuggets—all
tossed together and shaken down into a solid mass. The ship's manifest valued the cargo at 1,400,000 pieces of eight.

Drake and his companions could only gape and burst into incredulous laughter. "This is too great a weight for a ship to carry,"
he said. "We shall have to ease her of it." And so they did.

While the sailors were on wages and recognized that the value
of the prizes did not concern them, they could all share in the wine,
so Drake allowed them one quick drink and then, before the alarm
could spread too far, manned two pinnaces and rowed to Santiago,
a larger settlement upriver. But the Spaniard who had escaped from
the *Grand Captain* must have told a hair-raising story, for Santiago's eight or ten families had discreetly disappeared, leaving behind their altar ornaments, their stocks of wine, bacon, grain, and
bread, and here the Englishmen spent a restful three days laying
in provisions. Then they moved up the coast, raiding as they went.

By now the alarm was spreading, the Spaniards, with no ships
fast enough to outrun the *Golden Hind,* sending horses north
through the mountains, but so swift was Drake and so rough the
roads that almost always the first intimation of danger was the sight
of his Queen's flag, and he struck and was gone before the appalled
Spaniards could rally for resistance. His name became the Dragon,
and was spoken in hushed tones everywhere the eighty wild men
had been.

He did not, of course, come off scot free, as for example at
Cyppo, the next town north. Fourteen of his men had rowed to

land to fill their water casks and were thus occupied when, looking up, they saw a number of Spanish horsemen, each with two naked Indians running alongside like dogs on leashes. The Englishmen dashed for shore and were picked up by their vigilant comrades before the Spaniards could follow, but Richard Minivy, with ill-timed courage, stayed behind to have a shot at the pursuers and received a ball through the head. The exasperated Spaniards seized their one small chance of revenge, and in sight of the ship cut off Minivy's head and right hand and dug out the heart, filling the carcass with arrows till it bristled like a porcupine.

His force thus slowly diminishing, Drake moved northward with eyes peeled for his lost ships. Coming ashore outside Tarapacá, they found a man asleep on the ground, thirteen bars of silver lying by his side, which he had taken out of a sack and been admiring. As they approached stealthily he woke and sat up, yelling.

"Oh," Drake murmured with a long face, the point of his sword just touching the other's throat, "our apologies for disturbing your rest. But since we have done you that injury let us make amends —relieve you, perhaps, of your burden." He stood guard while his men, puffing and groaning in a great show of exhaustion, removed the bars to the boats, after which he followed them. "It was the least we could do for him," he said gravely.

For some distance up the coast they continued this sport, relieving a man here of eight hundred pounds of silver, a bark there of fifty-seven bricks. It was so easy they forgot the dangerous passage of time, and took a few days off for fishing without noticing a small skiff that hurried past on the way from Arica to Chuli. When they got there, piloted by a local Portuguese with a dagger tickling his ribs, they found that the breathless little skiff had alerted the captain of a ship lying in harbor and that not two hours before he had dumped his cargo of three hundred thousand pieces of eight into the sea. Drake's temper had a certain towering magnificence, and now, suspecting the Portuguese, Nicolas Jorge, of deliberate sabotage, he laid into him with his fists and then disgustedly shouted, "Hang him. Hang him three times." This was a routine punishment, in which the culprit, with a rope around his neck, was dropped over the side and took an unpleasant but rarely fatal dunking.

After his temper had subsided, Drake sat down for serious thought. Manifestly, fame could be a bad thing; his was spreading like an epidemic, and he would have to race it to Panama. This meant he could search no longer for the *Elizabeth* and the *Marigold*, nor take along any other prize ships, for all these things delayed one; and he reluctantly decided to cut loose the *Grand Captain*, which he had kept in tow simply because abandoning such a pretty ship violated his instincts. Her crew having already been set ashore, he ordered her tow line dropped, and she drifted seaward, empty and helpless. Then, full of business, he hurried on to Lima, the capital of Peru, stopping only to snatch a thousand yards of linen from this ship, rakes and plows and more wine from that.

Lima stood in the high country twelve miles inland, with a harbor, Callao, which existed solely as a link between the wealth of Peru and the outer world. At ten o'clock on the moonless night of February 16 the *Golden Hind*, trailing two pinnaces, approached this harbor and slid in without a sound. Seventeen large ships lay at anchor, unlighted and silent, unsuspecting.

Drake and three companions dropped into a pinnace, daggers in teeth, and started to a nearby bark. In the complete silence they had practiced so long they slipped aboard and heard snores rumbling up from below. Leaving Nele the Fleming on deck, Drake and Moone and Martin tiptoed down to the cabin where the snores were loudest. Drake pressed the point of his dagger very gently against the throat of the sleeper and whispered in his ear, "Make no sound."

The man started awake and opened his mouth to yell, but the dagger pricked his skin ever so slightly and he gulped and shut it again. Drake bent to his ear. "Tell me what ships lie here and what each one contains."

The man gasped and made inarticulate noises, so Drake waited till he was calmer and then repeated the demand.

"Miguel Angel, his galleon," the man stammered, "fifteen hundred barrels of silver. So I hear."

"Not bad. Where does Miguel Angel lie?"

"Second ship on the north side. Galleon with two decks."

Drake nodded. "Very good. Mr. Moone, you and Mr. Martin

may take this gentleman back to the *Hind* for the present. Nele and
I will see to those fifteen hundred barrels."

But luck was running against them, for Miguel Angel had not
yet loaded his silver on board. Indeed, there were not even any
men on the ship. Never dreaming of marauders, the crews had all
gone ashore for the night and for two hours Drake and Nele entered one ship after another without meeting a soul. It became quite
lonely.

In the meantime Moone and Martin and their captive were
waiting in the cabin of the *Hind*. Suddenly a large ship, blacker by
a little than the black of the water and sky, entered and anchored
alongside and the crew turned in. Soon a small boat bustled out
from shore and the Englishmen, scarcely breathing, heard two men
rowing around the new arrival.

"I think she's from Panama," one said in a low voice. "It's all
right." They started back to shore, and Moone and Martin breathed
again. Then the boatsman said, "Wait. This ship here . . . That's
a strange-looking ship if ever I saw one." In a louder voice, but still
cautiously, he called, "Who are you? Where do you come from?"

English eyes met each other in silence. Thomas Moone, with a
slight pressure of his dagger, whispered to the captive, "Say you are
Miguel Angel, from Chile."

The Spaniard, his eyes never leaving Moone's face, cleared his
throat and obeyed.

"Well, well," the man outside shouted gaily, "Miguel Angel! My
old friend! What do you say, shall we come aboard for a cup of
wine?" And without waiting he climbed aboard.

The first thing his hand met was a long, round metal object, and
running his palm along it, he came to a muzzle. No Spanish ship
had ever carried a gun of this caliber, and with a clatter and a cry
he fell backwards into his boat and made off for shore.

Now the Englishmen became restless, and when Drake arrived
they greeted him with their news and a demand for haste. But
he had news of his own. On a ship fresh from Panama he had
found a sailor who, too drunk to discriminate between an Englishman's Spanish and the real thing, had poured out the latest news,
notably about *Our Lady of the Conception*. This was the most
magnificent ship ever seen in these parts, large, lavishly decorated

and, as her nickname the *Spitfire* suggested, equipped with two guns. She had left Callao for Panama on February 2 carrying, the sailor said, more than three hundred thousand pesos de oro, part of which was the property of King Philip and the rest that of private parties. A dizzying prize, if the rumor was true, one worth making a strike for. But February 2 was two weeks past, and what chance was there of overcoming such a head start?

The men looked at each other, the same question on every face, and each saw the same answer. "First, just let us burn the ships here," young Hawkins suggested, "to prevent their following us."

But Drake was more interested in acquisition than destruction, so from ship to ship the pinnaces rowed, quietly cutting the cables of all seventeen, and a fresh east wind did the rest. The crewless ships drove helter-skelter, butting each other and snapping off their bowsprits, or running alone onto the lee shore, so that by dawn half were far at sea and the others beached and helpless. The *Golden Hind*, meanwhile, was beating up the coast after *Our Lady*.

Badly in need of careening and greasing and almost awash with her cargo, she was still so much faster than her quarry that when they called in at the port of Paita on February 20 they learned that the *Spitfire* had passed only two days before. They were catching up. Indeed, if she was dawdling like that there was time for them to dally a bit, so they stopped a passing bark to lift eighty pounds of gold and some rope as well as a huge crucifix studded with emeralds a finger long. Then on the twenty-fourth they waylaid a ship off Guayaquil. The pilot shook his head blankly at all questions, but the master, interviewed separately, admitted the galleon had passed three days before. They were losing ground. Drake piled on all sail.

Meanwhile the coastal towns of Chile and Peru were in a ferment, for every day or so another ship was struggling home without her cargo and with the pilot abducted. The officials alternately cursed the Dragon and each other. "Why has not word gone out to these ships in time to save them?" they demanded of each other, and a solemn conclave was called at Lima.

The primary concern being *Our Lady of the Conception*, the two swiftest ships available were dispatched to order Captain San Juan de Anton to put in at the first safe port and rush the treasure into a guardhouse. Orders also went to all ports to scrutinize every vessel trying to enter, and to post guards night and day against a raid. Ships fitted with guns were rushed up the coast to do battle with the English ship, if they could catch her, and others set forth with tiny skiffs to sniff out marauding Englishmen hiding in the creeks and inlets.

Within a few days they all limped sheepishly home, having found nothing but one crippled galleon set adrift by the Dragon. Everywhere they had heard the same thing, that he had passed eight, ten, twelve days before.

Even more galling than his depredations was his cockiness. The passengers of each ship left drifting told of his swaggering about boasting that San Juan's doom was sealed, that it would be only a matter of days till he was overtaken. And no one could reach the gallant captain to warn him.

But worst of all was his forbearance. There was something patronizing beyond endurance in his habit of handing back a portion of the loot he had just taken, like an alms. And one captain reported the ultimate insult—Drake, having seized his ship and found it fast enough to rush ahead and warn San Juan, had removed her sails, wrapped them around her anchor, and dropped the bundle into the sea. This was maddening, but at least it was the behavior of one fighting man to another. But when the Englishman had smilingly tossed him a length of coarse linen, saying, "Make yourself a sail to get you back to land," the Spaniard's blood had churned. He should have been a complete brute. This condescension, this easygoing gentleness of the strong towards the weak, of an adult towards a child, was more than the pride of a conquistador could endure.

But they would catch him. Someday he would want to go home, and as naturally he could not go west around the world (no one but Magellan had ever done that), he would have to return the way he had come. So the Viceroy dispatched the Captains Pedro Sarmiento de Gamba and Anton Paulo Coros to lie in wait by the Strait.

Drake sailed on serenely, crossing the equator on February 28, with the most recent report placing the *Spitfire* just a day ahead of him. He had promised the gold chain he wore on state occasions to the first man sighting the quarry and on Sunday, March 1, his fifteen-year-old cousin won the prize. Young Drake, on watch at one o'clock in the crow's nest, saw a speck sixteen miles to the northwest. With a great shout he cried, "Ship on the port bow," and the others ran to look. It was a galleon, certainly, tall and cumbersome, yet lying low in the water as if heavily loaded. Drake peered ahead and then looked around at his men.

"*Now!*" he grinned, rubbing his hands. "At last!"

They were advancing under full sail, and so was the galleon, but so much faster were they than the Spaniard that at this rate they would overtake her in an hour or so—in broad daylight. Drake had a liking for the obscurity of night, and moreover, the men and the artillery needed some last-minute going over. He might shorten sail to delay the encounter, but this would render the *Hind* less quick on the getaway as well as arouse the suspicion of San Juan, the last thing he desired, so he resorted to a trick learned from a French pirate. In the hold were a quantity of empty earthen jars for water and oil which he now filled with sea water, rigged with lines, and dragged from the stern. These dead weights cut the ship's speed so sharply that, though still under full sail, the agile little *Hind* was now plodding through the waves like a great sea turtle. San Juan, watching from *Our Lady*'s poop, must be remarking to himself on the slow and inept vessel on her starboard quarter.

Now that their prey was comfortably within reach a spirit of elation pervaded the *Hind*. The cook prepared an extra-tasty dinner, the men polished and oiled their firearms, and Drake conducted a short service. Then they waited for twilight, when they would haul in their drags and make after the *Spitfire* with all speed.

But San Juan was altogether too friendly a man, and his curiosity and the loneliness of the sea impelled him to turn inland to cross the other's bow some miles ahead. Drake noticed the new course and frowned; then he shrugged. If the Spaniard elected to meet his fate in the daytime, so be it.

It was eight o'clock before the two ships met, however, and in the deepening dusk San Juan dipped a sail. Receiving no reply, he shouted, "Who are you? Are you come from Chile?"

Drake had been maneuvering his ship alongside the galleon, and now from her railings grappling irons were run out, catching the other's rigging, and he shouted, "We are Englishmen. Strike sail, in the name of the Queen."

San Juan stared, unbelieving. Drake shouted again, more peremptorily, "San Juan de Anton, strike sail or go to the bottom."

San Juan now had recovered his voice. "What English bastard tells me to strike? Board me and strike yourself, if you can."

"Just what I had in mind," Drake chuckled, and blew his whistle. The trumpet aft responded and six arquebuses spat a noisy volley at the galleon, followed by a cloud of arrows. Simultaneously a large gun on the poop sent three chain balls at the ship, one of them catching the mizzenmast and carrying it into the sea with its sail and lateen yard. Again Drake bellowed, "Surrender!"

San Juan glanced about his deck. The two guns were deserted, for his sailors had disappeared below; on his one side the grappling irons held the two ships fast while a group of men leaped aboard, and on the other ten or twenty more were swarming up from a pinnace. He looked wildly from port to starboard and back again, and threw up his hands. The *Spitfire* had surrendered without sending a shot.

Drake, mindful of his position, had remained on his own ship but now Elyot leaped onto the Spaniard and strode to San Juan. "Seize him," he ordered two men, "and take him to the General." Others he sent below to lock up the passengers and sailors.

Drake was removing his helmet and cuirass as San Juan was led before him, and the two men studied each other. The stocky Englishman with the amused eyes waited for the other to speak while San Juan, breathing hard but magnificently composed, gave his captor a long, almost insolent glare and remained silent. Drake put out his hand. With slow dignity the Spaniard bent and kissed the knuckles.

Clapping him on the shoulder, Drake said with a smile, "Too bad. But this is how war is," and he waved to Ffortescu. "Have His Excellency locked in the poop cabin and set twelve men on guard. But see that he is comfortable."

That night San Juan, lying in the narrow cabin, had to listen to the sound of loud rejoicing outside, for now the long chase was over and it was time to relax.

Next morning Drake, forbearing to wake his captive, left orders for the chief sergeant to lay dinner in his own cabin and serve the guest good wine and meat. Then he stepped aboard his prize and went below.

Always there was a breathless moment when he approached a new storeroom, and now he opened the door with a pounding heart. Since this wild chase had been begun on the word of a single drunken sailor, he had secretly prepared himself for disappointment. But now as he stared at the rows and rows of chests he whispered, "Holy Jesus!"

Calling for the ship's register, he slowly read aloud, " 'One chest of jewels; two silver-gilt drinking bowls; thirteen chests of coined silver; eighty pounds of gold; twenty-six tons of uncoined silver.' " He turned to the clerk, hiding his excitement. "Open the chest of jewels." Inside were loose pearls of all sizes and shades, emeralds and rubies and sapphires and diamonds, tossed together like pebbles, massive gold chains and bracelets and rings, crucifixes and vessels. And lying half buried, a gold crown surrounded by emeralds each the size of an egg. Drake disengaged it and held it up. "For my Queen's head," he said.

He turned to Domingo de Lizarza, the clerk. "The register values the total at three hundred thousand pesos de oro. But I would have valued it higher."

"This is the official count," the clerk murmured, "for taxation purposes, but truthfully, there is more like four hundred thousand here." Lizarza was watching Drake's face nervously, and at his pleased expression moved a little closer and continued his obsequious murmur. "Your Excellency, may I be permitted to mention an unfortunate fact? Should Your Excellency have the goodness not to put us all to death, we shall one day have to account for this cargo to His Majesty and the other owners." He looked very woebegone. "We stand in considerable danger of losing our heads."

Laughing, Drake called for a pen, and laboriously wrote a receipt for the full amount and signed it with a flourish. "Show this to your precious King. It would give me great pleasure to be present when he reads it. Ever since his Viceroy Don Martin broke his pledge at San Juan de Ulúa your King has been acting as treasurer of seven thousand pesos belonging to Hawkins and me, and now it is fair that I act as treasurer for some of his. You can tell him how I divide the booty, that what is earmarked for him goes to me, every-thing else to my Queen." The clerk bowed and accepted the receipt.

For the next three days, while the *Hind* led her captive out to sea far from passing vessels, San Juan and Drake sat long talking together as seasoned sailors will. The Spaniard admired a huge navi-gation chart of South America Drake had had made in Lisbon, but the Englishman pointed out how falsely the Portuguese cartogra-pher had drawn it, for the map showed the Chile coast far west of its actual position. Had he believed it he would never have found land. "That Portuguese did it on purpose to fool me," he snorted. "But it takes more than that to throw me off." He looked his guest full in the face. "However, *you* I trust. Let me ask you a question which it will do you no harm to answer. Where can I find water and a place to careen?"

San Juan studied him for a moment. "Yes, I will tell you. You are a rogue, but the kind of rogue I would like to be if I were not an honest sea captain. Fourteen miles off Costa Rica is the Isle of Cano. It lies one degree, seventeen minutes south of the equator. There is fresh water and livestock and fruit, and the beaches are wide and flat, an ideal place."

Drake's lips memorized the directions, and he nodded. "I thank you."

"Now let me ask *you* a question—purely out of curiosity," said San Juan. "Where are you going after this?"

Drake glanced at the Spaniard and then clapped him on the shoulder with a laugh. "You expect me to answer that? You must think me as much of a fool as I look. But tell me, where do you *think* I am going?"

San Juan leaned back and crossed his handsome legs. "I think you are going eventually into a Spanish prison—or to the execution block."

"Oh, your friends will never catch me," Drake grinned. "Within six months I shall be at home in England."

The other shrugged. "Perhaps."

On Saturday, far from prying eyes, the two ships put down sea anchors and the pinnaces shuttled back and forth transferring the treasure. After that came the food, two casks of water, tackle, sails, canvas, and a cable. And finally there were farewells. Drake called the Spanish company on deck and began gravely, "My friends, I have recently had the good fortune to come into a considerable sum of money. You have all been pleasant guests and I would like to give you some small mementos of our time together." To each sailor he gave forty pieces of eight; to a few, lengths of Portuguese linen and wool; and to the farmers among the passengers, hoes and pruning knives. Two men received cloaks from his own extensive wardrobe and Domingo de Lizarza a steel shield and a sword to make him look more manly. A merchant, Cuevas, who had been more than generous with the details of his love affairs—the less the men saw of women the more they liked to talk about them—received several fans with mirrored backs to aid him in his chosen line of endeavor. And to San Juan himself went a firelock from Germany which Drake particularly prized, a gilt corselet and a silver-gilt bowl with his host's name engraved in the center. He would also have received a large supply of ammunition and powder, for Drake was in an expansive mood, but his colleagues whispered urgently in his ear, and he desisted.

This whispered reminder of his enemies in the Pacific prompted Drake to another gift. "There are two more ships of mine somewhere about," he told San Juan. "Their captain is not like me, merciful and gentle, but kills on sight. Therefore I will give you a safe-conduct to present should you run afoul of him."

He wrote a letter: "Master Winter, If it pleases God that you should meet with this ship of Señor Juan de Anton, I pray you use him well. And if you want anything in his ship, pay him double the value of it and I will repay you later. Furthermore, command your men not to do the ship any damage. This is written not only to you but to Mr. Thomas, Mr. Charles, Mr. Caube, and Mr. Anthony, with all our other good friends, whom I commit to Christ. I am in good hope that we shall be in no more trouble, but that He will help us in adversity, and desire you for the sake of Christ, if you fall into any danger, not to despair of God's mercy, for He will defend you and save you from all danger and bring us all home, to Whom be all honor, glory and praise, for ever and ever, Amen. Your sorrowing Captain, whose heart is heavy for you, Francis Drake." This letter *might* insure good treatment for the two ships, and it would certainly bring them news of him.

When the moment for adieus came the two men shook hands cordially, Drake beseeching the other not to take personally the inconvenience of the last few days, and the captain, as he stepped aboard his empty ship, turning with a twinkle. *"Our Lady* has often been called the *Spitfire*. A better name for her now would be *Spitsilver."*

While the whole ship roared, Drake replied, "I wish you were not Spanish, I like you so well."

After this pleasant and profitable interlude the time had come for thought. The voyage was more than made—indeed, there was hardly room for another peso—and common sense counseled that they leave off raiding and turn to the next phase of the trip.

This phase had nothing to do with treasure, but it was more in the spirit of the contract signed in London, the semi-public one concerning Pacific exploration. Naturally he could not explore Terra Australis, since no such continent existed, but there were other questions that England and the Queen would appreciate having cleared up. Chief was that of the Northwest Passage.

Every explorer from Cabot to the present had been convinced that a stretch of water joined the Atlantic and the Pacific on a line running from Labrador southwest to the coast of Mexico. No one had been there to see, but if Drake could find it his homeward route would be shortened by thousands of miles, he would avoid the Spaniards at the Southern Strait, and its discovery would win him such fame as had come to Magellan fifty years before.

But first he must look to the ship, for barnacles and seaweed on her bottom were slowing down her speed, cracks let the Pacific through in a hundred places, and her precious burden, tossed in so hastily, was in danger of shifting in a heavy sea and sinking her altogether. No long voyage could be undertaken until repairs had restored her to her very able self. Their next stop, therefore, must be the Isle of Cano.

They found the island situated where San Juan had promised, but that was all, for instead of a gentle mound of green earth surrounded by wide beaches where a ship could lie and be reconditioned, they found a pile of rock with indented perpendicular sides against which tides rose and fell thirteen feet. Sailing around its three-mile length, they peered into each craggy fiord and shook their heads.

"The devil take that Spaniard," muttered Thomas Moone, but Drake shrugged philosophically. "Let him have his joke. He deserves this much revenge."

Finally, on the northeast side, they came on a small bay with thirty feet anchorage and a stretch of steeply sloping beach, not enough for careening but at least a place to beach the pinnace. They scrambled up the rocks to survey the island. The "livestock" was rats, a few wild monkeys, and goats, the water was poor, the "fruit" was underbrush and cactus. But there was a horde of great turtles so tame that the men could kick them onto their backs without resistance and these, with the fish in the water, would solve the food question.

The questions in Drake's mind were of a different order—how much treasure did he have, and how could he recondition his ship in this inhospitable harbor? For answer to the first, he could, of course, wait till his return to England. But he was nothing if not human, and while the men hunted and fished, he and young Hawkins and Fletcher sweated down in the hold. All morning they stacked bars of silver and ingots of gold in piles and counted the piles; laid vessels and candlesticks and altar ornaments on the scales and totaled their weight; measured gold dust and nuggets in the cook's copper bowl and added up the bowlfuls; and finally evaluated crowns and crucifixes and bits of jewelry. Twelve hundred bars of silver there were, each worth three hundred pesos de oro; three large chests full of gold ingots; four chests full of silver pieces of eight; four chests full of dust and nuggets and odd pieces. Drake cocked an eye at Fletcher. "What would you say—half a million pesos de oro?" And the chaplain nodded.

But now Drake's eyes were not flaming with delight, for at this moment the metal represented not so much enormous wealth as enormous weight. Indeed, it was almost pushing the planking out of the ship, and if he could not careen her to caulk her leaks the whole expedition was likely to sink to the bottom.

While he stood in heavy thought, chance, as so often before, supplied the answer, a little bark making north for Panama. "Ah-*ha*!" he shouted. "After her!" And thirty gunners and archers tumbled into a pinnace. At a distance Ffortescu fired his arquebus into the air and called for surrender, but the Spaniards bustled about waving their swords and making noises of defiance. After a further volley, however, which nicked one of the passengers in the face, they meekly lowered their sails.

Going aboard, Drake shook hands cordially with Captain Roderigo Tello and the passengers, and was much pleased to find on the register the name of one Alonzo Colchero, a pilot of the China Sea. He brought the bark back to his private cove, and after ordering the injured passenger brought aboard the *Golden Hind* and cared for, he set to work.

First transferring to his pinnaces the bark's cargo of butter and honey (the evil-smelling sarsaparilla he ordered overboard despite Tello's insistence that it was a prime cure for the "French disease" so often contracted ashore), he cleared her decks completely. Then he grappled her to the *Golden Hind* and transferred the artillery onto her deck. As the *Hind's* weight decreased she rose a little, and for the next two days his men scrubbed her newly exposed topsides down to the water line, while the bark's passengers, under guard, watched from a little distance. Barnacles and seaweed were scraped off and grease, brimstone, and tar rubbed in, and the seams caulked. But her draft was still too much, and many leaky seams could not be reached.

They lightened her further, discharging her lumber and food ashore, but still she had too much draught. Drake went out again looking for a beach, but everywhere the island rose straight and rocky from the sea. "San Juan de Anton has got his revenge, damn him," he muttered. And then, "We'll careen her here and be damned to it."

As close inshore as the ship would go he brought her, then, putting her into a sharp list by shifting her entire cargo to the port side, he cleaned the exposed starboard side. Next, righting her and reversing her position, he shifted the cargo to starboard and cleaned the port, after which they restored the cargo and the vessel was again on an even keel.

Down to the hold went Drake and his men to have a look. And there still—he drove his fist against a stanchion in his fury—were innumerable trickles of water filling the bilge.

He drew a long breath and, looking around at the circle of worried faces, he said grimly, "We will jettison some of the silver."

There was a roar of horror, but he spread his hands in a helpless gesture. "What else can we do? Better to get home with most of it than go to the bottom with it all."

"But there must be some other way," they protested.

"What other? Sail without guns? Live without food and water? She must be lightened."

They had no answer, but their faces were dark. They had followed him contentedly these months, for success formed a natural bond. But throw away solid gold and silver, the magic stuff of life? There were sounds of growling, like those of the bad days of Thomas Doughty, and he knew that this sound was deadlier than that of many guns.

Once more heaven or something else came to his rescue. The sea suddenly gathered itself together and rose, round and glistening, in a huge single wave; like an elephant rising with riders on its back it lifted the vessels high into the air, held them there, and then as suddenly receded, dropping them back into a trough so deep it seemed its sides must close in over them. The fall shook the *Golden Hind* till her teeth rattled, while the wave passed on and crashed against the cliff and was followed by other smaller and yet smaller ones till the water flattened out again.

Drake and the chaplain had dropped to their knees, praying furiously. The others hastened to follow, for earthquakes make for reverence. And when the vessels had stopped rocking they looked with awe at this man upheld so vehemently by his God.

Quick on his feet as usual, Drake stared them down. "Now who will disobey me?" The silence was his answer.

Having got his way, he softened. "However, I would not have you dissatisfied. Before the sea gets any silver you shall each have a share. What will you have, bars or coins?"

Instantly all were happy again. "Coins," one laughed, "they are more easily gotten rid of." And the rest agreed.

But first the artillery was brought back and stowed away, for this, no matter how heavy, had to go along. Then a locked chest of coins was brought up on deck. "We will divide this among you, and then we will dump until the ship is light enough."

Young John ran below for the cook's copper bowl. The gentle-men, who were themselves part owners of the enterprise, scorned to line up, but the seventy men, each holding a shirt or a towel or a cloak, passed before their General and received a bowlful of coins. When all had been around once the line came again and yet again, and at last each had sixteen bowlfuls and was satisfied.

Then Drake went on to more painful business. Over the side into the thirty-foot water went bars and coins and candlesticks and dishes, many thousands of pounds. Lumber went too, and a certain amount of supplies, but he knew there would come a time when food and firewood would be more precious than silver if they ran out of them, and he went on mercilessly till enough of the ship was out of water to permit a better repair job.

At a distance the Spaniards watched, aghast, and later, when they were released and went ashore, told the scandal of the jettisoned silver all up and down the coast. The Isle of Cano became known as the Isle of Silver. Subsequently English sailors called it Drake's Island, but the Spanish mapmakers preferred their own name and always put it down "Isla de la Plata." Many people thereafter came looking for La Plata's treasure, but some mistook the cove and most had no way of retrieving it if they found it. A hundred years later English pirates, watering at the island, spent a few idle days peering over the side of their ship, sticking lumps of tallow onto sounding leads and letting them down, like boys fishing, with the hope of bringing up something stuck in the grease. But the sea had churned up the bottom and buried the pile, and all they got was sand and a sunburn on their necks. The forty-five tons of silver remained for a later time.

After several days' work the *Golden Hind* was adjudged tolerably safe. She still needed caulking low by the keel, but for that they could wait for a better beach somewhere along the coast. Lest they never find one, Drake entertained the idea of taking Tello's bark along, but finally he gambled on his luck and settled for the pilot, Colchero, who knew the China seas. Then they bade Tello farewell and weighed for Mexico.

Now, he thought, his plundering days were over, but the sight of a prosperous Spaniard was still more than he could resist, and when he overtook Don Francisco de Zarate at dawn on Saturday,

April 4, and the helmsman called out, "Who are you?" Drake reacted automatically. Prodding Colchero awake, he whispered an order, and the pilot called out, "Miguel Angel. Coming from Peru."

The Spaniard dipped sails to this well-known mariner, and in the time this gave him Drake came alongside, bellowing in his own voice, "Strike sail!"

Since no more than six Spaniards were awake, and even they were unarmed, Drake's men boarded the ship as if on invitation, bowing right and left to the passengers, relieving them of swords and keys, and politely greeting the General, a courtly gentleman of middle age and rich appearance.

Don Francisco de Zarate was the most impressive prisoner Drake had ever interviewed, a man who, coming into his presence on the *Golden Hind,* managed to bow and kiss his hand without loss of dignity. Drake studied his rich black velvet doublet, his jeweled earrings and long silk hose. "Sit down, please," he said.

He paced the cabin a moment. "Now I want you to know that I am a friend of those who tell me the truth, but with those who lie I lose my temper. How much gold and silver do you carry?"

"None, sir."

Drake frowned, but patiently. "I said, how much gold and silver do you have?"

"None, sir, in truth. Only some small silver plates and cups."

After studying him a moment Drake asked, "Do you know Don Martin Enriquez?"

"Yes sir, of course. He is Viceroy of Mexico."

"You do, eh?" Drake's eyes lit up. "Is any relative or property of the Don's on board? No? Too bad, I would like to meet him again. I would show him how a gentleman keeps his word. Perhaps you have heard how he broke a pledge to John Hawkins and me some five years ago?" The Spaniard bowed ever so slightly. "Well, you can tell him that if I ever meet him I will burn him alive. That is *my* pledge, and I will keep it." This time the Spaniard gave a noncommittal shrug, and Drake laughed. "Well, never mind, I won't hold you responsible. Come, since you are a gentleman—a cousin, your men tell me, of the Duke de Medina—I will not put you in the iron cage. But I notice your fine clothes. Perhaps you will let me have a look at your wardrobe."

During his very thorough examination the fine linens and silks and delicate China dishes suddenly put him in mind of the wife he had not thought of these many months, and when he had finished going through them he apologized to Don Francisco for making so free with his belongings.

"Take the linens and silks if you will," pleaded the Don, "but leave me my own apparel. You know yourself how important it is that a General present a certain appearance." And he was so agreeable that Drake left his clothing intact. (The Don, with his five feet nine inches, was exorbitantly tall anyway.)

Drake had waited for years to encounter Don Martin, and though that pleasure still eluded him, this nobleman, member of the order of St. Iago and friend of the Viceroy, was a pretty good substitute. Now he could either kill him or overwhelm him, and not really being a killing man, he chose the latter.

Next morning Don Francisco was brought up from his cabin. Young John had been dressed in his best when he delivered the formal invitation to dinner, but even so, as the Don stepped on deck his eyes bulged. The *Golden Hind* was a-crackle with banners and pennants, bunting decked the yards, the drums rolled a salute. And the host stepped forward in a purple velvet peasecod-bellied doublet, his fingers heavy with emeralds and a red scarf, gold-embroidered, around his neck.

The guest murmured polite compliments which the host tossed aside, remarking carelessly, "This suit happens to be one in which I called on the Queen. And this scarf was embroidered by one of her ladies of honor especially for me." The Don pursed his lips, properly overwhelmed.

"Before we dine," Drake went on, "we will have our usual service. We are Protestants here, and if you do not wish to join us you may retire to the forecastle. But we shall expect you to keep quiet." Retire the Don did, but not so far that he could not watch.

The entire company gathered around a table on the poop deck, on which lay the *Lives of the Saints*. The General stepped forward and struck the open book twice with his palm, after which the ten noblemen seated themselves, prayer books in hand, while the common sailors gathered behind. Drake, kneeling on a box, lifted his eyes in prayer, remaining thus mute and still for fifteen minutes,

and then spent an hour reading psalms, with the company responding. This was followed by ten minutes of lamentations by voices
and violins, very loud and moving, and the service was over.

Pleased with the morning's effects so far, Drake called Don Francisco to him. "You are probably saying to yourself, 'This man is a
devil, who robs by day and prays by night in public.' Well, that is
what I do. But you must remember I am not a captain but a lieutenant. When your King gives your Viceroy an order he performs
it, and when my Queen orders me to these parts I come. King
Philip has used her very ill, and Don Martin has done the same
to me, and we are both determined on revenge. I regret having had
to take articles that did not belong to those two, for their under-
lings should not have to pay for their sins; nevertheless, I shall not
stop until I collect the two million Hawkins and I lost at San Juan
de Ulúa."

The Don's eyes widened a trifle at this "two million" but he said
nothing. And Drake went on jovially, "But that is enough of unpleasant business. John Drake, come and entertain us." The boy
laid two swords crosswise on the deck and did a hornpipe, after
which they all went to the General's great cabin.

As they entered, the violinists struck up a lively tune, young
Drake hurried to his place behind his cousin's chair, and the ten
noblemen waited respectfully behind theirs. Nuño da Silva, the
Portuguese who had made the entire voyage without being heard
to utter one word, stood in his long black gown and black beard,
sepulchral as midnight, and everyone, he included, bowed as Drake
and the guest seated themselves. "Gentlemen, I pray you be
seated," he said, waving a hand, but though they bowed with proper
humility, no one moved. "Indeed, do sit down with the cousin of
the Duke de Medina and myself," he begged, and, at last persuaded, they sat in silence.

Food was brought on silver dishes edged with gold—fresh fowl
and sheep, salted turtle, herbs, fruit, wines of Spain and Chile—
but Don Francisco sat with his hands in his lap looking uncertainly
at his plate. His host, taking up his knife, glanced at him. "Do you
mistrust me?" He took one large bite of his fowl and lifted the rest
of the carcass onto his guest's plate. "There. You will see we don't
poison our guests here."

After that the meal went gaily, the two discoursing on geography, seamanship, and the art of war, and at its end perfumed water was brought to wash their hands. "This perfume was given me by Her Majesty," Drake murmured offhand, and later he exhibited the paintings he and young John had made of the people and places they had passed.

The Don made a close examination. "I am sorry to see these," he said with a rueful smile. "They are so accurate any Englishman coming after you will have a perfect guide."

Drake gave a happy laugh of gratified vanity. "And there will be many of them, too, make no mistake."

"We shall do our best to make it unpleasant for them, make no mistake about *that*, either." Both men laughed, altogether at ease with each other.

On Monday, Drake released his prisoners, and after the crew had gone to their ship he escorted the Don there himself, as a last gesture presenting each man with a handful of coins. "So now it is good-by," he said to the Don with real regret. "You will tell Don Martin all you have seen, will you not?"

"In the greatest detail." The Don nodded. "And His Majesty as well."

The Englishman's cup was full.

The rest of the voyage was by comparison uneventful. After a careening place had been found on the coast of Mexico and the *Golden Hind* was made tight, they considered returning for the jettisoned silver, but Drake realized that by this time it must be sunk in the sands of the cove, and besides, their thoughts were turned homewards.

Mindful of his commission to explore, he determined to go in search of the Northwest Passage. Leaving the coast on April 17, he pushed west and north, and on June 3 sighted land on the 38th parallel. This was the latitude of tropical southern Spain, but Drake's luck had deserted him, for he landed in unheard-of weather. During the whole of June and July the ship was covered with ice. The ropes froze stiff and crackled like gunshots in the gales, sleet clattered onto the decks, and the food, taken with frozen fingers from the stove, congealed as they tried to eat. After the winds came thick fogs. "As filthy and stinking a land as was ever seen," stormed the Englishmen.

The natives likewise seemed overwhelmed. Tall brown people, who had wrapped themselves in fur skins and huddled together to share their bodies' heat, on sight of the white men's ship they rushed to the water's edge, took one look, and fell flat in wonder and horror. Convinced that there was some connection between these white-faced gods and the weather, they set up a terrified howl, tore their flesh with their fingernails, and crawled on their bellies to offer their land and themselves in propitiation.

Drake halfheartedly accepted the country in Elizabeth's name, christening it New Albion, but no one had any interest in such a place, and it was agreed that if the Northwest Passage was anything like this it was hardly worth the trouble. The claim was allowed to lapse and England forgot about it. (But much later a Spanish explorer came by and the place was opened up again, this time to be christened with the Spanish name of San Francisco.)

The northern route home having been cut off from him, Drake considered returning by the way he had come. But he had picked up word along the coast of the guards waiting at the Strait, and that way too was closed. So there was no way left but around the middle. No one except Magellan had done it; but what any Portuguese or Spaniard could do any Englishman should do better, and so at the end of July, after a thorough reconditioning, they struck out westward across the Pacific.

After sixty-eight days they made a landfall at the Solomon Islands, and in time reached that goal of many a mariner, the Spice Islands. Exotic lands these were, rich and beautiful, but since there were no Spaniards to chase the fun was gone, and Drake hardly bothered to log the rest of the voyage home. Indeed, its most exciting moment was its last, when, at the end of September 1580, the *Golden Hind* slipped into Plymouth Harbor, having been gone two years, ten months, and a few days.

Drake's first act on stepping ashore was to inquire for the health of the Queen. This was more than affection or respect; it was a deep concern for his own neck, for the Queen was childless, and if she had died and someone else, say Philip of Spain, had seized the throne, his next move would have been obvious to him. But she was alive and well, and moreover, she was expecting him. John Winter had returned the year before with an account of the storm that had sent the *Elizabeth* home and, doubtless, the *Golden Hind* to the bottom, and she had mourned the pugnacious little sailor and her thousand pounds' investment. Later, however, the Spanish Ambassador had begun bringing reports that indicated her mourning was premature. From each coastal settlement that Drake had attacked had gone up bleats of distress to the King's Viceroys. Don Martin Enriquez, who had been so sure after San Juan de Ulúa that he had heard the last of the English marauders, was becoming sick to death of hearing of this one, and the complaints Ambassador Mendoza in London relayed to the Queen became an indignant chorus.

The Dragon, she was told, had stolen 760,000 pesos de oro. He had sunk a hundred thousand pesos' worth of ships. Besides, he had treated his victims unmercifully, killing many and hacking off the hands and arms of innumerable others. This last report caused Elizabeth anxiety, for while the other was pleasant hearing this had not been included in even the most confidential of the plans. She sent word to the mayors of all her port cities to notify her of his return.

Therefore when the *Golden Hind* slid into harbor that Sunday morning the Mayor of Plymouth was ready to spring into action. The forgotten Mrs. Drake was hurried to Plymouth for a momentary reunion, and then Drake sent off reports of his adventures to Elizabeth and Walsingham and Hatton, reports that were very confidential, for England and Spain were still officially at peace.

The relations between the two countries were growing sicklier every day. Philip had recently added Portugal to his enormous realm and with it a fighting navy even stronger than his own, and the people of England were watching uneasily while the forces against them gathered strength. Appeasement, that medicine administered by officialdom to keep the diplomatic relations alive, was losing its efficacy, and soon the wheezing peace was to come to an unlamented death.

The moment Drake arrived Philip began demanding his stolen treasure, and though Elizabeth's fingers were itching for it, she was still administering the medicine, and so she sent Drake a formal order to register the treasure in the Tower of London while she discussed the disposition of it with the Spanish authorities and her own Council. This gave him momentary anxiety—he had been packed off to Ireland last time to keep Spain happy—but at the same time that she was publicly ordering the treasure held for possible return to Philip she was privately writing Edmund Tremayne, the Clerk of the Privy Council, to admit Drake into the vault to help himself to ten thousand pounds plus a bonus for his crew.

Not long afterwards Mendoza wrote indignantly to his King: "Drake is squandering more money than any man in England. He gave the Queen a crown, which she wore on New Year's Day—a crown of Peruvian gold with five emeralds, three of them as long as a little finger and two round ones valued at twenty thousand pounds. Not only that, he has given her a diamond cross for New Year's Day, of which the value is enormous." Obviously Elizabeth and Drake saw eye to eye on the disposition of the treasure.

Leicester, Hatton, and Walsingham, who were the chief investors in the venture (and eventually realized a 4,700 per cent profit) were getting worried, since the more publicity the treasure received, the greater would be Philip's hunger for it. As members of the Queen's Council they had considerable weight, and now they demanded—politely, of course—that instead of registering and publishing its value she issue a statement that the sum was, after all, not so very great—quite disappointing, in fact, considering the amount of talk about it. Let Philip fume, it was only his word against hers. She saw the wisdom of their argument at once, and as a consequence the real figures were never made public during her lifetime.

The councilors acted to spike Philip's guns in other ways, answering to the charge that Drake had mutilated his victims with depositions taken from the men on the voyage. Lawrence Elyot, who was the son of a nobleman and could therefore read and write, was asked to make a statement, which he did. "Regarding the value of the cargo I can say nothing, this being unknown to me; I do know that some silver and gold was taken, but it was a very small amount in comparison with what is rumored. It is true that some ships were taken, but that any were sunk or that any men or sailors were sunk with them is a false rumor. Also, no Spaniards were killed or had their hands or arms cut off or were in any manner mangled or maimed. One man, I remember, was hurt in the face, but our General had him lodged in his own ship and seated at his own table, and when he was recovered sent him away safe." Chester, Cary, Ffortescu, Gregory, Fletcher, and forty-three common sailors added their signatures. This disposed of that charge, and the Spaniards, realizing their position here was weak, let it drop.

But Philip still pressed Elizabeth for the treasure and she still made motions of thinking it over. Then she found the excuse she had been hoping for when news came that Spanish troops had landed in Ireland. At once developing a case of galloping indignation, she refused even to see the Spanish Ambassador until every Spaniard had cleared out of Ireland, and free now too to be friends with Drake, she journeyed to Deptford.

There the *Golden Hind* awaited her, refurbished with spit and polish and shining as never before. She was served a magnificent banquet, and afterwards, in the sight of all, the little sailor knelt and a sword struck him on the shoulder, after which he rose up Sir Francis.

Though the Spanish Ambassador's name for him, "master-thief," was a just one, to Elizabeth and the English people he was a good deal more than thief, for his hates and theirs happened to coincide, and whenever he took a piece out of his own enemy he was by that much reducing theirs. So he was the common hero, and any honor she paid him came from the hearts of all.

In time even men like Burghley, who deplored his methods, rejoiced at his achievements. And before he died he and the navy that had been foreshadowed on the Island of True Justice and Judgment had swept Philip's great Armada from the seas. The revenge for Don Martin's broken pledge took some time in coming, but when it arrived it was complete and sweet.

Cyril Harrow, disinterested in any facts about his country's hero except the spot where he had careened the *Golden Hind*, questioned Wilkie closely, matching the contemporary accounts with his own knowledge of the island. "You say it was a bay on the northeast. Yes, that's the only place on the island you can land. There are a few fishermen's shacks on a small beach there."

"What shall we do about them?" Jockel asked. "We don't want anybody knowing what we're up to."

"Oh, we can say we're getting a load of gravel or something."

Suddenly the little scientist, who had lived his life in an atmosphere of free exchange of knowledge, saw the nature of this venture in a clearer light, and his heart gave an uncomfortable thump. "I'd forgotten about the treasure-trove laws," he said. "Probably Ecuador's are very strict too."

Jockel, in the role of legal expert, waved his pipe grandly. "Oh, very strict. There's a big penalty for——"

"Oh, Charlie, you talk as if you knew everything," Harrow snapped, and turned to Wilkie soothingly. "As a matter of fact, when I first went to the bank I asked about that, and they told me it was quite O.K. to look for treasure, that all the government wanted was a little slice, you could work it out with them afterwards." He patted Wilkie's shoulder. "We wouldn't get you into anything illegal. When we've found something we'll go to the police nice and open and make a deal, but suppose we never do, why bother them ahead of time?" His voice became a little sharper. "And while we're looking for it, we don't want anybody sticking their nose in and swiping what we've got, do we?"

Wilkie thought for a moment before nodding. "Well, so long as we do go to them afterwards."

Harrow patted him again. "That's the ticket. You supply the gray matter, we'll supply the brawn, and between us we'll all get rich." He fell to meditating. "That bay faces the mainland about fourteen miles off Punta Canoa. I've taken fishing parties out there many's the time. The shore is so steep to, you anchor about two ship lengths offshore. And about the bottom—sandy and pretty clean, I think, and rocks, of course. This is a good time of year, because in the dry season the wind builds up a sea. But now it should be fairly calm. Wet, of course, but who cares about that?"

"Were you thinking of getting some native divers," Wilkie asked, "or are the sharks too bad?"

"You couldn't get one of these Indians into that water for a pension. No, I'll rig up a clamshell bucket and we'll dredge from the lighter."

By the time they had beached the *Goole* on Manta's gently sloping shore the over-all plans had been laid, Harrow and Jockel murmuring confidentially while Wilkie listened, agape and bewildered. Their first consideration had been the elimination of unnecessary partners. "I promised the Brain here fifty per cent," Harrow remarked, "so the fewer chaps I have to cut in on my share the better. We need Rafael in the engine room, me at the wheel, and Estevan in the boiler room, that's three. I guess you're in on it, Charlie, though God knows you're the worst deck hand on the coast. I'm wondering about Jose." He surveyed Wilkie's tubby figure. "Could you be a deck hand?" Wilkie nodded uncertainly. "O.K. Don't let on to Jose that anything's up."

The two craft manned by this disparate crew were as rackety and disreputable as anything afloat. Such an exercise as washing down a deck had never occurred to the languid dark-skinned seamen, and Jockel's main exercise was sitting in his cabin with his hat firmly on his head, drinking bad whiskey, an activity leaving little time for oiling machinery or cleaning up ship. Harrow and Dolly, who shared the pilothouse cabin, seemed not to notice the mess below, and Dolly cooked her Spanish-Chinese meals in dishes lucky if they got an occasional rinsing under the hand pump. The engine room's one shiny spot was the mirror before which Rafael combed his black wavy hair off and on all day, and its air was fetid with the smell of hot oil and wood smoke mixed with that of hot men and tobacco smoke.

The *Bridlington's* old bones creaked at every unaccustomed movement; when she steered a steady course her rattles and wheezes were at a minimum, but let Harrow whistle down for a hard a'port turn and Rafael throw the wheel hard over, and the great chains leading to the quadrant rattled with a deafening racket, while the strain on the rudder threw her into a paroxysm of shaking. Moreover, with a firebox burning twenty-four hours a day and an equatorial sun overhead, she was hot beyond belief.

The lighter was no nattier than the *Bridlington*, its two-drum winch, boiler, compressor, water tanks, and engine house all being in need of repair of some sort, and the fifty-two-foot boom swinging on its goose-necked swivel shrieked an unending protest against the neglect of its owner.

And now suddenly Harrow was faced with the penalty for this

neglect. Nothing but a clamshell bucket could scoop the sand and silver from the bottom, but months ago his had lost its closing cable and he had never bothered to replace it. The bucket could still rise and fall and swing from side to side, but its great toothy jaws hung open and impotent, and without 255 feet of new wire cable the silver stayed at the bottom of the Pacific.

As soon as the cargo had been unloaded Harrow discharged Jose. He had expected this dour Indian, who had rarely taken the trouble to communicate with anyone except by shrugs and grunts, to accept the dismissal with his usual impassivity, but the world-wide depression having seeped through to Manta, jobs were scarce, and Jose opened his eyes and his mouth in unlooked-for protest. Harrow denied having any plans for another trip, but Jose hung about like a sullen dog, and when the Englishman began tinkering with the clamshell bucket demanded suspiciously, "What for the bucket?"

"That's my business," Harrow snapped, but he knew it was no answer, for since reading Wilkie's article he had been asking questions about the Plata treasure all up and down the coast, and he could not now wash everyone's memory blank. If suspicions were aroused a trail of the curious would be following him to the island. Therefore he softened his tone and began pouring out such a complicated tale about a prospective buyer of secondhand equipment that Jose was left blinking and satisfactorily confused.

Wilkie, nearly as confused as the Indian by this conspiratorial secrecy, found himself maneuvered into meekly following directions. Harrow had suggested that he accompany him to the ship chandler, and after buying a length of rusty cable he turned to Wilkie heartily. "I say, old man, since I'm chipping in with the ships, what do you say to taking care of the rope?" And Wilkie, quickly embarrassed, had dug into his shirt for the traveler's checkbook suspended around his neck.

Secrecy and haste were the watchwords in fueling and victualing. Below and above decks the *Bridlington* was jammed with charcoal and wood (paid for by Wilkie, again apologetic); every inch in the galley was stuffed with dried and canned food ("What for the food?" asked Jose); the water tanks were filled ("If fresh water on Plata's too hard to get to," Harrow grimaced, "we're sunk"); extra anchors for the lighter were stowed aboard with six hundred feet of extra cable ("As I remember the bay, the water's ten or twelve fathoms"); the closing cable was fixed to the newly oiled bucket and the rest of its length wound on its drum ("For God's sake don't let the bloody thing kink"); and at last the *Bridlington*, with the *Goole* in tow, got up steam and shoved off one morning before the rest of Manta was awake.

So crowded were the cabins with extra provisions that Wilkie, who preferred the smooth deck to the flour sacks filled with straw anyway, begged to sleep outside. But Harrow put an arm around his shoulder tenderly. "And run the risk of you catching a cold in a rainstorm or something? What would we do without our little Brain?" So he was thrust into a lower bunk, with Rafael above him and his leather suitcase underneath.

Redistributing his belongings on the thirty-mile run to La Plata, he sat on the bunk studying the nickel-plated revolver in his hand. If his companions knew of the gun it was bound to suggest to them distrust, or even evil intentions, but he could not bring himself to throw it overboard, so he slipped it into the toe of a sock and tucked it at the bottom of the suitcase, locking it just as Rafael strolled in. The Spanish the two men spoke being hardly the same language, their communication was attenuated, but Wilkie grinned and nodded warmly, and Rafael picked up a package of cigarettes, grunted, and went out.

On approaching the island Wilkie was surprised to find the popular pirate resort so inhospitable-looking. Rising abruptly from the ocean for its full three-mile length of rock, it had only one open door, the semi-circular bay rimmed with dirty sand on which were dotted three or four palm shacks and a few dugouts. Standing at Harrow's elbow, he studied the bay, scratching about in his memory for details of Drake's careening, and then pointed to an area off-shore.

"X marks the spot, eh?" grinned his host affably, and the vessels came to anchor.

Operations began at once, Estevan being left in the boiler room of the *Bridlington* to keep up steam while the other men leaped from her deck onto the lighter and began sounding the clear bluish-green water. Finding themselves in sixty feet on a steeply inclining shore, they dropped anchor from the lighter and let it swing with the current. Then Harrow began shouting orders. Jockel had been driven protesting to the engine room, where, bowler on head, shirt sticking to back, he fed the firebox till the steam came up and the winches responded. Rafael took his seat at the controls of the lifting and closing cables, and at last the clamshell bucket began to fulfill its appointed destiny, plopping down openmouthed into the sea and presently coming back up, its slavering jaws clamped shut on a bite of the ocean bottom. Two guy lines running from the point of the boom onto winches handled by Harrow and Wilkie swung it back over the deck to disgorge its load, and Harrow watched Wilkie anxiously the first two or three times. "Don't work too hard and strain yourself," he begged.

A separator box—two wood walls a foot high divided by a number of parallel partitions—extended the full width of the lighter and a little over into space, and when the bucket had dumped its load into this a hose attached to a steam pump played on it to wash the sand back into the sea and leave behind anything heavy. It did dispose of the sand and caught numerous rocks, crabs, and small fishes, but for several days no metal appeared. The Goole drifted with the current as her anchor chain was slacked off, and when that area had been explored the anchorage was shifted and the dredging began again. Four or five times a day Dolly brought them stale bread and coffee, but after fifteen minutes Harrow whipped the men back to their posts, suddenly unsmiling with all save Wilkie, whom he still cherished like an expectant mother.

When a few days had gone by and the fresh water was running low, Harrow took Rafael and Wilkie ashore in the dinghy. Rafael he delegated to bargain with the Spanish fishermen for a supply of water ("And if they ask what we're doing, say we're after a special kind of sand"). Again Wilkie found himself on the paying end, but he reflected that Harrow had been so fair in offering fifty per cent of the proceeds that he deserved some help.

Two more days went by of screeching sheaves and rattling chains, of searing sunshine broken occasionally by light rain, of increasing tension and bad temper and exhaustion. Through Harrow's tender care for Wilkie, like a marshmallow stuck on the point of a pin, a certain sharpness was showing as he demanded, "Are you *sure*

Drake dumped his silver at La Plata, you're not just playing us a joke?" Then, on the sixth day, all doubts were resolved.

As on other afternoons, a sudden rain had pockmarked the surface of the water, but the giant bucket, with its mouth drawn wide like a Halloween reveler ducking for apples, had gone on ceaselessly dropping, coming up, and disgorging its wet load in the separator box. Late in the day, as Wilkie and Harrow played the hose onto the sand, a few unfamiliar shapes were uncovered, flat and round. Each bent and seized a black disk and held it up. Harrow's face was eagerly questioning, but Wilkie the metallurgist shouted, "Silver!" as wildly as any child, and for the next few minutes all was pandemonium. Dolly rushed from her stove and Estevan from his boiler, Jockel and Rafael burst out of the engine room, and together they laughed and thumped each other on the back and pawed through the sand for more black metal disks, caressing them like holy medals.

There were sixty-six in the first load, some octagonal and some imperfectly round. After the noise of rejoicing had died down and Harrow had counted them tenderly, he remarked in a careless tone, "Sixty-six. Exactly eleven apiece." His eyes were on the coins in his hand, and he did not raise them to meet Wilkie's startled gaze.

The three Ecuadorians continued to chatter in Spanish, but among the others a dead silence fell. Wilkie could feel Jockel and Dolly watching him while Harrow played with the coins in his hand. A wave of blood rushed to his head and away again; he dropped his eyes and pretended not to have heard, but his mind was spinning with shock and fear and anger. Now that the treasure was found, it seemed, he and his priceless knowledge were suddenly superfluous and his status had been reduced to that of deck hand. Perhaps, he argued with himself, a half share had been too much to expect; if fairly approached he would have agreed to a compromise. But it was the manner of Harrow's telling him, the obvious collusion with the others. . . . He felt like a man who finds the ground he stands on surrounded by swirling waters.

Meanwhile he kept his eyes lowered and his face expressionless, and to all appearances nothing clouded the joy of anyone. Each grab of the bucket brought up hundreds of coins and a few clotted masses of gnarled and shapeless black. "Is this stuff really silver?" Harrow asked doubtfully, and Wilkie nodded.

"The salt and oxygen in the water have had a chemical effect called oxidation. There may be some sulphur in the water, too, which turns it black. But it's all silver; even if we found only a lot of black powder it could still be reconverted in a refinery." Harrow laid down his clotted mass with reverence and picked up a coin, pitted, misshapen, and battered. "How much is this worth?"

Wilkie looked at it. "The world price is sixty-five cents an ounce, though of course it fluctuates. But these coins ought to have more value to a numismatist—a collector of ancient coins—than as bulk silver. I could take some back to New York and try to sell them there." He had spoken without thinking, but the others' sharp looks brought him up with a shock—distrust and suspicion were mutual, it seemed. He reddened and dropped the subject.

When the day's dredging was done Harrow said, "Now—not that anybody suspects anybody, of course, but I think we'd better count the stuff and make six even piles, and then we can all stand watches at night." So six piles were counted out, each containing eight oblong bars ("Probably thousand-ounce bars," Wilkie had said, "worth $650 each") and 413 pieces of eight. Rafael was given the first watch, and as the others left the lighter they turned for a final look of awe.

"We're rich right now," Jockel breathed. "My God, think of the next few days!"

That night everyone went about in a trancelike state, beaming at nothing—everyone but Wilkie, whose self-respect demanded at least a token show of resistance. As he sat with Harrow and Dolly over a cup of coffee he cleared his throat and began, "Er . . . Harrow, I quite agree with you that the fifty-fifty split you originally suggested isn't reasonable, but I do think——"

Harrow's eyes widened in amazement, "Fifty-fifty split! What are you talking about? We always understood we'd share and share alike, you know that." Though his face wore a metallic grin his eyes bored into Wilkie's like the twin barrels of a gun, and with a start the little man became conscious that the other's hands, lying idly on the galley table, were fingering the edge of a kitchen knife. His eyes wandered uncomfortably to Dolly, standing silent by the hand pump, and he found her eyes trained on him unmoving. A wave of panic raced over him as he recalled that three times a day he ate Dolly's cooking. Full of shame at his own cowardice, he beat an ignominious retreat. "Oh well, if I made a mistake . . ."

Alone in his cabin, he pulled his suitcase from under his bunk and felt for the comforting shape of the revolver. His heart gave a great plop, for it was not there. Numbly he sat down on the edge of the bunk to think. Whoever it was had robbed him now possessed a revolver and cartridges, and also probably concluded that Wilkie had had evil designs on the rest. Well, though it was unthinkable to bring up the matter of the theft openly, he could at least try to remove that suspicion against himself.

The next morning, when Harrow and Jockel had broken the dredging for coffee, he began a rambling tale about prospecting in the jungles and about the savage Indians among whom no mineralogist would dare venture without firearms. No one responded; he could not tell from their blank faces whether any one of them had ever heard of his revolver, and for all he knew the thief might be one of the Ecuadorians. The one thing he did know was that the waters were climbing up about him very high.

Next day his nervousness increased when a couple of gold doubloons turned up, for though at the moment he might have some value as a pair of hands on the guy line, when the dredging was done he would be merely a claimant of a share of the fortune, and the larger the fortune the less popular the claimant. But the doubloons appeared to be simply strays that never repeated themselves, and he went about his duties docilely, swinging the bucket back and forth, digging for coins and bullion in the sand, and thinking, thinking, thinking.

At last Estevan served notice that the fuel was running low, and on the tenth day they agreed to return to Manta for provisions. The *Bridlington* required all five men to take her in, but despite the proximity of the shore fishermen, Dolly was left behind alone on the lighter. However, Wilkie reflected, perhaps Dolly was well guarded; that might be where his revolver was. At any rate, he did not ask.

But on the way to Manta, like a man worrying a sore tooth, he found himself asking a question whose answer he guessed all too well, "Harrow, what was the point of leaving the silver out there if we're going to turn it in to the government when we finish anyway?"

Harrow stared incredulously. "Turn it in! And let them take half?" His eyes turned cold with threat. "If I found anybody letting on where we'd been——"

Wilkie gulped and went on, "Government takes half, eh?"

"You're bloody right. And if you *don't* turn it in and they catch you with it, they confiscate everything and fine you double. And jug you too, like as not." His eyes held Wilkie's blinking ones steadily. "So you see, we'd all better be pretty careful, don't you think?" The little man nodded.

He noticed that during the whole day at Manta he was never left alone for a moment.

When Jose appeared on the beach, his dull eyes restless with suspicion, and asked where they had been, Harrow snapped, "Down the coast for a load of sand, you idiot," but the Indian's eyes did not change. "You been to Plata?"

The *Bridlington's* men stood frozen, but Harrow waved him away with convincing carelessness, and Wilkie had to admire the assurance with which he went on refueling and revictualing the rest of the day under Jose's scrutiny.

The next morning, back at the island, the dredging was resumed and the piles mounted, and as they increased so did Wilkie's tension. He would gladly have relinquished all his wealth just to be safely ashore, and he even considered making such an offer, but he realized that since their greatest fear was betrayal they would never trust him out of their sight, and that he would be with them until the dredging had come to an end. Or until *he* had.

As to that, he never knew whether his highly charged imagination was playing tricks or not, but the following day, as he was standing near the edge of the lighter with a length of guy line uncoiled at his feet and his back to the winch, the line was suddenly jerked taut and he was thrown to the deck, saving himself from going overboard only by grabbing at a ring bolt. When he turned to see what had happened Jockel was rushing towards him with deep concern on his face.

At this point the little man's self-control shattered and he charged, head down and fists swinging, but Jockel stuck a foot out to meet him and he hit the deck thuddingly a second time. The final triumph was his, nevertheless, for in the tussle the green-black bowler flew off into the ocean and underneath was revealed a dome glisteningly bright and bald, with a wen as big and nude as a hen's egg perched at the very top. When Rafael and Estevan caught sight of the two shining spheres they gave a shout of amazed laughter and thereafter doubled up helplessly every time they looked at him.

Wilkie knew that now his position was shakier than ever, and all he could think of was how to get to shore. Then Harrow's negligence gave him a clue.

From the start the Englishman had been worrying audibly about his rusty closing cable, pointing out to the men the fragility of its 114 individual wires and imploring them to use care in winding and unwinding. "If you let it kink," he warned them, "and even a few of its wires get broken, they get fouled in the sheave and won't clear it any more. Then we're cooked, that's the end of the dredging."

So that night during his twelve-to-four watch he stole into the engine room, where the twin drums of the cables stood still and silent; with a file from the *Goole's* toolbox he silently cut through three of the closing cable's wires and turned the winch so that the raw ends were out of sight. Then he returned the file to the box and sat down to complete his watch.

In the morning he listened with immobile face and eyes lowered for the consequences. At first the bucket rose and fell as usual, but then it stuck, suspended in mid-air. He heard Rafael call Harrow; there were anxious words, a quick examination of the wire, and a burst of blistering profanity. The word "seizing" was invoked like a prayer, and after a desperate search a length of fine wire was located and bound round the injured area. The cable was rewound on the drum and the dredging resumed. But every face now wore a doomed look, for the diagnosis was certain death even though the seizing might hold it off a few days more. But no one had suggested sabotage, and the little scientist's heart rose like a balloon.

Now each time the bucket went down, the cable's sheave squealing with a little catch as the wire wrapping passed through, everyone stood tense. The seizing was wearing loose, they could hear the sound of it. Then one last time the bucket was dropped; the smoke poured from the stack and the engine panted. Perhaps the bite it was attempting was no bigger than other bites before, but now as the drum turned and the cable struggled to draw the jaws together nothing moved; the winch groaned to a stop and suddenly, with a sound like a pistol shot, the cable snapped.

After the first shock had been absorbed Jockel pointed out the crowning irony—the last load had been the richest of all. The end of the treasure was nowhere in sight.

There was no serious thought of continuing, for all knew they were under surveillance and that an attempt to buy cable anywhere along the coast would merely advertise their activities. Sickly they accepted the end. But with ten tons of silver bars on board, five of coins, and three of wrought silver plate no one could mourn too long. Over a thousand stacks of coins each six or seven inches high stood in rows on the deck, while 241 bars a foot long and five inches wide were laid side by side like building blocks, and candlesticks, ornaments, altar pieces, dishes, buttons, and sword hilts were jumbled together at one end of the lighter. Each night Harrow, Jockel, and Wilkie had counted up the day's haul and added it to the rest, and now they stared in awe at the total. "Over a quarter of a million dollars," breathed Jockel. "And there's still more at the bottom."

A single question remained for discussion, but by the time Wilkie was drawn into it the others had made their plans. "We're going down the coast and find some quiet place to put in," Harrow told him, adding, "What about you?" in a detached tone. Wilkie thankfully seized his opportunity. "I think I'll put off here somewhere, if you don't mind."

"No, I don't mind what you do," Harrow said agreeably enough, and then the steel came into his eyes again. "There's just one thing I *would* mind very much—if anybody ever heard about the last two weeks. Anybody. Any time. Anywhere." And Wilkie nodded meekly.

He listened to the others discussing him as if he were a bale of hay, "The best place to put him off is Salinas. That's directly on our way and I've often thought what a good place for smugglers it would be, with all that cactus brush and the deserted beach."

He wondered whether they intended to put his share off with him, but he reasoned that in their eyes he would be less dangerous in possession of part of the loot, on the principle that in reporting them to the police he would be also implicating himself, and his calculations proved correct, for fifty-five miles down the coast, where a finger of land reached out into the ocean, the *Bridlington* shoved the lighter within a few feet of shore and under a full moon all six began pushing piles of coins and bars and plate overboard. When a sixth had been removed Harrow and Jockel each took a hand and let him down into the gently lapping wavelets.

He stood waist-high in water, uncertain how to say good-by, but Harrow held on to his left hand with a commanding grip. "Now remember," he warned, "there's no reason for the police to ever catch us, so if they do, we'll know it was your doing. And so help me God, if it takes twenty years, we'll get you for it."

Wilkie looked up at him, silhouetted against the moonlight between the flat-faced Dolly and the bald-headed Jockel with the egg on top. "I know you will. I'll remember."

"Here," said Dolly, and dropped a paper bag into his hands.

During the next few hours he was more thankful for the bag than for the great mound of metal lying at the edge of the water, for it contained a loaf of bread and two cans of sardines. When the *Bridlington* and the *Goole* had made off south he stood surrounded by his treasure, with seven hours of darkness ahead in which to hide it. All night he ran back and forth carrying the silver into the brush at the beach's edge, scratched a shallow grave and covered it over with sand, and at last, under the morning light, laid a design of stones for a marker and fell asleep, exhausted.

Waking a few hours later, he surveyed the prospects. The beach was indeed a place for smugglers, a long flat sandspit sparsely grown with palm trees and almost uninhabited. Far off to the left he saw a tiny settlement of huts, while in the opposite direction, near the end of the headland, a few beach villas suggested a colony of city folk who, he devoutly hoped, used them only on weekends. More to his taste was a broken-down hut not two hundred yards away, for its thatched roof, sliding off at a crazy angle, told him it was deserted. He smiled; he was in luck.

At this point he gasped at finding himself planning to keep the loot, and his conscience lit into him sharply. He countered with a plea against inviting his own murder, and for a few minutes the struggle within raged, but at last, his pink peeling face drawn, he said out loud, "Who am I deceiving? May as well face it, I'm going to keep the silver if I can." And having accepted his own iniquity and decided to live with it, he sat down to think, putting all the ingenuity of the explorer-mineralogist to work.

Leaving the silver buried under the sand and sun like ripening turtle eggs and clutching his wad of traveler's checks, he started towards the village. At Salinas his white skin attracted surprisingly little notice from the natives, for which he thanked the city folk of the beach villas, and he sauntered into a *pension* and ate an enormous meal. He proffered a check in payment, which the *dueno* refused indignantly until reassured by a Chinese merchant who had heard of such things, but so dubious was he still that Wilkie agreed to accept half the face value. With the change he bought a bag of charcoal, an iron pot and gridiron, and some food. The summer colonists being apparently very eccentric indeed, not an eyebrow was raised over his purchases, and he trudged back to his cache undisturbed.

He dug a hole in the sand floor of the hut and fitted the pot down into it, laying the gridiron across the top. On the gridiron he spread a thick layer of charcoal and, having brought some handfuls of silver from its burying ground, he sprinkled them on the glowing coals. As the heat intensified, the soft metal melted and trickled down through the gridiron into the pot, and when an inch had gathered he allowed it to cool and removed the round whitish cake. Then he decided to test his luck.

Early the following morning, with his cake of silver in Dolly's paper bag, he made for a railroad track he had noticed the day before, and followed it to a station where he boarded the autocarril. Four hours later, shabby, blistered, and peeling, he strolled the crowded streets of Guayaquil trying to look unconcerned but internally aquiver. He had never done anything illegal before, and now he was risking not only police questioning and confiscation of his treasure, a fine and perhaps jail, but also, if by accident he implicated his confederates, even worse later on. With customary detachment he smiled at his fantastic situation, but the humor of it did not lessen his nervousness as he walked along the Malecon looking for a silversmith.

The word *Plateria* on a shop front told him he had come to his moment of truth. He sauntered in and laid his silver on the counter, saying, as he remembered saying to pawnbrokers in his college days, "How much?"

The man glanced at him and then studied the silver, turning it over, running his thumbnail over its rough surface. At last he said, "Come back in a couple of hours," picked up the cake, and disappeared through a back door.

Wilkie stared in dismay, visualizing the man running to the police station, but too bewildered to protest. He stumbled out, and for the next hour walked the streets fighting off panic. Nothing but his pride kept him from fleeing, but after a struggle he got himself back to the shop, which he found closed with the shutters down. His heart stopped for a moment, but then he noticed that other shops were likewise closed, and with a snort of impatience remembered the two-hour siesta of the tropics. He sat on a sidewalk bench and waited for two o'clock.

Finally his silversmith drew up his shutters and Wilkie entered. As he did so the man glanced at him and went into the back room for the silver cake, which had had a deep notch filed in its edge and the gash painted with a liquid that had dried a cloudy cream color. Reaching into a drawer, the man brought out a handful of paper money. "Forty-four ounces," he said shortly. "A hundred and ninety-eight *sucres*." And laid them on the glass counter.

It was as easy as that. Wilkie's nerves had been strung so taut that now the relaxation was almost a shock to his system, and he started to tremble all over. But as calmly as if he had just bought a pound of cheese and received his change he picked up the bills and strolled out.

Now he wanted to laugh and stop people and tell them about his ridiculous good fortune; his body suddenly felt light and bouncy, and he could scarcely maintain the dignity expected of his years. Then, as he walked along the Malecon, admiring its beauty, his mind began doing a sum in arithmetic, converting *sucres* to cents, dividing cents by ounces. The silver, it seemed, was not bringing sixty-five cents an ounce but forty-five and thus the whole treasure was less than $200,000.

Well, he was not going to make a fuss, he was in no position to make a fuss, and even if his share was only something like $32,000 he was still absurdly rich.

But he did have one other experiment to make. Purchasing a cigar with the care of a connoisseur, he casually pulled out of his pocket a piece of eight, pock-marked and misshapen, ready if challenged to explain that he had picked it up on the beach. However, the storekeeper peered closely, shook his head, and thrust it back with a touch of indignation. "No good."

So that was how it was; the silver could be disposed of in bulk, but the coins were of no use as currency. Through his lighthearted sense of well-being he sighed as he thought of the days and days ahead bent over the charcoal fire and iron pot.

The following autumn Thaddeus Wilkie met his friend the publisher for lunch at the University Club. "You're looking very fit and prosperous," E. G. Duane remarked. "Where have you been keeping yourself?"

Wilkie smiled easily. "Oh, you know us mineralogists, we go shooting off to the ends of the world on jobs. I've been quite a few places, Central America, South America, all over."

As they spread their napkins the publisher went on, "That article of yours about the sunken treasures was quite a success. We had an unusual number of letters asking for more details—people wanting to go and look for themselves." He smiled incredulously. "Does anybody ever really find one of those treasures?"

"Oh, I suppose so, sometimes," Wilkie replied. "But no one ever admits it, so you never really know."

For many years historians have argued over the identity of the author of Buccaneers of America, *the prime source of pirate material for all writers coming after him. A. O. Esquemeling, or Exquemelin, a seventeenth-century writer who described himself as a Dutch barber-surgeon and member of Sir Henry Morgan's pirate navy, is the generally accepted author, but some men, respectable authorities themselves, angrily deny the very existence of a barber-surgeon named Esquemeling and declare the celebrated book to have been a work of pure fiction.*

In the 1920s, however, the disputed name was discovered in a contemporary register of barber-surgeons in Holland. This, it seems to me, through establishing his existence, automatically establishes the authenticity of his adventures as well.

To a lesser degree the authorship of the 1831 Seaward narrative has likewise been in dispute, but here again internal evidence is all on the side of personal participation as described. I am indebted to Miss Mary A. Brebner, Librarian of the Institute of Jamaica, who obtained for me a copy of the Memoires of Louis XVIII *containing the narrative.*

III

The Treasure of
the Puritan Pirates

IN THE CARIBBEAN SEA, just off the coast of Nicaragua, lies a tiny island forgotten and almost deserted. Its few inhabitants hardly remember its history, so long ago did anything memorable happen here, but this little pile of rocks has been a Jekyll and Hyde among islands, at one time the haven of a colony of English Puritans and at another that of the bloodiest pirates in the Western Hemisphere, while its schizophrenic personality was due originally to an English earl who was both Puritan and pirate at once.

After it had been deserted by both these elements no one else cared or remembered about its existence, and then unexpectedly, many years later, Puritan and pirate crossed each other's path again.

Innumerable men and ships have lost their fortunes in the waters of the world and never found them again; that is an old story. But when a fortune is found that has no discernible antecedents, that is something else again. One such foundling treasure fell by accident into the laps of a prim young English couple shipwrecked on this island, and neither they nor anyone else ever traced its ancestry.

One thing is sure, however—it was put there by *someone*, some unknown man who might have been anything from a single marine pickpocket roaming the sea without plan or preparation to a member of a strictly disciplined fleet sailing under the King's charter and, in a way, part of the King's own forces. At all events, piracy was in its history, and whether its owner was a vagrant or an admiral, he belonged to a tribe whose traditions reached far back into antiquity.

The story of the island, actually, and of the hopelessly incompatible elements that tried to make it their home, is the story of piracy itself.

Wherever honest ships have sailed, human scavengers have trailed them. The ancient Romans were plagued by Mediterranean pirates, for since slavery was a universal practice able-bodied men and women were always in demand and everyone taken on a captive ship was solid gold in the pirates' pockets. Rich and influential passengers were held for ransom, Julius Caesar himself once falling into their hands and being redeemed for fifty talents. (Later he recaptured the entire crew, along with his own ransom, and though he had sworn to crucify every one, in the case of thirty who had shown him some kindness he softened to the extent of cutting their throats before the crucifixion.)

When Rome died, and along with it Roman trade, the parasites starved. For nearly a thousand years there were no ships to support them, and only with the revival of trade in Turkey and Genoa and Venice did they come to life again. Now their headquarters were across the Mediterranean, on the Barbary Coast. These dark-skinned Berbers were expert sailors, though the art of tacking was still unknown to them, and, banded together into fleets, they forced the rulers along the coast to guarantee them safe harborage and an outlet for their goods for ten per cent of the spoils.

By 1535, already tyrannizing all Mediterranean craft, they occasionally even dashed out into the Atlantic to snap up a Spanish treasure ship, but this at last, though he had endured much before, Charles V could not endure. Andrea Doria, his greatest general, assembled six hundred vessels of various nationalities and challenged the corsairs in a great encounter. They were defeated; an even larger force failed a few years later, and this time the Berbers captured so many Europeans that the slave markets of North Africa were glutted; in Algiers alone, where ten thousand whites were put up for sale, their price dropped to the equivalent of one onion each.

Success like this naturally attracting many followers, Christians from all over Europe adopted Moslem ways and names and outdid the Barbary Coast men in daring and cruelty, thus earning for the name of Barbarian a very special meaning. After the Dutchman Danser had taught them the art of tacking, the Atlantic was as charged with them as the Mediterranean, between 1569 and 1616 England alone losing 466 ships; sometimes they were taken not even on the high seas but in the owners' very front yards, one corsair impudently chasing an English ship right up the Thames to London. Another Dutchman, Jansz, helped organize a pirate republic and was elected President and Admiral, which so touched him that he married a Moorish woman in spite of the wife and family back home in Haarlem. Jansz led the fleet against Iceland, bringing back eight hundred men, women, and children, and so ubiquitous were these fleets, and so deadly, that private ships were slowly being swept off the sea.

While renegade Europeans were keeping these Berbers prosperous corrupt Europeans were keeping them safe. Allied for the common good, the rulers could have wiped them out, but each thought only of his momentary advantage; when France was fighting Spain she egged the corsairs on against that country, Holland used them against England, England against France and Spain, and the Swedes got in a lick whenever they could. Thus the pirates were in the happy position of being everyone's hired assassin, privileged to call on each ruler for subsidy against someone else.

Occasionally a country would send a feeble fleet to Algiers or Tunis or Tripoli, and after spitting out a little gunfire for the looks of the thing the commander would go inshore to entreat the corsair to spare his country's ships; the Pasha would graciously agree; the commander would pass over a handsome gift; they would shake hands and part. This bribe was effective exactly as long as the Pasha chose, and ofttimes the commander had not reached his home waters before the corsairs were at it again.

England's Oliver Cromwell sent an energetic admiral to clean up Tunis, and for a while there was peace, but only for a while. Louis XIV made the noble experiment of fighting instead of bribing, and it worked as long as the French stuck to their guns. The United States also had a try; but well into the nineteenth century Americans were buying slaves from the pirates so cheap that their hearts were not in extermination, and it was only in 1820, when France sent 37,000 troops who really meant what they said, that the Barbary corsairs were polished off for good.

The Moslems had used the excuse of religion to justify their attacks on Christians, but the motive was actually plunder. The Norsemen were no different. These romantic-looking seamen with long fair hair and mustaches, horned headdresses and towering physiques, did incidentally contribute a little something to the human race, exploring the coast of Europe as far south as Italy and as far west as America five hundred years before Columbus, manning their ships with volunteers rather than slaves, planting sturdy colonies in Ireland, Scotland, and France, but they were savages, nevertheless, who cut such a swath of terror that the prayer books of the period included a petition, "From the fury of the Northmen, Good Lord deliver us."

But these Vikings were not the only pirates in the North Sea and the Baltic, and were gradually superseded by others calling themselves "Friends of God and Enemies of the World," who became so invincible that their attacks on Baltic herring boats literally put an end to the herring industry. Famine ensued, and only then did the rulers take action. A stern and virtuous Admiral with the emblem of the Spotted Cow at his masthead took on the pirates in battle. Their commander was captured and executed. Then it was discovered that the Admiral's virtue was indeed its own reward, for when the mainmast of the pirate vessel was cut down it was found to be filled with enough molten gold to pay the whole cost of the war and the losses of the merchants, as well as providing gold leaf enough to cover the spire of a church in Hamburg.

Thus, in 1402, the reign of these North Sea pirates ended.

Their brothers in England were, at this same time, just coming to full flower. True, there had always been pirates in England; in 55 B.C. Julius Caesar met them when he invaded the country; in A.D. 897 King Alfred had sent his little navy against them; and by 1300 they were so prevalent that Channel merchants were forced to form a league for mutual protection. But even this effort failed, for the very ships the league sent out to police the Channel turned to preying on each other. The ships were owned and captained by mayors of towns and members of Parliament, and so, stylish people having taken up piracy, piracy became stylish.

Meanwhile a subtle change had been coming over the profession. As the countries of Europe gave up the practice of slavery, human beings were no longer salable commodities (except of course those black people from Africa, who presumably were not human beings at all but animals with the power of speech), and with the elimination of that unsavory aspect of the profession it acquired a new respectability.

Still it was national cannibalism, Englishmen preying on Englishmen, and Henry VII, in an effort to turn the predators' attention outward, originated the letter of marque, a device by which any shipowner who had been the victim of a foreign pirate (or said he had) might hold up any other ship of that same country and reimburse himself by the amount lost. This merely drew others into the trade, however, for a man who might shrink from ordinary robbery could now secure royal authorization for a particularly magnificent kind and still maintain his social standing, and so by the time Elizabeth came to the throne four hundred pirates were buzzing happily in and out of her ports, and piracy was bearing to its zenith.

Like her grandfather, she tried to control it, but she was hampered by the fact that had she gathered her Ambassadors, Admirals of the Navy, Lords Lieutenant, High Sheriffs, members of the Privy Council, and other such high dignitaries into a bunch she could hardly have stuck a pin between the men who had some stake in the trade. Take the Killigrew family.

Sir John Killigrew, head of his family and of a great pirate combine, was Vice-Admiral of Cornwall and Royal Governor of Pendennis—and closely related to the Queen's Prime Minister, Lord Burghley. There were Vice-Admirals, Vice-Presidents of provinces, members of Parliament, all pirate Killigrews; and of course, being such talented men, they ran the business with the utmost efficiency. Payment of crews, bribes to officials, purchase and provisioning of ships, underwriting of finances, all were handled with dispatch from some castle or palace, while the men who did the work, the captains of the ships, were mere employees who received a flat fifth of the plunder, but they had the comfort of knowing that if they landed in jail the Killigrews would buy them out. This was typical.

Elizabeth was nothing if not realistic, and so long as Englishmen left Englishmen alone and concentrated on Spaniards she did not punish them. Indeed, such a man as Francis Drake, who practiced his piracy at a distance and against her enemy, fared very well at her hands. So did others under James I and Charles I, one Captain Mainwaring being created Gentleman of the Bedchamber and member of Parliament for Dover. And thus the rise of the Rich family was hardly surprising.

The Richs had made their money, in a small way, by piracy and other such means. With that loot they purchased respectable political jobs. As sheriffs and mayors they were in turn able to provide more protection for their fleets; and at last, becoming really wealthy and grand, one of the family bought himself the earldom of Warwick for ten thousand pounds from the King, who always needed money. He was not the only nobleman with such a side line, but the Earl of Warwick had the third interesting dimension of Puritanism.

At this time the Puritans were making themselves more and more conspicuous. After Elizabeth died, the Stuart kings, James and his son Charles, had defied them and tried to rule as absolute monarchs, once sulkily refusing to call Parliament into session for ten long years, but as the Puritans in Parliament were snubbed and ignored their indignation boiled over. At length John White, an eminent Puritan divine, cried to his followers, "Get out!" and the exodus to America began.

Though this rebellion was hardly flattering to the King, he was glad to get rid of these troublesome subjects and at the same time get an English foot in the West Indies' door before Spain was too firmly entrenched. He therefore gave them the necessary exit papers.

Even before 1628 many countries had started seizing Caribbean islands for pirate bases and cultivation of tobacco. England claimed Barbados in 1605; Bermuda fell into her hands soon afterwards, and through the influence of a prominent Puritan, Sir George Somers, it was renamed Somers Island and granted to the Puritans for a colonial settlement.

Other similar groups were fanning out across the Atlantic—to Virginia and New England in North America, to Guiana in South America, to Guinea in Africa. Rich English Puritans were organizing companies of planters, the crown was granting them lands and trading rights overseas, subscribers were being solicited on a share-of-the-profits basis, and brave inquisitive men and women were hopping into uncertain little ships and assailing the unknown.

Most important among those who made this possible was the nobleman pirate Robert Rich, Earl of Warwick. The young Earl, wealthy and handsome, never gave up those personal indulgences not ordinarily associated with a Puritan, but in other ways his heart was unqualifiedly in the cause, and along with his heart, his fleet of powerful vessels. The Rich family's ships bustled back and forth, transporting colonizers to Somers Island, to Plymouth, to Virginia. And then, on April 28, 1629, Sir Nathaniel Rich, a brother of the Earl, received a letter from one Captain Philip Bell, Governor of the Somers Island Company.

Bell had been hearing intriguing reports about a certain island off the coast of Nicaragua. This Santa Catalina had, he wrote Sir Nathaniel, every advantage for an English colony, rich soil, good water, and a fine climate. There were no snakes or venomous insects. Six miles long by four wide, it possessed a natural harbor and sites for fortifications that could make it practically invulnerable, and another island, sixty miles away, added a touch of security. Santa Catalina was inhabited only by a few harmless Dutchmen, San Andrés Island not even by these; and, most fortunate of all, the Carib aborigines with their taste for human flesh had been exterminated.

This potential naval base lay on the 13th latitude about a hundred and fifty miles off the coast, which, as the Rich family recognized at once, placed it dead center between Porto Bello on the Isthmus of Panama, Cartagena on the Spanish Mainland, and Jamaica in the West Indies—directly in the path of the treasure fleets going home to Spain twice a year.

The Earl lost no time. With Sir Nathaniel and three friends, Gabriel Barber, John Dyke, and Gregory Gawsell, Puritans all, rich men all, he got together two thousand pounds to outfit two ships which he named after himself, the *Earl of Warwick* and the *Robert*. Another brother, the Earl of Holland, who was a personal friend of the King and Queen, secured a letter of marque dated September 28, 1629, by which the ships were enabled to feed off other ships in the area, and armed with this the captains Elfrith and Tanner set forth. They sighted the island of Santa Catalina on Christmas Day, 1629.

At the north end of the island was a peninsula with a narrow neck of land, and nestling in this neck an inviting little harbor. But around it ran two protecting reefs, like a double lock on a front door, and only after much wearisome sounding did the ships find an entrance and anchor in the harbor. Then Elfrith and Tanner looked around. There were indeed woods and water, there was a high hill suitable for a fort, bluffs overlooking the harbor, and a flat plain perfect for the town of New Westminster. The few Dutch settlers greeted them with the warmth of men too long alone, and everyone briskly started building huts and planting tobacco and grain. Two months later, having found the islands highly suitable in every way, Elfrith and Tanner left behind the nucleus of a colony and sailed for Somers Island to pick up more settlers. The new Puritan colony was coming into existence.

Now the Earl of Holland was called on again. At meetings held at the homes of Lord Brooke and the Warwicks which were open to all Puritans in Parliament, and at which twenty wealthy men subscribed five hundred pounds each, it was decided to petition the King for a charter. Holland suggested that since the island of Santa Catalina was to be renamed Providence, in keeping with its Puritan nature, a useful gesture would be to rename the other island Henrietta after the Queen. This was easy and cheap; the Queen was pleased, and on November 19, 1630, a royal patent was granted to "The Governor and Company of Adventurers of the City of Westminster in London for the Plantation of the Islands of Providence (formerly Catalina) and Henrietta (formerly Andrés) and the Adjacent Islands lying upon the Coast of America." In grateful recognition of his labors Holland was given his share in the company free.

These aristocrats were, of course, not going out themselves. Their money provided the ships and provisions for selected middle-class men (women were not invited at first) who wished to worship God in their own way and support themselves by raising tobacco, the proceeds to be shared equally with their backers. For the hard labor, paupers and convicts were sent along, many of them decent men in trouble for political reasons alone, who would be freed after three years' service and given a plot of land.

In the third week of February 1631 the *Seaflower*, with the first contingent of the Providence Company, set sail from Plymouth. Many of the ninety men were actuated by the highest of motives and settled down to work and pray in good faith. But the healthy body carried within it the seeds of its own death, for piracy was one of its parents, and when, after the settling of Providence and Henrietta a third island, Tortuga, petitioned for membership in the Company, the Puritan colony was doomed.

This island, lying north of Hispaniola, now adopted the innocent name of Association Isle. But the change could not disguise its nature, for it was the home of pirates and its own brand of cutthroats, the local *boucaniers*. These men were a race apart, the slumgullion of many races of Europe. Filthy, illiterate, murderous, they drew their name from the *boucan* where they worked, a gridiron suspended over a fire on which was smoked the flesh of hogs and cattle. The *boucaniers* ("buccaneers" they became later) had in turn learned their techniques from the Carib Indians, who used their *barbecus* to cure not only their hogs and cattle but their prisoners. Human beings they preferred well toasted, and whatever arms and legs they could not eat at once they smoked and salted and kept hanging from the rafters. Treated thus, the flesh would last six months, a distinct advantage in that hot and humid climate.

The buccaneers, mainly of French and English extraction, were as leaderless as a herd of their own wild hogs. Without habitation other than a shed of leaves or belongings other than arms, a knife, a drinking cup and a hunting dog, they followed the moving herds, flaying them where they dropped and, as a special treat, breaking open the bones and sucking the warm marrow before dragging the rest to the *boucan*. Clothing consisted of a shirt dipped in blood and superstitiously never washed, leather pants and shoes made of the skin of a hog's leg, a brimless hat and a sack tied around the waist. The sack was pajamas, sleeping bag, mosquito net, and home; at night they tied themselves into it for protection against the insects that crawled and bit and stung, and in it lay back to back and on guard, for almost as hungry as the insects were the Caribs who frequented the forests. Living solely on smoked meat and liquor, supporting themselves by trading with the pirate ships that anchored in Tortuga's bays, the buccaneers often went twenty years without tasting bread, entering a chapel, or seeing a white woman. Gradually some of them joined the mariners and went to sea, while occasionally a mariner yearned for a spell on land, so at last buccaneer and pirate mingled trades and names and shared the worst qualities of both.

These were the men who were now incorporated into the Puritan colony of Providence. The Company, therefore, started off with a split deep into its soul. Many of the colony, which by now had increased to five hundred men and fifty women, took their charter seriously, expecting it to be a place ordered by justice and equity where they could subsist on the sale of madder, corn, cotton, indigo, and tobacco, and where religion was the ruling force. Insisting on the severest discipline—cards and drinking were forbidden, and a man caught drunk and swearing was in danger of deportation— they did their utmost to be virtuous, honest, and high-minded, but they were struggling against an element stronger than themselves and their failure was foreordained.

It was the accessibility of the silver fleets on one side and of Tortuga Island on the other that defeated them. The very year after the colony's founding, the frigate *Hunter* under Captain Thomas Newman sailed from England with the patent of the Providence Company to, as the papers read, "cut logwood on Tortuga." But once the ship was there logwood was forgotten; crowded with buccaneers and fitted out with guns, the *Hunter* set off on a raid of the Windward and Mona passages.

The first step having been taken by the Company, the next was inevitable when certain Dutch privateers ventured into the harbor of Providence and offered to sell their stolen goods cheaply. Goods were scarce on Providence and the prices high, so the purchase was made. More privateers followed with more stolen goods, and then

Elfrith, himself a leader of the colony, quietly outfitted a ship right there on the island and set off after Spanish vessels.

But Spain, after two years of seeing Tortuga's pirates, under the patent of the Providence Company, becoming ever bolder and bolder, determined to sweep both islands clean. Two hundred and fifty men suddenly poured over Tortuga, burning every house as they came to it and killing every man, and when they left the Puritan colony was no more.

From here they turned to Providence, but this attack was less successful, for the island had fortifications and a protecting ring of reefs, and its Governor Philip Bell repulsed the Spanish Armada without too much difficulty.

When the news of these Spanish attacks reached London there was secret rejoicing in the hearts of the Lords and Gentlemen of the Company, for the dispatches from Providence had been most bewildering. Five years of righteous struggle against the temptations of piracy had worn the planters' tempers thin; the Puritans who wanted to stick to planting and prayer complained about those who sought the abundance of heaven by other means, while these inveighed against Puritan narrow-mindedness. No one was being very pleasant, and the Council was increasingly irritated. But now the attack on Providence had cleared the atmosphere, for even the most pacific-minded agreed that Providence must be rendered impregnable against further invasion, and all together they plumped for aggressive action. The Earl of Holland secured for the Company letters of reprisal against the Spaniard, and war was official.

The first requisite for a war was money, and in order that Tortuga Island might be reinhabited and Providence fortified—both expensive operations—the *Blessing,* the *Expectation,* and the *Hopewell* were sent out on a privateering cruise.

The orders under which these ships sailed were typical of such expeditions. The master was to keep the destination secret till the ships had left port and then come to an agreement with the crew on compensation. The principle of shares was to be urged on them rather than that of wages, as inducing a greater enthusiasm for the chase, and all above deck of any prize ship or one third of the entire spoils, cargo and provisions, was to be set aside as their share of the loot. When the ships, sailing in consort, sighted a prospective victim, no independent action was to be taken but all would consult together and the will of the majority prevail. Any prize ship of negligible value was to be manned and sent to Providence for unlading; if of some worth it would go straight to England. All white prisoners were to be set ashore quickly, while Negroes were to be sold in Providence, with the exception of pearl divers, whom the Company would keep for its own use. Captured Spanish pilots familiar with the region were to be retained, but any brought to Providence must be blindfolded to conceal the paucity of the defending forces.

Captains landing on the mainland were ordered to keep a lookout for plants suitable for the islands and not scorn, in their search for bullion and money, such modest prizes as cochineal, sarsaparilla, ginger, rice, and indigo. When the ships were filled and the voyage made, the captains were to make for Somers Island and turn the prize over to an employee of the Earl of Warwick, who would use it for trading with New England's ships.

Despite their meticulous coaching the voyage of the *Blessing*, the *Expectation*, and the *Hopewell* was a dud, for Giles Welch, master of the *Expectation*, dragged the entire enterprise down. He was a thief (he retained part of the Company's goods for his private sale later), an inept sailor (his poor seamanship permitted a rich ship to escape), a coward (he ran out on the engagement under fire), a bully (when a plague hit the ship he allowed his men to die rather than let them go ashore and thus reduce his fighting force), a cheat (he withheld victuals from the crew until they died from starvation), a pig (while they starved he and his mate drank and stuffed themselves in his cabin), and finally a fool (he brought his ship to Providence with but ten per cent of the company able to stand up).

Discouraging though this try was, Captain Thomas Newman, late of the *Hunter*, was nevertheless eager to prove that such expeditions could succeed, and he persuaded the Company to give him one of their ships for a fifty per cent share of the profits; nine noblemen and gentlemen put up £1250 between them, and he was off. This time things were different, Newman delivering to Massachusetts a shipful of hides, tallow, and sarsaparilla, and taking to England a really royal purse, twenty-five packages of indigo, twelve packages of sarsaparilla, a gold chain nine feet long, a sack of ambergris, four

diamonds, a sack of pearls, several bags of gold and silver, some
silver plate, and two large lumps of gold as heavy as a man could
lift, the whole worth thirty thousand pounds. The Company con-
ceded that Captain Newman had made his point, and the business
of subsidizing pirates expanded.

Though the agreement between Company and captain was always on a profit-sharing basis the directors in London had no way
of checking on the actual amount taken, and large sums were frequently slipped ashore without ever going through the official
countinghouse.

It could have been one of these fortunes that was found by the
innocent young Seawards many years later.

Or it could have been a hoard belonging to Captain Nathaniel
Butler.

This protégé of the Earl of Warwick had in the past gone on
numerous cruises for his patron, he had been appointed by him
Governor of Somers Island (and been impeached for malfeasance
without losing the Earl's confidence), and now he was sent out as
Governor of Providence. He was met at the dock by a trio of earnest
divines, Leverton, Sherrard, and Halhead, and there was instant
antipathy all around. The Governor was more interested in fitting
out ships than administering the affairs of the colony, and finally
he set off on a cruise at the head of a fleet and left the colony
leaderless.

One coastal town after another he surprised and robbed, at last
approaching Truxillo, chief port of Honduras and one of the prides
of Spanish America. Earlier English attackers had been repelled successfully here but conditions were different now, for the Spanish
spirit was declining. That unexcelled daring of a hundred years ago
was petering out; the conquistador had been invincible when striv-
ing for personal glory and sustained by religious fervor, but he found
discipline antipathetic, and first here and then there he crumbled
under routine and drudgery. So Butler's troops found Truxillo ready
to shatter at the first rough touch. Unimpeded, they marched in,
seized the mayor, sat down in his chair, and demanded sixteen
thousand pieces of eight as bribe not to burn the city to the ground.
Cries of dismay went up that there was not more than half that in
the treasury, and graciously Butler agreed to accept the difference

in indigo. After collecting he ransacked the houses of an immense amount of table vessels, jewelry, and sacred images, and when the once proud Truxillo had been shorn clean the fleet stood away, each ship taking its share and going home.

After returning to Providence, Butler found the island a dull place, not like London society at all, and now that he was wealthy he yearned to go home for a fling. However, most of the fortune really belonged to his patron, and if he declared it he would not be so very wealthy after all. . . .

In his diary for February 1640 he noted that he left for England "in haste." There was no mention of a solitary walk along the beach first, nor of finding a cave conveniently constructed, but *someone* left a fortune there in the dark and Captain Butler was one of the possibilities.

At this period Spain's overseas empire was like a huge sick animal, grown too big for its own muscle and brain, that lay sprawled helplessly under the onslaught of innumerable flies. In full health capable of crushing her tormentors with a move, now she could neither crush them nor ignore them. From a wound here and a sore there the blood oozed and the flies gathered. On her Brazilian flank the Dutch were boring in; while she flailed angrily at them the French started biting on the Bay of Biscay. For ten years the English on Providence had been sucking her blood, and now the Governor had impudently sailed right into her prized Truxillo and sacked it. She trembled with exasperation. Until now she had been slapping and flailing at random, but this insult steadied her attention for a moment, and in May 1640 she got ready to take action.

Providence, meanwhile, was in an uproar. Governor Butler, before his hasty departure, had bypassed the Puritan Council in appointing his deputy and chosen a personal friend, Captain Andrew Carter, who forthwith assumed the titles of Deputy Governor, General, Admiral, Councilor for War, and Councilor of the Land. The Puritans, dismayed by the decay of their colony, recognized in Carter a man without principle or courage, and said so, tartly, to the Council at home. Carter in annoyance jailed a few of the dissidents, and then, in the midst of the quarrels, the aftermath of Butler's raid fell on them all.

The harbor of Providence Island was protected by three forts, Warwick, Black Rock, and Brooke. On May 27, Captain Carter was dressing in the Governor's house inside Warwick when he was interrupted by the captain of an English frigate who rushed up the hill and demanded entrance. "Ships," he gasped, "ten leagues to the north. I saw them. A great fleet of sail."

"Sail?" Carter smiled. "Boobies more like, a flight of boobies on the horizon," and went back to his dressing.

Word spread about New Westminster of the captain's boobies and a few men looked at each other, while Leverton privately oiled his musket; but no action was taken. Next day at dawn the boobies turned into thirteen sail of ships. "There is your flock of boobies," snarled Leverton to Carter.

The Deputy Governor now sprang into disjointed action, throwing orders about right and left. Three of the fort's large guns were fired and men were summoned from all over the island by beacons on Mount Prosperous, Split Hill, and High Peak. A man-o'-war and two frigates awaited the intruders in the harbor and all soldiers took their appointed posts. Towards evening nine Spanish ships anchored inside the reefs but just beyond reach of the fort guns, and the flagship's commander rowed towards shore, reconnoitering. Captain Carter, who had withdrawn to Fort Warwick with the women and children, watched the commander's boat return to the flagship and then, shortly afterwards, many little craft start rushing about among the fleet with their Admiral's orders.

The defenders instinctively turned to their captain for orders, but in the face of the impending attack he had come completely unglued. "Do what you think best," he cried, and the baffled men disgustedly fell to doing whatever seemed useful.

The minister, Hope Sherrard, in a towering rage, shouted to the women, "We are in the hands of a coward. There is no hope for us there. But now is God's opportunity; while the enemy is laying siege to us, we will lay siege to heaven with our prayers, and that is a powerful enough weapon." The women knelt and raised their hands.

Carter turned to look at them. "Yes, pray," he whispered, "pray, for the love of God."

Outside the Spanish fleet, fifteen hundred men strong, was moving towards Fort Black Rock. The English, watching from the towers, perceived their intention and rushed to meet them; passing Fort Warwick and remembering the women inside, all shouted together "God will save us," and ran on. Meanwhile the flagship's twenty guns had started pounding and the English four replied tartly, and for the next two hours they traded shots. Under protection of his guns the caravel of Don Antonio Maldonado y Tejada moved shoreward, while like a mother hen she in turn covered with her guns nine smaller boats brimming with soldiers.

Mixed with the racket of the artillery a song could be heard, the boatloads of Spaniards chanting in unison, "*Pero diabolo cornuda, sa, sa, sa.*" Here and there a man toppled into the sea, but the rowers pulled on, and as the distance narrowed, the musketeers in the boats joined in the gun battle. Now as the chorus changed to "*Victoria, victoria!*" those in the two nearest boats sprang to shore and started climbing the rocky slope to the fort.

At this moment, the Puritan ministers claimed later, the prayers of the righteous were answered, for the attackers' hard-soled shoes skidded on the wet and slimy stones and threw them down in the path of those behind, so that the shore was soon alive with sprawling men in armor. Still the crowded boats pushed forward in the face of the English fire; a ball crashed through the bottom of one and the men jumped out as it began to fill. Then another ball opened up a second boat, and presently the water was clogged with Spaniards floundering under the weight of their own arms and armor, peppered by musket shot and snatching at each other in their panic.

The invasion, which had begun at sundown, was all over by half past eight, though in the dark the English could not know that the gunfire that landed on the beach came from the distant ships alone, and that the bodies in the water were those of dead men. They kept shouting for more powder and shot, and Halhead called down from the fort, "If you keep calling for ammunition they will think we are beaten. Throw stones if you must, but keep quiet."

Carter, meanwhile, had disappeared. He had been seen earlier crouching among the cannon, in order, as he explained, to watch the enemy through a hole in the wall, but as the Spaniards approached he became uncommonly solicitous of a gun whose touchhole had been stopped with a spike, and generously offered to run to Fort Warwick for a pair of pliers. Once there, he and a few friends searched the men's quarters for all spare victuals and carried them to a ship in the bay, after which, prepared for flight, he bravely awaited the verdict of the battle.

In the darkness Maldonado had sent out a second wave of boats, but the oars kept catching on the bodies of their own dead and wounded, and with failing hearts the men returned to their ships.

Next day, while Carter waited nervously for another onslaught, his men went out and gathered up the casualties, friend and foe. On the Spanish bodies they found, besides weapons and bread and cheese, evidence in the form of pumpkin seed and peas that the men had expected to stay and establish homesteads and plantations. Their own losses were astonishingly light, three wounded and two killed, while two others displayed hats with gunshot holes through the crowns as evidence of divine protection.

Parties of three and four went through the woods in search of escaped Spaniards, and one group, seeing the top of a man's head behind a pile of boulders, let fly. A volley answered, which caught one of the Englishmen in the forearm, and with a round of oaths he shouted in bad Spanish, "Come out, we have you cornered."

Recognizing the truth of the statement, the Spaniards began to bargain, "We are here to fight for the King and the true faith. There is no such thing as surrender."

Interpreting this aright, the Englishmen shouted back, "If we guarantee you good quarter, will you throw down your arms?"

"Spaniards never make bargains," a haughty voice replied, and then there was a pause. "Besides, how can we know you have authority to make such a guarantee?"

"By a letter from the Captain General of the island," they answered, and ran to Fort Warwick, where Carter hastily scribbled a note of indemnity. They thrust it towards the boulder on the point of a pike and a hand inched out and took it. After a moment the haughty voice called, "I am he who was appointed by Don Melchoir de Aguilar, our commander in Cartagena, as new Governor of this island. You may take me to your Captain General to discuss the future." Throwing their weapons into a pile, the Spaniards filed out, led by a frowning man who bowed disdainfully, as if conferring a favor on his captors.

As they were led into Carter's council room, the prisoners' eyes ranged from him to Halhead to Sherrard to Leverton, searching for the leader. Carter barked, "Step forward. Kneel."

After a long cold stare he turned to the guard. "Kill them."

Sherrard gasped, "You promised them mercy."

"I am Governor here. Take out these enemies of the King and execute them at once."

Reluctantly the guards dragged the Spaniards to the courtyard and ran their swords through their hearts, while the outraged Puritan leaders stormed.

The rest of that day there was no further attack from the water. One more prisoner was brought in, but, alarmed by the reaction to the murder of the other five, Carter allowed this one to live. He was later sent to London and finally to Spain, where his story of the Carter treachery was filed away, to be avenged as later circumstances permitted.

The following day, as Maldonado's armada was seen putting on full sail and retiring over the horizon, Captain Carter's courage returned. For a few months thereafter his office was shaky, however, for the indignant Puritan leaders had composed a sixteen-page letter full of incriminating details for the Council in London to consider, and it came near unseating him. But any appointee of Captain Butler was vicariously an appointee of the Earl of Warwick, and so he lived to fight another day—to fight, in fact, that same battle over again and this time lose it.

While Maldonado was meeting defeat at Providence, Don Francisco Diaz de Pimienta, General and Admiral of the Royal Armada of the Indies, was setting out on his yearly voyage to Cartagena to collect Peruvian silver. Fragile and tubercular though he was, Pimienta was nevertheless one of Spain's great warriors, and when news of his country's humiliation reached him at Hispaniola he left the flotilla with his second-in-command and returned in a swift barque to Spain to secure permission to avenge it.

For five months he made his preparations, interrogating everyone in Cartagena who knew the waters of the island, making hydrographic charts, and selecting his forces with meticulous care. His King had consented to the attack only if it did not interrupt the regular semi-annual sailing of the treasure fleet, which left him but a month. But so thoroughly had he planned that five days after he sighted the island it was in his hands.

His first move on landing was to make for the fort where Governor Carter had immured himself. Pimienta had prepared for a desperate last-ditch fight, but with almost comic haste the gates opened before him and Carter's emissary approached, accompanied by four Spanish friars, prisoners in the fort, who trotted back and forth carrying messages from vanquished to victor and return. Most of the English gasped at Pimienta's terms—immediate surrender and a free passage to Cádiz—but Carter kissed the General's hand in gratitude for his clemency and the next day the Spaniard took formal possession of Fort Warwick.

All English males were sent in chains to Cádiz while the women and children were allowed to return to England; the six hundred slaves, along with a great quantity of gold, indigo, and cochineal, were held at Providence for future sale. The entire booty, estimated at half a million pounds, was added to Pimienta's bulging cargo, and his fame, already glittering enough, shone like a fixed star in Spanish history thereafter.

The island itself he left under his second-in-command, Don Jeronimo de Ojeda, with a handful of soldiers. Later it was transformed into a prison, and for the next twenty years few came and went but criminals in chains.

The loss of Providence would have distressed the London Council more had they been free to put their minds on it, but the contest between King Charles I and Parliament, which culminated in his execution, was so all-engrossing that the demise of the Puritan colony took place almost unnoticed. Thus the island's ten-year struggle to reconcile two irreconcilable elements was over the moment the Puritan colonists stepped on a prison ship for Spain.

The other element, although not dead, was lying dormant, and before it returned to the island would have undergone certain changes. In England times were advancing, and though piracy did not become immoral overnight little by little those who indulged in it did so with a certain becoming shame, until at last public opinion succeeded in driving it from the home waters. Overseas, however, this loss of all links with respectability left the men to sink to depths unimagined even by the buccaneers of Tortuga; they seemed to know themselves to be lost, and sought ways to outdo each other in dreadfulness.

The island of Tortuga had reverted to its original character, English, Dutch, French, Swedish, Danish, Portuguese robbers mingling with the native buccaneers and to simple larceny adding the others' brutality and degeneracy. Most of them were immensely daring; some were brilliant generals who won victories against twenty-to-one odds; a few were quite insane—the Frenchman Le Grand, for instance, who developed a tigerish hatred of Spaniards just through reading about them and came to the Caribbean to indulge his hate, going to such lengths as to nail one end of a living man's intestines to a tree and unwind them by forcing him to run backwards, or L'Olonois, who cut out men's tongues and tore their limbs from their bodies, once gouging out a man's heart and eating it in a blind rage. Such men as these attracted hundreds of followers by the sheer magnitude of their recklessness, and in beating them into a disciplined group laid the foundations of the fighting force their greater successors inherited. Also under them grew up a system of laws and customs which were honored by all.

Whenever a group of buccaneers had spent their last penny in alehouses and brothels and felt the need of another cruise, word was spread abroad by word of mouth, and all like-minded men gathered at a specified spot equipped with arms and ammunition. Since provisions were of prime importance a council was held immediately and sources of supplies discussed, after which the farm getting the highest number of votes was raided. Enough beef and pork and tortoise were salted and stored aboard ship to provide two meals a day to every man, as much as he could eat.

This being a co-operative venture based on two principles, "share and share alike" and "no prey, no pay," its conditions were worked out beforehand and set into contracts. The strictest law in the books concerned the disposition of spoils; every piece of swag must be thrown into the common lot and any man found holding out so much as a penny was evicted from the organization. Indeed, so meticulous in this regard were these men that all locks, bolts, and other fastenings were prohibited, on the grounds that their very presence impeached the honor of the rest.

As the first piece of business at the end of a voyage certain obligations were discharged: to the owner of their ship, a sum previously agreed on; to the carpenter who had fitted it out, a hundred or 150 pieces of eight; to the surgeon for his services and drugs, 250 pieces. Casualties were indemnified on a sliding scale—right arm, six hundred pieces of eight or six slaves, left arm, five hundred or five slaves; right leg, five hundred or five slaves, left leg, four hundred or four slaves. Loss of an eye brought a hundred pieces of eight, and a finger the same. After all claims were paid off the remainder was divided into equal shares, which were allotted according to rank, captain rating five shares, master, mate and other officers two, common mariners one, and the boys one half.

Since members of the Brotherhood of the Coast had all experienced the dissensions engendered by the presence among them of a woman, one of the firmest rules was that prohibiting females aboard (unlike ordinary navies, which permitted women on long voyages, any child born under such circumstances, generally of uncertain parentage, being registered in the log vaguely as "a son of a gunner"). Not from choice but from necessity, therefore, other emotional attachments were made, and a couple shared belongings as acknowledged consorts. These couples were not bound onshore, however. The brothels were never so full as when pirate ships were in port, and pirates being the greatest drinkers of rum and spenders of money known to mankind, they were welcomed with wide-open arms.

These buccaneer fleets were a useful if unacknowledged arm of government, for England's small possessions in the Caribbean were surrounded by French, Dutch, and Spanish enemies, and Sir Thomas Modyford, Governor of Jamaica and cousin of the celebrated Duke of Albemarle, who was one of the King's intimates, was only too glad to encourage their raids on foreign shipping and their visits to Port Royal. Modyford's position required him to write continual accounts to the Duke, and in February 1666 he reported that he had recently given letters of marque against Spain to an elderly pirate named Edward Mansfield. To justify the move he reminded his patron that though Spain and England were as usual officially at peace it was more practical to keep these raiders in the English camp than to allow them to form foreign allegiance; that friendly pirates could keep Jamaica alerted to unfriendly Spanish doings, could bolster prosperity in local shipyards and shops, and would, if given co-operation (this the Duke was to pass along to the King in a delicate manner), yield to the crown a tenth or a fifteenth of some very considerable prizes.

Thus in a short time the hoary Mansfield, a fine navigator if a poor leader, set off to Costa Rica with a young man as second-in-command who was to learn all that the elder could teach him and then go on himself to teach the world. Henry Morgan came of a respectable Welsh family with several eminent soldiers in his background. Of medium height, with pig eyes and a bulbous nose, his appearance was not improved by his addiction to rum, though in his later grandeur he sported a pair of magnificent mustaches and an overwhelming wig. At twenty, restless and ambitious, he had hurried off to Bristol and signed on for four years as an indentured servant in the West Indies, but when he got there he transferred to a buccaneering outfit. From then on, like bubbles in champagne, he rose naturally to the top, and when he joined Mansfield had had seven successful years at sea.

Mansfield's attack on the town of Cartago was such a flat failure that to redeem himself he resolved to take on something so easy he could not help but succeed. He had long dreamed of a homeland for pirates, a small island convenient to Spanish shipping where they could relax among their own, and Providence, for twenty years now a prison, commended itself to his attention. The rest of the men in his six ships agreed, and on the night of May 2, 1666, while the garrison's commander, Don Estevan del Campo, was asleep, they slipped through the narrow channel, crept onshore, and surprised the defenders, who gave up with hardly a shot. The two hundred Flemings, French, Genoese, Greeks, Levantines, Portuguese, Indians, and Negroes captured everyone on the island except three men who escaped, holding the slaves for later sale and firing all forts but the one in which they cached their own ordnance and provisions. Then Mansfield and Morgan held a conference.

The older man had fired Morgan with his enthusiasm for a pirate stronghold, but now they had it, it needed more men than they could spare to hold it against a hostile world. So leaving behind a slim one hundred under Le Sieur Simon, a Frenchman, they rushed to Jamaica to bring back more volunteers. But Modyford was in a timid mood, and instead of receiving the news of their conquest with delight he was coolly reserved. Since Mansfield's letter of marque had been against Spanish *shipping* alone and nothing had been said about Spanish *territory*, the Governor feared that this time his protégé had dragged him a little too far over the legal line. In his accounting to the Duke for his actions he made it clear that he had severely reproved the old pirate for his depredations, but added that since the parcel of land had, so to speak, fallen into his hands, he had thought it best to accept it on account of its strategic position, and was, therefore, dispatching a token force of thirty-two men and three volunteer gentlemen, Major Samuel Smith, Sir Thomas Whetstone, and Captain Stanley, (that same Stanley who was so poor at treasure hunting) to take over.

Mansfield, disappointed and furious over his reception, flung off to Tortuga, for there he was sure of finding plenty of men to join him, but on the way he was seized by a Spanish ship whose captain, knowing his name all too well, executed him without more ado. Thus Le Sieur Simon and his hundred men waited in vain for reinforcements.

Don Juan Perez de Guzman, Governor of Panama, old and so tortured by erysipelas that he could barely endure clothes upon his body or shoes upon his feet, had been notified of the loss of Providence and wretchedly realized that since it lay more or less within his bailiwick he would have to take some action, so he dispatched Joseph Sanchez Ximinez with four hundred men to recapture Providence. Anchored beyond the reef, Ximinez sent in an officer with a letter accusing Mansfield of having seized the island during a time of peace and therefore illegally, and demanding surrender on pain of instant death. Captain Stanley sent back word that it had been settled, planted, and cultivated by the English, that it was rightfully and eternally theirs, and Ximinez knew what he could do.

While Ximinez was wondering just exactly what he should do, three Negro slaves, under cover of darkness, swam out to the ship with the information that the entire garrison consisted of only seventy-two men, which so stimulated the Spaniard that he immediately stormed the island. The English returned the Spanish fire as long as ammunition held out, and when that was gone broke up the chapel organ and fired the pipes. Nevertheless, the invaders landed and Providence was once again in Spanish hands.

Captain Andrew Carter's treachery had never been forgotten, and now, when the defenders offered to surrender on condition of good quarter, the besiegers agreed, but the moment they disarmed threw them into irons. Smith, Whetstone, and Stanley were sent to a Panama prison and the rest put to building Spanish forts.

Since no one had escaped to tell the tale, the fall of Providence was unknown in Jamaica for many months, but at last three men who had slipped out of the Panama prison turned up with evidence of such shocking ill-treatment on their bodies that public feeling boiled up in indignation. Nothing could have pleased Governor Modyford more, for whatever justified hatred of the Spanish justified his collaboration with their enemies, and the pirates were proving indispensable in the growth of Jamaica.

This island's life depended on its ports, and Port Royal was a veritable jewel, with a sandspit reaching out like an arm around a harbor seven miles by four. Along its length stood such truly royal slums as few cities have ever boasted, with a drink shop for every ten males and almost as many brothels, and the pirates were its most treasured visitors. No matter if some staggering reveler dragged a pipe of wine into the street to sprinkle the passers-by, no matter if the shouting and brawling kept the air hideous; the men tossed their money away with no thought of how dangerously they had got it or how long they might be in getting more, and the merchants and politicians, the pimps and prostitutes and tavernkeepers grew wealthier by the hour. And if in their drunkenness they ran up bills impossible to pay they could always be seized and sold to outgoing ships to liquidate their obligations.

Now that the escaped prisoners had infected the Council of Jamaica with a good case of indignation against Spain, Modyford adjudged the time ripe for a raid. Mansfield was no more, but his second-in-command was at hand, resting on an estate near Port Royal with his cousin and bride, Mary Elizabeth Morgan, whose father was also living in the vicinity. Since leaving Providence, Morgan had been trying to arouse support in Virginia and New England for the projected pirate stronghold, but without success, and when Modyford beckoned he was only too glad to get back into action. So in a very short time Colonel Henry Morgan could be seen at the head of twelve sail and seven hundred men, sailing against Porto Principe in Cuba.

His first solo raid was in the nature of a trial flight, in which he learned several useful tricks. When the citizens resisted invasion he set fire to their houses, whereupon they surrendered rather than sacrifice the entire city. Then, in order to be free to ransack the town in peace, he locked its citizens inside the churches and left them to suffocate and starve, excepting only those rich men and beautiful women who might prove useful some other way. Finally, when the time for division of the spoils came, he dared to commit the pirate's number one crime. Boldly staring down his colleagues' demand for a recount, he taught himself the valuable lesson that with sufficient gall he could get away with anything.

But despite his faults he was a magnificent leader, and though the men distrusted him they were shortly back again for another cruise, this time to Porto Bello, third-richest city in America. His technique was constantly improving, and this raid yielded a quarter of a million pieces of eight, providing large percentages to himself, Modyford, and the King, and sixty pounds to each of the four hundred pirates alive at the engagement's end. It was followed by two more, on Gibraltar and Maracaibo in Venezuela, which brought another quarter of a million pieces of eight to the grogshops and brothels of Port Royal, but then followed a time of enforced rest, for the useful Albemarle had died and taken his buffer influence with him, and the Spanish Ambassador was so indignant over Porto Bello and Gibraltar and Maracaibo that Morgan was advised to lie low. So with the wife whom he loved—or at least never repudiated —he drank rum and planted tobacco and sugar cane on his estate while Modyford handled London. Then suddenly a certain Spaniard with a daring as great as his own released him for the greatest feat of his lifetime.

Spain was not without its own privateers, who went about nipping lightly at French and Dutch and English shipping in the neighborhood. One Manuel Pardal had committed a few of these raids on Jamaica, causing more annoyance than damage, and at last, with an engaging impertinence, he landed onshore and nailed a paper to a tree. Addressed in both Spanish and English to the Chief of the Squadron of Privateers in Jamaica, it read: "I, Captain Manuel Rivera Pardal, am he who this year have done that which follows. I went onshore at Caimonos and burned twenty houses and fought with Captain Ary and took from him a ketch laden with provisions and a canoe. And I am he who took Captain Baines and carried the prize to Cartagena, and now am arrived at this coast and have burned it. And I am come to seek Admiral Morgan, with two ships of war of twenty guns, and, having seen this, I hope he will come out and seek me, that he may see the valor of the Spaniards. It was only because I had no time that I did not come to the mouth of Port Royal to speak to him by word of mouth. In the name of my King, whom God preserve, Manuel Rivera Pardal."

Nothing more opportune could have happened, and Modyford pushed through the Council a resolution "desiring that commission be granted to Admiral Henry Morgan to be Admiral and Commander in Chief of all the ships of war belonging to this harbor and of all the officers, soldiers, and seamen belonging to the same, requiring him with all possible speed to draw into one fleet and with them put to sea. And to seize and destroy all the enemies' vessels within his reach, also destroy the stores and magazines . . . That he shall land in the enemies' country and march to such places as he shall see fit and take, destroy, and dispose of the magazines and forces therein." Morgan was furthermore ordered to offer mercy to all Spaniards and slaves who would swear loyalty to the English King, but otherwise to burn the homes of all, leaving the place a wilderness, and to put the men slaves to the sword and bring in the women slaves to be sold for the account of the fleet and army. Word went out to the Caymans, Cuba, Tortuga, the Bahamas, even to Somers Island, that volunteers could meet Admiral Morgan at Cow Island for a mighty effort against the Spaniard.

Morgan remained at Cow Island several months whipping into shape a well-disciplined organization with colonels, lieutenant colonels, majors, and captains under his own generalship. The army was on the familiar "no prey, no pay" basis, but compensation for injuries was at a very high rate, and any man first to enter a castle or fortress or to haul down a Spanish flag was guaranteed a bonus of fifty pieces of eight.

On December 2, 1670, he called a meeting of the thirty-seven captains on board his flagship *Satisfaction* and drew up a resolution: "Having seriously considered what place might prove most feasible to attack and carry and be most advantageous for the safety of the English and particularly of Jamaica, for preventing annoyances and invasions of the Spaniards, we do unanimously conclude that it would stand most for the general good of trade between Jamaica and the rest of His Majesty's plantations in the West Indies to take Panama, the President thereof having granted several commissions against the English to the great annoyance of Jamaica and of our merchant men."

They next discussed the need for guides into Panama City, and since most of the garrison on Providence were known to be Panamanians, the harried little island was again slated for invasion.

By now the island was one vast fortress, with many small forts and one great one, St. Teresa, in the middle, while St. Catalina, the smaller island (recently formed by cutting through a thin neck of land) was a citadel with ten redoubts. However, only 90 of the 450 inhabitants were soldiers, the rest women and children and slaves. So when Morgan landed with over a thousand men the Spanish Governor, after one hard look, retired with the entire population across the drawbridge between St. Catalina and Providence and pulled it up after him.

Next morning, Morgan having sent a demand for immediate surrender, two officers came back with a counterproposal from the Governor. This gentleman was quite ready to comply, but he begged General Morgan's co-operation in a slight stratagem of war, to wit, that night the General was to bring troops to the drawbridge and attack the fort of St. Jeronimo, while his ships turned their guns on the fort of St. Teresa, and still other troops landed near the battery of St. Mateo. The Governor would rush out valiantly to the defense of St. Jeronimo, and as he passed through the courtyard the English were to seize him, demanding loudly in the hearing of all that he give up the fort. Thus vastly outnumbered, he would lead the English into the castle, both sides meanwhile keeping up a constant fire with blank cartridges.

Morgan, with nothing to lose, agreed, and that night, sputtering fiercely, he and a body of men chased the Spaniards from one fort to another till all citizens had fled into the churches and shut the doors after them, whereupon the firing ceased and the two warriors shook hands. He took all the arms on the island, all the provisions, and any likely-looking men and, leaving the Governor somewhat plucked and forlorn, made ready to move on Panama, three hundred miles to the south.

Panama City lay on the far side of the Isthmus. The river Chagres, guarded at its mouth by a formidable castle, cut halfway across as far as Venta de Cruz while the rest of the route lay over land. Before Panama could be reached the castle must be taken, but rather than go himself Morgan sent Lieutenant Colonel Bradley, one of Mansfield's officers, to take it, on the theory that an unknown man with a small force would arouse less suspicion of further attacks to come. Scarcely two weeks later a sloop returned bearing mixed news —Chagres Castle had fallen in a fierce battle which left not a single Spanish officer alive, but Bradley himself had been badly wounded and, even more disquieting, interrogation of prisoners had disclosed that Morgan's plans were known to Governor Guzman. Ambuscades were waiting all along their path, and Panama was an armed city, with every male alerted.

Though Morgan would have had plenty of excuse to call off the attack, his only change was in his Providence plans. He had thought to leave a garrison behind to greet him on his triumphal return, but now he could not afford to; neither could he leave the forts empty for the enemy to take over. Regretfully he ordered all shore fortifications demolished, pushed the cannon into the sea, and burned down the town to the ground.

This was a sorry end to the dream of a pirate homeland he had inherited from Mansfield, but he had early learned to adapt to the inevitable and, leaving the island smoking behind him, he set sail for Chagres.

He found Bradley dead and his men gloomily anticipating fierce opposition all the way to Panama. Reports of conditions on the river were equally disheartening, for their spies said that it was blocked by shallows and rapids in some spots and clogged with fallen trees in others. None but the lightest vessels would serve, therefore, so, anchoring the ships in the harbor and stationing a rear guard of five hundred in the castle, he piled fourteen hundred men and the artillery into seven sloops and thirty-six canoes and flat-bottomed boats. On January 8, 1671, he set off.

At the outset he took a dangerous gamble; needing every inch of boat space for men and ammunition, knowing that Venta de Cruz was but four days' row upstream and Panama one day's march beyond that, remembering that his forces had always lived off the lands they conquered, he allowed each man to pack only a few cobs of maize and strips of dried beef. And the first day they did not suffer, for only nature was against them so far. True, the tropical sun beat down on their steel helmets till they could feel their brains cooking, the hours of squatting or kneeling or lying in the crowded boats drove pins and needles through their inflexible muscles, and the clouds of gnats turned them into a ballet of flailing arms; but at least they had something to eat. That night, however, man turned against them too. At a little Indian settlement which was to have been their first depot of supplies they unwound their cramped limbs and jumped ashore in anticipation of a small battle and a large meal. But when they entered the first palm-thatched hut, pistols cocked, a shock ran through them. The Indians had cleared out, not panic-stricken and helter-skelter, leaving all their belongings, but purposefully and methodically, taking every grain and burning everything they could not carry. The village provided not one bite nor drop and the men began to look at Morgan hard and bitterly, but he only laughed and said, "Only Spaniards are so weak they need to eat every day."

Next day the river became shallower, and from time to time they had to portage around fallen trees, stumbling through dense swamps along its bank. And that night again they found the same desolation, not a cow in the fields, not a grain in the bins, though some of the fires were still smoking and the inhabitants had left only a few hours before. The men were frantic with hunger and their anger at Morgan simmered near the surface.

They were further unnerved by the knowledge that they were being watched, for occasionally a twig snapped when they had made no move or a macaw screamed in sudden alarm, and they realized that through jungle so thick their knives could cut only a foot at a time Indian spies were observing them and slipping ahead to put starvation in their path.

On the third and fourth days the portages were more frequent. At every step the men, weighted down not only by the boats but their own muskets and cutlasses, sacks and ammunition, sank into black slime, dragging up each foot with a nasty sucking noise to set it down a yard farther ahead among the interlaced mangrove roots. Alligators and snakes slid past their feet, making each move a gamble with death. And all this time they had had nothing to eat but leaves and twigs.

Each day they had prayed to meet an ambush, for where soldiers were there would be food, and towards the end of the fourth day luck threw them a bone. Their spies rushed back to report a party sent from Panama to intercept them, and they strained forward eagerly to meet them, but at the last moment the defenders had voted for the scorched-earth policy instead, and when they arrived nothing remained but some empty leather bags. Such was their desperation that even these looked appetizing.

The leather, covered with coarse hairs and almost as hard as wood, was first sliced into strips and then softened by being alternately dipped into water and beaten between two stones. Next the hairs were scraped off with a sharp knife and the strips cut into bite-size pieces, after which it was ready for the fire. They washed each bite down with many gulps of water and gradually felt the gnawing in their stomachs ease a trifle.

By the fifth day of deserted villages and empty food bins the men's rage at Morgan was becoming dangerous, but his luck held, for just in time one of the pirates found two sacks of grain, a bunch of bananas, and two jars of wine in a cave. And when his authority was tested, that miraculously held too. Like a herd of animals the men were rushing to the cave when he stepped firmly before them and with blazing eyes yelled, "Get back, you dogs. This food is for the sick and I myself will decide who gets it. No one else is to lay a finger on it." Hating him as they did, still his authority was so firmly rooted that they turned and stumbled away.

On the sixth day, shaking with weakness and tortured by insects, chewing grass for moisture and cursing Morgan at every step, they came upon one more deserted plantation. But this one was different, for the Indian had had no time to scorch his earth and an entire barn stood filled with hard dry kernels of maize. Thus they were momentarily sustained.

Next day, when the smoke of Venta de Cruz was seen rising over the trees, they dreamed for a moment of meals ready cooked and waiting, but on rounding the last bend in the river they saw to their horror that the smoke came from the town itself, which was going up in flames. Not a soul, not a spark of life but a few cats and dogs, remained. However in the deserted stables they did find sixteen jars of Peruvian wine and a sackful of bread, which they wolfed like animals, with the result that their abused stomachs finally rebelled and in a few minutes had the entire camp writhing in an agony exacerbated by the earnest conviction that they had been poisoned. Each man in his extremity turned to his consort and made his last will, only to realize in the morning rather sheepishly that he had not died after all.

Venta de Cruz being the terminus of their water route, they hid their boats in the riverbank and proceeded on foot, and on the ninth day things improved, even the dawn being pleasant for a change, with soft white clouds that kept the sun off their weary heads. Then, on reaching the top of the highest ridge and standing where Balboa and Drake had stood before them, they saw the great South Sea. At last they were in sight of their goal, and with cheers and yells they tossed their hats in the air.

At that moment two ships were just sailing out of the distant harbor; they saw them, but to their ignorant eyes these ships looked no different from any others, and they were more interested in the broad Pacific and that welcome sight nearby, a herd of grazing cattle.

While some of the men stabbed and flayed the animals and cut them into quarters, others built fires, and at last, after nine days, everyone ate his fill. And such was the magically pacifying power of one good meal that the men who, two days before, had been ready to kill their leader now marched down the hill behind him, trumpets and drums sounding.

As they advanced, a party of two hundred horsemen appeared on the horizon, well out of musket shot. "Dogs!" they shouted, shaking their fists, but when Morgan gave chase they dashed away, turning in their saddles once or twice to bellow as they ran, "This is your last day alive." Morgan would fain have caught a couple for interrogation, but his adversaries proved as slippery as ever, and he had to go forward in total ignorance of what lay before him.

He did know, of course, the main fact, that Panama was the richest city in America, with a population fluctuating seasonally between thirty and fifty thousand and annual trade worth twenty or thirty million pesos de oro. Seven thousand mansions of lavishly carved cedar or rosewood and thousands of other humbler dwellings housed the free citizens, while the Genoese Company, holder of the slave trade monopoly, maintained a slave pen through which thousands of blacks annually passed to the mines and plantations. A magnificent cathedral, tallest and most imposing on the continent, dominated a group of two smaller churches, seven monasteries, and one convent. In short, this hot and humid city was the center of a secular and ecclesiastic empire, a target worthy of a pirate's attentions.

However, though he knew it not, Panama was not as rich as it had been, for news of Morgan's advance had rushed ahead of him and those two large ships loaded with priests and nuns, wealthy citizens, and eight million pesos de oro in plate, money, bullion, and jewels were every hour putting more miles of safety between them.

Meanwhile, fully fed and happy as larks, the men were pushing downhill unopposed. Guzman had made a feeble attempt to rally his people for an offensive before the pirates reached the city, but had received no co-operation, and now citizens and troops together waited, trembling, within the gates. In subsequent reports to the King, Guzman complained bitterly of the quality of his fighters and the quantity of his arms, for though he had twice as many men as the English and some very decorative cannon, none of them could be trusted, and on the day of reckoning he rushed to the Cathedral of St. Anastasius and in the presence of Our Lady of the Pure and Immaculate Conception made an oath to die in her defense, first giving her a diamond ring worth four thousand pesos de oro and invoking her aid. Then he went forth, shaking, to battle the heretic.

In expectation of a head-on offensive Guzman had lined up his twenty-four hundred foot soldiers in orderly rows, with the four hundred horsemen behind them and in the rear three thousand wild bulls ready to be released from their chains for a masterly *coup de grâce*. At the appearance of the enemy the first three ranks of foot soldiers were to drop to their knees and fire, their place then being taken by the next three, and then the next and the next, while the horsemen drove through and decimated the remaining invaders. But Morgan had other plans, and while Guzman's lines waited for him to emerge from the jungle at one point he turned aside and slipped around another way, so that, with a bloodcurdling yell, he erupted suddenly upon the startled Spaniard's right flank. The defenders' cannon and infantry had been firmly planted northward, where the light was good, and now in disorderly haste they had to swing to the east and take aim at the yelling hordes with the sun directly in their eyes. Guzman's heart, never very bold, at this moment hit bottom.

The pirates, in their turn, felt a momentary stab of fear on seeing the hundreds of horsemen and rows of kneeling musketeers. But the time was past for hesitation, and slapping each other on the back, they turned smartly to the business at hand. Morgan had risen at dawn to study the terrain, and now, forming his men into three battalions under his favorite captains, Edward Collier, Lawrence Prince, and Blodre Morgan, a cousin, he led them downhill to a selected spot. This piece of ground, though dry in itself, was surrounded by a swamp masked with tall grass, and he waited there for the cavalry to charge. When the first horses reached the bog their front legs sank, pitching their riders over their heads, while the next rank, following too close behind to stop in time, plowed through on top of them, and all went down together in floundering disorder. Meanwhile the pirates knelt and leveled with deadly accuracy.

Wave after wave of horsemen poured blindly into the choked swamp, while the foot soldiers, firing from behind, caught more of their own in the back of the head than pirates in the face, and the cannon, at last re-emplaced, added noise and confusion to the scene.

All at once, like fire in a lumberyard, panic struck and spread. From all over the field at once, it seemed, a cry went up, and catching terror from each other, the men turned tail and ran while their leaders swung at them with the flat of their swords to halt the retreat.

Guzman in dismay yelled to the rear, "Release the bulls," and the three thousand bellowing beasts were unchained and driven forward. But the flash of powder and rattle of musket and cannon so bewildered them that the drivers soon lost control and left them to run about goring everything indiscriminately.

Guzman was watching in despair. A priest (so he insisted later in his report) twice begged him to retreat and save himself, only to be severely reprimanded, but the third time the priest declared it was neither Christian nor sensible to commit suicide, and Guzman agreed to retire. With their Governor in flight, any remaining wisps of courage faded in the Panamanians, and their last sight as they withdrew into the city was the buccaneers, with skill born of long practice, slashing right and left at the stampeding cattle.

Now left in complete possession of the field, the pirates, relaxed and confident, lay about resting while Morgan, with the endurance of a goat, questioned prisoners. Then they were on their way again.

From within the walls the Panamanians watched them come. Though the forts were many and the streets were barricaded and armed, though, indeed, the cannon gave forth a last sputter of resistance, terror swept over them like a tidal wave. Guzman could think of nothing better than blowing up the forts, in one of which he caught forty of his own men, while the people rushed about with torches setting fires, and the result was that when the English arrived they found the town ablaze. Churches, warehouses, and homes, with all their merchandise and valuables, were on the point of disappearing; the Genoese Company's slave pen, with its two hundred inmates, had already gone, and, blow up buildings and douse flames as they might, by midnight a mass of red embers and a ring of suburbs were all that remained. Then the men paused and looked around, ready for relaxation.

Morgan knew what to expect next; even while his men were fighting the fire they had taken time out to catch the arm of a fleeing woman or suck up a swig of rum, and now that the emergency was past there would be no restraining them. But he still needed his men sober, for there were rich folk to be seized for ransom and Spanish soldiers to be flushed from cover, so instead of issuing orders that would never be obeyed he let it be known that the Spanish wine had been poisoned, and as a result had a disgruntled but still sober force to wind up the business of the day.

Foremost item was the interrogation of prisoners as to the whereabouts of valuables. Anyone giving the appearance of wealth was questioned not only about his own belongings but those of his friends, and refusal to co-operate was handled promptly. One manservant, dressed in his master's stolen taffeta breeches from which a silver key happened to be dangling, was seized on the suspicion of hidden wealth. Although he screamed the truth he was put on the rack and his arms and legs pulled slowly out of their sockets, while a knotted rope was twisted around his head till his eyes bulged like hard-boiled eggs. Others were hung upside down and beaten, noses and ears cut off, faces singed with torches, and red-hot wires pushed under their fingernails. The only prosperous people who escaped mutilation were young and attractive women.

During the course of the interrogation the news had leaked out about the two escaped treasure ships, one of which was said to contain an altar of solid gold as large as a tub, and Morgan had lost no time in sending after them Captain Robert Searle in a barque seized in the harbor. But Captain Searle got only as far as Tobago, a small island off the coast, for there his men found a store of Peruvian wine, and made up for lost time. While they were at their mellowest a galleon anchored nearby and sent ashore a boatload of Spaniards for water, whom the pirates seized instinctively, and were enchanted to find they were from the very galleons they had come to seek. But, too mellow for a fight at the moment, they merely held the sailors captive and went on drinking.

The captain of the *Holy Trinity*, waiting offshore for his boatload of men, became suspicious after some hours and made off without them, followed by the other ship of the team, and though Captain Searle gave sheepish chase when he woke up, the golden altar was lost to him forever. By some miracle he was allowed to live, but until Morgan's dying day he never forgot or forgave the loss of those two ships.

After three weeks nothing was left in Panama to steal, so Morgan ordered the pack animals led from the royal stables and the spoils piled onto their backs. A hundred and seventy-five mules were re-

quired to carry the tapestries and oriental rugs, the table services
of gold and silver, and the sacks of jewels and coins and bullion.
Certain titled ladies being held for ransom were granted horses to
ride on, while stumbling along on foot and prodded with knives
when they lagged behind came six hundred starving men and
women, slave and free, who threw themselves at Morgan's feet
whenever the caravan halted and begged either for food or death.
Knowing that the more famished they became the greater effort
they would make to raise a ransom, he lifted his eyebrows and replied in a mincing voice, "I did not come to Panama to listen to
lamentations." The prisoners would, he told them, have ten days
at Venta de Cruz in which to raise money to buy their freedom,
otherwise they could expect to be sold into slavery.

The ten days at Venta de Cruz were occupied variously—by the
captives in begging relatives and friends to buy them out of slavery,
by the pirate forces in drinking, eating, sleeping, and raping, and by
Morgan in making an inventory of the spoils. This was a task, he
said with a weary sigh, for the Admiral alone, and no one else need
trouble to help him. Indeed, if any tried he sent him back genially
to his drinking and whoring, and carried on alone.

After several such days in the countinghouse he called his men
together and with narrow eyes and tight lips demanded, "Who has
been withholding?"

The men stared, first at him and then at each other. "Withholding?"

Like a stern schoolmaster he went on, "You know the laws of the
brotherhood, everything thrown into the common lot and divided
according to contract." They waited, knowing the law so well they
did not even need to nod. He glared right and left at the besotted
faces. "The prize is only a fraction of what it should have been.
Some of you have been withholding."

A murmur of incredulity rose, but he raised his voice over it.
"There will have to be a general search." He motioned his special
friends, Blodre Morgan and Collier and Prince, to begin it but,
the murmur taking on an angry pitch, he shrugged with patient
good humor. "Very well, I too will submit to the search." Osten-
tatiously he pushed himself into the hands of Lawrence Prince,
turning his pockets inside out, tearing open the collar of his shirt,

removing his shoes; and having thus silenced the men he directed the rest of the search with even greater care, overseeing the opening of personal baggage, the removal of clothing, and the breaking apart of the muskets' barrels and stocks. When nothing was forthcoming he clapped the nearest man on the shoulder, his pig eyes crinkling in a hail-fellow grin. "You must understand that the Admiral has a duty to all alike. But now that everyone has been cleared we can all be comrades again." The looks that answered him were sullen and sidelong, but his eyes caught those of his special friends with deep content.

At Chagres, Morgan gave the prisoners one last chance to produce ransoms, and while waiting attended to a few other affairs. The castle he ordered completely demolished, walls, turrets, and edifices, but its guns were too good to discard and he had those taken aboard his flagship under the supervision of Prince and Collier and Blodre Morgan. Though many of the men glanced distrustfully at the bristling *Satisfaction*, none dared question their leader, for the division of the spoils was still ahead and all were technically friends.

At last came that great day. They had gathered in a semi-circle by a pile of chests and sacks, and Morgan took his stance before them, a long list in his hand. "Before anyone else," he said, "comes His Majesty. One fifteenth of the whole to the King." He scanned the assemblage. "You understand?"

They nodded impatiently and he checked a name off his list.

"One tenth to the Duke of York, Lord High Admiral of the Fleet."

They nodded and he checked again.

"To myself"—he shrugged modestly—"a mere hundredth part."

They stared stolidly, their faces expressionless, and he made another check.

"To the owners of the ships, one hundred pounds each," he went on blandly, ticking off each name as he came to it. Next followed the roster of ship's officers, so much to each, the surgeons, carpenters, blacksmiths, and other artisans, so much to each. After that came the compensations for losses of eyes and legs and arms, and as he droned on the men nodded absent-mindedly, for they themselves had computed these figures long ago. They were waiting for the residue, the prize all shared.

Now Morgan drew a deep breath. His eyes steely, his bulbous nose tightening about the nostrils, he lifted his head and stared at the ring of faces. "The balance is eleven thousand pounds——" There was a shocked pause and then a roar of indignation, but without change of expression he went on doggedly, like a swimmer breasting the breakers, "—which makes ten pounds a man."

The howls broke over his head. He stood rigid, immobile, while the men crowded around shaking their fists, cursing, demanding an accounting.

"There was more than eleven thousand pounds in ransoms alone," they shouted, "besides the jewels and furnishings and church pieces. There should be sixty or seventy thousand pounds. What have you done with the rest?"

He shrugged, a patient man reasoning with children. "The entire prize was thirty thousand pounds. The rest went to the injured. Would you," he suggested sarcastically, "prefer that I take away the compensations to the wounded? Or shall I give up my own poor hundredth part?"

Though some of the men were silent, most continued to growl threats of murder and mutiny; little groups, gathering confidence from sharing their rage, advanced fingering their knives. But he calmly went on apportioning the eleven thousand pounds, laying it in the hands of those who held them out and superciliously dropping it at the feet of those who turned away. "There was sixty or seventy thousand pounds," they kept muttering sullenly.

"I have told you," he said in a loud firm voice, "the total was thirty thousand pounds." With supreme control he casually turned his vulnerable back, and such was his authority that, though few believed him, none dared stick a knife in it.

But he still had a number of followers who, for their own reasons, were faithful to him, and suddenly and swiftly, in the middle of the night, these men went about the fort spiking its guns, setting fire to its wooden buildings, and demolishing its wall. Then, in the succeeding melee, Morgan and his close friends set sail in four or five vessels, leaving the sputtering remainder marooned and ready to explode with rage. On board with him, those left behind were firmly convinced, were the forty thousand-odd pounds for which he had given no accounting.

The deserted men would have followed and murdered him on the spot, but not an armed ship remained to them, and since the fluff in their skulls could not retain any idea long, after a few days they shrugged and started refitting the ships for a cruise of their own.

Morgan's departure from Chagres had taken place on March 6, and he did not turn up at Port Royal for nearly a month, which even allowing for contrary winds was a very long time for the voyage. Where he was all those weeks he never revealed. But certain facts remain: the men he trusted were with him, the deserted island of Providence was nearby, and everyone believed he had with him a huge fortune he could not own up to. All the rest was conjecture.

The General entered Port Royal like a conquering hero, and it was no wonder, for in two years he and his men had brought back nearly half a million pounds to be spent thereabouts. He became a power in the community. True, his fortunes had their summers and their winters, reflecting the temperature of England's relations with Spain, and after an initial burst of warmth they cooled off rapidly under the indignation of the Spanish Ambassador. Modyford was even brought to London for questions and spent three years in the Tower (very comfortably housed, for he was a wealthy man), and Morgan was likewise called home. Then it was that he became an intimate of the new Duke of Albemarle, infecting him with a permanent fascination for the West Indies, and since his interrogation was purely window dressing, he returned home with a knighthood and the lieutenant governorship of Jamaica.

So here he was now, Sir Henry Morgan, Lieutenant Governor, sometime Commander-in-Chief of the Forces on Land and Sea, sometime Inspector of Customs, and as always using his power where it would do him the most good. For a while he provided safe harborage for his Brothers of the Coast, with whom he went on wild rum-swilling bouts; he became ever richer and richer, his plantations spreading over twelve hundred acres and several parishes and his name attaching itself to half a dozen hills, rivers, roads, and forts. Simultaneously he became sicker and sicker, for the stomach he had pickled in alcohol was beginning to rebel, at first by refusing food and then by swelling so prodigiously that his form took on the shape of a pear. With an eternal hiccup and a complexion the color of a banana, he rolled from plantation to grogshop, from the Council Chamber to the Loyal Club, steering his course this way and that but always guided by the north star of expediency.

Then his influence began to crumble, and to prop it up he who for years had lived by flouting the law with a dizzying switch became a pillar of the law. Pirates were bloody renegades now, and piracy a dangerous pestilence that must be swept from the seas. He passed ordinances outlawing them from the islands, he pursued and caught and executed them. "I abhor bloodshed," he wrote to the Secretary of State in 1681, "and I am greatly dissatisfied that in my government service I have been so often compelled to punish criminals. But the discouragement of pirates has always been the utmost endeavor of the Council and myself, and I have put to death, imprisoned, and transported to the Spanish for execution all English and Spanish pirates that I could reach."

Despite his piety the political winds kept blowing colder, and he was at last displaced by a man more interested in the welfare of the island. But before winter set in altogether his friend the Duke of Albemarle brought him a short Indian summer. The Duke was the new Governor, come to the island not so much to rule as to treasure hunt, for after investing in William Phips' successful salvage operation on the Silver Shoals he wanted to be on the spot for another try. So for some months the Duke and Morgan, both in the last stages of alcoholism and peripheral complaints, sat through long hot nights over a rum bottle, talking and killing themselves off.

Morgan beat the Duke by two months, dying on August 25, 1688, only fifty-three years old but decayed to the bone. With no children of his own he willed his fortune to his nephews on condition that they take his name, and as a consequence Morgans were splattered all over the island for many generations.

The pirate would have been pleased with the funeral the Duke gave him. There was a salute of twenty-two guns, one more than for ordinary dignitaries; his body was carried in state to its grave on the palisades of Port Royal; and in order that proper homage might be paid by his former colleagues, a one-day amnesty was proclaimed from his own anti-piracy laws. A crowd of ruffians, cleaned up for the occasion, rolled in and stood around the coffin gravely. Many of them, men he had cheated at Chagres, had a right to loathe him, but they knew they would have done the same thing had they dared, and they laughed and shook their heads with frank admiration. "He was the greatest of us all."

Whatever his plans had been, Morgan never got back to Providence, and after his death the island was almost forgotten. A vessel dropped in for water and wood occasionally and anchored under the lee of a forty-foot rock that towered over the point of Santa Catalina Island. On one such visit a pirate gazed up in meditative mood, and before his eyes the rock took on a curious shape, the head of a man, a craggy old ruffian in profile. "By God," he said, "that looks like old Morgan himself." Others agreed, and the name stuck, and Morgan's Head continued to watch forever over the harbor.

Gradually even these pirate visits ceased, and cedar forests that had been cut away to make room for Fort Teresa pushed back again and closed in over the crumbling walls. The ashes of New Westminster disappeared under brush and grasses. Roads accepted the encroaching weeds and the beaches became as barren as when the sea first carved them out of the land. At last, sixty years later, the island was ready for the astonished young couple who thought they were stepping on land never before inhabited.

In the early eighteenth century England's trade with the New World was booming. Sailing ships scudded back and forth with tobacco for the English and all manner of commodities for the colonists, and on April 5, 1733, the brig *Mary* set out for Chesapeake Bay.

With her was Edward Seaward of Bristol, nephew of the owner, who was going as supercargo more or less for the ride. When he returned, however, he had liked sea life sufficiently to listen with interest to a proposal from his uncle, whose son had gone to Honduras as a trader some years before. Now the uncle wanted to retire and bring his son home to take over his business, and he suggested that young Edward go out instead and make his own fortune. Edward was agreeable, provided he could take along the girl of his heart, the daughter of the Reverend William Goldsmith.

The two youngsters, twenty-one and twenty and as green as lettuce, sailed with their King Charles spaniel Fidele for the logwood cutters' community of St. George's Cay on the coast of Honduras. Six weeks later the *Mary* put in at Jamaica, sold her cargo, and took on another for St. George's Cay—lumber, household and farming implements, American flour, maize, coffee, sugar, and rum. The Cay was described as so desolate and primitive that for themselves they providently purchased three goats, a dozen hens, ducks and guinea fowl, barrels of yams, plantains, oranges and limes, pumpkins and watermelons, pineapples, capsicums, sugar canes, and bird peppers.

The son of a farmer, young Seaward faced pioneer life undismayed, as did Eliza, who had been well trained in the housewifely arts. They were young, healthy, in love, and strongly given to prayer; moreover, their date of departure, December 23, fell on a Sunday, which the sailors assured them was a most propitious circumstance, so they set off for their new life bursting with confidence and gaiety.

From Kingston the *Mary* ran down to Port Royal with a good breeze, from whence the captain shaped her course southward to keep clear of the Pedro Shoals. Meanwhile the Seawards were settling themselves in the only passenger cabin, Eliza's enormous skirts almost suffocating Fidele as she swished about the tiny room laying out washbasin and drinking mug, crimping irons and hair pomade. Overhead could be heard the contented shouts of the crew and the healthy creaking of ropes as the wind strained against the sails.

During the afternoon the creaking stopped and, looking out of the porthole, they saw that the ship was no longer moving. Edward, a lively inquisitive mind always sniffing like a terrier at new experiences, ran up the companion to see what a ship looked like when she was becalmed. All that evening the crew stood about, mildly annoyed, and when the couple went to bed the sails were still hanging slack.

About midnight the trade winds set in, shoving the brig before them briskly, and by morning freshening to something nearing a gale. Edward, holding onto a davit, watched the sailors struggling grimly to keep her head before the wind. Towards noon the weather broke up into squalls, the sky darkened, and the crew took in much sail, while the new uneasy motion of the vessel drove Edward below to see to his wife's comfort. He found her white but smiling firmly. The washbasin had skidded off onto the floor and, taking the hint, she had stowed away everything movable and then lifted Fidele onto her lap, where he lay motionless except for the temblors that ran through his body periodically like a pulse.

Edward ran up on deck again and found his way to the captain. Over the wind he mouthed the words, "What can I do?" but when the captain waved him away impatiently he wandered about looking for something to occupy his energies. Two of his hen coops were slithering about the decks, so he lashed them down and comfortingly patted the heads of two goats cowering near the companion door.

In the afternoon the weather changed repeatedly, one minute calm, the next whipping into a sharp squall, and the entire sky was blue-black, like an umbrella spread over them, save for a rim of pale green around the horizon. In the eerie light the men frowned at each other. "We're in for a hurricane," they muttered.

"Idiots," the captain shouted uneasily, "the hurricane season is past." But he glanced at the sky with foreboding, and bellowed orders to make the ship very snug. The men were moving now with contained urgency, hauling in sheets and lashing down everything loose, while the seas, climbing over the gunwales, foamed white against the black sky. Suddenly, topping the roar, came a crackle of lightning and a gunshot clap of thunder, and at the same moment the sky, like a bucket overturned, emptied itself on them. Wet through in a flash, Edward rushed below to reassure his wife.

He had just closed his arms about her when a gust of wind laid the ship over on her side, and the two were flung across the bed, while at the same time something crashed on the companion ladder outside. Silently they clung together for a moment, then he whispered, "I must go and see what I can do," and, tight-lipped, she pulled herself to her feet and sent him off. Out in the passage he found the two goats scrambling to their feet; a hasty hand had shoved them down the ladder before slamming the door shut to keep out the rush of water.

Edward climbed the ladder and pushed against the door, but all the weight of the gale was against him; he yelled till someone heard and pulled it open, and stepped out into the storm. The brig was running before the wind, which howled over her quarters first from one point of the compass and then from another, and each time she veered around the waves washed over her decks. Two hands and her yawl had already been thus swept overboard.

Far into the dark hours Eliza sat huddled in the cabin nursing her quivering dog, while Edward from time to time struggled to the galley, candle shielded with one hand, for hardtack and salted meat. In the early morning, as they were forcing the morsels down their throats, they heard a yell overhead, "Breakers! Land ahead! Breakers!"

Instinctively they stood up, as one rises to face any danger, and after a few moments the vessel struck. Thrown violently forward, while the lamp crashed to the floor and Fidele set up a dismal howl, they forgot their fear for a moment in stamping out the burning wick and its trail of oil. Then Edward muttered, "Stay here," and felt his way up the ladder. At the top he found the door tight shut again, and though he bellowed and beat it with his fists no one responded. At last remembering that he had stumbled over a stone bottle in the passage earlier that evening, he retrieved it and beat on the wooden door till the captain let him out.

He found the ship lying hard over on her starboard side, her sails in ribbons. A few of the men were sawing away the mainmast, which lay broken over the side, while others struggled with the davits of the long boat. "We are lost," shouted the captain. "The *Mary* will go to pieces on the reef any minute. The boat may swamp but the chances are better there. Get your wife."

"Yes. Wait for us," Edward gasped, and rushed below.

In the dark he and Eliza picked up the spaniel and crept along the listing passageway, but as he pushed open the door the vessel righted herself violently and a wave poured over her deck, flooding man and woman and slamming the door back in their faces. Again he fought to open it, and when at last they did stand on deck the vessel was upright, free of the point of the reef, but they were alone. The boat, and the entire crew, had gone. When a flash of lightning whitened the scene they caught a glimpse of it fifty yards away in the trough of an enormous wave, and then darkness shut down and they saw it no more.

The brig, which since her release had been sweeping along before the gale, now struck upon a second reef and came up sharp, heeling over onto her beam end. Man and wife were thrown to the deck and, heads bent, clung together waiting to be engulfed, but after an interminable time the heaving motion of the vessel subsided and she became quiet. Little by little they accepted the fact that they were to be neither sunk nor washed overboard and, unclasping their arms, stood up and looked around.

Day was breaking and the dim light showed them a ship with mainmast gone and fore-topmast broken and hanging by its rigging. Gone were the booms, gone were the boats, the caboose for cooking, the binnacle. The hen coops were still lashed in place but the hens and guinea fowls were drowned, though in another coop four hens and the ducks droopily survived. At a distance they discerned the outlines of a high and wooded land, a curving beach and, towering over all, a rock vaguely shaped like a man's head. Edward held out his hand to his young wife. "We're alive anyway," he smiled faintly.

She nodded, white lipped. "But where are we?" And he shook his head.

At noon the wind came to their rescue as, blowing comfortably, it worked the brig fore and aft and in half an hour swung her stern off the reef into deep water, leaving her hung up by her bow. Later the false keel forward broke away, setting her free altogether, and she began to drift. Quickly Edward tried the tiller, and when the rudder responded he set the remaining forestaysail and gently steered the *Mary's* head towards shore, where she struck sand in a little cove alongside a pile of rocks. At last the water was smooth and the sky clearing; the immediate danger was past.

When they went below to survey the devastation they found the furniture smashed and lumped along the starboard bulkheads, but, rummaging through the wreckage, they discovered an unbroken bottle of wine and a bag of biscuit which they dunked, gratefully, the one in the other. Next move was to secure the ship by lassoing a tall rock with a rope, after which they knelt for a solemn prayer of thanksgiving and immediately fell into the exhausted sleep of youth.

The following days called forth all their ingenuity, the first meal consisting of drowned hen boiled in sea water over a fire started with the lens of the ship's spyglass. But a search of the hold turned up not only the supplies laid in for St. George's Cay but the tools, instruments, and firearms common to every ship on a long voyage, while the problem of fresh water was solved by a rivulet which trickled daintily down a hillside. In short, though they would have to work hard they would not starve.

A climb to a lookout point showed their landfall to be an island, with a smaller sister island just across a channel. During the first few days they never ventured forth without a musket, but when no human creature ever showed himself they realized slowly, with a mixture of relief and dismay, that they were the only inhabitants on either place. Until some ship passed by they were completely on their own.

Eliza, the well-trained housewife, had hastened to hang out their clothing to forestall mildew, and on the first Sunday they took down their best and conducted the day as nearly like an English Sunday as possible. Standing erect with his prayer book in hand, Edward read the Church of England service, while Eliza, seated primly on a bench, read the lessons. The dinner having been prepared Saturday night to eliminate Sunday cooking, they sat down to a cold meal of boiled salt pork, roasted plantains, and tea, and afterwards Edward said, as his father had said to his mother a hundred times, as the Reverend William Goldsmith had said at least as often, "My dear, shall we go for a walk?"

Eliza took his hand and, modestly keeping a grip on her wide skirts, let him help her down the plank from the ship's gunwale to the rock. Arm in arm they strolled thus along the beach, curiously happy for a pair of stranded youngsters, and speculated on important matters, the one of the moment being the question of how to keep the sand out of their shoes. Eliza, eager to show off her housewifely skills, undertook to make both of them canvas gaiters from a bit of sail, while Edward, his mind ranging a little farther afield, began dreaming of a garden and a run for the livestock.

Fidele, meanwhile, was roaming far and wide. At the edge of the thick woods that ended abruptly at the beach he stopped, ears lifted, and barked. He rushed into the underbrush growling, there was a scrambling and crackling of twigs, and when Edward followed cautiously he found him standing over the dead body of an iguana nearly as large as himself. Eliza drew away from the huge lizard, but Edward reminded her of the captain's reference to iguana meat.

"We can't be choosy," he said. "However, we must eat it soon, for fresh meat will go bad quickly in this climate." So on Monday Eliza dutifully roasted the skinned reptile and admitted rather unwillingly that it did indeed taste like chicken.

With it they ate the ripest of the fruit, saving the seeds with care. "We can plant them," Edward said, "as soon as I can find a place with good soil," and some time later, when more seeds had accumulated and the immediate task of cleaning up the ship had been accomplished, he took his spade and musket, called Fidele, and sidled down the plank onto the rocks. Eliza, who had plenty of courage but saw no reason to use it unnecessarily, had requested her husband to stay within call whenever possible, so for his search he chose the long arm of land, thickly wooded and rising to a ridge, near the ship.

He paced the beach with his eyes peeled for an open patch among the trees. Fidele, more interested in hunting than planting, again combed the underbrush, and when Edward followed his barking through the thicket he found him with an iguana as large and as dead as the first. Eliza and he were by now weary of salted meat, and he slung it over his shoulder with a grateful pat for the dog.

Once drawn into the woods, he decided to climb to the ridge. The land ahead rose sharply in front of him, and as he pushed through the trees he came upon a cavern, a wide mouth yawning in the side of the hill, with bushes at its lip. On the point of moving on, he stopped, his inquisitive mind having noted that within, where it should have been pitch-black, a dim light shone. On investigation he saw that at the far end a crack in the roof let in a feeble illumination. Beneath his feet the ground was thick in bird dung, and a flock of blue pigeons was flying overhead, while others perched in the niches of the rock walls. The farther he penetrated into the cavern, the cooler became the atmosphere.

"A pantry!" he exclaimed suddenly. "A place to keep the fruit. Eliza will be so pleased." And with the satisfaction of a husband who has done something intelligent he rushed home and reported.

His wife's response was all he could have hoped for, and under her admiring eyes the fresh foods were transferred to the cool of the cave. "This will make a good home for the hens and goats as well," she said, and thereafter they visited their combination larder and stable almost daily.

By now the island had become home, and a home not too unlike what they had anticipated at Honduras, with the exception of the solitude. As to that—they were a couple long in love and newly married, which made them as nearly independent of outside society as was humanly possible, and their every minute was occupied with improvising a new life. They told themselves a ship must come by eventually, and in the meantime the daily challenge to their wits and inventiveness left them no time for moping.

However, the ethics of using any of the ship's cargo other than their own fretted the Reverend William Goldsmith's daughter until her husband pointed out that as the owner's nephew he was the next best thing to its rightful proprietor, and furthermore, that if they had not salvaged the ship the entire cargo would have gone to the bottom anyway. Her conscience thus appeased, Eliza gave consent and Edward, with a terrific burst of energy, rushed down to the hold for lumber with which to start building a house ashore.

This developed into a square hut set on the summit of the ridge, the planks laid flat on top of one another to form walls a foot thick and dovetailed neatly at the corners. It went up slowly under its single pair of hands, and by the time the roof was on Eliza had made a pen nearby for a small armadillo Fidele had turned up and a garden was prospering with a rapidity astonishing to the couple from England.

From the beginning their lives had been lived, as far as possible, in the mode to which they were accustomed, with prayers daily and on Sunday a service, cold meals, and enforced leisure. But before long the clambering about the ship and struggling through under-brush had worn down Eliza's insistence on her accustomed attire. At first she had simply dedicated one hand to her skirts and done her chores with the other, but this became increasingly difficult, and after a discussion with Edward she shortened a dress and two or three petticoats to the top of her ankles. Still the irreplaceable gar-ments were being torn to shreds. Of course no more leg could be exposed, but as a compromise she made one of her gowns into loose trousers caught in at the ankles, and wore over them a knee-length skirt, a Turkish effect which amused Edward no end.

The question of washing could not be avoided indefinitely. They had done very well with their little basin at first, but when the carpentering and gardening increased, the need for a cooling bath became ever more pressing. Since sharks had pre-empted the lagoon, ocean bathing was out of the question; finally Edward devised a showerbath on deck, in which one of them could stand wearing a single long garment while the other overturned pail after pail of salt water. But in time even their garments needed attention. The work of a laundress was so menial that Edward recoiled from letting his wife undertake it, for no one had ever heard of a young lady washing clothes, but eventually they faced the inevitable, and he carried a bundle to the rivulet where together they beat them with improvised paddles until they came nearly as white as new. Once having made the break, they repeated the operation a number of times thereafter.

By spring the hut was completed, and when Edward had carried some of the ship's furniture up the hill and installed it, they moved into this first home of their own. As a final homelike touch Edward, who had discovered a few wild flowers in his rambles, planned a flower garden, and went to the cavern for pigeon manure.

In preparing their larder they had scraped the floor clean on one side and piled up the dung on the other. Now as he filled his pail the spade struck a foreign object, which on investigation proved to be a belt, very old and rotten but plainly worn by some man sometime in the past. He rushed home in breathless excitement; they had supposed themselves the discoverers of the island, and this intimation of predecessors left them gaping. Turning it over and over, they studied the leather and the metal buckle and speculated on its owner, but when nothing further turned up gradually let it pass from their minds.

On one of their Sunday walks along the point Fidele startled a herd of peccaries in the thicket. A big male grazed the dog's side with its tusk and dashed on before Edward could raise his musket, but at the same time another charged at Eliza, who with a feminine squeal and very masculine efficiency jabbed her walking staff right into its open mouth. The herd rushed on, leaving the dead pig at her feet, and since food was of constant concern and anything new worth trying, Edward congratulated his wife on this addition to their diet. They would have to corn it immediately, however, for it was too large to keep fresh.

To keep it away from the ants until Monday morning Edward cut a short strong twig for a peg and, running his palms over the rocky interior of the cave, found a fissure into which he drove it. Then, tying the animal's feet together, he hung it up.

As they walked home he was thoughtful. "Did you notice anything unusual," he asked, "when I drove that peg into the wall?"

"I don't think so. What do you mean?"

"I thought there was a queer sound—a hollow sound—when I struck the rock with my hatchet."

She smiled at him affectionately. "I didn't hear anything, but if I know you, you'll be back there tomorrow to find out."

Next morning they were both back. In the darkness he tapped here and there with a large hammer, and certainly there were two different notes. In many places the sound was dead, like any other rock, but near the peg it was hollow, and for several yards thereabouts the note persisted. "There must be another cave inside there," he said. "I wish I had a candle."

It was ten minutes' run to the ship for one, and then, in the flickering light, a number of fissures became visible. But the cracks were regular, organized, with an unnatural neatness. "Somebody *put* those stones there," Edward whispered.

Eliza's eyes opened wide in sudden excitement. "Remember the man's belt? Quick, get a chisel or something." He tore to the ship for a handspike, and while she held the candle he inserted it between two rocks and began jimmying. Soon the first rock moved slightly, and after ten minutes' frenzied work came loose and fell out at his feet. The second rock was easier to dislodge, the third easier still, and now he could thrust his head and shoulders inside the aperture.

The interior was not entirely black, for a crack in the roof gave a faint illumination. "It's a kind of cave," he shouted, his voice banging back and forth within the hollow. "Hold the candle for me so that I can go inside." He tore away a few more rocks and squeezed himself through, taking the candle from her and lifting it high to look around.

The floor was of loose white sand, while the walls faded away into deep surrounding shadow, but as he moved about his eyes fell on an object on the ground less dark than its background. It seemed at first a row of round stones, but as he came closer he saw they were not stones at all but small canvas bags ranged precisely side by side, and behind them a long box. He gaped a moment, felt them with his fingers, and rushed to the opening.

"Eliza, come here. Come inside and look!" He pushed a few more rocks out of the wall and she clambered through, gasping, "What have you found?" He led her to the row of bags, and while she watched he slit one open and laid back the canvas. Under the light of the candle the contents gleamed and winked metallically.

Eliza's reaction was away from the point. "Dear God preserve us from harm!"

Edward was already on his knees digging his hands into the loose coins, lifting them, savoring them with his fingers and his mind. He stared up at his wife. "Harm? What harm can it do us?"

She shook her head vaguely. "What good can it do us here?"

Without answering he went on examining the bags, which were of uniform size and shape. "They all seem to be full of silver dollars. Let's look in the box." The lid was nailed down fast, so they left the cave to fetch a chisel from the ship. Out in the sunlight Edward took a closer look at the coin in his hand and gasped. "It's gold. A doubloon."

"How much is a doubloon?"

"About three or four pounds, I think. Pounds!" He stared at her, absorbing the idea, then took her shoulders and gave her a little shake. "We're rich, Eliza, rich!"

Together they ran to their plank hut for a quick meal, then to the ship for a chisel and mallet and back to the cave. The box was too heavy to move, so in the uncertain candlelight Edward hammered it open and laid back the lid. Inside were a jumble of crucifixes, images of the Virgin and Child within intricately wrought shrines, sword hilts, earrings, tissue, ingots. The silver had turned black, but the gold pieces were bright as on the day of minting.

Eliza stood frowning down at the box. "Edward, this doesn't belong to us. I don't know what we should do with it."

"The Reverend Mr. Goldsmith's daughter speaking," he smiled. "Well, we can always put it back." And slowly and gravely they did so and went home.

At the moment the treasure was of less value to them than the peccary that had revealed it to them, and in an absent-minded daze they went about the business of corning it, following their daily routine of household and garden chores. But their thoughts kept endlessly returning to the cave, Edward's frankly eager and Eliza's wistful but firm. "It doesn't belong to us," she said over and over.

At last Edward went back to the cave and carried one of the bags out into the daylight, where he examined the coins one by one, and then rushed back to the hut. "It's all right," he told her. "I don't think the money can possibly belong to anybody. Judging by the age of the coins, it must have been there sixty or seventy years. Probably it was hidden by some buccaneer, and everyone connected with it is dead long ago."

The parson's daughter considered for a minute and then softened. "I suppose in that case it's all right for us to have it."

With that decision they began by common consent to make preparations for going home, Eliza sewing forty new bags for the coins and Edward fitting them into new wooden boxes, three bags to each with one bag over, and replacing the whole in the inner cave and closing it up. And now, though they resumed their daily regimen, their favorite walk was to the lookout point with the widest view of the sea.

On April 15, Edward's entry in his diary noted that while he and his wife were eating breakfast they were struck speechless by the sudden appearance of a large sailing canoe in the lagoon between the islands. They hurriedly hoisted a white napkin on a pikestaff and waved until the occupants, two men, two women, and a young girl, all Negroes and all wearing next to nothing, turned in towards the harbor and, rounding the point of land, saw the anchored *Mary*. Their reaction, though voiced in a foreign tongue, was so unmistakably friendly that Eliza, blushing furiously and clinging to her husband's hand for moral support, accompanied him to the beach to make them welcome.

"Amigos," the five called out together, grinning and ducking their heads in a kind of obeisance.

"We are friends too," Edward replied, and he and Eliza helped them to disembark.

With the advent of the Negroes the island took on the aspect of a benevolent little feudal system, each slave fitting into his appointed niche. Diego, the elderly husband of Rota and father of Hacinta, turned out to be an expert carpenter and was put at once to building huts for the new arrivals, while his wife took over the cooking. Xavier and his wife Mira were given charge of the gardens, and Hacinta became a kind of general housemaid.

Eliza, whose first move had been to make garments for the three women, had next begun daily classes in the rudiments of Christianity and English, with the result that the Negroes were shortly able to make known their history. Purchased at Trinidad for a planter at La Guaira, the five had been shipped thither in a schooner which had struck a reef and filled with water. The whites had taken the ship's boat and made off in it, leaving them to their fate, but with the canoe and a small sail they had managed to save themselves, and finally fetched up here on the Seawards' front doorstep.

For a year the group lived amicably together. The couple said nothing to the slaves about the cave's contents, and indeed they rarely mentioned it even to each other, for it belonged on the far side of a curtain which by now seemed unlikely ever to be lifted. In self-defense they had tacitly agreed to pretend indifference, each vowing he would be content to live his life out here. But the pretense was abandoned in a moment when one day a vessel was sighted in the distance, apparently caught on the outside reef. Wildly they ran to the promontory waving a white cloth, but the tide lifted the vessel off the reef and it sailed away without noticing their signals, and then in each other's faces they saw the truth.

After that Edward mounted a flagstaff on the point and they frankly watched and waited. A month later a distant booming caught their ears and they rushed out to see a little schooner beyond the outside reef and, a few hundred yards behind her, a larger brig firing in hot pursuit. Edward hoisted the *Mary*'s colors and, after a short interval, the red ensign of the Mercantile Navy appeared at the peak of the schooner's main gaff. At the same moment the English ship turned in towards the island and the brig closed in with her. Edward sent Xavier running for three muskets while the rest, hardly breathing, watched the schooner sounding for a channel, and by a miracle she found her way inside the reefs, followed ever closer by the brig, which was firing mercilessly. Edward waited until both ships were within gunshot and then all three men fired on the brig simultaneously, which so astonished her that she came about to watch and await developments. The English vessel proceeded towards the harbor, and after anchoring beside the disabled *Mary*, dropped a boat, while the brig, apparently feeling herself outnumbered, turned and went away.

The Seawards in uncontrollable excitement had rushed down to meet the little boat and her six occupants, but the master of the schooner, a Norfolk trading vessel returning from Honduras, was at first so preoccupied with cursing his Spanish pursuers that he could hardly be civil to his English rescuers. Eliza retired behind Edward till the storm had passed, and then at the first pause both young people asked simultaneously, "Will you take us home?"

The blank stricken look on the Negroes' faces that followed this request made the Seawards stop and reflect. Suddenly they realized what abandonment would mean to these refugees from Spanish slaveholders, and Eliza hastened to reassure them that no final decision had been made.

That night, after the visitors had returned to their ship, the young couple sat up late talking with great earnestness. "Edward, we have a responsibility," Eliza said firmly. "Both the island and the treasure were put into our hands for a purpose, and we must do what seems best for everyone, not just for ourselves," and so on the morrow the request for a passage home was amended to one for Jamaica.

On the night before sailing Edward and Diego, carrying a long plank between them like a stretcher, slipped through the dark to the cavern, and while the gaping Negro watched, Edward removed a few stones from the wall and climbed inside. One by one he lifted out the boxes, and finally, with many a groan, hoisted the chest through the hole.

He had expected one trip to the harbor to see the entire lot delivered, but when he and Diego attempted to lift the ends of the plank on which the boxes had been set, their palms and their backs rebelled, and it was two hours before the last box was loaded into the boat.

When the time for farewells came the couple called the five Negroes before them and Edward gave final admonitions about the care of the houses, the gardens, and the *Mary*. "And now we are leaving you," he said, smiling, "but we will be back, with more supplies and perhaps some companions for you. But in case some disaster prevents our return, we have a present for each of you," and he passed around five papers, certificates of freedom.

The passage to Jamaica was accomplished without event, and the master, having got his initial rage off his chest, was chattiness itself. On the last day out he invited them to the bridge to watch him bring the ship in, and as they swung around a point of land he nodded off his port shoulder. "That's where the old city went down." In answer to their questioning looks he said, "Port Royal. Didn't anybody tell you about how Port Royal disappeared?"

Making the most of a fresh audience, he gave them the details of the city's last day on earth. On June 17, 1692, an earthquake had hit the island. The long finger of land on which Port Royal stood trembled for a moment, and at once its thousands of citizens, shaken by something worse than the temblor itself, started rushing about like frightened chickens. The walls of the buildings cracked and came apart, and the trees swayed from side to side as if whipped by a high wind. The tip of the finger started sinking, while at the same time the earthquake churned great waves up over the disappearing land, and in a few minutes the long spit of Port Royal, its underpinnings gone, tilted down into a newly formed cavern at the ocean's bottom, and people and houses and animals slid with it into the sea.

"That wasn't all," the master said, enjoying their shocked looks. "Just a few years later the rest of Port Royal was wiped out by a fire. They used to say it was the wickedest city in the world, and that this was a judgment from the Lord."

Eliza, the parson's daughter, nodded breathlessly. "Like Sodom and Gomorrah," she agreed.

The Seawards were busy people in Kingston, the first piece of business being the conversion of some of their doubloons into cash. Edward made a complete inventory: boxes of coins, 13; bags per box, 3; coins per bag, 250; contents of chest: gold—crucifixes, 36; sword handles, 12; chains, 4; medals with scriptural figures, 9; silver —candlesticks, 2 pairs; ewers, 2; salvers, 4; crucifixes with chains, 53; perfume cases, 2; shoe buckles, 5 pairs; plus four pieces of gold tissue and five of silver. This inventory did not include the bag of doubloons which he had already opened for current expenses.

As the next step in furtherance of their new mission they purchased a group of likely-looking slaves whom they intended to free after seven years' service on the island, and wrote letters to a brother of Edward and a brother of Eliza, sending five hundred pounds each and an earnest invitation to bring out their wives and settle. Edward also bought a schooner, which he named the *Porghee,* and took back to the island a crew for his uncle's disabled brig.

For a year or so the colony prospered amazingly. Houses went up, gardens flourished, livestock propagated; the Seaward and Goldsmith relatives brought fresh companionship, and on later visits to Jamaica, Edward recruited several more families. The *Porghee* and the refitted *Mary* carried on a lively trade between Jamaica and Honduras, and altogether, unlike other Providence colonies, this one seemed on a fair way to permanence.

At this point word arrived from England that the Reverend Mr. Goldsmith was not well. As their island seemed now capable of sustaining itself, they decided to take the *Mary* home to their uncle, visit Eliza's father, and recruit more settlers for their "Seaward Island Colony." But when they arrived at Bristol and joyfully called on Edward's uncle to announce the salvage and return of his ship, and to tell him of their own good fortune, he responded with a sharp demand for a hundred pounds each for their passage home, plus the price of the original cargo.

This was the first cold wind to blow in their flushed young faces, but it was not to be the last. Edward sought permission of the government to purchase his beloved island. Much time was consumed, for people of influence had to be sought out and won over, but for a while things looked hopeful. Then within a short space two items of intelligence were received which swept the entire project into the ash heap. The Seawards' island colony had been ruined by a hurricane that demolished almost every one of its buildings, and the Spanish Government, having learned of the unauthorized settlement of its Santa Catalina and Providence islands by a group of English, had protested sharply and demanded their immediate withdrawal.

The Seawards found not a single champion in high and influential circles, for no one wanted to offend Spain for the sake of a few tradespeople and slaves, and sadly they relinquished their plans and brought the colonists home. But at least their fortune remained, for Edward proved a surprisingly good businessman, and they settled down in a small village in the south of England to enjoy their wealth to a benign old age.

Except for a few scattered fishermen, Providence was taken over once more by the grass and the forests. Some time later it was the bone in another dogfight between England and Spain, but that was the last time, for in 1808 the island was formally ceded to the Province of New Granada and, still later, to Colombia.

Piracy still clung to it, however. In 1817, with all Spanish America revolting against the mother country, a bold adventurer took advantage of the muddy situation to obtain a commission to the island. This Captain Aurey rebuilt the fort, settled a town, Isabella, on the ashes of New Westminster, and in one final fling sent pirate fleets darting about the Caribbean to despoil the occasional Spanish vessel that ventured along the sea lanes.

But Spain as a great maritime power was dying, with no more Silver Fleets running and even the slave trade drying up, and since piracy could prosper only when there were rich ships to feed on, by 1860 it had come to an end in the Western Hemisphere. And with that end a final obscurity fell over the little island whose history paralleled that of the profession that had given it its *raison d'être*.

This story was first told by David Scott of The Times *of London in two excellent books,* Seventy Fathoms Deep, *and* The Egypt's Gold, *after living nearly two years on the* Artiglio. *Much information was also obtained from SORIMA and many newspaper sources, British, American, and Italian.*

IV

Gold Four Hundred
Feet Down

THE RECOVERY OF TREASURES from the sea and its environs, while occasionally accomplished easily and by accident, has generally entailed much dangerous effort. For thousands of years men had to make do with their own faulty bodies as tools; like William Phips' Indian diver Franko, they grasped a stone to pull them down, wore a belt to pull them up, and simply held their breath meanwhile. Seventy-five feet was usually the extreme depth of these dives, and a minute and a half the maximum time, though occasional individuals did go much deeper and a few were clocked holding their breath over four minutes—longer than some men have taken to run a mile.

But even at best there were many obvious disadvantages, and men were always seeking means to increase both the range and term of the dive. Such creatures of the natural world as the elephant had given them ideas, for, the whole trick being to get the body underneath while securing air from above, the elephant, who could wade far out over his head until nothing but the tip of his trunk remained above water to breathe through, showed it could be done.

As early as A.D. 77 people were using a sort of breathing tube by which they could duck a few inches below the surface and remain a very short time; in the Middle Ages some were using a leather hood with a flexible tube to the surface, and Leonardo da

Vinci, who seems to have invented everything, made a number of designs for a helmet with eyeglasses and tube, all on the principle of drawing down surface air to a man a foot or two below.

But lower than a few feet he could not go, for at that point came into play the diver's nemesis—atmospheric pressure.

At sea level air weighs approximately fourteen pounds to the square inch, pressing up and out as well as down, and thus cradling all living things in a matrix of equal pressure—including the air inside the lungs, which supports the rib cage and prevents it from being crushed in like an empty matchbox. Water, too, has weight, which increases with every foot of depth and, added to that of the air above it, becomes so great that when a diver descends the pressure of the normal air within the lungs is not enough to withstand the combined pressure of air plus water outside. If the early experimenter tried to go more than a few feet down his lungs were squeezed until breathing became impossible and, in the enormous effort of trying, hemorrhage occurred.

Over the centuries all kinds of devices were tried, air bags, tubes, complete diving dresses with helmets and force pumps to drive air down; but nothing worked satisfactorily until, in the nineteenth century, experimentation was diverted from the suit to the air itself. Then, *compressed* air was pumped down, and they were on their way. A complete coverall was worn, loose-fitting and waterproof, and into this, which for the moment had become the diver's world, was pumped air with sufficient pressure to equalize that of the water outside. Thus again the diver was cradled in a protective matrix of air which pushed back the water seeking to crush him.

Although this revolution in underwater work took place in the 1830s, the dress, of rubberized canvas, with a metal helmet equipped with air hose and, later, electric light, telephone, and the nonreturn valve by which air can be retained inside in case of accident to the hose, has remained virtually unchanged from then on, and for many years virtually all deep-sea salvage was accomplished by men thus equipped.

But there was always one tremendous hazard in such work, the bends. Since first men tried using compressed air in their dresses, they had been going down and coming up again, apparently perfectly well, and then suddenly collapsing. A diver's tenders would unscrew the window glass from his helmet and find him blue, paralyzed, unconscious. Perhaps he died without ever coming to, or else he lay on the deck writhing, twisting in agony and screaming aloud. This was a regular occurrence, and was regarded as almost inevitable.

There had seemed to be some connection with the pressure of the water, but what that connection was, and how to circumvent it, was not discovered until about the close of the nineteenth century. While the diver is at sea bottom, inhaling compressed air with perfect comfort, his body is, unknown to himself, undergoing a change. The charged air is forcing more nitrogen into his blood than it can properly absorb, with the result that the excess is being forced into the fleshy tissues. He becomes thus a human bottle of soda water, pressure from the ocean outside holding him *in* as the glass bottle holds in the carbonated water. But let him be raised to the surface and this external pressure be removed, and the stored-up gases expand, fizzing like the familiar bubbles in the drinking glass. This fizzing is the bends, and the bubbles, rushing off into the blood, may go straight to the heart and kill instantly, to the spinal cord and cause paralysis, or to the joints and muscles and cause the excruciating pain that is the least of the hazards.

It was given to Professor J. S. Haldane of England to rescue divers from this perennial danger. A physicist, he discovered the remedy to be a matter of timing. During a given length of time at the bottom the man has absorbed a given amount of nitrogen; it takes a given length of time for the body to throw it off; so keep him down only so long, haul him up only so many feet at a time (taking longer for every minute below), and thus allow the gases to work out of the blood and tissues at a rate they can manage. This is called natural decompression, and the use of Haldane's decompression schedules, worked out to the minute, has saved thousands of men from illness, permanent damage, and death.

But at best this system wastes untold hours of the men's time hanging about at various levels—from a very great depth three hours may be required—so Haldane, working with Siebe, Gorman and Company, invented a *recompression* chamber in which a man could be artificially decompressed on the surface after coming straight up, non-stop. Even with this, however, deep-sea salvage vir-

tually stopped at the 120- or 130-foot level, anything below that
being uneconomic, and the result was that underwater salvage was
about as efficient as if the only fruit picked from a tree were that
within the reach of a small boy with very short arms and his feet
stuck in the mud.

But the restless spirit of man, not content with such limitations,
for two hundred years had been trying the alternative of *avoiding*
the pressure instead of *combating* it. But no one had succeeded.
And then suddenly, in the 1920s, it was achieved with such abrupt
and vast success that the world of science—indeed, the world in
general—took note with gasps of admiration. The scene was the
coast of France, and the time the drama began, May 1922.

A white, clammy fog had been hanging over the shipping lanes
between Brest and Cape Finisterre all afternoon. The air was motionless, the sea dead-calm, and foghorns mooed sadly at each
other, muffled like voices under an eiderdown quilt.

The wireless operator in the Préfet Maritime in Brest, his ears
trained to distinguish the unusual from the routine, jumped to attention. From the tiny Pointe du Raz station down the French
coast a message was coming in:

"Have located steamship in distress bearing 277° at 19 hours 01."

Almost simultaneously came in, very feebly, "SOS, SOS, SOS.
Position 40° 10′ N, 5° 30′ W *Egypt*."

Six minutes after that the station on the nearby Island of Ushant
signaled "Received from *Egypt* SOS, position 40° 10′ N, 5° 30′ W."

Two hours later the operator received another message from
Ushant, "Since 19 hours 12, when the *Egypt* gave her position,
there has been no signal from that ship. The steamship *Cahiracon*,
which was nine miles from the *Egypt* when the accident occurred,
went to the spot and signaled to us at 20 hours 50, 'Here in position of *Egypt* we cannot see sign of her or hear her siren or
wireless.'"

Not very long thereafter the *Cahiracon* signaled to Brest, "At
22 hours 30 have failed to find any trace of *Egypt*. Now proceeding
on our voyage."

That was all. The Ushant operator noted everything in his log.
The *Egypt* was a liner of 7,941 gross tons in the P & O service

between London and Bombay. She had left England for India on Friday, May 19, 1922, with thirty-three passengers and a crew of 291, intending to pick up the rest of the passengers at Marseilles. Built in 1897, she was an old ship, but on this voyage a very rich one too, for she carried ten tons of silver and five of gold—£1,054,- 000, or well over five million dollars.

Saturday evening at dinnertime she was steaming down the coast of Brittany in heavy fog, her whistle sounding at three-minute intervals, when, shortly after seven, she heard a whistle and suddenly the bow of a large cargo steamer loomed right on top of her. Before either ship could change course the *Seine* struck the *Egypt* a deathblow on her port side. Reinforced for ice breaking, the *Seine's* bow crashed through the other's plates like a knife through jelly, and in twenty minutes the *Egypt* had gone down bow first.

Captain le Barzic circled the *Seine* area for three hours, he and his crew saving all but ninety-six lives, but the ship and cargo were a total loss.

Lloyd's of London, with whom the bullion was insured, paid up in full immediately, for the *Egypt* had sunk in four hundred feet of water, more than twice the depth at which any ship had ever been salvaged, and the company assumed that recovery was impossible. It always *had* been, at that depth.

But at that same time a short fat man in Genoa, whose name in Italian meant "Quail" and who looked very much like his name, was making his separate way towards a test of the *Egypt's* inaccessibility.

Giovanni Quaglia was a rich man's son, but being a native of the energetic north of Italy, he could not stand being idle. At school and university, short and round though he was, he went in for many sports, becoming amateur "palla" champion (palla being a cross between fives and pelota basque played with a pad strapped to the wrist) and winning prizes as a rifle and pistol shot. Though he had studied for the law he soon found life indoors intolerable, and like his fellow Genoese Christopher Columbus, took naturally to the sea. When the 1914 war came Italy had almost no ships, and what she did own were old sailing vessels plying the coastwise routes. Even these Germany soon finished off, and then Italy began to starve. Seeing a perfect opening for himself here, Quaglia bought up old windjammers and, after fitting them with oil engines, sold them to the government, and in no time was rich and a *commendatore*, the youngest one in Italy. Then the war stopped; all of a sudden there was a glut of ships, their value skidded from $145 to $14 a ton, and the little Quail was ruined.

Now, stripped of everything but guts and a good credit rating, he started a new kind of shipping, oil tankers, and soon the Citoma Company's tankers were steaming back to Italy from the Black Sea, from Africa, from the Americas, from anywhere that oil was produced. Indeed, energetic and restless despite his fifty-nine years, he was even becoming a little bored with prosperity, so he looked around presently for something new to do.

The adventurous little Italian's business principles had always been the same—look for something that had not been done before, or, if it had been tried, had proved palpably impossible—and do it. So in the early twenties the Quail went into deep-sea salvage. But this was really *deep*-sea salvage, deeper than anyone had ever reached before, and though he finally set all kinds of records, he would first be stripped even further down than ever before, past his credit rating, right down to his guts. Those he never lost.

Having obtained from the Italian Government exclusive rights for diving below 150 feet in the Mediterranean, he formed a company called Società Ricuperi Marittimi, SORIMA for short, and acquired the Italian rights to a remarkable device developed by Neufelt & Kuhnke in Germany.

This company had been working on the principle of *avoiding* the pressure at great depths instead of the old one of *fighting* it, and had developed a plan to put a shell of uncrushable metal around the man inside to withstand the pressure, instead of a shell of compressed air. With the metal holding off the weight of the water he could be fed ordinary air for breathing—which meant no more decompressing, no more time lost coming up and, best of all, no more bends.

The many inventors who for years had been trying to evolve a satisfactory metal shell had recognized that they must forego certain advantages of the flexible rubber suit. In this the diver could move about freely, use his bare hands, walk down companionways and along corridors, crawl into narrow openings—indeed, take any position his work demanded, even upside down if necessary. The metal shell would set up a whole new pattern of work.

In order to withstand enormous pressure the shell must be made on the principle of the arch, that is, its helmet, trunk, and limbs had to be round, without weak spots, and since joints were an invitation to water leakage, there must be as few as possible. That meant rigidity. The body of the shell must be large enough to allow the man to move about inside comfortably, and that meant clumsiness, enormous weight, and limited movement. Since it was suspended from a cable it could not move sideways, but only straight up and down, and could operate only in an open space; furthermore, its hands would be nothing but a pair of pincers at the end of the arms—all disadvantages. But inside it the man could breathe ordinary air, he could go down to depths undreamed of before and could come up without decompressing; and these features made all the inventors' efforts worth while.

Many designs along the same general lines had been developed over the years, but when the *Egypt* was sunk so little progress had been made in deep-diving techniques that she and her cargo were automatically written off as lost. Among Lloyd's underwriters only two privately believed salvage to be possible, neighbors of a British engineer, Peter Sandberg, but these three did spend many an hour worrying the idea like bulldogs over a bone, and the upshot was that Sandberg contracted with the Salvage Association and a Swedish ship, the *Fritjof*, under the command of Captain Hedback, to locate the wreck. The captain made one attempt to find her, but failed, and there the whole matter dropped.

In the meantime Quaglia had been making history of a sort in the Mediterranean with his jointed metal shell. The *Washington*, lying two miles off Genoa in three hundred feet of water, had been the first test of the new SORIMA, and so successful had this salvage operation been that experts had come to watch and admire from all over the world. It took four years for the job to be completed, but during that time seven thousand tons of material, including seven locomotives, were brought to the surface, and that was good enough for a start.

But they still had much to learn, and for further apprenticeship went to Lake Garda, where a seaplane had crashed while practicing for the world's speed races. There Alberto Bargellini, in the diving shell, brought up the young dead pilot in his jointed metal arms.

Later, on the French coast, near Belle Isle—their first experience in tidal waters—they searched for a tiny packet of uncut diamonds inside the *Elizabethville*, which had sunk on her way home from Africa. They missed the diamonds but recovered a fortune in ivory, and then, having proved themselves, were ready for the biggest job of all, the one the experts called impossible.

The *Egypt* undertaking turned out to be a double-header in that, while Quaglia had been engaged simply to bring up $5,078,000 out of the ship, the search for the vessel, which had already defeated Sandberg and his associate Terme, was a longer and tougher job than the salvage itself.

In 1929, Quaglia brought his four divers, Gianni, Franceschi, Raffaelli, and Bargellini, and his two salvage ships, the *Artiglio* and the *Rostro*, to Brest equipped with the latest apparatus. He had concluded an arrangement with the Salvage Association on a "no cure, no pay" basis, whereby he assumed entire costs but got a fifty-fifty split of the returns. Thus he stood to lose everything if he failed to bring up the gold. But he had been highly successful in his previous jobs; he possessed, moreover, a private fortune and excellent credit. So he worried less about finances than about the other difficulties, which were considerable.

Most salvage experts thought the job impossible. A few admitted that the jointed shell might withstand the pressure of 177 pounds to the square inch, which they would encounter at four hundred feet, but almost everyone agreed that even if the men did reach the wreck the currents would be too strong and the light too bad for actual work. And the personal danger was obvious. Dangling far below the surface in a strong current, a diver could be swung uncontrollably against the wreck and his armor smashed or his window glass broken. Should he get fouled in the rigging of the ship and his mates be unable to pull him loose, there was only one chance of escape—he had a clip device inside the shell whereby he could cast loose his entangled lines and then he could empty his ballast tank and pray that the current would work him free to float to the surface. But his prayers had to be of a very high order.

The corner of the Atlantic where Quaglia and his men were to spend the next years was thick with dead ships. Brest, the second most important port of France, lies well back in an estuary called the Goulet, and from there the shipping lanes fan out across the Atlantic like the spokes of an umbrella. A long chain of rocks and islands also stretches out into the ocean, many under water, making for hazardous navigation. Charts of the ocean fifty miles west of the harbor are dotted with the victims of the fogs, storms, and collisions common thereabouts. The *Egypt* was number fifty-eight on the map.

Quaglia and his chief diver and director of operations, Alberto Gianni, formulated their plans together. These two men were different and yet alike. Both were from Genoa; both were squat and vehement and fond of drama. But Quaglia was wealthy from boyhood, while Gianni was self-made. Gianni was like a bulldog, square and powerful, with huge hands; on his right one he wore a gold signet ring weighing a quarter of a pound which was given him by the captain of a ship he had salved and which he used as a weapon as occasion demanded. Like a bulldog he was courageous and persevering; and though he devised many brilliant schemes and inventions he was, like a bulldog, a little stubborn about adapting himself to new conditions. He was also sure of himself—too sure, as it turned out.

Quaglia resembled his namesake. He skittered about on short fat legs like a quail flushed from a hedge, and weighed over two hundred pounds, with a stomach that went well ahead of him and for whose sake the bottom three buttons of his vest were kept undone. His nose was beaklike and he carried his head high, like a fowl drinking, with a double chin that spread around his face right up to his ears. He was a Winston Churchill for cigars, the best and most expensive, and was never without one under his nose. He liked his name and always wore a jeweled tiepin in the form of a quail.

The two men sat in the small cabin of the *Artiglio* and considered their maps and charts. They had a choice of places to begin sweeping. A fix was plotted on the chart at the point where the bearings from Ushant and Pointe du Raz wireless stations intersected. That was one possibility. The captain of the *Egypt* had broadcast her position before she sank, and his hurried calculations *might* have been accurate, so that was another possible starting place. A British destroyer had found mailbags and wreckage floating on the water the morning after she sank and noted their position. That offered a third, provided the force and direction of the current could be determined. And then there was Hedback's point. This was all that remained of a 1923 expedition when Captain Hedback, in the *Fritjof*, swept the area and touched something he thought might be the wreck. He had taken bearings, but had not buoyed the spot, thinking to come back immediately, but suitable apparatus was never available and no one returned. Hedback's point, however, was duly noted on Quaglia's chart. Thus he and Gianni had plenty of possibilities.

"Nothing to do," sighed Quaglia, "but cover all of them." And since the *Egypt* lay thirty miles from shore with no landmarks to check against, and since sea bearings are notoriously inaccurate, "We'll sweep a mile to each side of all of them, too, to be safe," he said, chewing his cigar savagely, with the resentment of a seaman used to the tideless Mediterranean. "And there are these damned currents, too. You never know where you are from one minute to the next."

Gianni shrugged. He did not take currents very seriously.

Finally they drew a rectangle on the chart, including within it all the possibilities. It was five miles wide and eight miles long. Somewhere inside that forty square miles, every inch of which had to be swept, must lie the *Egypt*.

Their two ships were unimpressive, except to a knowing eye. The larger, the *Artiglio*, was a steam trawler of 300 tons gross. Though built in 1906 for the North Sea fishing, she had had a few years of glory during the 1914–18 war when, as the *Macbeth*, she had boldly swept for mines instead of fish. When bought by the SORIMA and refitted with a heavy mast to support her 15-ton derrick operated by a steam winch, she still was quite a vessel. Her decks were fitted with winches from stem to stern. The *Rostro*, lower and squatter, had been likewise transformed, and both ships seemed to be made of rubber, for the number of humans they absorbed into their inward parts was a miracle by ordinary standards. The company of nine officers and more than twice that in crew, plus a correspondent from *The Times* of London and, later, representatives of the Salvage Association and Sandberg's firm all managed to shoehorn themselves in somehow. The ships, furthermore, accommodated an amazing amount of equipment, coils of rope, hooks, grapnels, grabs, spare buoys, wire hawsers, and all necessary gear for the unusual work. In the hold lay an enormous electromagnet that looked like a manhole cover with an umbilical cord. Four-ton anchors were secured about the decks. And in the holy of holies, the divers' room, stood the diving shells, nine feet tall, with Gianni's young nephew to care for them. There was a bathroom, but it was used for storing lumber. In the hold was half a ton of macaroni.

In May 1929 sweeping began. These husky Italians, used to beginning work at four, without breakfast, took their little black ships bristling with equipment out of the dark harbor at dawn that first day. Between the wooded arms of the bay the mist drew up from the deep blue sea, forming in front of them a solid golden cloud bank on which the rays of the rising sun made a rainbow like a triumphal arch over their course, which the Italians, eager and superstitious, hailed as a good omen.

The first day was to be purely exploratory, a look-see at the diving conditions and ocean floor. They chose Hedback's point with the thought that if by some wild flight of good fortune the captain had really touched the wreck six years ago they might hit the jackpot the first time. If not, it was as good a place as any to try their instruments. But at the very outset, though they did not know it, they were defeated—both ships in different ways but by the same enemy.

When their plottings showed them on Hedback's point the *Rostro* attempted to mark the spot by anchoring, but it was twenty minutes before the anchor held. By that time the current had carried her a mile. Mario Raffaelli, the second diver, noticed the drift but decided this spot was as good as Hedback's point for diving, since after all the chance of finding the wreck was infinitesimal, so he dived where the current had taken them and saw nothing but firm sand and broken sea shells.

The *Artiglio*, on the other hand, did anchor immediately, and on Hedback's point, but the current defeated them in a different way.

Gianni sent down young Bargellini, whose first experience it was in these waters. Preparations were tedious for the dive. While Bargellini dressed, two men made ready the shell in the hold, screwing the great round white arms into place and oiling its flexible joints. The glass windows were polished, the telephone was tested and installed, as were the respirator with its small face mask through which the diver breathed out old air and the canister of chemicals which purified and returned his breath to him clean but "dead." The cylinder which supplied the air with its needed oxygen was also gone over.

Meanwhile Bargellini dressed himself against the cold. A great hairy sweater went on over his ordinary clothes, a thick waterproofed overall, wool socks, and the traditional diver's red knitted cap with tassel. When he had dropped through the neck of the shell, the domelike head was screwed on and the telephone again tested, after which the steel cable lifted him carefully out of the hold and swung him over the side, where he dangled like an enormous white panda with an aluminum pot over its head. Gianni, at the phone, tried out the connections,

"One, two, three," and Bargellini answered:

"Four, five, six."

A nod from Gianni to the man at the winch, "Down the shell," and Bargellini slowly dropped into the water. The white mass sank, gleaming greenly through the water, while Bargellini kept up a running comment on the phone:

"Light's good . . . Water's clear . . . It's getting darker now—a little darker." Then there was a long puzzled pause. "It's not getting darker any more. That's queer. Give me more line, I must not be going down."

"Yes, you are," Gianni answered, "you must be. We're giving you plenty of line. You've had a hundred feet."

"But I'm not sinking. The light is the same as before."

Suddenly Gianni burst into a string of oaths, beginning with "God dog!" and pointed to the suspending cable. Instead of going down straight it was dragging on a slant. Bargellini was right, he *wasn't* sinking, the current was keeping him at a 45-degree angle, and though they kept paying out more and more cable he could never get down to the bottom. He never saw what was down there until years later. If he had, many lives would have been changed and a few saved.

His dive, and Carli's on the *Rostro*, used up a full day, and the boats returned to Brest to report. Quaglia, not knowing how much better things might have been, was delighted to hear that the water was clear and the bottom firm.

"Now," he told Gianni, "lay buoys along the lines we marked out"—he glared up at the darkening sky with a disgusted look—"before these damned clouds open up."

Gianni took the *Artiglio* out, laying buoys at the four corners of their searching rectangle, two intermediate buoys on its long sides, and one at the center point; and after the *Rostro's* previous experience with the current he paid it the respectful compliment of dropping the buoys the moment he hit the spot. The buoys were anchored with a four-ton anchor connected with 450 feet of heavy chain and cable, and Gianni laid all seven in one fourteen-hour working day, which is more remarkable than it sounds.

Then, as Quaglia had foreseen, the weather broke, and next morning it was blowing a gale. He threw up his arms in an enormous shrug and rolled his head in despair. "In Genoa, the papers say, there's sunshine. In Paris, they say, it's hot and dry. And here, rain and wind." The mist rolled in from the Atlantic clammy and cold, and the miserable Italians wandered the streets, shivering, looking for something to do. Quaglia spent his mornings at the docks and his afternoons and evenings at the Hotel Continental, having taken a room for the season in a transaction that shook the establishment to its foundations. He had entered and looked the bedroom over, striding to the windows, examining the fit of the shutters and the windows, inner and outer. Next he turned back the bed and felt the quality of the sheets and sniffed at the pillowcases, tested the taps in the bathroom and the cock on the hotwater heater, and then with a disdainful snort shook out one of the bath towels at the shrinking chambermaid and demanded ten of the same.

"I am a *tremendous* man," he boomed.

For the men there were few places of amusement in Brest save one moving picture house supplying class B drama. One elegant "dancing," the Brasserie de la Marine, supplied the naval station's officers with high-toned dancing partners, but it was at the less pretentious Ermitage that Quaglia's men danced with the local girls. Of course there was a narrow street of iron-shuttered houses with large red numbers over the doors, and there were bars galore. But these men were deep divers. None of them smoked, and though one or two might wave a glass of red wine at his friends with many a cry of "Salute!" their drinking meant nothing to them, and in all the years of the *Egypt* expedition not one ever got drunk.

After a week of wretched idling in Brest, the first of many weather interruptions, the sky cleared and sweeping began. In the stern of the *Artiglio* stood an enormous steel drum on which was wound the sweep, a steel cable two thousand yards long. The *Rostro* was to take the other end of this sweep, they would drag the area between them, and thus they would catch the *Egypt*. As simple as that.

The *Rostro* came lumbering alongside. Carli caught the line thrown from the *Artiglio* and made it fast to her own stern, then the two ships parted till fourteen hundred yards of cable were dragging along the bottom between them. They moved forward along parallel lines, a mile to one side of the buoy, then around with the *Rostro* as pivot and a mile to the other side; another swing around the *Rostro* and the same all over again, like a farmer plowing a field.

Before long Lorenzo the Magnificent, one of the *Artiglio's* crew, waved the flag that said to the *Rostro*, "Stop quick, we've caught something." The engines were stopped and the stern winch hauled the sweep in. The thing at the bottom was holding the cable fast, dragging the two boats closer and closer together, and anything that held like that, Gianni reasoned, might be a wreck, for cables slipped easily off rocks. He was considering going down to investigate when the line suddenly fell slack. "It was a rock," he said. Every few minutes the same thing happened.

Quaglia, Gianni, Carli, and a visiting representative of the French submarine service put their heads together. They had assumed that the *Egypt* was lying solitary on a flat floor, offering herself to the sweep like a single flower to a scythe, but now it appeared that she was virtually surrounded by tall jagged rocks, and to catch her was like slicing the head off the tallest tree in a forest without tangling with the rest. A nice problem of gauging the proper depth. They were all staring this obstacle in the face when the weather broke again.

By the time it cleared Gianni and Quaglia had devised a new type of sweep. Each ship let a three-ton anchor swing over her side, the ends of the cable were attached to these anchors and pulled taut between them at the desired depth, and again the *Rostro* moored herself to the buoy at Hedback's point and the *Artiglio* steamed around her. Again the cable caught and slipped free. This happened over and over and over, half an hour being lost each time in straightening the cable out, and if it frayed or broke that section must be repaired. This kind of sweep was no good either.

The next inspiration was a series of small buoys attached every hundred feet to suspend the sweep evenly along its full length, but this was expensive and meant Quaglia had business to do in Brest and in Genoa, credit business. Meanwhile the ships would carry on with present equipment.

They went back to Hedback's point and started sweeping north of the point, but soon the rocks began catching again. Farther south they caught once more, but this time instead of falling free the cable held fast and the two boats hauled and hauled till they almost collided, the sweep running tautly down to the bottom in the shape of a huge V. A fresh northeast wind rushed waves under the ships' overhanging counters and, unable to rise with the swells, they smashed down each time in a cloud of spray. Still the sweep held.

This looked interesting.

Gianni excitedly got into his red wool cap and warm clothing, and was put down over the side in the shell. But he never got down, for so fierce was the current that he merely swung out at a 45-degree angle, like a pennant in the wind, and dangled there cursing and sweating.

Carli at once dropped a small buoy to mark the spot, and Gianni spent the next hour in the motorboat dragging a heavy grapnel, but this caught nothing and again he gave up, swearing. At last he lowered a charge of explosive in the hope that some part of the wreck might come loose and rise to the surface. Even a scrap would tell them something of what lay below. But all Gianni got was a dead conger eel, and that told him nothing.

The profanity became ever more fiery and complicated. Three

hours had the ships been anchored to the bottom and to each other, then suddenly they both shuddered and the sweep fell slack. Their sterns, released, bobbed up and down. The men rushed to the winches and hauled in the cable.

It was broken, the two ends frayed and cut. The steel was marked here and there with red glints, like rust, and there were faint white smears, perhaps of paint.

Gianni looked around at the circle of anxious faces and gave a long low whistle. Bargellini pounded everybody on the back and burst into song. The *Times* man, David Scott, gulped and grinned, and Franceschi, shuffling his enormous feet, broke into a little dance. Then the sparkle went out of Gianni's eyes.

"There's just one thing . . ."

Bargellini shouted impatiently, "What?"

"This paint—if it is paint—is white. The *Egypt* was a P & O liner, and all P & Os are painted buff." It was true; according to their model, she had had a black hull and funnels, and elsewhere was painted buff to prevent dazzle in the tropics.

The turmoil quieted down. Franceschi nodded sadly. "That's right. And even if it is a wreck, it may not be the *Egypt*. The *Vapeur*—on the French chart she's sunk just about here."

Bargellini said eagerly, "I'll go down again. I might find out something."

Gianni shook his head. "You couldn't get down past that damn current any more than I could." And he waved Bargellini aside. "There's nothing more we can do today. Carli's buoy is marking the spot. We will come back tomorrow and find the wreck."

That night in the little eight-by-three dining saloon of the *Artiglio*, under the photographs of Mussolini and King Victor Emmanuel, the argument ran high. "The only white paint on the *Egypt* would be the inside fittings of her cabins, and that would mean she had split wide open. Very unlikely." Carli shook his head. "It's probably the *Vapeur*. Or there's another wreck on the chart somewhere around here. You can't trust charts within two or three miles."

Suddenly Scott, the *Times* man, exclaimed, "Listen, I've just remembered—the *Egypt* was a hospital ship during the war! She was white all over then."

Again the saloon was in an uproar, everyone shouting and slapping each other and drinking red wine to the absent Quaglia. This meant they could begin diving in a day or two—there might be gold before autumn—bonuses for Christmas . . . They went to bed early, to be ready to begin first thing.

In the morning a gale was blowing, the waves bouncing them up and down, tossing them about, slinging the loose machinery across the deck. Gianni looked around and, sighing all the way up from his shoes, ordered both ships back to Brest.

The weather was dirty for a week, and the men paced the streets in a mood no better than the weather. When the sea calmed they hurried back to look for Carli's buoy, but it had broken away in the storm and was not to be found.

After that Quaglia tried a fresh approach. The slow plodding method having failed, he would try the flash technique. Magic might do the trick. And he did not want for volunteers.

A Capuchin friar, Father Innocent, who had earned a reputation in Italy for finding water and ores with a hazel twig, offered to locate the *Egypt*, and Quaglia, bristling with excitement, brought him to Brest in spite of the embarrassment and skepticism of the others, who tried to conceal his arrival from the newspapermen hanging about. But a monk, complete with robe, sandals, tonsure, and bunch of freshly cut twigs, is a conspicuous object, and Father Innocent was pure delight to the newsmen, by now bored with the long search.

The friar, in spite of a bad case of seasickness, gave the men on the *Artiglio* a demonstration of the divining art as they steamed out to Hedback's point. He started well; holding the ends of the hazel twig in his upturned hands, he shuffled about the deck "feeling" for various metals, iron, steel, copper. When he made a find the loop of the twig twisted upwards, and this happened several times, with the consequence that the men were becoming more respectful, and demanded that he try for gold. Holding out his twig towards various members of the crew, he found two gold coins in Cuniberti's pocket and Gianni's enormous signet ring in his. So now, really warming to the little man, everybody organized a game of hide-and-seek, with the gold coins hidden in various spots all over the ship.

The little friar did swimmingly for a while, and then—whether the seasickness undermined his powers or they just petered out—Father Innocent went all to pieces. He kept wildly finding the coins in all the wrong places, and, put to work on the *Egypt*, located the wreck in two different places at once. At last Gianni, losing patience, sent the embarrassed little man back to Brest and home.

Quaglia's fling at the supernatural having been a field day for the newspapermen, he heard from people all over the globe offering help for ten per cent of the proceeds. Now it was his turn to shake his head in disgust while Terme accepted the offer of one M. Poireau to get a perfect bearing on the wreck with a magical invention of his own. Poireau came up with not one but two widely separate places to investigate; somehow no one was impressed, and this was the end of diviners.

By this time morale was low and where there had been laughter and horseplay and guitar playing after work, the decks were quiet now. Franceschi no longer stamped out rhythms with his huge feet, Gianni shadowboxed no more, Bargellini, the handsomest and youngest of the divers, gazed moodily off towards Porto Vecchio, where his young wife was making him a baby. They had already used up a month, and most of that time had been wasted in the cafés of Brest taking refuge from the storms. It had become evident that a day at sea afforded no more than four hours of actual work, between tides; and now they saw that ten days in the month, and three months in the year, were all they could count on. That added up to an entire diving year of 120 hours. At that rate, they would be all their lives . . .

Though none of the divers or officers defected, others did and had to be replaced by men with more loyalty. Quaglia himself still carried his round stomach proudly before him, head high, beak cutting the atmosphere, but his temper was shorter than customary and he bellowed "*Sacramento!*" with stunning regularity.

After a particularly bad spell, when the *Rostro* and *Artiglio* had been lost in a fog and nearly rammed each other, Quaglia called Gianni and Carli into the Café Continental bar. In this teeming

place with its white-topped tables the waiters scurried about screaming, "Draw me one," and "Beer me two."

Quaglia, looking very serious, told them to sit down and beered
them one each. He had been away on one of his many trips, and
now, his black beret forgotten on his head, he sat working his large
cigar nervously from side to side in his mouth.

"Things aren't good," he said.

Gianni and Carli nodded agreement, but Quaglia shook his head.
"It's more than you know about. I've told you the kind of deal I
made with Lloyd's—that is, that I supply all the working capital
myself because that way SORIMA gets a bigger share of the proceeds. But"—they waited, knowing the kind of thing to expect—"I
never thought we'd be so long finding the *Egypt*. It's fouled up my
timetable."

He told them particulars. Confident of quick success, he had put
up all his personal assets, plus those of his two companies, as security for working credits. And not a cent had been coming in to keep
him going. "I've been trying to get another loan but our record
hasn't been too impressive so far. And besides, there's all that talk.
It doesn't make for confidence."

"What talk?" Gianni asked.

"Everybody says we'll never find the *Egypt*, that nobody could."

"They've always said that," Carli objected. "That's nothing new."

"There's other talk now too. Damn-fool stuff."

"For instance?"

Quaglia shrugged his massive shoulders, reluctant to elaborate.
"It's too stupid even to talk about. And anyway, it'll all stop the
minute we find the *Egypt*."

"Is there anything Carli and I can do to help?"

Quaglia gave Gianni a weak smile. "Nothing except find me some
gold. You'd be surprised what one gold bar would do in a London
bank." They nodded; they knew what one gold bar would do right
there.

Quaglia had tried the flash technique and found it wanting, so
next he turned to science. Several years before, a Mr. E. E. Brooke
had sold to the British Admiralty an electric search gear with which
they had had considerable success in locating submarines during
the war, and now Quaglia invited him to bring his knowledge to

bear on the problem of the *Egypt*. An elderly but animated professor, he would have gone down in the shell if Quaglia had not
nervously given strict orders to keep him topside. His invention was
a kind of galvanometer, which was to pick up minute electric currents originating in the metals of the submerged ship. It had worked
well for the Admiralty, but since the actual formula was owned by
the Admiralty, Brooke had had to improvise certain variations,
which vitiated its usefulness. One more effort to supplant the sweep
had failed. Quaglia gave up for the winter.

Next spring Quaglia swore there was going to be no more nonsense, no more diviners or cranks or half-baked specialists.

Well, almost none. He had had an offer of help from a man who
certainly should know where the *Egypt* lay, since he was the one
who put her there. Captain le Barzic had been in command of
the *Seine* when she rammed the *Egypt* and had spent three hours
on the spot rescuing the passengers. He joined the *Artiglio* in June.

Quaglia had given strict orders, delivered, as always, with a violently wagging forefinger, about the sweeping. They were to work
carefully along lines of buoys, leaving no area uncovered, covering
no area twice, and checking every position as they went. There was
a suspended sweep now, and the cable could be lowered to the exact depth they desired, high enough to escape the bottom, low
enough to catch the ship. The *Egypt* could hardly elude them very
much longer.

Efficiency reigned, except in the case of the expert. Le Barzic had
a personal antipathy to Hedback, whose very name drove him into
a frenzy. He was convinced that the *Egypt* had gone down at a point
far north in the rectangle, while Hedback's point lay far south, and
he was so violent about it that Gianni bowed under the blast and
they started out in June working along the northern edge. For two
months they crept back and forth, never missing an inch, always
working farther south, and on the way flushing a number of other
wrecks, which at least proved their mechanism was working. And
at last the luck that till now had played so hard to get suddenly
switched and literally threw itself at them.

Gianni had laid a line of buoys just below Hedback's point and
begun sweeping along it. Nothing happened. Next day he moved

his buoys and swept again. This time the drag caught. But this had happened countless times before, and as it was near sunset and a storm was rising, Gianni buoyed the spot and went home. It was the last night they slept in uncertainty.

Next day, after a twelve-hour blow, they came out anxiously, for once before a storm had robbed them of their precious marker, but this time the buoys were all in place. The one they had dropped last night was bobbing pleasantly, and so was the line of five others stretching off towards the horizon.

After a second look Gianni scowled; no, there were only four. The missing fifth he saw a good half mile away. Buoys cost money, and so he went to bring the runaway home.

Ranging alongside the buoy, Gianni made fast the tackle and pulled. It came just so far, then stuck. He pulled again; still it stuck. Gently, firmly, the winch put its weight on the line, and instead of the buoy giving the ship gave. The *Artiglio* began to heel over. Yet the buoy's mooring only weighed one ton, and it could not be that alone that was holding it so fast.

With patient insistent drag the winch pulled on, then suddenly something gave way far below and the *Artiglio* rolled back to an even keel. Now hauling was a somewhat easier matter, and at last a tangled slimy mass broke the surface, the one-ton weight—and all entwined in the buoy's wire a shaft of rusty steel that might be a davit.

Gianni, Franceschi, and Bargellini measured the shaft—six feet exactly—and went in a tense silence to the saloon to study the blueprint of the *Egypt*. Gianni checked the specifications. The rusty davit up there should match some davit here in this scale drawing. Not this one—not this. They were all too big.

But here, right out on the farthest reach of the stern, here was a shaft barely an inch long on the drawing. Figuring on a ratio of one inch to six feet . . .

The men looked at each other and laughed out loud.

The identification had to be verified, so Bargellini went down in the shell and was hauled gently along the side of the hull, taking measurements, checking dimensions. He came up and reported, "It's the *Egypt* all right." And later Franceschi went down as well.

He too was satisfied, and that night the sound of men singing, of mandolins and guitars, put the seal on the *Egypt's* discovery.

Quaglia, always busy with a thousand affairs, had been away in Italy, but now he hurried back and the glorious reunion thundered through the corridors of the Continental. He greeted his friends in white silk pajamas, clasping each to his stomach and smacking him on either cheek. Somehow suddenly taller and grander, he shouted and boasted and shook his head in happy incredulity, receiving adulation like royalty and putting in telephone calls all over Europe. After he had dressed and wiped his face with eau de cologne he went out and bought a new hat and paid a state call on the Admiral.

A financial problem arose almost at once. Captain le Barzic, who had sunk the *Egypt*, now claimed a large premium because he said the ship had been found through his efforts. There was no question that he had been on board at the time, but whether he had helped was another matter. However, Quaglia was in a liberal mood; and reasoning that if Le Barzic had not been around in the first place there would have been nothing for anyone now, he grinned and paid up.

Now, after so long, everything was going well. The *Artiglio* dropped its automatic grab, a pair of gigantic jaws that went down open and clanged shut as directed by the diver from the shell, and brought up a steam winch weighing six tons. This was more of a dramatic gesture than useful salvage, but it served to prove they had really found the *Egypt*. An actual photograph in the papers always shut up a lot of talk.

The sweep which had combed the bottom for so many months was sent ashore amid mingled groans and cheers—they were done with *that*, thank goodness. And then the captain's safe was brought up from his cabin on the boat deck. The grab gently nipped the edge of the deckhead, ripping it off and tossing it aside, and then reached in and bit down hard on the safe. No special information about the ship or cargo was found in it, but anyway it was a nice thing to have and it might aid Quaglia in raising funds.

Then, after this short spell of smooth sailing, catastrophe hit—something worse than delay, worse than failure. It happened partly because everyone was impatient to be home for Christmas, partly because Gianni was a shade too self-confident.

The diving season in this region was over, but Quaglia planned to give his men other work through the winter, on an American ship, the *Florence*, which was lying at the bottom of the channel into St. Nazaire, partially obstructing harbor traffic. She had been a munitions ship during the war, carrying explosives from the United States to France, and a bomb had been smuggled on board before she left New York, timed to explode in the harbor. The town was to have been wrecked, shipping blocked, and the entry of the American Expeditionary Forces obstructed for weeks, but fortunately for the war effort, she had been delayed outside and had blown up in a comparatively harmless spot. It was now Quaglia's commission to remove her.

Containing as she did an unexploded cargo of munitions, the job might last one day or many months—one day if the explosives could be induced to blow themselves and her up, many months if they were duds and the ship had to be cut to pieces. In any case, plenty of distance must be put between the *Artiglio* and the *Florence* whenever a charge was blown.

"Now, strict orders, remember," Quaglia told Gianni, shaking a finger in his face, "be careful. No chances, no risks."

Gianni nodded impatiently. Nothing had ever happened yet.

The first charges were laid down, one on either side of the hull, and when the divers had been hauled back on board, the *Artiglio* steamed away to the far side of the channel, Gianni paying out several miles of electric wire. But nothing happened beyond the usual thud on the ship's keel. The charges had made only a couple of small holes in the *Florence's* sides.

Next time they laid six charges outside the hull. Then they dropped charges right through the hatches among the munitions. Still the *Florence* made no sign.

The men were getting restive. Plainly her explosives, after thirteen years under water, were duds, and they would have to blow her apart plate by plate, so better get at it if they were to be home for Christmas, home to that baby Bargellini had never seen, home to that small child Franceschi was always shopping for. The blasting went on impatiently.

Quaglia's strict orders had been, "After laying a charge retire a full two miles." But that was a ridiculous waste of time. A mile would be far enough. Or even half a mile. . . .

It was December 7, 1930; the *Florence* lay like a picked carcass, nearly down to the required thirty feet below water, with her munitions still in the hold, obviously dead as a dodo. Bargellini had laid an unusually heavy charge under the overhanging stern, and soon the job would be done, after which they could all go home.

The *Artiglio* moved slowly away from the *Florence*, connected with her only by the electric wire, while the nineteen men aboard lolled along the railing watching for the big bang. One of the wires in Gianni's hands led to the charges on the wreck, the other to the dynamo in the engine room. All he had to do was bring the two ends together. He stood waiting while the *Artiglio* steamed down the bay. When he decided it had gone far enough he called "Dynamo."

The response came from the engine room, "Dynamo."

"Contact," he called, and brought the two ends together.

At that moment the *Artiglio* was just three hundred yards from the *Florence*.

When the waters went back to normal seven men remained alive, the others having been drowned in the tidal wave that engulfed the *Artiglio*. The *Florence* had gone up in a mushroom-shaped cloud that rose and grew and multiplied and turned over and over in the sky, and all that was to be seen now of the *Artiglio* was floating wreckage.

By the spring of 1931, Quaglia had partially recovered his birdlike strut. Everybody knew he had always emphasized that no chances must be taken, and no one blamed him because Gianni had been impulsive once too often, but the tragedy had been a bad blow to him, nevertheless, for these men were his friends.

It had not eased his financial situation either. The long-drawnout search had already put a strain on his resources; and now he must replace the *Artiglio* and her equipment, so that it was imperative that they find the gold this year—just how imperative none of the crew knew, for he did not want to cripple them with anxiety.

The new salvage ship was a shabby tramp whose best days had been spent transshipping fish from the Newfoundland Banks to

French ports. She still smelled strongly of old fish, and was covered with rust and grass, but they scraped and painted and oiled, and trusted the clean Atlantic air to deodorize; and called the new *Artiglio*—not *Artiglio II*, for that would have been a jinx no ship could survive—she finally became quite a prideful little vessel.

Among the twelve men who had been lost were three of the *Artiglio's* divers, Gianni the ebullient, with his dramatic inventions and schemes (Gianni had planned to cut the bullion room right out of the *Egypt* in one piece and raise it like a box); Franceschi, the practical joker who was all efficiency the moment he was under water; and Bargellini, the boy with classic features who would have been one of the world's great divers if he had lived. Two of them had been picked up while still warm, smashed to a horrid pulp by the force of the explosion.

Quaglia transferred some of the *Rostro's* men to the new *Artiglio* and put Mario Raffaelli in charge. Unlike Gianni, Mario was quiet and cautious and unobtrusively efficient, but he had a tongue that could burn through iron if his orders were disobeyed. Before joining this expedition he had spent years in rubber-suited work, and SORIMA came in time to regard him as the world's best salvage officer.

His subordinates, Mancini, Sodini, and Lenci were newcomers by comparison. Remarkable divers, they still had much to learn in the matter of judgment, and sometimes they were overoptimistic, on one occasion their faulty reports nearly ruining Quaglia.

It required everybody, working eighteen hours a day, to make the new *Artiglio* ready. They were racing against the calendar, since the sooner they got started the sooner they would find gold and cash in on the bonuses they expected. No one knew exactly what the bonuses would be, but all knew Quaglia's reputation for generosity and trusted him to do the right thing. Fascist labor organizations regulated wages stringently, putting a ceiling on wages which was hard to pierce, and though at times Quaglia managed to slip through something extra, there was plenty of room for generosity —the annual wage was $306, with no limit on working hours.

The job ahead was stupendous, for the *Egypt's* bullion room, a chamber twenty-five feet long and only five feet wide, was situated at the very bottom of the boat under four decks. Had she lain in shallow water where the divers could use ordinary rubber suits the task would have been comparatively simple; since she was resting upright on the bottom, a diver simply would have walked down from deck to deck and along the passageways, dragging his lifting and telephone lines with him, and entered the bullion room, or as an alternative made one hole in her side outside that room and entered sideways. But with the diving shell this was impossible. Dangling like a fish on a line, he could go only straight up and down. The same was true of the hooks and grabs; everything was operated from directly overhead.

Mario and Quaglia, conferring during the past winter, had discarded Gianni's spectacular plan of raising the bullion room in one piece, for Mario preferred the conservative way. First, sections of the four decks directly over the bullion room must be cut away with explosives and the debris removed; then, when the room was opened up, automatic grabs could be lowered to lift out the gold like tongs lifting out sugar. Simple in theory, staggering in practice.

Working four hundred feet below the surface, the men would be able to see only fifteen or twenty feet through the water, which, muddy and full of silt stirred up by the explosives, would be nearly as black as the wreck itself. Nor would artificial light help, for white floodlights created a glare as if in a fog, and red lights, while making no glare, gave little illumination. Natural daylight, dim and chancy as it was, would have to serve.

Even more than the darkness, they dreaded the current, which, always running, created difficulties and dangers unknown in the Mediterranean. It complicated the laying of explosives, sweeping them out of position; if it carried the *Artiglio* out of position the diver hanging from her might be dragged under some overhanging ledge and cut off; and, because in moving water the arms acted as fins and kept him always facing downstream no matter where he wanted to face, it finally caused the abandonment of the jointed diving shell altogether. Thus the armless, legless wonder came into use.

Through Siebe, Gorman had invented an "observation chamber" some years before the Italians' time which had received little attention. The impracticality of the jointed shell had inspired Gianni to invent one of his own, a plain cylinder nine feet high with a series of bug-eyed windows in its oversized head. Like the jointed shell it had phone connections, respirator, mask, oxygen tank, seat, and all the other comforts of home, but instead of resembling an animal it now resembled a fire hydrant. Its occupant's sole function was to see and, seeing, to report and direct, and using it, the divers were to cut a hole down through the decks of the wreck and extract five million dollars from its belly.

Towards the end of May the new *Artiglio* made off to the scene of action. When Gianni had left last year he had set out four buoys over the *Egypt's* resting place, and now he moored the ship to them and began to blow the wreck apart.

The usual charge was a sixteen-foot tube, which was lowered respectfully halfway down and then allowed to hang while the diver went ahead and scouted for the spot to place it. This might take ten minutes or an hour. Then he called for the bomb to be lowered, taking care not to let it hit him on the way down, and spent an hour or many hours having it endlessly lifted and dropped till the spot was hit, while at the same time both he and the bomb were rising and falling uncontrollably with the movement of the ship on the waves above. Four hours of this was as much as the respirators could comfortably handle, and more than enough for the nerves of any man.

When the bomb was finally placed the diver was brought up, the thud on the keel gave notice when the charge was fired, and after an hour, or whenever the water cleared, he went down again to check. A good charge would cut a long gash in the steel plating; since they were cutting sections out of the deck like a chef cutting a pie crust out of dough, several of these gashes were needed before the section was freed all around. When it was, it would be lying under a pile of debris torn and shaken down by the explosions, and at this point the grab would come into play, its wide-open jaws held poised to strike, while the man with the earphones above listened to the man in the shell:

"Up the grab . . . Down the grab . . . No, not so far. Up again . . . A little more . . . Down six inches . . . Now half a yard to the right . . . Now down . . . A little more . . . More . . . Not so *much!* Oh hell, take it up and start over." The man on the earphones had to guess what was meant by "a little more" and tell the winch man how much line to let out. Not all of them were good at this job; some got angry and impatient, but others were almost psychic in guessing and transmitting messages.

Though the current and the darkness were tough enough, the real enemy was the weather, which, that year of 1931, was famous; in June they got but twelve days' work, in July five and a half. Once the weather remained fine for eight days together, and the men stayed at work till they ran out of water and had nothing to eat but broth and biscuit. But in those eight days they removed sections of three decks. The crater they were making across the fifty-foot width of the ship was fifty feet at the top, diminishing at each successive deck till at the bottom the hole was to be just big enough to let the smallest of the grabs enter, mouth open, and bite.

By July 30 the wreck was coming apart in big rusty chunks. One day, for a change, they salvaged something of intrinsic value, a piece of solid copper pipe worth eighty-seven dollars. One end flared like a trumpet and Beck, the Lloyd's representative, suggested that it be made into (how English!) an umbrella stand for the chairman of the board.

August came in, and the men worked lower, pulling up deck plates twenty-four feet long weighing eight tons. The divers were working with ever greater efficiency as they became more familiar with their black surroundings, and by the end of August, in twenty-eight working days, they had made two hundred dives and lifted fifteen thousand square feet of plating. At the start of the season Quaglia had estimated it would take thirty working days to get down to the goal, and here, after twenty-eight, they were within shouting distance of it. Or so it seemed.

Quaglia had been spending most of his time away on unnamed business. Now, after receiving a wire from Carli, he was back, though he was invariably seasick on board and had to lie down during meals. The end was in sight, Carli had wired him; the three young divers had reached the main deck, which formed the roof of the bullion room, and reported that after clearing away a few bulkheads they could begin on the room itself.

Quaglia was all one great grin. "It's going to be all right after all," he boomed. Then he took Mario and Carli and Scott, the *Times* man, aside. "This has come just in time," he told them.

"You've known I was worried, of course, but I didn't tell you details. I've spent all my own money, four hundred thousand dollars, and I've made several large loans besides. One of them was from a private firm, raised on its notes to a bank, and now, recently, the bank failed. The firm has been pressing me to repay, and I've been trying for weeks to raise another loan. But with nothing to show but failure"—he lifted his shoulders in a shrug and shook his head —"they just laugh at me. Things have looked very bad. I'd hate to tell you how near I've been to scuttling the whole works."

The three men stared, aghast. "It'll be all right now though, won't it?" Mario asked.

"Oh, this will fix everything. You should have seen those newspapermen's faces when I showed them Carli's wire this morning. They've been laying bets we'd never get to the gold—and even that you fellows had got lost down there and been blasting in the wrong place. But now—" he pounded them on the back—"this will show them."

That afternoon Mario, who had not been down recently, got into the shell to have a look at the wreck. He was back up in a rush, and the moment the shell was opened a flood of white-hot rage poured out on the three divers. "You damn fools," he stormed, "we've got the whole main deck to go yet."

In the darkness and welter of debris the young men had misjudged the situation; instead of a few loose bulkheads, as they had reported, there was still a whole steel deck to be removed, and they were weeks away from the gold.

Mario's fury was terrible, and Quaglia held his head in despair. Indeed, everyone on board was stunned, but only the few knew how serious this mistake might be. Mario insisted that the divers be called below and told the brutal facts.

"After this false alarm," Quaglia said to them then, "God knows who will ever believe in us."

The divers' faces were grave and ashamed. Then Lenci, who was very young and saw a joke in everything, laughed. "Don't worry. They think the gold's got us beaten, but it's lying down there right now, quaking."

Quaglia said, "Listen, you don't realize how serious this is. It's not only that I'm broke and all over Europe people are laughing at us. There's something else they're saying—and it's another reason why we've got to come through. They say we're spies."

They gave that a scornful snort, but Quaglia went on, "Why, certainly. That's why we've been taking so long. We're stalling, we don't ever *intend* to get through. Don't you realize—" his lips pulled back in a kind of sneer—"for three years now we've been hanging around the bars of Brest listening to the pilots and naval officers talk . . . Brest, the second largest naval base in France!" He slapped his forehead in mock horror. "My God, can you imagine all the priceless secrets we must have picked up!"

The air was blue with the divers' rage, but after a few wild suggestions of a murderous nature Quaglia interrupted them, "That's all very well, but the main thing is, just get the hell down there and wind this thing up. I'll go back to London or somewhere and see what I can do about more money."

And so, while Quaglia chased a loan through the month of October, Mario drove the three men till they slowly sickened under the long hours of darkness and bottled oxygen. On the days when the weather forced them into Brest they huddled together in a corner of the bar, shying away from the wisecracks of the sailors and their former girl friends, and they were gladder than ever now to get back to the *Artiglio's* fishy stink.

But the blasting went on, and at last they had a hole cut clean through the main deck and Lenci reported that its edge was curling up invitingly. The grab was dropped, and as the *Artiglio's* derrick pulled, the ship heeled over. Those on deck watched the grab break the water, the square of metal grasped daintily by one corner. It was a momentous sight, for it meant that a corner of the bullion room was open and nothing but water separated them from their goal. A photograph sent out over the world by Scott of *The Times* would do much to lay the talk; it might also ease Quaglia's struggle to raise more funds.

Then—it seemed needlessly cruel—the teeth of the grab slipped and the metal plate fell back into the sea. No picture now to prove their claim, nothing but their word, and after the previous fiasco their word had not much weight.

They became a little numb after that, but swept along by Mario's furious determination, they went on diving long after good sense told them to stop. Though the season normally ended the last of August, so desperate were they to show some concrete results before the winter's hiatus that the last dive took place on December 1. But when Lenci went down it was as black as midnight, and all he could report was that he had stood up to his knees in the bullion room—he thought. With that they had to live through the winter.

Quaglia's winter of fund raising was his own private war. No one recorded the number of banks he visited, the hours he spent haranguing, the times he spread the *Egypt's* blueprints on a deck and pointed out how near they were to the gold. If ardor, plus the sheer weight of conviction, is eloquence, Quaglia was an eloquent man. At any rate, by spring he had raised enough to carry them down to the bullion room.

In May 1932 they gathered at Brest. Most of the men had been home on leave and five babies were expected in September. The months of rest had restored their good spirits and optimism, and literally flinging themselves on the roof of the bullion room, they soon had the hole started last fall big enough to admit the smaller grab. On June 9 actual treasure hunting began.

The first grabful was unenticing, bits of wood, broken china, metal wire, all covered with evil-smelling slime. Then some broken boxes with the name of a gunsmith, Westley-Richards—which meant guns in the bullion room, an unexpected development. Out of the next load of slime came a Bible (Lord Inchcape had had one put in every passenger's cabin), and this too seemed a strange thing to find. Then part of a book of essays—photograph of Lord Douglas Haig—*Paradise Lost*—English dictionary—program of a Port Said movie theater printed in Arabic, all waterlogged but legible. By then they were inured to anything.

But as the grab went deeper the stuff got a little more interesting, some silver-plated spoons and forks, a broken cashbox containing a few coins, a silver rupee with the head of Queen Victoria, a square five-cent piece from Ceylon, a Belgian ten-centime piece, and three silver dollars from Malay. It was at least money, though hardly what they had dreamed of. Well, they could work up to the big stuff gradually.

Next came a loaded pistol and a bundle of sticks tied together, golf clubs without heads, which had come unglued and dropped off, and then two magnificent guns in cases, engraved with the initials M.B.S., and an oriental crown. Then, getting more nearly down to business, came bank notes, packet after packet of hundred-rupee notes printed in native script, "THE GOVERNMENT OF HIS EXALTED HIGHNESS THE NIZAM OF HYDERA-BAD." Five million dollars' worth, spread in bundles over the decks to dry. Everyone wondered why they had not been listed as part of the treasure, and then Quaglia noticed that they lacked the governmental signature. Duds.

More Indian stuff came up, twenty-nine guns for M.B.S., who turned out to be the Maharajah of Patiala, and then something really incongruous, half a dozen rolls of delicate silk, varicolored and lovely. The *Artiglio*, draped with pink and pale green and blue, was suddenly as feminine and festive as a Mardi Gras float, but everyone was much annoyed by these delays. (Finally the Mystery of the Bullion Room Trash was solved. The *Egypt's* captain, worried about his precious cargo, had buried it under a welter of trivia to discourage possible thieves.)

On June 22 the star of the show made its debut. Quaglia, who had been with the *Artiglio* since the start of the season, unremittingly seasick, examined each grabful of muck as it came up. With pince-nez dangling off the end of his beak, his shirt collarless, and all but the top button of his vest undone to accommodate his shape, he hardly qualified as a glamorous treasure hunter, but suddenly his face lighted up dramatically. "Look," he shouted, and held up his hand, "a sovereign!" It was bright gold, King Edward VII, 1901. The hunt was on.

Every hand reached for the black slime, feeling for hard round objects, and another gold sovereign appeared, George V, 1921. Quaglia, his eyes shining, silently dropped the two coins into his pocket.

They stopped for lunch then (their days were always the same, six hours' work on an empty stomach and, at noon, a good meal of spaghetti) and then to Lenci went the honor of the next dive. The rest stood and waited while the grab rose dripping, swung round, and disgorged an uncertain mass. Then as the mud and slime hit the deck there was a new sound, heavy, important—two gold bars, hardly soiled and winking in the sun.

Now everyone laughed and shouted and pounded each other, feeling the slabs of gold, stroking them, laying them against their cheeks. Kisses rained on each other and on the gold.

Suddenly Quaglia broke the moment of exaltation with a raised arm. "Quiet!"

Someone had thought to break out a new Italian ensign from the jack staff, and Quaglia pulled off his beret. "Is everyone here?" he called, and then, realizing that Lenci was below, waited till they got him up from the bottom, and spoke to the ring of silent men. "Today we are at last successful, standing here together in our moment of triumph. But let me say to you, we must not forget those others, the ones we have lost. Let us all bow our heads and think of our beloved friends, for I am sure they are rejoicing with us now."

There was a long silence. Numbers of the men wiped their eyes, for among the lost were brothers and fathers and childhood friends. Then everyone shouted, "*Viva l'Italia!*" and they got back to work.

Now the job was all pure pleasure, as gold bars came up steadily, seventeen with one grab, eleven with the next, silver bars in profusion, and individual sovereigns that dropped and rolled and had to be chased ere they skittered off into the sea. The bars were of various sizes, the largest worth $7,290, and all of them bright and unsullied despite the slime. Quaglia settled himself in his deck chair with an umbrella to keep off the sun and gathered them around him like a hen on a setting of yellow eggs. Beck, the Lloyd's man, made a careful record as they came up, and then they were tied into bags and stowed in the improvised strongroom, though, as it turned out, this precaution was a mere formality, for the only gold that disappeared was one coin which no one had missed till old Zio handed it to Quaglia and said, "Here's a sovereign I found when I was sweeping the deck."

The first day the divers brought up 254 pounds of gold, and by the end of the second day $291,600 in gold and silver and coins was on hand. They averaged six shots of the grab an hour, a phenomenal rate, and each load averaged $44,300. At the end of the third day the *Artiglio* was radiant with $874,800 worth of gold. Thus in three days Quaglia was out of the red, for according to his arrangement with Lloyd's, whereby everything recovered belonged first to the company and then was split fifty-fifty, he had got back more than the four hundred thousand dollars sunk in the venture. It was no wonder his face, in the June sunlight, shone with something other than common sweat.

Besides the gold, there was the moral victory, and that first afternoon he sent out forty triumphant telegrams. One went to Ciano, Italy's Minister of Communications, who replied with a wire conveying Mussolini's "warmest congratulations to yourself and all your crew." Lloyd's wired their rejoicing, and Italy's press was full of praise. (Later *Punch* published a cartoon and a long poem neatly bracketing the salvage of the *Egypt* with the salvation of Europe.)

After three days of this glory, which he was enjoying only by remote control, Quaglia could stand it no longer and announced they were going to England to deliver the gold in person. Their strong room was not filled to capacity, but after so many years of humiliation the thought of a triumphal entry with crowds and flags and cheering was irresistible. The *Artiglio* sailed north.

The reception was worth going for, too. On the morning of Sunday, June 26, 1932, the ship entered Plymouth, where a motorboat with a pilot came out to meet them, followed by two more motorboats containing Peter Sandberg and his wife, Count and Countess Buraggi, and assorted pretty girls. Debarkation took place in a space on the quay draped with British and Italian flags, where gentlemen of title and reporters and photographers awaited them, and there were cheers and a ceremony and a speech by the head of Lloyd's.

Later Sir Hubert Brand, the Admiral, himself paid a visit to the ship, bringing more beautiful women. Quaglia nearly exploded with pleasure, and the men who had done the work, all neatly washed and dressed and shoed, lined up to be presented to the dignitaries and explain the monstrous diving shells, the armless, legless wonder coming in for special attention. Then everybody said good-by; the Italians said good-by to the treasure, which went on a train to London with Quaglia; Beck and Scott said good-by to the *Artiglio* and her men; the *Artiglio* said good-by to Plymouth, and everyone went back to his job, which in the case of the divers meant to the *Egypt*, for the bulk of the treasure had still to be brought up.

It took them the summer of 1932 and three more summers besides to strip the *Egypt*, but this they did, making a record that has only once or twice been equaled. Towards the end, when the few remaining coins were scattered widely throughout the hold, Mario devised a gadget, based on an earlier English one, which was to revolutionize deep-sea salvage, a metal tube whose lower end was closed by a glass cover. The air was pumped out of it, forming a vacuum, and it was then lowered to the bottom; when the glass was broken the water and everything in it were sucked to the surface, and thus, on the very first trial, six thousand gold sovereigns and some small bars were salved.

By the end of 1935 the job was done, ninety per cent of the coins, 97.4 per cent of the silver, and 98.25 per cent of the gold bars having been recovered. Though Operation *Egypt* had cost him nearly a million dollars, Quaglia was again a rich man, and no one begrudged him his fortune. Likewise the sturdy Italians, who had thrown themselves with fervid loyalty into the enterprise, knowing they themselves would never be rich but satisfied to do a good job, were famous and respected, for they had set a record for depth of working level which would stand for a few years longer, and even those who broke it would speak with wonder of the men who showed them the way.

Down to the present day SORIMA, headed by its president and chairman Quaglia until his death in 1955, has continued to raise gold, bank notes, metals, and such offbeat cargoes as two-thousand-year-old Roman pottery. Its fleet of salvage vessels, at work in most of the waters of the world, has grown to five. But none of its achievements has surpassed Operation *Egypt*, and none of its other ships has the proud history of that smelly old tramp who in fair weather and foul so well lived up the motto painted on her bridge, MEMENTO AUDERE SEMPER—"Remember always to dare."

Since most of this story has never been told before, I have had to rely for the facts on correspondence and interviews with participants in the events described. The confusion prevailing during the last days of Corregidor, and the deliberate destruction of all papers, meant that neither Army nor Navy could supply any details of the 1942 jettisoning, and for much the same reason there are available no official records of the 1945 salvage operations. However, I have had unofficial help from many kind and generous people: first and foremost, Brigadier General Charles C. Drake, Ret., without whom much of this information never could have been obtained; the Honorable Francis B. Sayre, former U. S. High Commissioner to the Philippines, who lent me his Report to the President; His Excellency Brigadier General Carlos P. Romulo, Philippine Ambassador to the United States; Rear Admiral William A. Sullivan, Ret.; Brigadier General Hugh J. Casey, Ret.; Lieutenant Colonel Sidney L. Huff, aide to General MacArthur; Colonel Joel F. Thomason, of the Office of the Chief of Military History; Colonel Andres Soriano; Mr. George F. Peabody of the Philippine Association; Mr. Celso Al Carunungan of Manila; Mr. Roman J. Azanza, Vice-President, and Mr. Maximo E. Fernandez, Auditor, of the Philippine National Bank, New York Agency; I am also indebted to Messrs. Byron P. Hollett, Walter E. Harmon, and Russell S. Osborn for the use of their logs and other material.

The Clark-Daves salvage operation was first told by Allan Clark himself in the Saturday Evening Post, and Mrs. Woodbury Willoughby described, in her delightful book, I Was on Corregidor, incidents involving the State Department.

V

Operation
Sunken Pesos

CHRISTMAS EVE, 1941, was hot and humid. A department-store Santa Claus, perspiring heavily into his tow beard and red flannel, piled sandbags on the sidewalk outside the windows of his shop in gloomy silence. There were few shoppers; some weeks earlier panic had sent the city into a whirl of buying and hoarding, but now a sort of daze had fallen. Now it waited numbly for the periodic bombings and the inevitable invasion.

General MacArthur meanwhile was pacing the flag-draped office in his headquarters at 1, Calle Victoria, in the old Walled City that had been his father's office before him. Tremendous decisions were in the making—whether to fight it out on the beaches of Luzon or withdraw the troops to Bataan, whether to hold Manila or give it to the enemy. Number one objective was to keep Manila Bay, the finest natural naval base in the Orient, out of the Japanese hands, but with the disasters both to the Navy at Pearl Harbor and the Air Force at nearby Clark Field, with Guam and Wake Island gone and Singapore hanging by a thread, with the Cavite naval base a burning pyre and Japanese troops pouring down from the north, MacArthur's original plans had become suddenly outmoded. Instead of trying to hold all of the Philippines, the best he could hope for was to save those south of Luzon, and so he must concentrate on Bataan, the peninsula that threw a protecting arm around the

bay, and on Corregidor, the rock that stood like a watchdog athwart
its entrance. By noon he and the Philippines' President had reached
a decision and the long retreat had begun.

A few hours later President Manuel Quezon, his staff, his wife,
and his children Maria, Nini, and Nonong, got into a PT boat at
Admiral's Landing opposite the elegant Manila Hotel. Into another PT boat stepped the United States High Commissioner
Francis Sayre and his wife and son Billy, with his staff, and both
diplomatic parties, transferring to the inter-island steamer *Mayon,*
crossed the twenty-six miles to the Rock.

At 6 P.M., MacArthur left his office. Major Carlos Romulo, remaining in Manila as press aide to Brigadier General Richard J.
Marshall, was at work in the office next door, and as MacArthur
passed him he bent over to say in a low voice:

"I'll be back, Carlos."

At seven the military moved out, and at nine-thirty of that beautiful moonlit night the General and his staff disembarked at Corregidor's North Dock from the *Don Esteban.* Next morning, Christmas Day, Headquarters of the United States Army Forces, Far East,
opened for business on the Rock.

The evacuees had been limited to one suitcase of personal belongings each, but what they took with them was considerably more
than that. Ten days before, the Philippine National Assembly had
hastily appropriated all its available funds, about ₱240,000,000, and
turned them over to the President, and now with him to Corregidor
went trunks and trunks of paper bills in one-hundred and five-
hundred denominations. The government's gold and silver reserves
were already in the Fort Knox of the Philippines, a vault on
Corregidor.

The United States High Commissioner likewise took a bundle
with him. Some days before he had been ordered by the Treasury
Department in Washington to accept for safekeeping any money
or other valuables which any bank, corporation, or individual
turned over to him, which valuables, in the event of their loss or
destruction, would be later restored to the original owners. (This
was the order that four years later caused the recovery, under peculiar circumstances, of a tremendous treasure from the bottom of
the bay.) A second order authorized Sayre to possess himself of any-

thing valuable, not voluntarily given him, to prevent its falling into the hands of the enemy. All these millions, along with President Quezon's ₱240,000,000, went into the Corregidor vault.

Besides being authorized to seize and protect, Sayre was told to destroy if necessary. Indeed, this self-destruction was in its place as much a policy of war as self-protection, and each department had orders on evacuation to leave nothing of value behind. Colonel Royal Jenks, Finance Officer of USAFFE, spent much of Christmas Eve in the quartermaster building opposite the Army pier stuffing his war plans and other strategic papers into the furnaces. Several other officers before him had, in their haste, simply dumped their bound volumes and left them to consume or not as chance dictated, so while the air raid warnings moaned miserably overhead, he stirred up their papers into flames and then emptied his own in on top. Meanwhile upstairs Lieutenant Colonel John R. Vance and the rest of his staff were collecting several locker trunks, and now all together they stuffed them with twenty-four million pesos cash for soldiers' salaries, food, and other such expenses. While he and Vance were sitting on the trunks on the Army pier waiting for a boat, a bomb flattened out the building they had just left. Jenks wondered if General Drake, whom he had seen in the corridors a few moments before, had got out in time.

Brigadier General Charles C. Drake, Quartermaster, had escaped that bomb but had been hit by another almost as lethal. He had been called to the office of MacArthur's Deputy Chief of Staff and told of the switch in war plans, which meant that he had to move his base of operations to Bataan and at the same time put enough reserve supplies on Corregidor to supply ten thousand men for six months, a staggering job. A small fleet of vessels was rounded up, some of them requisitioned (which means they were acquired after official written request), and others commandeered (which means nothing so formal), and within twenty-four hours the required stocks were laid in. Bataan received the balance of transportable goods, vehicles, craft, and supplies, and what could not be moved was given the prescribed scorched-earth treatment.

By the day after Christmas the staffs of the Philippine and United States governments and the Army Headquarters, perhaps a hundred in all, had gone to Corregidor, leaving the city under its

Acting Mayor, Jorge Vargas, formerly the President's Executive Secretary, onto whom now fell the unsavory task of proclaiming Manila an open city. The blackout was lifted, large amateurishly printed signs, OPEN CITY and NO SHOOTING, were strung across the streets, and the city offered no more resistance.

But the self-destruction went on, as radio stations were wrecked and Colonel Hugh J. Casey's demolition squad went about systematically destroying everything of value. The doors of the quartermaster stores were thrown open and excited Filipinos rushed in and filled their arms with canned and frozen foods until the warehouses were stripped bare. Fuel supplies at Fort McKinley were set on fire; what remained of Cavite naval base was blown up, the explosions shaking the city nine miles away; the Pandacan oil tanks, bursting, spread flames to the surrounding warehouses and sent burning oil down the Pasig River to set ablaze everything on its banks. At the same time Vargas and five high government officials, including the National Treasurer, went to the National Treasury in the Intendencia Building. While the main body of the paper currency and gold and silver was already on Corregidor, some paper and silver had been left for immediate contingencies. (Indeed, when the Intendencia had received a direct hit a few days before, thirty people had been killed, including the watchman, who was crushed under a shower of silver coins.) This committee now made an inventory of the bills and their serial numbers, signed it, and turned it over to Vargas. Then they spent an entire day burning them in the furnace of the Manila Electric Company. This much the Japs would not get.

There was, however, other money, which, having never been legally issued, had no gold or silver backing. This nobody got around to destroying before the Japs came.

Meanwhile the city attempted to carry on as usual, and on New Year's Eve a dance was held at the Fiesta Pavilion of the Manila Hotel, where the garments of the Filipinas with their huge transparent sleeves, like butterfly wings, lent a light touch to a scene never very festive. The bars were open and a few people drank and danced, but many of the dancers had other clothes already packed in anticipation of the concentration camps ahead, and at the end of the evening bartenders smashed the remaining bottles lest the oncoming Japs have too good a time. "A scotched-earth policy," some wags called it.

Hour after hour and day after day Romulo had sat in his news office answering frantic questions and sending out news releases, until on New Year's Eve, with the phone in his hand, he fell forward onto the desk, asleep. The jolt awoke him and he continued the conversation without interruption, replying helplessly to the same unanswerable question:

"When will the Japs be here?"

On January 2 the Japs answered the question for him. Dr. Claude Buss of the High Commissioner's Staff, who had stayed behind to keep the office open, and Acting Mayor Vargas improvised a white flag (no one had dreamed such a thing would be a necessity) and went out with cold grave courtesy to admit them to the city. Immediately the Commanding General, Homma, moved into General MacArthur's handsome penthouse apartment on the roof of the Manila Hotel, where, if he had time, he was able to avail himself of the finest military library in the East.

The invaders at once released the Japs interned after Pearl Harbor. (Though many loyal Filipinos, being of Japanese blood, looked like Japs themselves, a distinction had been easy to make, for the man born and bred in Japan, who had spent his babyhood hanging on his mother's back with his legs wrapped around her waist, had grown up abnormally bowlegged, and the resulting heavy splayfooted walk had betrayed him in a moment.) Americans and British were simultaneously interned, the only Europeans left at large being Germans, Italians, and Spaniards.

Next morning Vargas was summoned to the Intendencia Building, where the Japanese colonel in charge of finance demanded that he open the vault. Vargas protested that nothing was inside but some unissued paper money, useless because unbacked, but the colonel repeated his demand a little louder and Vargas produced the safe's combination.

The direct hit on the building had sprung the door's hinges, and a mechanic was sent for to get it open. At last the colonel entered and found, as Vargas had warned, no gold or silver, only boxes of paper money. These he appropriated. Vargas demanded a receipt, and the colonel scribbled on a scrap of paper, "Received of Mr.

Vargas twenty-six boxes of paper money containing twenty-four million pesos, more or less," and signed it.

Though the money would be technically worthless until backed by gold reserve, it carried nothing on its face to show this fact, and in appropriating it the Japs had enriched themselves by twenty-four million pesos of highly negotiable local currency on their second day in town.

This was one of the few American failures of its sort; in actual fact, the main achievement of the entire pathetic struggle was in denying the enemy some of the tools for victory, from the gold and silver to Manila Bay itself. And even this achievement was not complete; Bataan did fall, the entire Philippine archipelago finally did fall to the enemy, but the Japs' timetable was badly disrupted, and when they got what they wanted it was so marred and mutilated that it did them little good. Like the Battle of Britain, it was not perfect but it was enough.

The island that was now headquarters had been rightly nick-named the Gibraltar of the East. A solid rock over three miles long and shaped like a tadpole, it was a fortress impregnable from the sea. But the Japanese, disobligingly, had not come by sea, and the enormous guns, facing in the wrong direction and rooted in cement, were doomed to stand paralyzed and impotent under the bombardment from air and shore.

There were three levels on Corregidor: Bottomside, with its docks, warehouses, and native shacks; Middleside, with its hospital, schools, and soldiers' quarters; and Topside, with its clubs, officers' homes, regimental headquarters. Overlooking everything was an old Spanish lighthouse which the Japs must have had their eyes on from the first, for never once did their guns hit this useful adjunct to naval warfare.

Late on Christmas Eve the trunks and lockers, old whiskey cases and metal containers with their hundreds of millions of pesos and dollars, were dumped on the docks, and the High Commissioner's Staff tried to disengage them from the piles of ammunition, guns, and food suddenly being poured onto the island. The wife of Woodbury Willoughby saw a young MP standing guard over a tin locker. Thinking to give him something pleasant to remember out of the war, she smiled and said:

"There's two million dollars in that thing."

He stared down at it, expressionless. "I'd rather have my forty-acre farm in West Virginia," he said finally. Money, as young Captain Leslie Doane said later, was the most valueless thing on Corregidor, and indeed, guns and food and water always did take precedence.

The staffs were assigned homes and offices on Topside, Colonel Jenks and his locker trunks settling in the guesthouse of the Officers' Club, while MacArthur's party, Quezon's, and Sayre's received wooden houses. All, however, were advised to make for Malinta Tunnel, and there, on close-packed cots, they spent their first exhausted night.

Waking on Christmas morning, they were overwhelmed by the unexpected beauty of the place. Rocky though the island was, its dense vegetation covered it with a coat of velvet, birds sang fiercely, and below its high cliffs the wide bay coveted by the Japanese stretched blue and dazzling in the morning sun. To the north rose green Mariveles Mountain on Bataan and from the west the China Sea sent in the breezes that saved the island from the humid heat that plagued the mainland. It would have seemed, had they not known otherwise, the perfect place to live.

For four days Topside, with its breezes and spaces and views, seemed the best place for the newcomers to work at their various jobs, but suddenly, on the fifth, hell broke loose. A five-hundred-pound bomb was dropped thirty feet from MacArthur's headquarters, a second took the southeast corner off the quartermaster headquarters, and a third went through the roof and three concrete floors of the barracks. The fifty-thousand-gallon water tank, after a direct hit, opened up with a rush and a roar that carried everything loose before it. For four hours bombing formations passed over in waves, unopposed, because the Far East Air Force had been shattered soon after Pearl Harbor and the island's anti-aircraft guns would not reach that high. In one morning Topside had met the enemy—and it was his.

Before the bombing the manager of the PX had been pressing Colonel Jenks to release some of his financial experts to audit his

books. When the five-hundred-pounder tore the office out by its
roots, Colonel Jenks, a large southerner with a hawk nose and hu-
morous blue eyes, remarked dryly to the earnest young officer:

"Well, boy, your office has been audited."

His own office received an auditing later the same morning. He
and Quezon sharing a taste for the finer things of life, he was smoking one of the President's personal cigars with his picture on the
band when the five-hundred-pounder removed part of his office and
moved in all the furniture from the quartermaster office next door.
Jenks leaned against the wall and let the office fall. When the dust
had settled, his sergeant poked his head out from under a table like
a turtle and said:

"I just wondered if that cigar was still going."

Jenks blew a smoke ring to show nothing really valuable had been
destroyed; nevertheless, he had fallen out of love with the officers'
guesthouse on Topside. The entire Army payroll, he felt, should
be somewhere less exposed, and he asked President Quezon for a
key to the vault.

Although Corregidor was United States territory known officially
as Fort Mills, a small area had been reserved for the Philippine
Commonwealth, and here, dug into the side of a hill with twenty
feet of dirt over it and a thick jungle on top of that, was the Fort
Knox of the Philippines. Invisible except for its deeply recessed door
and two windows, each protected by three layers of bars and shutters painted the same dark greenish gray as the landscape, it escaped the notice of the uninitiated. The whole thing was reinforced concrete, and its interior vestibule and small gray rooms
lighted by unshaded bulbs hanging from the ceiling were as cheer-
less as a prison's.

Like a prison's, too, was the elaborate formula for getting in and
out. It took three officials of the Philippine Government plus the
keeper to gain entrance, each unlocking one layer of doors with his
own particular key. The keeper at this time was the widow of the
former incumbent, a large smiling middle-aged woman suffering
from varicose veins who lived nearby with five dogs. Into this concrete cave moved Jenks and his millions. Formalities were carefully
observed; it took three keys to get him in and three important gentlemen, Major General George F. Moore, Commanding General

of the Harbor Defense, Señor de Leon, Treasurer of the Philippines, and Colonel Jenks, as well as Mrs. Wingate, who turned up faithfully, in spite of her varicose veins, each time he had business to transact. (Later these formalities were so far relaxed that a twenty-three-year-old captain was allowed the run of the place.)

Even before the war the vault had held in its small dark rooms ₱16,422,000 in one and one half peso silver coins. Some had been there as long as thirty years, ever since the United States had begun weaning the Filipinos away from the previous Spanish coinage with paper certificates and salting away the corresponding silver. There were 269 gold bars weighing 1,343,493.95 grams, the proceeds of melting down $805,410 worth of coins when the dollar was devalued in 1933. (A peso was worth fifty cents.) There were a few odd pieces of gold and silver, and there was in paper currency ₱78,-261,825. The vault was unquestionably loaded.

Now President Quezon had added the ₱240,000,000 paper he had brought over with him. And stuffed in on top of that was the hoard Sayre had collected in Manila. Following his sweeping authorizations to take whatever he deemed necessary and destroy anything else of value Sayre, his two advisers Woodbury Willoughby and E. D. Hester, and the rest of the staff had accepted, packed, and shipped how much they did not know. Into the vault it had gone, the doors were locked by the three officials and Mrs. Wingate, and a guard of United States soldiers stationed outside. These men kept a strict watch at all times, but it was suspected that their tender care was directed more urgently towards Mrs. Wingate's garden nearby. One banana and two papaya trees were growing there, and while silver and gold were money, bananas and papayas were fresh fruit and edible.

Although the staffs had thought happily to do their work in clean air when they came to Corregidor, after the Japs' welcoming salvo of the twenty-ninth they faced the facts of life and retired to Malinta Tunnel.

Their readjustment to this tunnel could hardly have required a greater effort than that of the tunnel to them, for it had been designed solely for storage purposes, and its only advantage as a living quarter was that there were tons of solid rock between it and the surface. Thirty feet in diameter, it bored right through Malinta Hill east and west, with laterals branching off like the ribs of a skeleton from the spine; of concrete and clean tile, it was perfect for storing guns. But guns need neither washrooms nor ventilation, and when men and women moved in their discomfort was extreme. The concrete walls dripped moisture, which augmented the prevailing stench of sickness, gangrene, death, impromptu latrines, and plain unwashed bodies, and while suction fans were installed in an effort to accommodate the place to human requirements, whenever bombings filled the air outside with dust these fans drew the dust down in clouds that almost suffocated the inmates. If in desperation the fans were turned off, the heat and humidity and smells pressed on the top of the head like a bag filled with buckshot, and after a time the open air, even with bombs dropping about, was the only refuge.

The day after the first Japanese bombing, as if in defiance, President Quezon was inaugurated for his second term. He was an ill man, dependent on a wheel chair and soon to die at Lake Saranac, New York, but his thin body seemed afire and his eyes indeed did blaze. Outside the entrance of Malinta Tunnel some planks had been laid under a canvas awning and a few rows of benches set facing a table. There sat General MacArthur, High Commissioner Sayre, Vice-President Sergio Osmeña, Colonel Andres Soriano, the President's financial adviser; and Chief Justice Jose Abad Santos. On one side stood a small portable organ and the crossed flags of the United States and the Philippines. (Months later Colonel Jenks, sacrificing precious space, brought these flags to the United States in a submarine.)

Its circumstances made the simple ceremony strangely solemn. Before a few American and Filipino officials Justice Santos administered the oath of office; there were short speeches by Quezon, MacArthur, and Sayre, a message from Roosevelt himself, and finally a young society lady, Miss Bewley, who with her mother had somehow got swept along with the evacuating officials, played "Hail to the Chief" and both the national anthems on the hand organ, thereby unexpectedly winning a place for herself, however small, in history.

Meanwhile the military situation was, as the dispatches put it gently, deteriorating. Since Pearl Harbor the Japanese had performed a blitzkrieg, cutting the Philippines' communications with Australia, the nearest base of reinforcements, and establishing complete aerial and naval control of the area. General MacArthur summed up grimly:

"Enemy penetration has resulted from our weakness on the sea and in the air. Surface elements of the Asiatic Fleet were withdrawn and the effect of our submarines has been negligible. Lack of airfields for modern planes permitted the Japanese unhindered day bombardment. The enemy has had utter freedom of naval and air movements." Had he been given to undignified expression he could have put it in five words: "We are now sitting ducks."

General Marshall was doing his best back in Washington; he promised to send "all help possible," and indeed all help possible was sent, but even he could not do the impossible, and daily the Philippines saw more clearly that they were expendable. And as certainty of defeat grew, those on Corregidor charged with the safekeeping or destruction of valuables began to make their preparations. The gold and silver were a problem, but the paper, which could be burned and later reissued by Washington, was child's play. Or so they thought. With the fervor of ignorance they started briskly preparing for the cremation.

For nearly six weeks Woodbury Willoughby, James Saxon, and their assistants counted and recorded millions upon millions in currency and securities. At first they worked at the vault where everything was stored, but whenever the power station was bombed the lights went out and they had to work by flickering oil lamps; furthermore, the vault was mistakenly supposed to be bombproof, and was often crowded to suffocation by people with a prejudice against being blown up. So they moved to the tunnel.

Here the conditions, though safer, were stuffier. Their desks, jammed together in the entrance to the men's sleeping corridor (there were no doors anywhere), were too few for the personnel; the typewriters were ancient and ill-natured; paper and carbons were scarce, and there were only two erasers. Headaches and short tempers became an occupational disease. But the counting went on.

The unissued ("stock") money, still in its Washington Bureau of Engraving containers, was no trouble, for each metal box held the same number of bills and only the containers themselves had to be counted. But when they got into the bank accounts of private corporations and individuals the variety was overwhelming. Each bill, each certificate, had to be recorded separately in complete detail to provide proof of ownership for later reimbursement. Some were in foreign languages and foreign currencies, and some deposit boxes contained valuables almost unclassifiable. How, for instance, was the High Commissioner's office supposed to deal with a baby's shoe?

Nevertheless, everything must be recorded—and in sextuplicate, one copy to be retained by the Commissioner's office, three to go to Washington, one to the owner, and one with the property in a sealed envelope. Finally all was counted and they knew what they had, $2,741,225 in paper, ₱28,375,420 in paper, and £10,800 of gold bullion, besides the stocks and bonds, which were harder to evaluate.

Lest these records never reach Washington by plane or ship, the details were sent immediately by radio, and the air waves were kept throbbing with names and figures.

Colonel Jenks, head of Army Finance, also kept the air waves alive with his own records, and though these hard-working financial departments knew nothing of it at the time, and were thus deprived of some innocent pleasure, these radio messages were giving the Japanese High Command some very bad hours.

Before coming to Corregidor many soldiers had carried no insurance, but now Jenks daily wrote out hundreds of applications and nightly radioed to America the names, serial numbers, amounts of policies, and beneficiary names, signing the messages with his name. Months later, when Corregidor was taken, all key men were interrogated. Jenks by that time had been ordered to Australia and Lieutenant Colonel John R. Vance had succeeded him. The Japanese, badly in need of currency for trading with local Filipinos and enraged at the emptiness of the Corregidor cupboards, put Vance on the grill. "There should be three hundred million pesos here," the Jap colonel said. "What have you done with it?"

Vance looked vastly innocent. "My superior, Colonel Jenks, burned all that."

After a short pause for swallowing, the colonel persisted, "Then where is the silver?"

Although Jenks had had nothing to do with civilian funds, Vance knew a good thing when he hit upon it. "Colonel Jenks handled all that in person," he said gently.

"And the gold?"

"Jenks again," Vance murmured, shrugging.

The colonel was visibly swelling with rage, but at the same time a certain respect came into his eye. "Jenks," he murmured, trying the name over on his tongue, "Royal Jenks. Now I remember. That's the man who kept sending out those radio messages in a code we couldn't break. Just names and numbers." How many hours the Japanese Intelligence decoding department had wasted trying to wrest military secrets from those G.I. insurance applications no one ever knew, but perhaps this deflection of their energies put off the conquest of Corregidor a fraction of a minute. At any rate, a few Americans derived a little satisfaction when they heard about it later.

Sayre and Quezon had prepared their countries' treasures for disposal (though Quezon's task was simpler in that his was in good round sums already audited: 16,422,000 silver pesos, 240,000,000 paper currency, and a few gold bars), but while there was hope of rescue they held on to it wistfully. Every day men and women crowded around the loud-speaker in the tunnel entrance and discussed the war news: When would the planes from America come? February? Surely by March. One day news came of an Allied naval victory in Macassar Strait. Now the tide had come, surely now Singapore would hold. Then Singapore went, and Corregidor was a lonely lion holding at bay a ring of jackals. But the ring was closing in, and they could no longer delay.

Someone brought a fifty-five-gallon oil drum and set it up outside the vault, and a fire was lighted in the drum. Five men with keys went into the vault and brought out a number of boxes two feet long, which were opened and the packages of bills broken apart. One by one the bills were dropped into the burning oil. For a few days Sayre's committee worked at the oil drum, Hester, Saxon, Colonel Howard Smith, and Lieutenant Colonel Sidney Huff of the United States, and Lieutenant Colonel Manuel Nieto of the Philippine Army, with casual help at various times. On one day two million dollars went up in flames, on another twenty-seven million pesos, on other days much more. At least one man of the committee was present at every session to sign the certificate of destruction.

It was wearisome work, for the money burned slowly, especially the new bills in their original packages. At times it could be even dangerous, since each day Willoughby removed as many cases from the vault as he thought the committee could dispose of, locked the vault again, and left them to the burning; but the Japanese artillery across the bay, a thing with a personality of its own, explored the Corregidor landscape like a dog after fleas, and the column of smoke from their oily bonfire made a finger rising into the sky, beckoning. Once the battery got its range they clung to it, rejoicing.

Colonel Huff, MacArthur's aide, especially desired no interference on a certain fine evening, for small ships were still running the blockade between Corregidor and the southern islands, where food was plentiful, and he had been invited for dinner aboard the *Legaspi* by President Quezon, a notable gourmet. There would be fresh fruit, meat, wine. . . . He kept his fingers crossed.

Willoughby had given them some millions of dollars' worth of paper for the day, and burning began in a high wind with a ring of G.I. kibitzers, who could never get over their fascination at the sight. Although the fact had been well publicized that much of the money was "stock," it looked like any other, and if you had not known it was illegitimate you could have been very happy with it. The G.I.s stood in a ring watching the packages being broken open and the bills dropped into the oil, each dreaming his private wistful dream. Just then the gunner on Cavite saw the black finger beckoning, and a shell dropped, so close one man was wounded badly in the stomach. The group scattered for shelter, and in the high wind the loose hundred-peso notes rose and took off like a flock of starlings. As soon as the dust settled from the shell's burst the committee returned to gather up the scattered greenbacks with the help of the G.I.s, and sadly the men dropped their handfuls into the fire.

"This money never even got to buy a single beer," one mourned.

Then another shell dropped, nearer than the last. All normal instincts told the committee what to do, but there was that pile of unburned packages; the vault was locked and they could not get back in; so the conscientious group stuck by their bonfire while the Cavite gunner had his fun. Periodically they retreated to shelter, and periodically more green birds went sailing out over the bay, but at last the harassed committee tossed in the last of the bills. By that time, however, it was long past the dinner hour, and Colonel Huff had missed one of the memorable evenings of the whole campaign. (Later he heard about it; there had been soup, rice, fish, meats, and native vegetables with all accessories, each course served with its appropriate wine, and champagne and Spanish brandy afterwards from the host's private stock.) Huff, being of a large nature, rose above his personal tragedy and carried on.

Not long after this windy afternoon Colonel Jenks paid a call on Mrs. Wingate. Jenks was an individualist who could go without food indefinitely but once in a while had to bathe, and in the tunnel even sea water was rationed at one cupful a day for bathing and shaving. In the money vault one could sometimes get a shower but one was taking a risk—Romulo had once got himself lathered all over just in time to have the pressure fade and die on him; however, Mrs. Wingate's house, being on a separate system, had a fairly steady dribble, and Jenks happened to pass that way from time to time. Today Mrs. Wingate greeted him with a puzzled smile and produced her ironing board for his inspection. It seemed that some days before a group of enlisted men had borrowed it, and when it was returned, there, on the cloth, was the indelible print of green-backs.

Jenks sent for the men remembered to have been kibitzing that afternoon and lectured them gently. "Now, boys, you've got to return that stuff. I know you fished it out of the bay and you feel as if it's yours. But it isn't. And it's got to be destroyed . . . Keep it out of the hands of the enemy, and all that stuff." Sorrowfully the men brought in their harvest—though, of course, no one knows whether *every* hundred-peso bill came back.

When the American committee had had a few days at the burning drum the Philippine committee, Osmeña, Santos, Hester, and Smith, began on the ₱240,000,000, twenty million the first long steaming afternoon, and so on, day after day after day. Money became the most *boring* thing in life.

News was daily getting worse from both overseas and close at hand. Everyone looked at everyone else and said, "As Bataan goes, so goes Corregidor," and that was ominous, for by this time Bataan was starving. The meat was full of maggots, and helpless mess sergeants argued angrily that a few maggots did *not* make it inedible. The soldiers were foraging for themselves, shooting wild pigs, wild chickens, lizards, snakes, and monkeys. One man, obviously an epicure, complained wryly that eating monkey was not so bad, except when the little thing's hand turned up on your plate.

The Japs were getting closer, and as they closed in the need became more pressing to do something about the gold—gold, which, unlike paper money, was good in all places and under all circumstances. Information as to its ownership was sent out by radio and submarine mail, and then an inspiration was awaited.

Although sinking or burying would be quick and relatively easy, so long as it was physically within reach of the Japs they were likely to find it, and so other means were sought. Early in February it came. Several submarines had made trips through the blockade to bring guns and ammunition to the besieged island; great with steel they came in, like a woman great with child, and after delivering their burden took on a similar weight of ballast, water if nothing better offered, to submerge for the return journey. Unfortunately one of those slip-ups that can occur in even the best regulated war had brought severe disappointment to the anti-aircraft batteries. They had requested high-altitude fuses for their three-inch ammunition, but the submarine had turned up simply with more three-inch shells with standard fuses. Faces were red all around, some with rage and others with embarrassment, and after some pounding of tables another submarine was ordered in to rectify the mistake. The problem of the gold having entered the conversation about the same time, it was decided to kill this second bird with the same stone.

The *Trout* was the stone that was to do it, and having been told to avoid combat on the way north, Commander Fenno ordered out all the torpedoes he could spare along with everything else disposable, blew out the ballast, and then loaded ammunition in every cranny—the right ammunition. Boxes of shells were stacked to the overhead in both torpedo hatches, in the companionways, in the wardroom and the battery compartment. If a locker were pulled open, out spilled shells, while in the bunks instead of men were piled equally important medical supplies. Thus bulging, the *Trout* slipped into Manila Bay on February 3. A motor torpedo boat met her, and in the darkness she crept to the dock and began unloading.

Meanwhile young Captain Leslie Doane, transportation officer of the 60th Coast Artillery, had been alerted. He was regularly in charge of the motor vehicle pool which supplied trucks and cars for jobs all over the island, and since there was a transportation job this night Captain Doane had been given some keys and told to take the detail personally. At the pool were several drivers who had been on duty all that day, and they stumbled sleepily to the trucks, cursing automatically. No one expected to have an undisturbed night's sleep, but it was obligatory to grumble a little, just to keep one's franchise. Now as they drove to the vault Doane explained their duties.

At about that same time Willoughby, Saxon, Hester, and Robert Huffcutt, asleep in the men's lateral in the tunnel, woke at the touch they had been expecting for some days. They knew of the *Trout's* commission, but no one knew when to expect her, for Japanese aerial surveillance was strict, and in clear tropical waters undersea craft, even very deeply submerged, were all too visible. Every day at noon a lone plane went over, never dropping bombs but circling inquisitively and then letting out one trial balloon to test the wind drift. "Photo Joe," who shot with his camera alone, was more dreaded than a loaded bomber, and if Joe caught sight of the *Trout* at the bottom, the jig was up. However, on February 3, in the dead of night, the *Trout* made it, and now haste was being made in the High Commissioner's quarters. Silently the men slipped on clothes and in the bright tropical night hurried down to the dock at Bottomside, where the crew of the submarine was passing out boxes of ammunition in frantic haste, for before daybreak they had to be loaded and gone.

Doane and his men had been met at the vault by Vice-President Osmeña, Chief Justice Santos, and General Valdes, the man in direct charge of the bullion. All the keys were brought into play, and the group stepped inside and switched on the unshaded bulb hanging from the ceiling. Through the front rooms they led a small group of enlisted men, past piles of boxes containing unburned paper money and bags and boxes of silver, to the rear rooms. There, stacked neatly against the walls, was all the gold the Philippines possessed.

At the description of their assignment the eyes of the sleepy young G.I.s had popped open with interest; here was something better than their usual nighttime circuit of the island picking up dead bodies. "Jeez, what next in this crazy war," they had grumbled, but that was only because grumbling was the recognized reaction to any order. Now they surveyed the gold, more wealth than any of them had ever imagined in physical terms, and their faces fell. It was far from the gold of Tiffany's window or childhood's fairy tales. It neither glittered nor shone, but was stacked in dirty brown bricks, with here and there a lighter yellow chunk, bars and blocks of all sizes, some wrapped, some naked, some with tickets attached and some with weights stamped into their surface. A young G.I. bent to lift one the size of a pound of butter, quickly adjusting himself to its surprising weight by bringing arm and back muscles into play, and one brick proved enough for each man to carry at a time. A small neat stack laid over the rear axle was, Doane decided, as much as the springs could handle, and as soon as it was assembled a guard jumped aboard and down the road to the dock they bumped.

Clinging to the side of the concrete dock was the black 298-foot-long object, like a whale with a hump, out of which ammunition was being lifted. By midnight the last of the fuses was being unloaded; the gold bricks had collected on the dock nearby, and the moment the tide of ammunition ceased flowing out of her, the tide of gold started in. From hand to hand they were passed in a kind of fire-bucket brigade, across the gangplank, down the ladder and into the torpedo room and under the bunks, anywhere there was any room. Six and a half tons of gold, all that belonged to the Philippine Commonwealth besides all that Sayre had collected. But when Commander Fenno tried to submerge, it was not ballast enough.

They had gutted the *Trout* so thoroughly that she was too light, so hastily they took in all the water ballast their tanks would hold, but still she lay on the surface. They looked at their watches—only a little while till daybreak—and jumping ashore, started grabbing sandbags and rocks, hand-passing them aboard. A low bark of protest went up from the island's defenders. "Hey, we need those sandbags," they snapped, and that was the end of the sandbags as ballast.

Then one of the finance personnel spoke up. "There's lots of silver up in the vault. Some of that might as well go out."

Doane had already gone (he kept on the move all night, visiting one driver after another in the lonely blackout stations), but the keys and the trucks and enough officials to make it legal went back and grabbed up some bags of silver. One by one they went in too, counted as they disappeared—630 bags, ₱630,000—and the last bag was dropped as the first streak of dawn appeared.

But still no paper records of stocks and bonds had got on board, so the commander agreed to lie at the bottom all day and return the following night. The Navy men who had helped with the loading, the Army men who had trucked the stuff down went back up the hill to catch an hour of sleep before the day's fighting began, the residents of the tunnel returned to their fetid home. And all of them watched the sky, praying that Photo Joe might fail that day.

When twilight came, Willoughby, Saxon, and Tip Parker loaded their boxed paper into a launch and under the protection of a torpedo boat made for the spot in the bay agreed upon. But no submarine showed itself, and for three hours they chugged back and forth, rechecking their plans, churning the screw of the launch to catch the underwater ear of the submarine, while the freshening wind bounced them about on the chopping waves. Finally the whale's hump appeared, and in a delight so great they forgot to be angry they completed their transaction. Although transferring cargo from one bobbing craft to another in open sea was like rifle practice on horseback, the securities were at last safely stowed below.

Before going down the commander grinned, "Anybody want to go along?" and there were several wordless sighs, but no one spoke and he disappeared down the hatch, waving. The High Commissioner's men returned to the tunnel knowing that when the Japanese came to the Rock they would be at least that much poorer.

Next day Willoughby received a shock, for returning to the vault for a routine inspection, he saw a square of gold the size of a matchbox hiding behind a grating. He pocketed it sadly; and they had tried so hard to be careful, too. Well, that was the confusion of war.

Meanwhile the *Trout* was escaping to America, and the following month, in a ceremony at Pearl Harbor witnessed by Admiral Chester Nimitz, Lieutenant General Delos C. Emmons awarded the Distinguished Service Cross to Commander Frank Wesley Fenno, and the Silver Star Medal to his ten officers and fifty-seven men. Next year the Presidential Unit Citation was added, and to Commander Fenno went the Navy Cross, with two gold stars for taking his S.S. 202 "past enemy shore batteries under cover of darkness . . . into Manila Bay before the fall of Corregidor and bringing out a vast amount of gold, silver, and securities belonging to the Philippine Commonwealth and to banks, mines, and residents of the Islands."

President Roosevelt, alarmed by reports of Quezon's failing health, had been sending repeated invitations for a visit to Washington, and at last in February arrangements were made for a submarine to pick up some of his party and some of the High Commissioner's. Before he left, Quezon removed from the vault some millions of paper currency to leave with the troops in the southern islands, but the rest of the paper, and the silver, ₱15,792,000, he turned over to General MacArthur.

"Do with it what you think best," he said.

At that moment the silver formally became the property and responsibility of the United States Army.

On learning they were to be evacuated, the High Commissioner's staff hurried to complete their bonfires, but they were so well known to the Jap gunners by now that they moved into Malinta Tunnel, where they cut each of the bills into three pieces and then dumped them into incinerators. It was hurry, hurry, now, but at last, on the day before the submarine appeared, the money was gone and only the securities, which were to go along, remained.

All day on the twenty-third the ten members of Sayre's party nervously pretended nothing was afoot, but everyone in the nearby laterals knew that the hasty destruction of money, papers, and records, and the sudden packing of a few selected garments, could not be coincidence. Their friends quietly handed them notes for their families, saying, "How glad we are for you," while their eyes said, "How we envy you." At seven General MacArthur came to say good-by, and the four women, who had been told to wear slack suits and be prepared for anything, waited tensely for their menfolk. At last the party was driven down to the dock and a launch picked them up for their rendezvous with the *Swordfish*.

Down the conning tower's ladder backed the men and women, down into hot weary air already worked over by sixty-eight men. Although she surfaced at night, during the days the submarine ran along the bottom, and so enervating were the heat and foul air that the passengers spent the next thirteen days lying flat on their bunks in an irreducible minimum of clothing. Only Sayre and Hester upheld the dignity of the State Department by keeping on their shirts.

Since enemy destroyers roamed the waters, periodically the *Swordfish* sank to extraordinary depths, her fans and ventilators cut off, while they waited tensely for a depth bomb, but at last they landed at Fremantle in Western Australia, safe though dehydrated, after having picked up the exhilarating radio news somewhere in the Indian Ocean that the *Trout* had landed at an unnamed port with her gold intact.

When they reached America, the calm beauty of countryside out of range of Japanese guns, the untroubled eyes that had not seen what they had seen gave them the same kind of shock that, a few weeks later, the starving survivors of Bataan were to receive on arriving at Corregidor, where people still wore shoes and ate two meals every day.

Immediately on disembarking in San Francisco, Woodbury Willoughby, with almost paternal pride, hurried to the Federal Reserve Bank to check up on the *Trout's* gold. His reception was cordial, but he noticed that although he was invited down to the vault he was never allowed within twenty feet of its door except in the presence of two officers. And passing through a room where twelve or fourteen girls were checking the inventories he and his assistants had made so laboriously on Corregidor, the officials signaled to the clerks to stop work and cover the papers while he passed. He smiled; routine security, no doubt.

The conversation opened with congratulations on the success of Willoughby's handling of the securities. They were in first-class order. When the gold was mentioned, however, the voices drooped slightly. Taking a deep breath and doing his best not to look embarrassed, an official wanderingly described the way their office had checked the gold against the Corregidor records, and the way the United States Mint had checked *their* checking. There had been a double checking all round after that, and an investigation of everyone's past history—the crew of the *Trout*, the crew of the cruiser that had picked it up *from* the *Trout*, even the crew of the trucks in San Francisco. The squirming official did not add "and yours," but the words seemed to hang unspoken in the air. Eventually he did manage to squeeze out the unhappy fact, which he hated to mention in view of the magnificent rescue of so many millions and which he trusted Mr. Willoughby would forgive his bringing up— the ridiculous situation was that in spite of all their checking there did seem to be a slight discrepancy between the records and the gold on hand, a very small piece of gold, really, worth only $306 —but still—government funds . . . The voice died away miserably.

Willoughby opened his brief case. "You mean this?" he asked, and laid the matchbox-sized bit on the table. The ring of faces, which had been quivering with discomfort, burst into sunshine. The gold had come home and the books could be closed.

By March no one in the Philippines believed any longer that the expected convoys of relief troops would arrive, and when General MacArthur was ordered to Australia to consolidate all Pacific operations, leaving Lieutenant General Jonathan Wainwright in his place, every face wore the dulled look of those looking inward and backward because they could not bear to look out and forward.

But even with defeat their only certainty, people went on numbly doing their duty. Before leaving, MacArthur had turned over the keys of the vault to Jenks with instructions to destroy at his discretion, and Jenks immediately named a committee consisting of his chief disbursing officer, Lieutenant Colonel Vance, Lieutenant Colonel Leroy Edwards, and Major Jardeleza of the Philippine

Army Finance Department. Now that the money was the Army's responsibility, Vance organized a group of junior officers for Lateral 16, and whenever nothing more pressing interfered they went at the paper millions.

Brigadier General Lewis Beebe dropped by Lateral 16 on a routine tour of inspection and stood, a dead cigar in his mouth, fascinatedly watching the group sitting around a table stolidly rending bills into two or three parts each, taking especial care of the serial number. As he stood, the distant power plant was shaken by a bomb and the lights went out. There were a few moments of aimless conversation to fill the pause, and when the lights went on, every man was sitting motionless, his hands spread before him on the table. This was rule number one.

Rule number two was that periodically all the pieces were to be gathered from the floor like autumn leaves and stuffed into a mattress cover in the presence of a member of the committee, who accompanied the mattress cover to the bakery oven on Bottomside and watched it shrink to ashes.

Beebe watched the eight pairs of hands resume their stolid cutting and tearing. "How does it feel, Jack," he asked Vance, "to be deliberately destroying good money like this?"

Vance smiled. "Want to know? Here." He touched a match to a note and held it to Beebe's cigar. "Now when you get back to the States you can tell people you lit your cigar with a five-hundred-peso match."

Thus, in supplying a light for a cigar, a smoke signal for Japanese gunfire, and fuel for a bakery, the Philippines' fund performed their last service and were no more.

Not every peso was burned, of course. There were the damp bills ironed out on Mrs. Wingate's board; no one ever knew whether they were all returned or not. There was a suitcase, filled with bills cut into three pieces, which was found buried in the rubble years later; no one knew who put it there or what he had thought to do with it. And there is still the gasoline can.

Under ordinary circumstances the money was taken by two men from the vault to the finance lateral, but in emergencies formalities were overlooked, and on one such occasion a load made the trip under the care of a single driver. Two hundred yards from the entrance he parked his truck and went inside to notify the finance people that the money had arrived. During those few minutes an unnamed man removed a quarter of a million dollars and hid them in a gasoline can, which he later buried. Although the money was later invalidated, at the moment he was for all practical purposes vastly wealthy, and might have had a riotous time had there been anything to spend it on. But the PX had practically nothing but cigarettes, which were rationed, and money was of so little use that many men did not even bother to draw their pay. Food and water were the important things in life.

On April 9, Bataan finally fell, and its starving thousands poured across the North Channel onto the Rock. This evacuation was a sister operation to that of Dunkirk half across the world, and as in that other, every craft, from the tiny native *banca* to the biggest Army mine layer and Navy submarine tender, snatched its share of glassy-eyed soldiers and terrified civilians out of the reaching fingers of the Japs and ferried them through the mines underneath and the shells overhead to the Rock. Every tiniest boat, every stick of wood, had its clinging refugee, many of them swept out to sea with the current, some to be rescued by larger ships, some never to be seen again. But when the wretched thousands crawled ashore to momentary safety, gaunt, half naked, and covered with thick black oil from the fuel tanks of sunken ships there was no similar exhilaration, no triumphant conviction of a spiritual victory. Instead, defeat weighed them down like a physical burden.

The quartermaster, Drake, who by a little fancy bookkeeping had managed both to obey orders to keep a reserve on Corregidor and get more to Bataan than the books allowed, now issued a double ration of food and as many shoes as the supply permitted. But within a few days the population of the island had increased from nine thousand to fifteen thousand, and the hospital beds were now triple-deckers.

And no matter how many bravely protested otherwise, despair had taken over. The Bataan refugees, resentful of the "soft" life on Corregidor, where no one had gone shoeless or eaten snake and where none had met Japs hand to hand, squatted numbly five deep along the walls in the main tunnel and refused to budge. The authorities tried to clean them and put them on coast defense; a few responded, but more stared back in a daze mixed of starvation and shock, compounding the prevailing despair.

Still, the motions and noises of defiance were not yet altogether subdued. Shooting went on, the Voice of Freedom went on, hypnotized by the island's *ideé fixe*; even if all they could do was draw a little blood from the enemy and weaken his striking arm, delay the *coup de grâce* until others could attack him elsewhere, that was reason enough for going on. So the radio shouted defiance and the Rock took it and took it, and meanwhile the dead piled up in the tunnels and the reek increased.

Beside all this silver was a trivial matter, but Jenks had had orders, and so after a consultation with General Moore a series of instructions went out.

One of the craft that had assisted at the Dunkirk of the East, evacuating five hundred key personnel from Bataan, was an Army mine layer, the *Harrison*, which had picked her way across the North Channel between the mines she herself had helped to lay. Now she was given another historic assignment.

The *Harrison* was designed, like a Leghorn hen, for laying especially large eggs. With booms and winches capable of handling excessive weights she could have been seen, before the war, planting mines in the North Channel between Corregidor and Bataan, practicing being at war, and then as regularly picking them up again, while between times she ferried passengers between Manila and the Rock. When the war games were played for keeps, her crew of forty-two under Captain James Murray, with Raphael Garofalo as chief mate, repaired cables at night, maintained mine fields in the daytime, and slept when they could. When the fuel situation became critical in February she had been laid up in a cove behind Fort Hughes, but recently her first assistant engineer, Arnold Bocksel, had salvaged enough oil from the double bottom tanks of a sunken freighter to give her a fresh lease on life, and now out she bustled to help win the war.

A few days after the fall of Bataan, Captain Murray was called into the headquarters of General George F. Moore, commander of harbor defense, and given an order, and when he returned to the *Harrison* he took Garofalo into his cabin and shut the door.

"We're going to sink that silver," he said.

Previously General Moore had given another order to a young lieutenant in the Battery Commander Station on Malinta Hill, where the gunfire was plotted. He was to plot the position of a deep spot in the South Channel between Corregidor and Caballo Island, away from the Army's contact mines. These bearings Moore had given Murray. If an accurate record had been kept of this transaction hundreds of hours and thousands, perhaps millions, of pesos might have been saved later. But during these days *any* record was unusual.

At dusk one evening in the third week of April the *Harrison*, with a thousand-pound anchor hanging from her boom, shoved off from South Dock towards the small island of Caballo. Halfway there, at the designated spot, Murray gave the signal, the winch was released, and the anchor dropped. The anchor's cable was attached to a marker buoy about two feet in diameter; when Murray turned to look at it on the return trip, it was barely visible, but that was just as well, considering the Japs' sharp eyes.

While orders had been going around, the young captain from the 60th Coast Artillery had been getting his share. Leslie Doane, busy in the motor pool, had been summoned to the office of Colonel Chester Elmes in Malinta Tunnel, where Jenks and others of the Finance Department were seated.

"You took the gold and paper money out of the vault," he was told. "Now here's a man-sized job. The silver is to go down to a barge, to be dumped. Probably every Jap in the Orient knows we have the stuff here, but try to keep it quiet that we're throwing it overboard."

In the Navy tunnel in Malinta some of the men from sunken vessels and the naval base were sitting drinking coffee made with sea water when a warrant officer hurried in. "Who's off duty tonight?" he asked.

Several sadly raised their hands.

"I want volunteers for a work detail. It's not burying—something different." No one moved. He pointed at half a dozen men. "Come on. This really is different, this is something you can tell your grandchildren about."

"I know these volunteer goon parties," one grunted. "I'd rather stay home so I'll *have* some grandchildren." But they trudged off wearily and joined a group at the South Dock.

The silver was nothing new to Doane, the transportation officer, for since the departure of the gold the vault had been no longer the sacrosanct place of old and the 3rd Battalion of the 60th C.A. had taken over the vestibule and right front room as a command post. He knew the peculiar thing about it that would make it more difficult to handle than the corresponding amount of United States currency would have been. Before the United States occupation of the Philippines the common currency had been the silver Mexican cartwheel, the dollar Mex. Filipinos liked it, for it was large and heavy and gave one the feeling of majestic riches, but in 1903 the United States had created a Philippine currency based on the dollar, with a peso worth fifty cents as standard. But that was not the same, for a peso with only fifty cents' worth of silver in it was so small it was no fun to handle, and the Filipinos continued partial to the dollar Mex. So to wean them away the United States minted an absolutely irresistible coin, one actually larger than the dollar although worth only half as much—416 grains against 412.50. At last the Filipinos began rejecting the dollar Mex; after three years the peso's content was sneaked down somewhat, to 308 grains, where it remained until World War II, but even this meant that it contained nearly eighty cents' worth of silver—and was that much heavier to handle than it should have been.

Doane had asked Jenks whether he would accompany the silver to the dock, but Jenks shook his head. "The silver's General Moore's baby after it leaves the vault," he said, "and the fewer people who know where it is dumped, the fewer can give it away if the Japs question us."

So Colonel Vance and Doane together, in the light of the glaring unshaded bulb, helped the men lift out the boxes of silver—a thousand coins to a bag, six bags to a box made of two thicknesses of hard wood and weighing thirty or forty pounds—and carry them to the waiting truck. Doane had figured how much would make one night's work at the dock, and as soon as that much was loaded, two enlisted men jumped up in front and down to the water front they went. There the Navy "volunteers" and the officials of the Philippine Finance Department, waiting with two-wheeled handcarts, took over.

In darkness and silence twenty or thirty men lifted out the heavy boxes and bags onto the carts, wheeled them along the dock to an eighty-foot Army barge tied alongside, and there tilted them onto its deck like so many wheelbarrowfuls of earth. The boxes were solidly built and the bags made of tough canvas, but a few had broken open in the unceremonious handling and a number of pesos were strewn about the docks. Some of the men, full of high spirits even in these dolorous times, were sparked to play by the sight of shiny coins lying ownerless and unclaimed.

"Bet you a million pesos I can throw more coins down that smokestack than you can," Robert Burnett challenged his neighbor in the dark, pointing to an inshore patrol boat lying sunk on the other side of the dock, her stack protruding a few feet out of the water invitingly, and for a few minutes, until the clang of metal against metal rang out too loud, one method of throwing money away gave place to another.

Eldon Byerly shook his youthful head. "Someday, if I ever get out of this here mess, I'm sure going to wish I had some of this money," he sighed.

Meanwhile four members of the *Harrison's* crew, in a small motor launch, had pushed out in the general direction of the olive-drab marker buoy dropped two nights before. They were armed with a flashlight, but even with its aid they went puttering back and forth scanning the surface. "Either some damn Jap's cut the cable or the current's running so strong it's pulling the buoy under," they muttered. Anyway, after more fruitless searching they headed to shore. The night was getting on, and if the Japs saw them the fat was in the fire.

As fast as possible they located a length of heavy wire which they slung under the launch from side to side, like a skipping rope, and slowly, cautiously, ran back and forth until a jerk on the wire told them it had picked up the buoy's cable. Then with the flashlight they blinked a signal to the *Harrison's* skipper, and he steamed out to meet them, barge in tow. Directly beside the buoy, directly over the deepest spot in the South Channel, they dumped the silver overboard.

"We'll drop a big white buoy beside that little one tomorrow," said Murray. "We've got to dump the stuff always in the same spot, and it takes too long to find it this way." So a large white one was dropped the next day and the dumping was always done at that exact spot.

This, at least, was the intention. But there were many things to come in the way—currents, lack of time, the dark—and many other things to seem more precious—human lives, for instance. Even a large white buoy could not always remain immediately above its anchor, the ebb tide sweeping it in one direction and the flood in another. The tides demanded, too, that the skipper sometimes make a swing westward before fetching up at his goal, and sometimes a swing eastward, which meant that if the men began unloading before reaching the buoy the silver might land anywhere within a mile radius.

And seldom did they wait for the buoy, for under the constant cross fire of Japanese guns from Bataan and Cavite the only thought was cover, and soon after they left shore the boxes began going over the side in long curving trails with a big pile at the end.

On the sixth night, when Billy Short had chugged out to the buoy for the last time, the small olive-drab buoy and the large white one were perforated by machine gun fire and sent to the bottom. Now the position of the main body of the silver was nothing but a memory, known to the skipper, the Commanding General, and the lieutenant in the Battery Station. Although many others in the half dusk had taken private sights, lining up a lighthouse here with a point of land there, not one of them was true, and only three people knew what the position really was. Of these, the skipper was killed two weeks later, the lieutenant's records were presumably destroyed along with everything else on May 5, and the Commanding General forgot the exact figures. They never turned up.

At the time, no one cared about silver, for on April 29, the Emperor's birthday, four hundred guns suddenly exploded into a gigantic attack that pulverized every inch of the island, while wave after wave of planes passed over in an almost continuous air raid. Corregidor knew the end was in sight now. A United States plane which had somehow got through to the island evacuated a few stra-

tegic officers and some of the women, and the *Spearfish*, a submarine, took out Colonel Jenks, loaded down with twelve trunks and
mail sacks (and those two flags used at the Inauguration), twelve
other officers, fifteen nurses, and one Navy wife. General Wainwright had been urged to leave too, but he refused, and his refusal
cheered the doomed men and women as only one other sentimental
gesture had done—during a blinding barrage the main flagpole on
Topside had been snapped by a bullet and the American ensign
started fluttering to the ground, but before it touched, a group of
men had leaped out into the fire, caught it, and raised it again.
This was the last pleasant sight anyone saw for three years.

On May 2 the Japanese in Manila lifted their blackout and the
city sparkled with synthetic gaiety. Station KZRH broadcast news
of a magnificent banquet being given by the High Command, but
at the same time the shelling increased in violence and the frivolous
news did not deceive the island's defenders. They were being softened up for the kill and they knew it. Sternly they set themselves
to fight off invasion, but the huge guns of the fortress, planted years
before to meet attack from the sea, were impotent to meet it coming from land, and like a shackled giant the island stood helpless
while a horde of ants crawled up its limbs and swallowed it bit by
bit.

The invasion began on May 5, when, shortly after dusk, the Japanese massed on the shore of Bataan, a group of expendable men
who called themselves "human bullets," "the living dead." Together they sang softly the high, thin, haunting melody of the
Prayer in the Dawn and then clambered silently into seven landing
barges. At exactly ten-thirty, as they moved across the channel, the
Japanese batteries opened a protecting barrage so terrible that everyone on the island knew instantly that this was it.

The staff in Malinta had gathered in Lateral 3, wistfully anxious
not to be alone, when General Beebe walked in. "It's happened,"
he said. "They're coming in near Cavalry Point and James Ravine."

Now the group sprang into action; it was time for carrying out the
last order. While the Voice of Freedom sent out its last appeal—
no longer for resistance from its friends, but now only for a peace
conference with its foes—and the Navy scuttled its radio station
with a final salute, "The Navy's twenty-five hundred officers and

men reaffirm their loyalty and devotion to country, families, and friends," while the isolation was being made complete, the destruction was being completed too.

In the Commanding General's office files were opened, desk and table drawers pulled out, field desks emptied. Maps were torn from the walls and cut into bits, records were shredded. Scraps piled up as high as the men's hips. While the steel war raged outside the tunnel the paper war was being waged within.

In the finance lateral activity was just as frantic, for while the Philippine Commonwealth's money had been disposed of, that of the United States Army itself, two million pesos and a tiny fraction of gold, was ammunition for the Japs that must be snatched from their hands. All night in Lateral 16, Colonel Vance and Colonel Edwards passed out packages of bills to a group of fifteen or twenty volunteers armed with scissors and photo trimmers. As the scraps fell they were gathered into mattress ticking, and by morning a striped bag seven feet long and three feet wide was stuffed like a sausage. Vance dragged it to Lateral 18 and left it lying. So ended the payroll of the United States Army in the Philippines.

Edwards had a smaller private fund in his safe for Fort Mills salaries, and towards morning, after a night with the larger funds, he returned to his own lateral. Several G.I.s lay sleeping on the floor, so exhausted that even dread of the future could not keep them awake, and Colonel Edwards, an elderly man, looked at the youthful faces, gray with fatigue and filth. In his safe were a few hundred bills, and very quietly he divided them into fifteen piles and laid forty pesos by the empty hand of each sleeping boy so that when they were captured they would have something to buy them a little mercy. The gold and silver, about two hundred and fifty dollars, he put into a large leather case and buried under the crumbling walls.

After a night of pounding that shook out the lights in the tunnel and drove clouds of dust along every lateral, General Wainwright decided that the end had been reached, and that a white flag must be run up at noon. So once more destruction was the order of the day, destruction of ammunition, firearms, food.

General Drake, with a double-barreled gesture, opened up every store of provisions, and canned fruits, canned meat and sausage, tomatoes and cigarettes, everything movable was hastily consumed or stored under blankets against the privations of prison camp. Like condemned men on the last day, they ate royally.

Meanwhile Wainwright and Beebe and their aides, carrying a sheet tied to a bamboo pole, had gone to meet their conquerors. For hours, while they dickered with General Homma in an attempt to surrender something less than all the forces in the Philippines, the thousands in the tunnel waited under a bombardment that increased instead of easing. Finally, so long were they away, it seemed they must have been killed, which meant that Drake had succeeded to the command, and thus to the task of surrendering all over again. So after enlisting the aid of Colonel Theodore Kalukuka, a linguist proficient in five languages, he arranged for a truce and the orderly evacuation of the tunnel. Slowly and in the strictest silence, while the fierce eyes of a Japanese major and a corps of flame throwers watched for any belligerent movement, the thousands of Americans and Filipinos filed out with their hands over their heads into the noonday sun. As they passed the last barricade someone's pet monkey, holding in his tiny hand a jagged can with one golden peach, chattered and grinned his mirthless death's-head grin.

Drake watched the last of the men stumble out to imprisonment and slowly turned back into the tunnel, where there was no movement except the rats'. Now, mixed with the torn paper and broken weapons and rubble and powdered plaster were bits of food, fruit skins, bones, crusts, left over from the last square meal of the departed men, and the joyous squeal and rustle in the suddenly empty corridors were lonelier sounds than pure silence. Drake dropped onto the bunk in his office and sat with his head in his hands, numb beyond thinking.

After a long time he became conscious that someone was near, and looking up, saw directly in front of him, feet spread wide in typical splayfooted stance, a Japanese soldier. Like the others who had taken over the tunnel, he wore black cloth shoes with silent rubber soles and a camouflage suit with a green-netted hood thrown back off the face. A rifle hung over his shoulder and a samurai sword dangled from his hand. His face was expressionless as they stared at each other silently for a minute.

"Can you sing?" the Jap asked suddenly, in passable English.

Of perhaps a hundred ways the conversation might have turned, this was the last Drake would have imagined, but wrenching his mind, numb with two days' loss of sleep, back to attention, he nodded. "Yes, a little."

"You know 'Old Brack Joe'?"

Wondering, Drake nodded again. "I suppose so."

"You sing it." Drake only stared, and the Jap repeated firmly, "You sing 'Old Brack Joe' for me."

As of noon of that day the Japs were giving the orders and the Americans were taking them, so the tall, military-mustached General opened his mouth and began uncertainly, "'Gone are the days when my heart was young and gay . . .'" Queer; was the Jap forcing these bitter words on his captive for a specially delicate form of torture? It seemed not, for he had sat down comfortably, resting his rifle against the bunk and his sword across his knees, and his head swayed gently as the melody gathered volume towards the close, "'Old—black—Joe.'"

At the finale the Jap beamed and nodded several times. "Sing it again."

With an inward shrug of incomprehension the General complied, louder this time and, apparently, better, for the Jap demanded another encore. By now the General's sense of the ridiculous was nipping at the edges of his mind, and as he sat in the shambles of his country's defeat bellowing a sentimental folk ballad to his conqueror, a hope that someone would appear to end it mingled with a hope that no one would ever know. Actually there did come a break in the endless repetition, for the Jap now joined in and began to sing with him:

"'Gone are the days when my heart was young and gay . . .'" Off key it was, and the voice curiously falsetto, but confident of the words and faithful to the last dolorous "'Old—brack—Joe.'"

Drake turned to him graciously. "You sing very well."

The soldier bobbed his head in delighted acknowledgment.

"Where did you learn such good English? Why are you so fond of 'Old Black Joe?'"

"I rearn Enrish in high school, Nagasaki. American songs part of course. 'Old Brack Joe' my favorite." He waved a finger like a conductor giving the upbeat. "Once more." And they sang it through once more.

As the last mournful "Joe" died away he stood up, bowed from the waist, and shook hands. "Good-by, sir," he said, and his rubber-soled shoes carried him away as silently as he had appeared. Drake sat down again, staring into space.

While he was still trying to fit together the disparate pieces of his day a distant murmur and rustle became, as it approached, a swarm of little silent-footed men pouring through the tunnels, picking up scraps, poking into drawers, turning over furniture. When they saw Drake two of them rushed forward hungrily as if to take his life, but all they were looking for was jewelry and watches—indeed, the left arm of each was wrist watches up to the elbow. Everything of value went but Drake's West Point ring, which he managed to slip under his shirt, and then they swarmed on and he sat down again to wait.

Later the island's two other senior officers were herded into the tunnel beside him, and finally, much later that night, Wainwright returned to report that his attempt to stave off unconditional surrender had failed. The occupation of the entire Philippines had begun.

The defeated troops were rounded up and everyone of importance held for questioning regarding money, food, and weapons, the most sought-after spoils of war, but the Japanese interrogators revealed by their chagrin how complete the Americans' self-destruction had been. Colonel Vance and the others concerned with the money were put on the mat immediately, but the ignorance of them all was monumental, the only man, it seemed, who knew *anything* being Colonel Jenks, who had left just three days before.

No, they all shook their heads blandly, the gold was no longer on Corregidor, it had gone out months ago. No, the silver was not here either, Colonel Jenks had attended to that too. No, no one had helped him, the disposal of everything had been his sole responsibility. For a while the absent Colonel Jenks came out as a combination of lone wolf and Paul Bunyan, who had not only devised a code no Jap could break but all by himself had performed miracles of weight lifting and transportation.

The paper money was a different matter, however, and since it was safely destroyed Vance had no hesitancy in telling about that. Indeed, he derived some grim amusement from ushering his questioners into Lateral 18 and showing them the mattress cover on the floor. The Japanese colonel did not seem nearly so amused.

But from that day on more important things than money occupied the minds of the captured Americans, food, water, survival, for then began the shocking treks from one prison camp to another, camps in the Philippines, in Formosa, Manchuria, Japan, Korea. The women and some of the United States officials were interned in Santo Tomas University; the Filipinos who had shown "hostile intent and activities towards the Japanese" went to Forts Santiago and Los Baños, names thereafter synonymous with torture; and some men remained for a while on Corregidor in labor parties. But by now communications with the outside world had been cut off and a tremendous silence had fallen over the Philippines.

Three months before the fall of Corregidor, and halfway around the world, an event had taken place which was seemingly unrelated to the pesos in Manila Bay but which was, some years later, to have a deep influence on their history.

The magnificent French liner *Normandie*, only recently taken over by the United States and renamed S.S. *Lafayette*, was lying in her berth at Pier 88, Hudson River, New York City. The second-largest ship in the world, costing thirty-eight million dollars and capable of carrying a whole army to Europe at a single clip, she was being remodeled and stripped of the pre-war elegancies unsuitable to a troopship. On February 9, 1942, a workman accidentally (there was never any proof of sabotage) brought his blowtorch too close to the kapok life preservers stacked in the grand lounge, and in a moment the flames were roaring to the ceiling. Within one hour the interior of the ship was an inferno.

The Fire Department, hoping to prevent the blaze from spreading to the nearby docks, poured tons of water into the burning upper decks. But certain passages that would have allowed the water to drain away happened that day to be closed, and while it did put out the flames it also collected on the upper decks and made the ship top-heavy. Slowly she began to heel. Into open cargo doors on the portside more water gushed, and twelve hours later, in the early morning of February 10, she turned full onto her side and lay half submerged, like a beached whale.

The disaster was the sensation of the day, and the question of what to do with her excited the minds of all, from crackpot to genius. The crackpots contributed a few laughs—fill her with ping-pong balls, urged one—but the experts' ideas were less picturesque. Commander William A. Sullivan, Supervisor of Salvage of the U. S. Navy, A. C. W. Siecke and Captain John I. Tooker of Merritt-Chapman & Scott, the world's largest marine salvage concern, mulled over a variety of possibilities. There was dismemberment, but that would cost too much. So would building a cofferdam. Uprighting her simply wouldn't work, so they were stuck with pumps. After they had sealed every opening below the surface and built bulkheads to convert her into so many watertight compartments, they would pump out each compartment, and the air thus introduced would float her back to normal. Two years and five million dollars should do the job.

But the *Normandie* was not the only problem ship of World War II, and the solutions of all of them had to be made to mesh. The disaster at Pearl Harbor had syphoned off most of the experienced divers, Army, Navy and civilian, for salvaging the U. S. Pacific Fleet; German submarines were playing hob with British and American ships in the Atlantic, and these too needed attention. In fact, every bit as important as the raising of the *Normandie* was the return of all these other ships to service. Salvage officers were needed, divers and divers and more divers.

This shortage of deep-sea men had never been especially marked before. The Navy had long maintained a school outside Washington, D.C., to train enough divers to rescue men from sunken and disabled submarines, but for stranded or sunken vessels themselves they had borrowed men from firms like Merritt-Chapman & Scott. And now even M-C&S was strapped. The Navy was on its own.

The Navy, suddenly confronted with the sick giant in Pier 88, had taken a deep breath and bravely drawn up its plans. Nobody had ever operated on such an enormous body before, but they would have to learn as they went along—and incidentally would get priceless training for future operations elsewhere—so they rolled up their sleeves.

Like medical students at a Johns Hopkins of the sea, they had studied the anatomy of their patient from her designer's blueprints, and they knew every passage and cabin and saloon by heart. But when they got down into her interior they found a ship sick beyond imagining. When she had turned over, everything not bolted down had slipped to the portside and was now crushed and wedged together so tightly that dislodging each chair and lamp would be a separate amputation. But every single article had to be removed, as well as bulkheads and even the funnels wide enough to accommodate two subway trains.

This was learning salvage the hard way. From the outset they were blind men. The waters inside were so muddy that not even submersible electric lights pierced the thick blackness, and the sense of touch was their only communication with their surroundings. They had to work under four-foot ceilings, for the ship was now lying on her side and all room dimensions were awry; corridors amply high before but only four feet wide were now claustrophobic warrens in which men could only kneel or crouch, feeling their way along. And as they penetrated deeper the dangers multiplied. Tons of decaying rubbish gave off hydrogen sulphide and other deadly gases. Dependent as they were on air hoses for breath and phone lines for contact with the outside world, every step was jeopardized by the twisted metal and broken glass surrounding them, and at times two auxiliary divers had to go down to protect the life line of a third.

More insidious than the broken glass was the fine spun glass of the liner's insulation. Since the divers' hands were also their eyes they had to work without gloves, and once these invisible fibers had worked into the flesh there was nothing to do but endure the pain until they worked out again.

Worst of all was the mud. The open portholes on the submerged side, pressing down onto the muddy bottom, had admitted tons of thick black muck, and oftentimes the divers worked up to their armpits in it. Around the open cargo doors, indeed, mud was twenty feet deep and they worked *completely buried*. (Men with claustrophobia had been weeded out early.)

Such was the school in which the men of Pier 88 learned by doing, and while these seventy-five were making their way through the spun glass and mud seven hundred other men were working topside.

The plans as finally worked out in detail by Sullivan, Tooker, and Siecke called for patches on every aperture rendering the ship less than watertight, and then pumps to suck her empty.

To seal her a Tooker patch, invented by Captain Tooker, was pushed through each porthole into the mud beyond and then pulled back against the outer rim of the hole, where it was firmed into place with concrete to withstand the external pressure expected later. Three hundred and fifty-six portholes were thus closed and sixteen cargo doors; it took altogether nearly five thousand patches, wedges, and plugs, in diameter from fifty-four feet to a few inches; but at last she was sealed.

She was not ready for pumping yet, however. As long as there was water inside, the *inside* water, pressing outward against the walls, equalized the pressure of the *outside* water pressing inward; the walls themselves were thus unaffected. But since water's weight is much greater than that of air, when the hundred thousand tons inside were replaced by insignificant air the walls would collapse inward like a matchbox.

This was no fault of the *Normandie's* designer; her walls were more than strong enough—when she stood upright. But now she was lying on her side and a deck was a wall, so all the decks had to be shored up with huge timbers by men working solely by touch. But finally, after eighteen months, pumping began. Compressed air, carried in a small pipe down the outside of a large one and evicted into it at its base, rushed up inside carrying the water along, and with it the mud in the vicinity. This was an air lift, a tool as basic to a diver's operations as a scalpel is to a surgeon's.

It was August 4, 1943, when the pumps began concerted action, and four and a half hours later, when the salvage officers nervously took measurements, she had moved half an inch. So now it was only a matter of time. And time did see her through, though only after many heartbreaking battles with leaks that did not show up until the pumping began. Three thousand bags of rags and hundreds of mattresses and rugs had to be stuffed into these cracks, and eight hundred tons of concrete poured into the double bottom, before the mighty ship was really watertight. But then, when the air was pumped in, it stayed where it belonged, and so did the water. The job was licked, and on September 13, 1943, the *Normandie* floated into position.

During these nineteen months the salvage officers of the United States Navy and Merritt-Chapman & Scott had accomplished the biggest feat of its kind in history. And, learning as they went along, they had meanwhile set up a school to train a continuing wave of new recruits, with the result that, although the *Normandie's* own fate was a sad one (she had been so badly ruptured by the rocks on which she lay that she had to be scrapped), the school she brought into being had, by the end of the war, sent out twenty-five hundred highly skilled men to save ships and lives.

The first wave of these graduates, indeed, went out long before the end of the war, for by 1942 a dangerous situation had developed in the Mediterranean. Land troops, fighting in Italy, in Egypt, in North Africa, and doing not too badly, had found their supplies running low, while supply ships lying offshore were unable to deliver the necessities of battle because of the ships the Axis powers had sunk in the harbor to block their entrance. So now, with their newly acquired know-how, Sullivan and some of his men were flown to Casablanca in November 1942; others went shortly thereafter to Tunisia, Oran, Marseilles. Sometimes they worked such long hours without rest that they collapsed and had to be hospitalized, but before V-E Day teams of Army, Navy, and civilian divers, working with their British colleagues, had cleared Bizerte, Ferryville, Naples, Leghorn, Elba, Salerno, Palermo, Port de Bouc, Toulon, Cherbourg, Le Havre, Dellys, Arzew, Antwerp, and thus brought V-E Day just that much closer.

Others, as soon as there was anything to do in the Pacific, had gone there. General MacArthur had promised in 1942 to return to the Philippines, and in October 1944 return he did, stepping ashore at Leyte for a long winter's battle. In February 1945 he reached Manila, to begin the liberation of that city and the island of Luzon, and Sullivan, now a commodore, followed a couple of days later. A large group of salvage and harbor clearance men had already been sent out from the States, but by the time Sullivan arrived the need for them elsewhere had been so pressing that he found only Commander Byron Huie and perhaps fifteen others left. (Indeed, the shortage of man power was so acute that Commodore Sullivan's office in a quonset hut on Pier 7 was manned by one enlisted man only, who did all clerical work, with the result that official records of the operation were almost non-existent.) With more than six hundred vessels clogging the harbor, MacArthur issued a hurry call for all Army units to send over any men with underwater experience to join the Navy divers.

The absolutely first job, agreed MacArthur, Sullivan, and Brigadier General Hugh Casey, was to open the harbor enclosed by the breakwater so that the Army could get ashore; anything else could wait. So while Japanese snipers were still at work the USS *Teak*, a Navy net tender, bustled up and began removing the encumbrances from the harbor entrance and the areas alongside the piers.

The *Teak* was a stocky, low-slung vessel 165 feet long with powerful diesel engines and winches ideally fitted for handling heavy objects, just come from the southern islands to join the harbor-clearance project. Under direction of her skipper, Lieutenant Byron Hollett, she had rushed in like a terrier and begun worrying at the sunken ship lying athwart the channel entrance, and by the end of that first day, March 14, the opening was wide enough to allow LSTs to land.

By May, 350 ships had been removed, with Army and Navy salvors working around the clock, assisted by hundreds of Chinese and Filipinos. Some of the hulks were beached for repairs, some were raised bottom up, towed to the ship graveyard in North Harbor and sunk again, and some were blasted into pieces, raised with a derrick, and hauled away.

This unit, known as the Ship Salvage Fire Fighting Rescue Unit, had quickly learned to call the Japanese sampans that lay strewn so thickly in the harbor by their local names, Sugar Charlies, Sugar Dogs, and Sugar Loves, according to their size, Love unaccountably being at the bottom of the list. A sunken and rehabilitated Sugar Charlie was soon refitted as a club, and around Sugar Charlie's bar the salvage forces congregated, Commander Byron Huie, Lieutenant Hollett, diving officer Lieutenant Jensen, and the latest arrival, Lieutenant Junior Grade Walter E. Harmon, winner of the Navy

Cross for his rescue work on the *Squalus* and one of the original Pier 88 men—a real old pro.

Harmon, now the unit's safety officer, listened to the prevailing scuttlebutt about sunken treasure. There was, he heard, a fabulous fortune at the bottom of the bay—thirty million pesos, fifty million pesos, fifty million *dollars*—almost any good round sum seemed to do; there was a Jap ship lying somewhere in the bay stuffed with gold bullion it had been carrying back to Tokyo when it was sunk; there was a gold bar worth seven thousand dollars in the mud beside the South Dock at Corregidor, dropped when a submarine had slipped out with all the Philippine gold in 1942. Equally fascinating was the report of wine and whiskey in gourmet President Quezon's sunken yacht and—rumors never stopped at the reasonable—an enormous fortune in jewels. All gossip.

But even the proven facts were good enough to keep conversation lively: some Filipinos in Manila had been found passing one-peso coins that were discolored in the peculiar green or black of silver long immersed in salt water. Simultaneously, although the bay near Corregidor was out of bounds for all but Army and Navy craft, several innocent-looking boats had been surprised fishing by night in this off-limits area. Q boats reported chasing them away, not once but several times. What they were fishing for was anybody's guess.

Late in May gossip got warmer: an Army boat and Army personnel were involved in these night expeditions, though exactly how no one yet knew. Everyone agreed, however, that with all the modern devices and a little enterprise one could be a millionaire in no time.

Then, suddenly, it became evident that the gossip had spread further than Sugar Charlie's and that Washington had heard about the fishing boats. The silver at the bottom had been hijacked and the Army was indignant, for while the pesos had originally belonged to the Philippine Commonwealth, when President Quezon turned it over to MacArthur it had become the legal responsibility of the Army and they had to return it. Pressure, the men heard, was being put on Commodore Sullivan to go and get that silver, but he and General MacArthur thought clearing the harbor was more important. . . . Then finally, it seemed, somebody in Washington had cracked down.

Anyway, on June 1, while the *Teak* was tied to a wreck getting ready to pump her up, a radio message called Hollett and Jensen to Pier 7. Sullivan was not there, but Huie's grave expression lent enough importance to the interview.

"Hollett," said Huie, "I've got a job for the *Teak*. It's been assigned by General MacArthur himself. Straight from Washington. Top secret." And young Hollett listened while the extremely hush-hush job was described. He heard about the silver's being dumped off a barge into deep water (everybody in Manila knew, of course, but Washington had said it was to be top secret so that was the way it was treated); he heard about his ship's being chosen partly because her sturdy winches could handle deep-diving dresses weighing over two hundred pounds; about the accurate bearings taken from the battery station on Malinta Hill that would be forwarded in code any day now. And he was assigned in the meantime to investigate the sunken Jap freighter in the harbor.

"The *Moya Maru*," Huie said, "is supposed to have a lot of silver in it the Japs salvaged from the bay. Our planes sank it just as it was leaving for Japan. That's the talk, anyway."

About this same time Harmon was called into the salvage office, where Sullivan and Huie were waiting for him. "Got a job for you, Willie," said the commodore. "Deep-water stuff, that's why we picked you. You'll go out as first diving officer and safety officer. Tell him about it, Commander."

Huie looked around; the office was open and people were in the habit of passing in and out. "Come outside," he said, and together they went onto the back porch of the hut and sat down. "It's highly confidential," the commander warned in a low voice. "You're not to breathe a word, over a glass of beer or anything." And Harmon heard about the silver.

He nodded deadpan. "I'll need a compressor. And, for work at that depth, a recompression chamber," he said, and Huie told him to get together with the *Teak's* skipper and fit the ship for her work.

"We must do a good job for the commodore," Hollett and Harmon agreed.

There was deep-diving gear to obtain, as well as charts of the area and data on Jap mines and United States mine sweepers. There were endless conferences with the commodore and the commander and the Army security officer assigned to the ship, Lieutenant Gordon Hagerman, and all of them guarded the secret of the job so carefully that it was not even spelled out in the ship's log.

Activities were temporarily interrupted when a member of the crew, returning one night too full of beer, fell off the pier into deep water and did not come up again until several of his diving companions had gone down for him. Funeral arrangements and the dispatch of messages surrounding the cause of death in merciful ambiguity took two days, but on June 10 the *Teak* steamed out to the *Moya Maru*.

For three days they dived on the freighter and brought up six boxes of Indo-Chinese paper money, which were all right in their way and worth about five hundred thousand dollars if anyone would accept them, but they found only about a hundred silver pesos. If the Japs had salvaged any silver from the bay, it wasn't here. The *Teak* therefore was moved to Corregidor.

By this time sufficient conferences had been held in the office on Pier 7 to cover all contingencies, and a few working rules were set up. Sullivan, considering that this assignment was something of a treat to men used to the dangerous harbor-clearance jobs, and that in addition each dive paid five dollars an hour over base pay, ordered that the men be rotated when possible. In making this rule he was, however, also considering another fact—that human nature was more or less the same the world over. He remembered what had happened in Mexico some years before, when divers, after salvaging a considerable number of gold bars from a ship, had failed to find the rest and gone home, only to resign their jobs later and return secretly for the bars they had buried, the theft being uncovered when the men tried to dispose of their loot. Sullivan sought to make this tactic difficult by issuing orders that if possible only men who were due to return to the United States within sixty days were to be used, and in addition, Lieutenant Hagerman was to inspect everyone as he surfaced to see that no pesos were hidden in the shoes or chaffing pants of the dress. If any diver wanted pesos as souvenirs he was to buy them at regular rates from the Army.

On June 16 the *Teak* arrived a mile west of the South Dock, grasping in her hot little fist the bearings supplied from Washington, and found that the spot they indicated was as open and unprotected as the Midwest prairies (and, they found out later, as difficult to pin anything down to, for their anchors dragged helplessly through the loose bottom and let the ship dance about over the surface like tumbleweed in the wind). Hollett and Harmon surveyed the prospects.

"We've got an area about a mile across to cover," Hollet figured, "half a mile *this* side of the fix and half a mile *that* side," and Harmon said, "We'd better start dragging at once."

It was afternoon, and windy, too windy for safe diving (they were to learn sorrowfully that afternoons almost invariably brought wind), so while they sent to the boat pool in Manila for an LCM, Harmon had an old oil drum cut in half, punched full of holes, and a long cable attached to its lip. A buoy marked "A" was dropped directly over the spot indicated on the chart, and from the stern of the LCM the scoop was dragged back and forth across it. Periodically the scoop was hauled up for a look at samples of the bottom, but when the red flash signaled an air raid they were not sorry to be interrupted, for this dragging was getting them nowhere.

The following morning, the weather being fair, Lieutenant Jensen, and after him A. J. Parrish, went over the side. Their first reports to the surface were, "The visibility's good, a hundred feet," but the minute they started moving about they stirred up a layer of mud several feet deep, and since there was little current they were soon surrounded by a dense unmoving cloud. The water was only 108 feet deep, however, and that made it child's play for men like these.

There were no pesos.

That evening the men looked at the chart in disgust. "This thing says there's silver right smack at this spot. Look how fancy it's fixed up—points on compass, points on land, backsights, other sights on the island. How can anything so fancy be so wrong?"

"Maybe the island's moved," one of the men offered helpfully.

"Tomorrow we'll try circling," said Harmon.

A stake was driven into the sea floor under the ship with a line attached to it, and with this in hand, like a Maypole dancer, the diver circled looking for boxes. When the tenders, watching his bubbles, notified him that he had completed 360 degrees, he let out his rope a little and did the same thing again. During the day five men in succession circled at various distances up to a hundred feet, so that not a foot in a two-hundred-foot diameter was left unexplored, but the results were always the same, plenty of mud but no pesos.

Next day, June 18, more buoys were dropped to enclose a wide area around buoy "A," and the scoop, with fourteen hundred feet of cable, was dragged from the *Teak* again. No pesos. Then the LCM dragged it for a bit, branching out from buoy "A" in lines drawn on the chart. Again, no pesos.

Next day the scoop itself got lost from the LCM and a man in a face mask went down for it. This time it was no pesos *and* no scoop. The thing was becoming embarrassing, in face of those fancy Army bearings and all this Pier 88 talent aboard.

Another day of fruitless dragging followed, but they went on looking for the lost scoop, and in truth it was this scoop that brought them, on June 20, their first sniff of encouragement—just a sniff, but enough to keep hope alive.

At noon that day they were badly in need of encouragement, for four days of intensive work in the area indicated on the chart had revealed nothing. Hollett said, "Well, there's a spot over there we haven't dragged, about a hundred feet east of buoy "A." Let's drop a three-point mooring and try there." So Parrish went over the side there, and at four-o-five he suddenly phoned up in an excited voice that by golly here was a box. It fell apart when he touched it, releasing a collection of black disks stuck together in clumps, but he stuffed a number into the chaffing pants worn over the regular dress and came up, the day's hero. As the men crowded around to examine and caress the 274 green-black coins the skipper shouted jubilantly, "Boy, we've really hit it this time! Let's tell the commodore."

A code had been arranged for just such a contingency, and now an operational-priority radio message went into the office, "We have made contact."

"I expect we'll have a lot of gold-braid visitors out here tomorrow," Hollett grinned, and when the excitement had died and every man aboard had had a good look at the coins he discreetly pried them loose and locked them in the safe to show the gold braid.

The braid skipped tomorrow, which was a bad day, weatherwise, while divingwise it was medium, yielding two more broken boxes, but next day the inundation took place. All attempts at secrecy had been suddenly dropped, and by noon, when twelve thousand pesos had been added to the pile on deck, Commander Huie and Lieutenant Colonel Nowlin of Army's G-3 arrived with Vic Jurgens, a photographer, and a flock of M.P.s to guard the treasure. There was a lot of pleased thumping on backs, and plans were made for a real photographic coverage of the operations. In the meantime a diving bell was built at Corregidor's South Dock to enable the photographer to get underwater shots, and Sullivan, Huie, Hollett, and various divers were caught hard at work.

But somehow the publicity seemed to make the pesos self-conscious, for immediately they retired into the mud and had to be dug out individually by men feeling about on hands and knees. Five more divers had been hurried out to handle the uprush, but an occasional broken box was all anyone found, and day after day Cole, Bradley, Harris, Cione, and McGuirk came up inquiring what all the excitement was about anyway. If the going was always this slow, they figured, allowing twenty-five hundred boxes at the bottom, they would be about twelve years on the job. The *Teak* returned to Manila for consultations, the skipper with Sullivan and Huie.

"It isn't that there's anything the matter with the divers or the equipment," Hollett said. "We're just not in the right *place*. Those Army bearings were a bust."

"Those fellows who were caught hijacking the stuff had evidently found the spot," said Sullivan. "You might see if you can get any leads from them. I daresay they're in prison somewhere around."

So Hollett got a jeep and went to see Colonel Nowlin and after a fine lunch at the colonel's mess they went to Bilibid Prison to talk to the Chief of the Criminal Investigation Department. Bilibid, which had won an unenviable reputation with Americans held there, was an old Spanish prison suggestive of the Inquisition, gray and bleak, with long brown stains where the dampness seeped through the stone walls.

In the office Hollett interviewed Captain Kane. Were they holding any of the men involved in the hijacking last month? Kane thought they might be, and would do his best to round somebody up. He asked if Hollett knew about the two ships loaded with Philippine silver said to be lying at the bottom of the harbor; it seemed that the Japs had soon found out about the silver, but instead of diving for it themselves, had forced Filipinos to go down, and after filling two ships, were about to send them to Japan when United States planes sank them.

"We've already dived on one of them," said Hollett. "We found almost nothing."

"Well, it may be just a rumor," said Kane. "You know how those things get built up. Anyway, come back tomorrow, and I'll try to have somebody for you to talk to."

Next day Hollett found Captain Kane and two Army secret agents waiting with a couple of uncomfortable-looking characters, a Filipino in dirty white pants and shirt, and a sergeant in ragged G.I.'s. The Filipino, he learned, had organized the hijacking effort in May with the sergeant and several other G.I.s, using Army face masks and tanks and an Army barge. The other G.I.s had not been apprehended.* They were said to have taken up about a million pesos (this figure was later reduced to half a million) and although they worked at night, presumably they knew where they had been.

* Early in 1956, after the *American Legion Magazine* had published my appeal for information about the sinking and salvage of the Philippine pesos, I received the following letter, reproduced in its entirety, without address:

Dear Miss Sterling: I understand that you are writing a book about the 8½ Million dollars that the U.S. Navy attemped to salvage in the Philippines. I wonder if you have uncovered the story about the Americans that worked at nite during this operation, and fled to China? There was four of them. I was supposed to get cut in on 500,000 dollars of this gold for some work that I did for them, but the rats left. I understand that two of them are in Tokyo today working for the US Foreign Ecenomic Advisers. One other has a job in washington D.C. . The other was did away with.

If you do not have this complete story, let me know; it might make intereting reading. Regards, Joe."

It would be interesting to know whether the sergeant in Bilibid Prison was the one that was did away with. If Joe should happen to read this I should be glad to hear from him.

This might be really something, and Hollett asked eagerly, "Could you go to the spot again?"

The Filipino nodded with great assurance, and in the peculiar Spanish-English of the Islands said, "Sir, I know exactly where it is. No questions about it, sir."

Hollett turned to the sergeant. "You know too?" The sergeant, pale and shaking from three wartime years in a Jap prison, nodded. "I think so."

The following day the *Teak* added to her regular complement one Filipino, one U.S. sergeant, and two Army guards. When they reached the general area of the pesos the Filipino, very businesslike and important, squinted this way and that, observed this lighthouse and that point of land, and then, waving his arm off to the West, declared that the spot was just *there*, because of the bearings. The crew anchored there, dropped a cork buoy, and Harmon sent down a diver. No pesos. The Filipino, in dramatic amazement, shook his head and held his brow in an attitude of deep thought.

Deadpan, the *Teak's* skipper turned to the sergeant. "Where do *you* think it is?"

In a feeble voice the sergeant said, "About there, I think," waving his arm farther to the East.

With slackening enthusiasm Harmon said, "What makes you think that's the spot?"

"I took a bearing. It was night, so I used the lighthouse on Corregidor and lined it up with the bilge pump and a bollard on the barge."

"And what else?"

"What else?"

"That's only a one-directional bearing. You need a two- or three-point bearing to really know where you are."

The sergeant's eyes, wide and distressed, filled with tears. "That's all I had."

The eyes of the others met sadly, writing him off, and Hollett sighed. "Well, since you're here, you might as well tell us where you think you were. Stop us when we get near the spot," and he gave orders to move the *Teak* eastward.

When again the divers came up empty-handed Hollett returned to the Filipino. "O.K., now, what do you say?"

The Filipino jumped up, all eagerness to be of service. He had, he explained, been mistaken before, of course, but now he knew positively where the pesos were. If the *Teak* would just move a little more over *here* they would without fail begin finding them.

This, too, proving an empty dream, he assured them that he was doing the best he knew, but that of course the divers would be a long time finding them since the pesos were all hidden in the mud. They would just have to go on diving and diving and diving.

This proved to be all too true. For six days the wearying men on the *Teak*, between rain squalls, shifted from spot to spot, while the atmosphere became progressively chillier. "That guy's not coming clean," muttered Hollett. "The sergeant's half shot, he may not be pulling anything, but that other fellow knows more than he's letting on." At last in disgust he sent them all back to Manila, and now the old pros were really on their own.

Utilizing a two-day weather break, they built themselves a spike-toothed scoop and, on July 8, washing out all former advices, charts, courses and ranges, and starting in a location suggested by absolutely no one, threw over the scoop and gave it a bit of a drag.

McGuirk, standing near the fantail as it came up, let out a yell: "Here they are! Here's what we're looking for." And there they were, stuck in the mud, thick, like nut fudge.

With each drag more pesos came up, and now the men were itching to go overboard, but there was a heavy ground swell and the anchors were dragging badly. Harmon, to whom the safety of his men was paramount, forbade any diving that day, for if the ship shifted position while a man was below, the anchor line could foul his life line or cut his air hose, and no pesos were worth that chance.

But next day the harvest really began. When Pope went down, his voice came back in a shout:

"Boy, it's like an apple orchard down here, a bunch of four or five boxes, and fifteen or twenty feet away another bunch." The bottom was hard here, no muddy cloud, and through the clear sunlit water he could see the boxes distinctly. But when he touched the first it fell apart in his hands. Termites had eaten away the wood until it was ready to crumble on contact; the canvas bags inside had likewise disappeared, and the salt water had chemicalized the coins into solid blocks encrusted with sea shells, while the more protected ones inside were stuck in twos and threes. The *Teak* had struck it rich this time, and the only question now was the fastest way to bring the stuff up.

A G.I. barrel of galvanized iron, reinforced and punched full of holes for drainage, was lowered on the descending line on a loop. With a ten-quart pail in one hand and a circling line in the other a diver could, in this rich apple orchard, fill the barrel in one thirty-five-minute dive, after which the barrel and he both came up and the next team went down. So eager were they all that, weather permitting (which it seldom did), one man was always at the bottom. In this 108-foot depth a diver required, after thirty-five minutes of compressed air, another thirty-five minutes' decompression, so that by the time he reached the surface his pesos had been shoveled into coal sacks and weighed on a hook scale, exactly a hundred pounds per sack. And since a hundred pounds contained 2,339 pesos it was an easy matter for the finance officer to estimate each day's take before the sacks were dumped into a bin to await the LCM that would deliver them to the Central Bank of Manila.

Now everything was going swimmingly, except that whole boxes were a rarity and most of the coins had to be picked off the bottom one at a time, like daisies. When word of this laborious method reached the divers' alma mater in New York, Pier 88 put their collective heads together, and a few days later flew out blueprints of a specially designed air lift.

Harmon and McGuirk studied the plans; if they worked, they should do for the divers what the threshing machine had done for farmers. And certainly the principle was sound—a suction hose operated by compressed air, which, like a vacuum cleaner, drew the pesos up off the bottom into a large drum above. The engineers at Pier 88 had experimented with washers dropped into the Hudson River and they had come up admirably, so now McGuirk and Harmon made an air lift out of a fifty-five-gallon oil drum and some sections of pipe and hose. It looked elegant.

McGuirk, with the loving pride of the artist, took his creation to the bottom, turned the nozzle down into a mound of mud and pesos at his feet, and signaled for compressed air. With a great "BRRRUMMPPP!" the earth beneath him disappeared up the pipe, throwing him flat on his face into the resulting cavity. So great was the disturbance, indeed, that a tremendous muddy cloud mushroomed up about him. Through the swirl he saw that not a peso remained.

"Perfect," said McGuirk. Now all he had to do was to wait for the cloud to drift away.

But the experts at Pier 88 had not known and those on the *Teak* had forgotten that the current was so very mild. The cloud hung on indefinitely, a quarter of a mile wide, and since in this operation they needed to see what they were doing they were immobilized. Furthermore, Pier 88 had experimented with thin, light washers in forty feet of water, and here they were working with solid silver in 108 feet. Their air compressor could not lift that extra weight that extra distance, and the handsome mechanism had to be laid away.

So also with other mechanical aids; against the days when the present plenty should peter out, an Army lieutenant was brought aboard with a mine detector. This was to send forth a *ping* that, hitting the metal on the bottom and rebounding onto the diver's headphones, would notify him of silver, and this too was a fine principle; but there were so many other kinds of metals down there, and such a crazy patchwork of sounds came back, one indistinguishable from another, that they reluctantly went back to picking daisies.

There were no complaints of scarcity as yet, however; having put out a four-point mooring, they hauled themselves about within its quarter-square-mile area from one rich spot to another, and the days went on in a dreamy routine stirred up only by a curious circumstance which all the divers noticed. Although many boxes were found all bunched together, in other places the coins were widely scattered and buried in the mud, and here the boxes, generally empty, had an end or a side staved in. These boxes suggested that other divers had been there before them, but how could anyone have missed this profusion of coins, running now twenty, thirty, forty thousand a day? They discussed the mystery at night in the galley, but the question was purely academic at the moment, for the pesos were still abundant. On August 12 the million mark was passed.

Now they looked for excitement to such things as the typhoons which provided a few days ashore at Sugar Charlie's, or the case of the bends brought to the *Teak's* recompression chamber on the same day that the Japs begged for peace. There was also, on August 16, a case of *fresh* eggs brought aboard, the kind that could actually be fried in a pan, and, one stormy night, a tug breaking up against the cliffs of Mariveles, from which they rescued twelve men just before she sank.

Then there was the visit from friendly sharks. In midafternoon of July 21, McGuirk was standing on the decompression stage, a cross between a platform and a bird cage, at forty feet, with quite a wait still before him, when overhead he heard the improbable sound of rifle fire. Looking up, he saw a school of sharks frisking about in an ecstasy of excitement, while at the same time the breathless young voice of the pharmacist's mate came down over the phone:

"Hey, McGuirk, in case you're wondering what the shooting's about, it's sharks."

"So I see," the old pro said dryly. "But it's the first time I ever heard of sharks shooting."

"That's us. We're driving them off. Don't worry."

If contempt could freeze, the phone line would have been an icicle. "Worry? In a full suit? All they can do to me is bump me." And McGuirk watched with mild interest the gamboling fish making a meal off scraps from the *Teak's* table.

For an occasional busman's holiday they made "practice" dives near the South Dock, but, not surprisingly, the seven-thousand-dollar gold bar never turned up, and all the divers got really *was* practice.

But young Lieutenant R. S. Osborn nearly got a man who nearly was a thief. In Manila loading supplies, he overheard the crew of a ship docked alongside saying to the *Teak's* men:

"We know about your hush-hush salvage job. A man on our ship was one of the men who gave that silver the deep six off Corregidor."

Osborn pricked up his ears, for although the silver was still coming up well, they had a long way to go yet and could use all the leads they got. True, the help so far from hijackers, mechanical devices, and Washington bearings had been no good, but he dutifully reported his news to the new skipper, Lieutenant William Hale

(Hollett had just gone off home sporting a Bronze Star for his salvage work). The salvage officer and Osborn paid a visit to the ARS (T)1 newly arrived from the States.

Yes, they were told, a man had come out with them claiming to be the only survivor of the group who had dumped the silver. He had been captured by the Japs on May 6, 1942, had later escaped and joined a company of Filipino guerrillas, becoming a second lieutenant, and when the American forces landed at Leyte was given his choice of leaving the service or staying in. He had asked to be sent to a Navy diving school in the United States, and after graduating got himself sent right back to the Philippines.

On the way out he had boasted of knowing some rich people in Manila who owned boats suitable for salvage work, and the moment the ARS(T)1 docked had requested a two-day liberty to visit an aunt. Very shortly he returned in an unnephewlike rage, storming:

"Damn it, I thought I was the only person alive who knew where it was," and demanded immediate separation. His period of pre-war enlistment having run out, he had accordingly left for the States just two days before.

The two men, who had been working themselves up to a peak of excitement, received this last statement like cold water in the face. Sadly they returned to the *Teak* and resumed their unaided struggle towards the second million.

Pretty soon events began triggering the question, How much is there really down there to *get?* The Japanese freighter supposed to contain a fortune had, it seemed, turned out to be a creature of gossip, but on the other hand, they learned for certain that back in 1942 some Filipinos diving for the Japs *had* brought up *some* pesos. Many people in Manila were positive that the coins dumped had been 1910 mint and that there were floods of 1910 coins in circulation, which should prove that the Japs had got a great many and traded with them in Manila, while Jorge Vargas, former Acting Mayor of Manila and a numismatist specializing in Philippine coins, said 1910 mint were comparatively rare; and *that* should have proved the Japs got very few—except that they might, of course, have melted them down into wire for airplanes. It was all purely conjecture and very contradictory.

Then a set of Japanese diving gear was found on Corregidor, and this was taken as a sign that the Japs had been active in that area, but on examination the gear proved to be of a kind incapable of sending air down 108 feet, so then the assumption was that it must have been used for shallow work such as changing propellers on ships.

Only two days later a diving helmet was found at the bottom—an English helmet of pre-war design used by the Japs in the thirties. But all this left the *Teak's* men about where they had been —in a dense cloud of speculation. And then, after V-J Day, facts began to fall into place.

Men passing through Manila on their way home from Japanese prisons were heard talking about the sea-blackened pesos they had been given in camp, displaying rings and other trinkets of silver. Chief Warrant Officer Charles Audet, from the mine planter *Harrison*, was seen wearing a ring with a Masonic emblem, fashioned by an Indian from New Mexico in exchange for a tin of corned beef. Father John E. Duffy, Army chaplain on Bataan, owned a silver dollar given him in Bilibid Prison which he said had been retrieved from the bay (though how a *dollar* got in among the pesos no one ever knew). Many other men either possessed these coins or had seen them in the hands of campmates.

At first no one on the *Teak* could figure how they had got into the prisons, but then they heard that in 1942 the Philippine Government, learning that the Japs had located their silver and knowing a weakness of their enemies, had put about gossip to the effect that the money had been owned and handled by lepers. The Japs, in superstitious terror of leprosy, had shrunk from handling it themselves and had forced local Filipinos and Moros to go after it. Later they found a few United States divers in their prisons and sent them down as well. The Americans successfully sabotaged the work while appearing to be doing their best, and finally were returned to prison; it was these men, bringing some back as souvenirs, from whom Duffy, Audet, and the others obtained their coins.

All of this came to the *Teak's* men at second hand, and was no help in indicating how much the Japs had got. But one tantalizing question—the mystery of the staved-in boxes surrounded by an abundance of coins—was resolved by a report from Rear Admiral

George G. Harrison, who had been in prison with the U.S. divers. These men had told him that whenever possible they had broken open the boxes before sending them up, so that the pesos had fallen out and lost themselves in the mud.

Meanwhile the pace on the *Teak* was mounting, ₱60,000, 65,000, 70,000; they could ask for nothing better than to go along like this, cozy and friendly and doing a first-rate job. On October 10, Lieutenant Hale was promoted to lieutenant commander; on October 13, Commander Anderson, the salvage officer ashore, gave a party for the group; on October 16 the pesos hit a new high of 78,000; on October 23 a tremendous shark was caught off the fantail, and on the same day a new record was set, 86,000; on October 24 the *Teak* celebrated her second million with a half holiday for everyone; on October 26, Lieutenant Osborn talked Commander Anderson out of a new washing machine for his ship, and on November 7 he brought aboard two hundred dollars' worth of tobacco, soap, matches, toothpaste, and brushes; on November 9 the *Teak* began getting a new coat of paint; on November 11 the staggering sum of ₱128,000 came up; and on November 12, returning to Manila with bulging pockets and a beam from ear to ear, the *Teak* received a new set of orders—and, with them, the sensation that she had been running downstairs very fast and that suddenly the bottom step was not there. The *Teak* was being relieved—she was to go back to the United States—from now on somebody else would be bringing up the pesos.

The news, of course, meant home, wives, sweethearts, and a chance to sleep late in the morning, but there was a mixture of feelings, nevertheless, for this had been, after all, a unique assignment with a company of very good men.

After transferring the diving crew and gear to USS *Elder*, AN 20, the low-slung *Teak* waddled off for Subic Bay and, eventually, San Pedro, California, sporting a Navy Unit Commendation. The decoration was deeply cherished, but not quite so much, perhaps, as the personal decoration the crew awarded their ship.

"She ought to have a medal to wear," said Willie Harmon, and so they made her one, a shield of brass five inches by eight with two pesos soldered on it, one showing the side with the Philippine woman on it, the other the side with the United States coat of arms. This shield they welded to the mainmast six feet above the deck, and they had intended to engrave some suitable legend on the brass, but in the subsequent rush to be discharged this formality was ignored. However, the shield told its own story, and the *Teak*, thus decorated with her own coat of arms, entered San Pedro harbor, not the only ship in the Navy to own a Unit Commendation but certainly the only one to display in proper heraldic style, two Philippine pesos, *argent rampant*, on a field *or*.

The ship to which the *Teak* relinquished her responsibilities carried on conscientiously, but an understudy, however adequate, is never as glamorous as the star she replaces, and the *Elder's* operations were, in essence, a repetition of what had gone before. Lieutenant William Mahan relieved Lieutenant Hale as skipper, and Lieutenant J. J. Macdonald took over as first diving officer from Willie Harmon when Harmon went to Bikini to help recover the ships sunk in the atom bomb test, "Operation Crossroads." Harmon had directed 583 dives without a single casualty, and Macdonald carried on this perfect safety record.

All that winter and on into the spring the pesos came up, but now they were getting harder and harder to find, and at last a day came in May when skipper Mahan, surveying the declining tally, did some paper work on costs and profits and went to the Admiral of the Philippine area.

"I don't think it's worth while going on any more," he said. The Admiral looked at the figures and nodded.

So Mahan notified the Philippine Government, "We shall discontinue operations in two weeks' time." And the commonwealth, which was going to be an independent republic in a couple of months anyway, and was getting ready to handle its own affairs, assented.

So that was the end of "Operation Sunken Pesos" as far as the Army and Navy were concerned, and the office on Pier 7 closed up shop. In its year of activity it had recovered ₱5,383,173.50, a third of the jettisoned total.

On July 4, 1946, in accordance with an old treaty, the United States turned over control of Philippine affairs to the new republic. Hitherto she had supported the Philippine currency (and actually the peso was still to be pegged to the dollar) and had assumed responsibility for the Philippine assets when war came, conscientiously making good on them later on, but now the young republic, like a daughter coming of age, became mistress of her own concerns.

One such concern, of course, was the fortune remaining at the bottom of the bay. If the rich United States had found it too expensive to keep a ship and men on the job, obviously the new young republic would. But it felt there should be private salvors with their own equipment who would like to take a chance, on a percentage-of-the-profits basis, so the Bureau of the Treasury advertised in the Manila *Bulletin* and Manila *Chronicle* for bids "to recover about ten million pesos." The winning bidder, after posting a ten-thousand-peso bond to guarantee a start by a certain date, would be furnished a map of the area.

The Bureau's assumption proved correct, for from then on there was a stream of salvors eager to take a chance. Most were local men, who brought up as few as ₱574 or as many as 286,962.50, but the two most successful operations, the very first under the new regime and the very last, both happened to be American.

The first was notable mainly for the fact that it ended successfully by a fortunate accident of timing. On publication of the Bureau's advertisement, Clarke Brooke, Jr., Allan B. Clark, and John Daves of Seattle, Washington, put in the winning bid, fifteen per cent of the first two and a half million pesos recovered, ten per cent of the next five million, and five per cent thereafter, and engaging an old barge and a motor-sailer to push it along, they started work in January 1947.

Relations with the six highly skilled Moro pearl divers were strained from the beginning, for too late the ignorant outsiders found themselves bound by an ironclad contract for fifty pesos per day per man. Contemplating their running expenses, they prayed fervently that the men were fast workers, but in view of the ten millions waiting at the bottom, they still felt fairly relaxed.

In their initial enthusiasm they had overlooked the word "about" in the advertisement, but soon after they arrived it was brought sharply home when someone happened to mention that the Japs had done some diving in 1942. No one could tell them exactly how much had been salvaged, but a Manila businessman, Chick Parsons, said he had seen piles of coins on the docks which he estimated at four to six millions. And hardly had they recovered from this shock when they heard about the Filipino hijacker and *his* exploits. Clearly the target was diminishing rapidly, and they were even more dependent on the skill of their divers than they had thought.

Out in the bay they anchored over the spot indicated on the Treasury map, and the Moros went over the side. But from the first the operations had a curious dreamlike quality, for one man would come up saying brightly, "Lots of money down there," without actually producing any, while the next would produce only an empty box or a couple of loose coins. True, they were active enough, busily bringing up unexploded torpedoes, bombs, even a skeleton, but money appeared in such small quantities that expenses were barely being met.

After some disappointing weeks Clark and Daves, who more by accident than design had said nothing about being divers themselves, gave their Moros a sharp shock by donning suits and going down to look for themselves. Then it became apparent that Teddy, the boss, and his men had not been doing so badly after all, for there were a number of buckets of pesos sitting about in the mud, and the plan had clearly been to stall as long as possible, earning fifty pesos a day, and when the Americans had given up and gone home, to come back and gather in the harvest.

Now there were sputtering noises of indignation, but when the word "firing" came into the conversation they were told to look at the fine print in the contract, which, it developed, specified that so long as the Americans worked on this job the Moros worked on it too. At this point Clark and Daves, feeling their position somewhat cramped, sat down to think.

If the divers' operations had had a dreamlike quality, the next series of events also had a fey intangibility. Event number one was the uncovering of an obscure law on the Philippine books disqualifying any diver who suffered from certain specified diseases. Event two was the visit to the barge of a doctor who felt irresistibly impelled to examine each of the Moros. Event three was the alarming discovery that not one but all six showed symptoms of the very TB, VD, and other ailments specified. It was obvious no contractor could employ men who might at any moment drop dead at his feet, so the bewildered divers took their leave and a crew of Filipinos was signed on.

Although these new men miraculously turned in whatever they found, it was still no more than a trickle of coins, a few here in the mud, a few there in a broken box—just enough to keep them out of the red. Obviously they were working in the wrong place, so, the Treasury map having failed them almost as signally as the earlier bearings had failed Hollett and Harmon, they requested the Philippine Government to ask Washington for more specific information. While waiting, they suspended an anchor from the barge a few feet above the bottom and rode it back and forth hour after hour, peering about for pesos.

After several months of these unsatisfactory efforts it seemed foolish to continue, for without the hoped-for information, which apparently was not coming, they could go on like this forever, or at least until their contract was up. Indeed, had it not been for Clark, a man with the look of a bloodhound and persistence to match, the whole thing would have been called off. Then one day, without any warning, as the anchor carried Daves forward through the water, the entire bottom as far as he could see suddenly became a landscape of tumbled boxes, single, in bunches, and heaped up into a mound. They had run square onto the end of one of the *Harrison's* trips—a two-million-dollar jackpot.

For the next forty-eight hours they dived and slept, dived and slept, and on the third day got the fright of their lives. They had long ago given up hope of hearing from Washington, but now a cable arrived. The Japanese, it said, had already recovered some of the silver, and the Army and Navy Engineers all the rest, so there was nothing left at the bottom and further search would be fruitless.

Had the cable come three days earlier they would have given up and gone home, and realizing the narrowness of their time margin, they sat down hard, grinning but with knees suddenly gone weak and shaky.

However, the cable *hadn't* come three days earlier, and so here they were with ₱2,800,000. And since their time was now up, they brought it in to Manila and for their pains received from the

Treasury something over ₱400,000. The rest of the millions remained at the bottom.

After they had moved on, a stream of other salvors followed, dark-skinned men with Japanese or Spanish or Chinese or Malay features and names like Gaspar, Manuel, Garcia, Bognot, who spoke with Tagalog or Spanish accents and made no more than a ripple as they passed. Then a high wind roared in out of the United States, and everyone stopped to watch.

In 1950 one Chester Womack, an American diver in the Philippines, had heard about the pesos in the bay and, calling on Ray Higgins, a big water-taxi operator and power in the community, had enlisted him in a treasure hunt.

Higgins was big in a number of ways, weighing nearly three hundred pounds, with a wide grin that broke down barriers like a battering-ram, an acquaintance spreading from the presidential set to the Filipino water-front boys, and a stack of press books three feet high. Any deal with him in it was sure to be notable. Yet, only five years before, the huge man had been a night-club bouncer with twenty-five dollars to his name and none but the suit he stood up in. And for a good many years before that—say thirty—he had been far from the newspaper picture of a prominent man of affairs.

Son of a rancher and sheriff in Helena, Montana, who had started as a blacksmith, young Higgins got as far as high school and then, deciding he knew as much as the teachers, lit out with a traveling carnival. Though not as tall, nor, at that time, as wide as it would be later, his frame carried enough weight to make him a passable wrestler, and he knocked around the country taking on anybody who would stand still and let him, George Zaharias, Jim Londos, Strangler Lewis. Generally he got beaten, but he first managed to give them a fall or two just to make it look real.

Then, in 1936, he got homesick. Deciding to shake the road dust off his feet, he settled down to a thoroughly legal job, reading fingerprints in the sheriff's office, and might have been there yet had he not gone to an Eagle Lodge meeting in Chicago and caught the boss's eye. The center of a group of laughing men, he seemed the type the Eagles were looking for, and so not long afterwards, armed with the names of eighty prospects the previous organizer had been unable to dent, he drove off for Marquette, Michigan, in the dead of winter, two thirds scared and altogether frozen.

The first encounter set him back on his heels, for, starting on the names alphabetically, he approached A, only to have A greet the word Eagle with a punch that left Higgins horizontal. It seemed that the last organizer had borrowed a five-spot and never been seen again, so Higgins gave A his five and started on the Bs.

The first B was going fishing, and Eagles was the last word he was interested in hearing, but he did need fishermen, so Higgins got a job fishing on Lake Michigan on condition he never said that word. However, after three days the prospect softened and asked what he was promoting, but Higgins shook his head. "I promised I wouldn't bother you," he said.

The man began to probe and Higgins played hard to get, but finally the man said, "Come to the fish sorting house on Saturday night and bring some blanks," and that Saturday 150 signed up, followed by hundreds more later all over the country. For a couple of years Higgins lived and ate Eagles, but then he resigned.

"I'm up to here in Eagles," he told the boss. "You're all right, I like you fine. But I want out."

Strolling down Spring Street in Los Angeles not long afterwards, he saw a sign, "Work for the Trona Borax and Chemical Co.," and though he was up to here in money, too, he wanted to bake in the sun and sweat town life out of himself. The Borax Company was having replacement trouble at the time, for all the good help left after a few weeks away from home and family, and they could get nothing but a constant stream of winos who would not work. Since each replacement cost the company a hundred dollars in reference checking and transportation, they were losing their shirts.

Higgins heard a foreman complaining about his turnover problem, and the born organizer spoke up. "I know how to get good people up here and keep them here." The trouble was, he said, that after work the men had nothing to do but drink. "I'd organize a softball team. I'd build a local orchestra—the hell with how bad it was—I'd bring a dance band up once a week and put in movies with two changes of bill. I'd make it a place for men to bring their families and *live*."

Soon the place was humming like a turbine, smooth and sweet, which made him restless, and the Japanese having just hit Pearl Harbor, he quit to sign on a merchant vessel as an ordinary seaman, the bottom rung on the ladder. He had never been to sea before, but over a glass of beer with the business agent a few weeks later he said:

"Don't you think I'm ugly enough to be a bosun?" and the agent agreed he certainly wasn't pretty. In order to hide his ignorance, he hung around the old-timers on board and listened to their jargon. If he received an order to drop the boom, he repeated loudly, "Drop that boom, damn you," and slipped behind a lifeboat to see how a boom was dropped; and at night he hid out somewhere and practiced tying knots. Thus by quick footwork he managed to keep enough ahead of himself so that when, at the end of six months, he confessed all, the skipper grinned:

"I knew you didn't know a thing, but I figured if you could get away with it, it was O.K. with me."

By now the war had closed in on the northern islands of the Philippines, but the southern ones were still open, and when Higgins' ship put in at Leyte he slipped ashore with a group to see the town. During the night their ship was sunk in the harbor and there they were, stranded in the Islands, and although Higgins did not know it at the time, that was the luckiest night of his life.

This fact emerged only a little at a time. He still had to join another merchant ship for a few runs and then, walking along the Escolta in Manila, run into an old wrestling crony turned promoter, who offered him a guarantee of three thousand dollars to jump ship and fight a match. This meant leaving his belongings and pay behind, but with three thousand dollars guaranteed how could he lose? He did indeed win the heavyweight championship of Manila, but when he went to the promoter's hotel the following morning for his pay the old pal had vanished, and there he stood in his one suit, with twenty-five dollars in the pants pocket.

Certain jobs are naturals for a wrestler, and he found himself, in turn, dice dealer in a gambling parlor, headwaiter, and finally bouncer in a notorious night club called, solemnly, Ye Olde Mansion. He made ten pesos a night and slept on the deck of an old transport to save rent, when that job folded moving by natural progression out to sea with a cargo of kerosene. This boat too was sunk under him forty-five miles offshore; he and the second mate took to a lifeboat with no idea how to steer, but a tug came by which not only delivered them home but opened Higgins' eyes to his natural métier.

The harbor of Manila, a portion of the larger bay enclosed by breakwaters, was full of small boats skittering about between shore and the ships anchored farther out, and Higgins fell in love with these little water taxis. After a tour as hand on one he enlisted three men with capital and went into partnership with them, eventually buying them out one by one and becoming sole owner of the business.

Shortly he was rich, a strange sensation; and one night he found himself experiencing another sensation equally strange. Lying in a hospital room recuperating from a minor chest operation, with nobody to laugh with or drink with and no business to order around, he started down the perilous path of introspection. He had a nice business, yes; he was getting to know important people and he could pick up almost any sized check. But was that all the fun there was to be had? Just then he heard a groan from the next room. A man, he learned, was dying from lack of blood.

"Why don't you go to a blood bank?" he asked the doctor, and was told there was no such thing.

Higgins jumped out of bed, pulling on his pants, and plunged down to the docks, where he grabbed ten sailors and, dragging them back to the hospital, squeezed a pint of blood from each. The man died anyway, for they had got to him too late, but he had not, as the saying goes, died in vain, for the wheels had been put under Higgins and he never stopped rolling again.

"Why don't you have a blood bank?" he demanded of the Red Cross, and they shot back the demand that he organize one himself. The first year they got five hundred pints. He staged donation ceremonies in elevators, business offices, at race tracks. No visiting celebrity got out of town with as much blood as he brought in, and the police department gave Higgins first crack at speeding motorists, who were allowed to pay their fines out of their own arteries. By 1954, 160,000 pints had come in, and he had started an eye bank as well, which necessitated a trip to Leland Stanford University in California for instruction in modus operandi.

But he was pushing himself too hard, and when his plane conked out over a rice paddy and the enormous man had to walk ten miles in a cooking sun, something inside him burst. The hospital got blood for him from Clark Field, but its type didn't fit, so some other was flown from Tokyo. This serving only as a stop-gap, an appeal was put on the radio, whereupon one thousand Filipinos offered a pint of their best and a convention of doctors dining at the Manila Hotel rose from the table *en masse* and moved to the hospital.

During the months that followed, President Magsaysay presented the ill man, who was gradually shrinking to normal size, the Philippines' highest decoration, the Golden Heart, and sent him by plane to Walter Reed Hospital in Washington; after a long and difficult recuperation there he finally returned to his old haunts, with half the poundage but grin unreduced.

"I beat the box," he yelled to the crowd at the airport.

It was long before this time that Chester Womack had brought him his proposition about treasure diving: Higgins had many small boats, did he have one he could spare for a salvage vessel?

This was the kind of thing that would have lifted Higgins right off a deathbed, so the boat question was settled forthwith, after which each put up twenty-five hundred pesos for a compressor and they were ready for business. They put in a bid based on percentage of gross, but lost. The successful bidder found only a few thousand pesos, so next year Womack and Higgins tried again and got it. It is not known definitely, but Higgins' well-known philanthropies may have had something to do with the generous terms of the contract—thirty-five per cent of the gross.

Womack was a deep-sea diver but no native of Manila, while Higgins, who was strictly for the surface, knew his water-front men backwards. He knew who could dive, so he just hired back the men who had worked for the Japs and previous contractors, Teddy, Jaime, and two of Jaime's Filipino friends, treating them with fatherly solicitude and at the same time taking certain practical precautions. He knew that on previous contracts, the Clark-Daves one for instance, Teddy had got away with extra pesos by hanging a bucketful on the end of the skeg under the boat and taking it away after work; so, deadpan, he simply had the boat checked every night. He knew, too, that while Jaime had a good reputation it was always possible to repeat what he had done to the Japs during occupation, go down and rest awhile on a box and then come up to report sadly, "Nothing there." So to encourage co-operation he paid his men two per cent of the gross each in lieu of wages, and they worked like beavers.

Having no maps or charts such as had plagued the Navy and civilians before them, the men were starting from scratch, but at least they knew it, and they plotted the whole area between Corregidor and Caballo Island in grids sixty feet square with lines ten or fifteen feet apart and the salvage ship in the center. The men worked these lines an hour at a time, two walking at right angles to the other two and crossing each other periodically, and thus covered every foot of the bottom.

As if even the bay were Higgins' friend, it gave up a box on the very first day. Each man carried a short bar with which to probe the mounds of silt, and when Jaime stumbled on his first box he prized the lid off and emptied it into a bucket, giving the signal to topside with five jubilant jerks on the line. From that day forward, for the nine months of the contract, there was a steady stream.

True, there were no great piles of boxes, only those curving trails spreading out from South Dock like the spokes of a fan, but the trails were very nice and kept up a comfortable supply.

After some time Womack was called back to the States and Higgins went on alone, leaving a foreman aboard while he attended to the really important business of the blood bank. Once every ten or twelve days the crews would bring the load ashore, ten thousand pesos or so, always starting at a different hour to avoid raids by the lawless Huks in the hills and going by a different route. For a couple of days, while the men drank beer and a dark rum potion called *tuba*, Higgins' Spanish-Irish wife reprovisioned the vessel, with a heavy concentration on eggs, for however content the divers were with their rice and fish and vegetables, Higgins' superstitious faith in raw eggs demanded that no diver go down with less than four inside. An equal faith in softball carried over from his Borax Company days prompted a series of games with the Army on Corregidor, and though his men never won a single time they did run off any extra fat and keep themselves partially out of mischief.

The only mischief, indeed, that he could not handle was their insubordination in the decompression department. Despite years of diving they stubbornly decompressed by ear, scorning the elaborate Navy schedules of relative depths and lengths of time submerged. Over and over they broke surface too soon, to be met with curses from the foreman and told to go down and wait a little longer, but one day, after Macario had come up briskly and been helped out of his diving dress, he suddenly seized his stomach and threw himself on the deck twisting and screaming. Wildly Jaime radioed to Higgins' office on Pier 11 while the others stood about in awe watching their agonized fellow. Higgins flew out and rushed Macario to a hospital, where he was given multifarious pills, tapped to relieve an excess of fluid, and coddled for three weeks, after which he was grounded for life and moved to a job in the office. This was the end of the foreman's decompression trouble, for now the divers tiptoed respectfully around the bends, timing their ascents to the second, like a woman with a pressure cooker.

Except during such crises as these, Higgins stayed ashore, but he still managed to keep in touch, for friends in the Signal Corps daily relayed a code message from Corregidor, "Six cans of beans delivered," having its own special meaning for him.

The diving contract lasted nine months, and during this time they recovered ₱819,797.50, the largest sum retrieved since Clark's and Daves' try. Higgins and Womack each received eighty thousand dollars, of which Higgins kept forty thousand for himself and his wife and gave forty thousand to his loved one, the blood bank.

During the next few years he was busy elsewhere, with other people's need for blood and then his own pressing need, but in 1955 he was back in Manila at work, having beaten the box, and on February 15, 1956, began diving again. This time ₱73,756.50 came up before his contract expired on the last day of the year.

By January 1, 1957, then, the figures were almost all in, official and otherwise. Of the ₱15,792,000 originally dumped, ₱5,383,173.50 had yielded to the Army and Navy in 1945–46. All the other contractors, according to the latest figures of the Central Bank of the Philippines, had accounted for ₱6,492,707.

These were the official figures, and they suggested that a residue of ₱3,916,119.50 should still be at the bottom.

But that would be reckoning without what the Japanese had taken up. As to that, ever since 1945, when the *Teak's* men began making inquiries around the water front, estimates had varied wildly, from "very little" to "six million," but palpably neither of these was correct. All that was known certainly was that during the first summer of the occupation the Japs had forced Filipinos, Moros, and American PWs to dive for them, and that they were believed to have stopped these operations that winter and done no more diving themselves. This was all local gossip, and nothing official was known.

As late as January 1, 1957, no more than this was known. Inquiry of the Philippine Consul General in New York brought the reply:

"With reference to the salvage operations during the Japanese occupation, no record has been found as to amount salvaged."

The head of the Philippine Reparations Mission in Tokyo, which might, it was hoped, have secured information as to how much Japan had profited from her occupation, for the purpose of reckoning her total war debt, wrote:

"I regret to inform you that I do not have any data on the subject in my possession."

The Philippine Bureau of the Budget answered:

"The Japanese may not have kept any records of the silver coins they may have salvaged out of the amount dumped into the Manila Bay . . . You will see or understand how futile it would be even to attempt to estimate just how much was salvaged by the Japanese during the occupation period."

The United States Army Far East Command in Tokyo was equally at a loss:

"Your letter has once again confirmed the futility experienced in past efforts to gain similar information . . . the lack of adequate documentary evidence of the success or failure of such an operation is an established fact. There are a number of valid reasons why such records are not available. They could have been destroyed by fire during some of the numerous bombing raids that the city of Tokyo was subjected to, they may have been destroyed on purpose to prevent such information from falling into our hands, or for that matter it is not even certain that such records ever reached Tokyo authorities provided they were maintained in Manila at the time of the alleged operations. No known agency of the present Japanese Government is able to say with any certainty where a search for such information should commence."

Since neither the Director of Naval History nor the Office of the Chief of Military History in Washington could furnish any information on the subject, this seemed to be the end of the story.

Then, on January 12, 1957, Lieutenant Walter Harmon, Retired, that same Willie Harmon who had been diving officer on the *Teak* twelve years before, was going through some old papers in the attic of his house in New London, Connecticut, and came across a limp piece of paper, tattered and yellowing in traditional old document style. He had no recollection of ever seeing it before, but when he studied the date, "8 Nov. 1945," he realized that it must have reached him months after he started work, and indeed just before he left the *Teak* altogether. It would have been of no interest to the divers by then and he would have laid it away with all other papers pertaining to that operation.

It was a copy of a memo, made in Ward 231-3, Navy Hospital, San Diego, California, to Bureau of Ships, and read:

"Dear Sirs; I wish to report diving operations conducted from July 8, 1942, until November 7, 1942, while we were prisoners of war of the Japanese Government. We were taken to a spot between Corregidor, P.I., and the mainland and told to dive for boxes of silver. The following USS *Canopus* and USS *Pigeon* 1st and 2nd class divers made dives in 120 feet water and recovered 98 boxes of 6000 Philippine silver pesos:

P. L. Mann	BM 1/C	18 dives
G. W. McCollough	GM 1/C	18 dives
V. L. Sauers	BM 1/C	19 dives
W. A. Barton	BM 2/C	16 dives
R. C. Sheats	TM 1/C	13 dives
G. Chopchik	BM 1/C	10 dives
H. S. Anderson	CCM	11 dives
M. Solomon	BM 1/C	19 dives

Other diving crews also were diving for this silver. The known recovered were:

Filipinos   18 boxes
Moros   257 boxes

Total known recovered 373 boxes.

On November 7, 1942, all salvage work ceased for unknown reasons. It was not known by us whether any later attempts were made to recover this silver. The silver recovered was turned over to the newly opened Bank of Taiwan at Manila."

Three hundred and seventy-three boxes equals approximately ₱2,238,000. In view of the fact that there has never been a report or even a rumor of the Japanese having subsequently done any diving of their own, it must be assumed that, with that one, all the missing figures have now been collected.

The stimulating conclusion to be drawn, therefore, is that despite the best efforts of Army and Navy divers, old pros and Pier 88 men; of sleek little Filipinos and Moros, including a hangdog hijacker; of eager American contractors and energetic ex-bouncers, ₱1,678,119.50 is still at the bottom of the bay. And so the story, although brought up to date, is probably not finished yet. As Willie Harmon said:

"They'll likely be diving on those pesos for a hundred years to come."

While the foregoing has dealt altogether with successful salvage operations, the successes are outnumbered a hundred to one by the failures. The two following are fairly typical failures, in that, while the ships were lost many years ago, interest in them has never died.

For help in the preparation of the Grosvenor story I have to thank Mr. P. J. Leggatt of Bulawayo, Southern Rhodesia, and Mr. J. P. Rowe, Editor of the Outspan, Union of South Africa.

Research on the story of the Duke's Galleon was made possible largely through the kind assistance of Mrs. Marian Smith Akehurst of London, Mr. Charles Lynch of Reuters News Agency, in New York, and especially of His Grace the Duke of Argyll, who supplied me with much hitherto unpublished material out of his family's history and his own experience.

VI
The Miser Sea

I THE GROSVENOR

IN THE SUMMER OF 1956 a member of the Order of the British Empire announced plans to go treasure diving off the coast of South Africa. This latest in the long procession of amateurs and professionals attempting to plunder the sunken *Grosvenor* was a former senior salvage officer in the Royal Navy decorated for outstanding service to his country, and as such an old hand at jobs like this. But it is safe to assume that no ship that Commander Peter Keeble had ever approached presented greater obstacles to success or boasted a more unusual history.

A smart vessel 120 feet long armed with twenty-six guns, the *Grosvenor* belonged to the Governor and Company of Merchants of London, Trading into the East Indies, that extravagantly rich private concern which in the eighteenth century held undisputed sway over 176,000,000 Indian peoples. Known familiarly as the East India Company, it was a sort of empire within itself and maintained a sizable fleet in which to transport oriental goods and riches back to Europe.

There has always been dispute over the exact value of the *Grosvenor's* cargo, but the accepted estimate includes 720 bars of gold worth £420,000; nineteen boxes of diamonds, rubies, and emeralds worth £517,000; 1,457 silver bars of unknown value, and £717,000 in star pagodas, an Indian coin equal to seven or eight shillings. All told there would be in excess of two million pounds when she sailed, and that was in 1782, when a pound would feed a family for a week. Besides this, popular rumor has added since the Peacock Throne of India, made of gold encrusted with gems and worth six million pounds. But Commander Keeble, in announcing his plans, claimed to be going merely after her silver, which in itself was no negligible prize.

Rarely has a treasure hidden out in a lonelier or more discouraging spot, Pondoland, on the eastern coast of South Africa, which at that time was a country of blacks who had never seen a white person—with the striking exception of one pale-skinned tribe whose name, Abelungu, meant White People, and who very obviously had seen more than one white person. Even Commander Keeble when he came many years later would find it lonely and bare, but at least in the meantime a village had sprung up, Lusikisiki—"Whispering of the Reeds"—and a road to Port St. Johns with a sign reading intriguingly, "To Grosvenor Wreck."

Although many men have tried many different systems to get at the sunken ship, Commander Keeble's plans called for full-dress diving. He had sent the *Steenbok* a good five years before to make a survey; she had moved about over the area until the sunken ship, which lay in a strong undertow and was frequently buried in drifting sand, by good fortune showed herself twenty-six feet down. The divers had stood on her broken timbers, bringing up cannon balls and anchors; they had located the part of the ship where the valuables were kept in such vessels, and the last news from South Africa in the spring of 1957 was that Commander Keeble confidently expected to succeed where many before him had failed.

The *Grosvenor* is potentially a very rich prize, but money alone is not enough to account for the fascination she has exerted for nearly two hundred years—not enough to inspire the publication some years ago of a novel *The Fate of the Grosvenor*, for instance, or the production of a play in London. There had to be something more romantic, and in her story there is romance indeed.

Setting out originally from Madras on the east coast of India, she was taking home a group of aristocratic Army officers and their families and some East India merchants perhaps not so aristocratic but very much richer, with the consequence that in addition to the official cargo the lazarette was reputed to hold a fortune in private property. Stopping briefly at Trincomalee in Ceylon, on June 13, 1782, she struck out on a ten-thousand-mile voyage that was to take her down through the Indian Ocean, around the Cape of Good Hope, and up along the Gold Coast. It would be five or six months before they reached England. Her captain, John Coxon, was a gentle, well-liked man, and that was a good thing during such a long confinement, but he was without executive ability and inclined to be overoptimistic, and that was very bad.

Pirates in those parts were an ever-present threat, but with the *Grosvenor* carrying twenty-six guns as well as many pig-irons for close fighting, the passengers settled down confidently to the long voyage. All went well until they passed Madagascar. Then on August 3 the wind freshened a little and a thick fog closed in. Although he had been unable that afternoon to take observations and was proceeding by dead reckoning, Captain Coxon assured his passengers at dinner that the ship was at least a hundred leagues from shore and in no possible danger of any sort. They all went to bed comfortably.

About four in the morning the wind freshened to a gale. The ship by this time was lying to under a foresail and mizzen-staysail; Beale, the third mate, was on the bridge—Captain Coxon was in his cabin asleep—and John Hynes and Thomas Lewis were aloft trying to send down the fore-topgallant mast. Suddenly Hynes saw white ahead, the deadly white of waves breaking on something that should not be there, and he hurried down to give the alarm. Beale, infected with his master's complacency, pooh-poohed the very possibility and sent him back aloft, but Hynes knew what he had seen and rushed below to wake the captain.

It was too late; the gale was driving the ship towards a ridge of rocks a few hundred yards from shore, and though the helm was put hard aweather, the sails were run down or loosed, and everything was done to bring her about, she charged onto them like a panicky horse and hung, half on one side and half on the other. Each surge of the waters lifted and dropped her with an extra blow on her keel, breaking her like a man breaking kindling across his knee. Coxon ordered the gunner to fire distress signals, though whom he expected to raise in this isolated spot is a moot question, but the powder room was full of water and it could not be done anyway. Then he ordered the mainmast cut away, and the foremast, but still the ship pounded on the rocks, head down and stern high, and they knew she could not last beyond dawn.

When daybreak did come, another terror was added in the shape of a crowd of blacks standing on the shore fascinated, but of the two these were preferable, and Coxon ordered the ship's yawl launched. At once the waves picked the boat up and smashed it against the rocks like a china teacup; the jolly boat fared no better, and in desperation a few men started the construction of a raft. Meanwhile the captain sent three strong swimmers, two Italians and an Indian, over the side with a deep-sea line. One was drowned but two reached shore, where they hauled in the line and the larger hawser attached to it. To their surprise the natives fell to and helped them secure the line to some rocks, which enabled several of the sailors to swing shoreward hand over hand, but many more who attempted to follow were drowned. The raft, meanwhile, had upset as soon as it was launched.

The back of the ship had been weakening fast, and now, with a series of reports like cannon shots, she broke in two, but by a miracle which the captain hardly deserved the starboard bow where the passengers were huddled was caught by a sudden sea breeze and driven handily into shoal water. Even the women and children were able to wade ashore, and thus unexpectedly all were saved except the Negro cook, who, in a fit of drunken loyalty, refused to leave his ship.

The stern stuck between two submerged ridges of rock—the stern where the millions of pounds were tucked into a cuddy under the captain's cabin.

The catastrophe had consumed most of the day. When night came, the Africans, who had gathered a pile of flotsam from the wreck, took their spoils and went home to their kraals, leaving the whites to take over the fires they had built against the biting winds. The sailors had recaptured some hogs and fowls escaped from the ship, while others salvaged a cask of beef and one of flour, and two precious ones of arrack which were warming their queazy insides until Coxon—good old Coxon—ordered the liquor poured into the sand lest the male Africans steal it, become inflamed, and make off with the women. These shivering creatures were sheltered in tents made from two salvaged sails, and finally all lay down and slept. A decent burial was arranged next day for the dead and consultation was held about the future.

Coxon, with his usual amiable miscalculations, told the assemblage that while he had at first planned to remain here until Mr. Ligoe, the chief mate, and the other wounded recovered, he now thought they had better be getting along because of the scarcity of provisions. They were, he asserted after some fancy paper work, only about 170 miles from the Cape settlements and could make it easily in sixteen days. Fear of the Africans' assagais, knobkerries, and shields was another reason for moving on.

One of the crew, who spoke a little of the native language, explained to Bungana, the Chief of the Hlubis, that the white men had lost the wooden fish in which they had arrived to the god of the waters, that they were very hungry, and in return for food would give handsome gifts to the whole tribe. Bungana accordingly kept them supplied for three days, but during the third night Coxon, regarding promises to blacks as no promises at all, led his charges away *en masse*, and next morning, when the Chief and his tribe came for their gifts, two only remained, John Bryan, a lame artificer who had made friends with the Africans by doing some ironwork for them, and Joshua Glover, a half-wit who preferred their company. Considering the fate of the ones who went away, this boy's wits may not have been as meager as they seemed.

Coxon, wrong to the last, had divided his charges into three groups, one composed of the hardiest of the sailors, the second of the passengers and the last of the servants, the rest of the crew and himself. Altogether 142 people innocently set out on one of the most formidable treks ever attempted, a walk without fresh water, without food, without even shoes in many cases, along not 170 but seven hundred miles of rocky coast line. They had got off, too, on the wrong foot by betraying their promises, for Bungana and his friends, hastily assembled, followed their spoors and in three hours were demanding the payment as arranged. The whites pleaded inability to make good until they reached their own people, but the Africans impatiently ran at them to grab off their valuables and, seeing one woman slip a diamond into her hair, ransacked the headdresses of all of them. This was too much for the men, who swung about wildly with their knives until the others retired from the battle temporarily.

After a few days dissension began splitting the party. The young and vigorous, held back by the women and small children, finally declared their independence and sprinted ahead in order to alert a rescue party for the rest. The others straggled behind, meeting along the way tribes of all shades of temperament, from the friendliest to the most suspicious. Some attacked on sight while others traded food for trinkets, one gold watch chain bringing a bullock which the Africans helped dissect, being given in return some entrails as their share. The carcass was cut into portable pieces and the hide made into foot coverings for the shoeless, and the party then split again into a fast and a slow group, Coxon remaining with the rear guard of women and children.

Not long afterwards the men's party encountered a suspicious-looking mulatto by the name of Trout, whose vague account of himself led them to conclude nervously that he was a murderer escaped from white justice. Instead of assisting them he warned darkly that any resistance to the tribesmen would be worse than useless, and when asked to guide the party to civilization made an evasive excuse about a wife and children waiting at home. The most chilling thing about Trout, however, was the garment he was wearing, for that morning gown could have come from nowhere but off the back of Captain Coxon.

This, in fact, was the last sign of Coxon, or of the women and children in his care, for many years. Then it came out that they had stumbled on through the bush and along the shore, living on shellfish and the drops squeezed from their clothes when it had the goodness to rain, till one by one they began to die of thirst and starvation. Bungana and his brother, accompanied by the hanger-on Trout and a few friends, had followed and seized two of the exhausted women, killing the men when they attempted to intervene and taking them back to the kraals as their wives. Trout had got the morning gown as his share of the spoils.

Six years later, Captain William Bligh, passing that way in his ship the *Bounty*, heard the tale of a white woman living in a village with Africans who was said to be always weeping, and later still other people heard the story from Bungana himself. Although the antecedents of most of the Abelungu have never been identified, there can be little doubt that a few of those long-haired pale-skinned people are descended from the stolen women of the *Grosvenor*.

While this rear party was falling to the Africans the forward party was moving ahead along the sand and rocks of the coast, some drowning as they attempted to cross rushing rivers, some drinking the brackish water and dying in delirium, some dying simply of starvation. The ship's steward and young Master Law, aged eight, having become close friends, the child did his best to keep up with the rest, but eventually he had to be carried, his wan little face exciting considerable pity among the African women and winning the entire party milk and food in one place. But as the days went on he faded rapidly. Finding a dead whale on the beach, he and the steward ate of the flesh and next day were too ill to move. Their companions agreed to stay till tomorrow, but tomorrow they were no better. The third day the others faced the alternative of leaving them behind or waiting indefinitely, but the gentle little boy solved their dilemma by dying quietly in the night with his eyes wide open. The steward, weeping weakly, was forced by his companions to tear himself from the stone-covered grave and come along until in a delirious moment he drank a shellful of sea water, whereupon he too lay down and gave them no further trouble.

Of one group John Hynes was the only man to remain alive. So starved had he and his two companions been at one stage that they had discussed cannibalism as a way out of their plight, but when the other two died a natural death he could not bring himself to eat them—or at least he so reported when he reached the Cape settlement.

One Hubberly was more fortunate, for on November 2, after three months of walking, he came upon a friendly tribe who fed him for four days before sending him on his way again. Later he found two of his shipmates, and the three were permitted to remain a full month in a native village eating and drinking, to start out again for the final push with renewed strength. At last, after nine more days of walking, they came on wagon tracks which led them to a Dutch farm where white people listened to their tale in open-

mouthed horror. Soon the entire Cape settlement was buzzing with
the story of the three men who had walked 167 days through the
hitherto unexplored country of the Amapondos. A relief party set
out immediately and Hynes, another white man, seven Indians, and
two black women were brought back to add their stories to the
others'. Many of them could give eyewitness accounts of the last
days of their companions, but of the end of Coxon and his party
no one remained to tell, the fate of the two white women, brides
of Bungana and his brother, becoming known as a certainty only
when Bungana told it himself.

During the years following, many affairs of greater moment than
the fate of the *Grosvenor* occupied the minds of the English rulers,
the Napoleonic Wars among them. But by 1840, these being settled
and the records of the East India Company having fallen into the
hands of the government, the Admiralty took a startled and pleased
look at the manifest of the wreck and sent down a salvage ship to
investigate.

When Captain Bowden's warship arrived on the scene he found
the hull still visible, but after staying several months and making
fifteen or twenty attempts to reach her strong room he admitted
defeat by the tumultuous waves.

This was the first but by no means the last such attempt, for presently white men settled closer at hand and certain local farmers,
notably one William Carter, began taking a proprietary interest in
the wreck that has stayed alive ever since. In the 1870s Carter
brought to land some beams of strong English oak which became
family heirlooms. Twenty years later he helped Captain Sidney
Turner pick up eight hundred gold star pagodas on the beach, and
in 1896 was assistant to Alexander Lindsay when, instead of going
down to the bottom for coins, Lindsay tried to bring the bottom
up to him by blowing up the rocks on which the cuddy was said
to be stuck. From the newly made pools they did collect approximately a thousand coins, a deep-sea lead and a cannon ball. Several of her cannon were also removed, of which Cecil Rhodes
acquired two, while another was set up on the hotel lawn at
Lusikisiki.

In 1907 the first big mechanized assault was made on the wreck.

The Grosvenor Treasure Recovery Company of Johannesburg chartered the salvage vessel *Duiker,* whose first job was to remove the deep sand collected on top of her. Situated as she was in a deep gully, a strong undertow alternately swept sand over her and swept her clean again, but they could not wait for the whim of the currents and installed a large air lift to do the job. Two divers were brought along, but the seas were so unruly that before they could even go down, the *Duiker* herself had been hurled onto a rock and damaged so badly that she had to rush back to Durban port for a quick repair. A month later she came out again fighting. Though the seas tossed her about unmercifully, divers Abrams and Jacobsen did manage this time to get down and catch the end of the suction pipe, which they forced into the sand over the wreck and in four days' work uncovered a part of her. Jacobsen excitedly reported seeing a coin glittering on a nearby rock, but just as he reached for it a small octopus caught at his arm, whereupon he slashed off a tentacle and so enraged the octopus that it inked up the water and the coin was hidden forever. That glimpse, however, had given everyone a pleasant glow of anticipation.

On the fifth day both divers went down again. After a period of investigation Abrams surfaced, but Jacobsen stayed so long that topside became anxious and signaled down to him. When no answer came back Abrams was hastily screwed back into his face plate and, going below, found Jacobsen lying dead on the sea floor. His rubber air hose had been cut on a sharp rock. Had his helmet been equipped with a non-return valve to prevent loss of air inside the suit he would have had five or six minutes' grace in which to surface, but as it was he had been instantly inundated.

In spite of artificial respiration Jacobsen was at last pronounced irrevocably dead and buried in the sea, after which the heart went out of the enterprise even though considerable odds and ends had been brought up—some small star pagodas and Venetian gold pieces, a few silver and copper coins, a shoe buckle, a silver label from a Madeira wine bottle, some horn spectacle rims, and much broken china and glass—enough to keep interest in the *Grosvenor* alive for some time to come.

About this same time the growing son of William Carter, being right on the spot, was fitting naturally into whatever activities were afoot, and the next one of any importance came along fourteen years later. This was something fantastically new. A tunnel.

Like New York City in a blizzard, when all traffic leaves the surface and takes to underground tunnels, the Webster Syndicate planned to circumvent winds and waves by digging under the ocean and approaching the ship from beneath. After making careful study of the wreck from documents and charts M. L. Webster of Johannesburg put up a thousand-pound bond and secured a lease on the foreshore. With the government claiming fifteen per cent of all treasure recovered, he then floated a company and sold shares at one shilling before operations started, two later, and four when things really got humming, some of the capital coming, improbably, from Conan Doyle, who seems not to have been as shrewd as his alter ego, Sherlock Holmes.

Under the direction of C. D. Chapman, an engineer who had earned his spurs in the gold mines of the Rand and tunneled through many a hill and mountain elsewhere, a camp was established at the site. The nearest village was Lusikisiki, twenty-five miles away, the nearest railroad 130, and so bad were the roads that supplies took three months to go that 130 miles by horse-drawn wagon. Large round huts with thatched roofs, called rondavels, were built for the workers. Since the forests nearby had been hacked down by previous treasure hunters, now neither white settler nor black native was allowed to cut, and Chapman had to get special concessions to secure enough fuel for the necessary steam.

Steam was the life of the operation. The tunnel, with an entrance set back some fifty or seventy-five feet from the water's edge, had to be cut through solid sandstone with compressed air drills. Ten or twelve feet wide at its mouth and narrowing as it progressed, the inclined shaft drove down at an angle for 127 feet and then flattened and ran horizontally towards the wreck. This excavation was to be 420 feet long and contain a series of watertight compartments. When the tunnel arrived directly under the wreck the workers were to drill up through the ceiling into the ocean floor above. Through these compartments they would blast their way into the hull, convey the valuables to the first watertight compartment, and then by closing one door after another on the principle of locks in a canal, work their way out, each compartment being pumped dry in turn.

By the end of 1922 the tunnel reached 416 feet out under the sea, and at a meeting of the syndicate in Durban in February 1923, J. H. Forman, presiding, mentioned first this happy fact and then went on with a large *But*. It had been discovered recently that the precise position of the wreck had not been satisfactorily established and therefore a steamer had been chartered to have a look from above. This had brought to light the embarrassing fact that the tunnel had been pointing a little askew, but now its nose was set in the right direction, and hopes were of the most sanguine.

At this point a major catastrophe nearly struck. As the tunnelers penetrated nearer the wreck they found their drills sliding too easily through the rock overhead. On examination the diamond bits were found to be bringing down with them not dust of sandstone but clay, soft clay. By the time they had gone 690 feet there was no solid roof of rock over them any longer. Water had begun trickling through the holes and eating away the clay still farther, and at last, with a thunderous plop, the roof collapsed into the tunnel. The men got out just in time.

But the legend of the *Grosvenor's* treasure was so unforgettable and the theory of the tunnel so plausible that not even this failure could utterly disenchant the hopeful. Once more Richard Carter was put to work, this time by a sugar planter from Durban who planned to pump out the tunnel and then shore it up. But when it proved impossible to pump the tunnel dry he changed his mind and instead charged Carter with the digging of a new tunnel which was positively to keep to solid rock all the way. Three hundred feet of it were, in fact, accomplished, but by 1927 the planter's means and his enthusiasm had both petered out and he turned it over to an American millionaire.

Mr. Pitcairn, like a gambler at a race track, had allotted himself a certain sum to play with and after that, win, lose or draw, that was to be all. His ten thousand pounds took the tunnel out to the wreck—they believed. Fifteen holes were made up into the hulk—they believed—at least, the workers brought down bits of wood and a trace of lead that seemed to suggest a hulk. But Pitcairn was a firm man, and when his Canadian engineer Frazee reported that the ten thousand pounds were used up, although they were now 230 feet towards the wreck, Pitcairn refused to go further. In accordance with the mining regulations of the Union of South Africa, all unused dynamite was exploded, and one more assault on the *Grosvenor* ended in a reverberating roar and a vast column of smoke.

In 1946, Richard Carter was getting along in years but once more, at the call for action, he rushed out like an old fire horse. By this time he was not to be startled by anything, and when the order came to build a pier with a crane on it to lift the wreck bodily out of the ocean, he sighed patiently and set to work. The pier never got very far though; somebody backed out and Carter returned to farming.

Many other treasure hunters have come and gone since then, the local residents watching them with a tolerant smile. Eager skin divers have come with surf boats. Bright-eyed inventors have brought rafts with magnetized cables with which they hoped to attract the treasure to them. And in 1956 Commander Keeble, the last and one of the most reasonable, added his name to the list.

If the sea ever gives up the *Grosvenor*, or the *Grosvenor* gives up her treasure, hundreds of men will read of it with rejoicing, for each success is a reassurance to other seekers. But at the same time it will be something of a pity, for of all the games of hide-and-seek on a really grand scale, the search for the *Grosvenor* has been one of the grandest.

II   THE DUKE'S GALLEON

DURING THE COURSE of British history there have been many dukes and many sunken treasures, but only one sunken treasure particularly identified with one particular dukedom, and only one duke who has made a hobby, almost a career, of his family's treasure.

The homes of Ian Douglas Campbell, eleventh Duke of Argyll, are filled with mementos of this most famous and long-standing of all treasure hunts. The small house one door off Grosvenor Square (with an empty lot next door where a German bomb landed), furnished with quiet elegance and remarkably warm for an English dwelling, has a second-story library with a long closet full of papers, maps, court documents, and relics of the Tobermory galleon.

"This is an amusing bit," smiled the Duke, prior to his 1954 search, as he exhibited an ancient pewter dish with two engraved initials as indisputable proof of the authenticity of his family's claims.

But, questioned as to the probabilities of finding the galleon's reported thirty million Spanish ducats, he smiled again. "I haven't the foggiest notion what we'll find. It's just a gamble, but a damned amusing one, don't you think?"

His home in Scotland, Inveraray Castle, is likewise full of Tobermory mementos. An enormous structure started in 1746 to which, in 1878, a new row of rooms was added along the top ("Why they thought they needed twenty-eight more rooms, God only knows"), it has a great fireplace ornamented by nineteen halberds, thirty-three Lochaber axes, twelve broadswords, three shields, three cuirasses, three helmets, two miniature cannon, and seventy-eight flintlock muskets—relics of the fighting clan Campbell, in the entrance hall six round cannon balls, and on the lawn a handsome cannon known as the Glied Gun, all taken from the wreck many years ago.

While such highborn folk of the past as the Duke of Albemarle and all of the Stuart Kings have been eagerly interested in treasure-diving expeditions, they were thinking exclusively of the money, but the interest of the Argyll family is a legitimate family affection; anything you have owned for three hundred years is apt to be close to the heart. And, as the present Duke said:

"The galleon is a physical relic of the great Spanish Armada that was to have finished off England and didn't. That was a critical time in our history, and even if no money is ever found in her, *anything* will be interesting to us here, because of its historical significance." That he assesses his countrymen correctly would seem to be borne out by the excitement created by a sword taken from the wreck some years ago. Exhibited in a jeweler's window in London, it gathered such crowds that traffic was disrupted and the police had to ask that it be removed.

The Argyll family were, of course, not the original owners of the ship lying under thirty feet of mud on the Scottish coast, nor were they, indeed, even interested in her at the time she sank. They were

Scots, and in the sixteenth century Scots, who had no love for England, looked on at English struggles with Spain with a dispassionate eye; this was not their fight. But in the country to the south all was tension and expectation in that summer of 1588. The long simmering quarrel between Elizabeth and Philip II was gathering heat, and finally, in July, the pot boiled over and Philip took overt action.

Philip's allies, the Duke of Parma and the Duke of Medina, had taken a large force to Flanders and were there poised to strike across the Channel; another large force of thirty thousand men and 132 ships was to come up the coast and land on the south shore of England, setting up a bridgehead and thus preparing the way for Parma to rush in and sweep over the land. This invasion, more than a political war, was for the re-establishment of Catholicism in England, and it brought a crown, blessed by the Pope, to be used at Philip's coronation, as well as a store of money and valuables with which to bribe local sympathizers. In July it swept north towards the Channel.

During the eight years since Drake had returned from his circumnavigation he had spent as much time as Elizabeth would allow him at his favorite sport of singeing the beard of the King of Spain. At times she had wavered in her support of him—she was a prime waverer—for she feared his audacity was driving Philip into a war she dreaded. But Philip was determined on war anyway, Drake or no Drake, and when she realized it was inevitable and that her hour had come, she took a firm grip on herself, the situation, and her people. Riding down to Tilbury to inspect the assembled troops, she suddenly became ten feet tall.

"I know I have the body but of a weak and feeble woman," she told them stoutly, "but I have the heart and stomach of a King of England, too, and I think it foul scorn that Parma or Spain or any other prince of Europe should dare to invade the borders of my realm." The men, soldiers and sailors alike, thought it foul scorn, and went out furiously to repel such impudence.

Drake was not allowed supreme command—that could only go to a nobleman, the Lord Admiral, Lord Charles Howard of Effingham—but he was made Vice-Admiral and that was good enough. When the Armada sailed up the Channel on July 19 it was the most formidable fighting instrument ever assembled, but for seven days it was outthought and outfought by Howard and Drake, Frobisher and Hawkins, and on the eighth Drake had the greatest satisfaction of his life.

Many years before, in the harbor of San Juan d'Ulúa, Drake and Hawkins had been brought to the depth of humiliation by the two Spanish fire ships that had set their tiny fleet ablaze and ruined them, and now it was appropriate that the humiliation should be avenged in the same manner. Eight English merchantmen, stuffed with tar barrels, were put to the torch and sent downwind among the galleons. The wooden Spanish ships, once set blazing, were helpless to save themselves, and what the incendiary ships began the winds took up and carried on, fanning the sails into sheets of flame and the hulks into prisons filled with suffocating, dying men.

Drake watched the remnants of the mighty fleet turn tail and run, not back south, because that way was cut off, but north, the long way around for home, and he must have sensed that Spain would never be the same again and gloried that her ruin was largely his doing.

The fleeing Spaniards, even after the pursuing English ships had dropped the chase, were pursued by the vengeful English winds, which gathered force as they rounded the head of Scotland and, bursting upon them in a merciless gale, ripped them to pieces and sent them crashing onto the rocks. Along the coast of Scotland and West Ireland more than sixty ships piled up; between Sligo and Ballyshannon eleven hundred men were found lying drowned on the shores, and enough wreckage drifted in to have built a whole new fleet. Eight thousand men struggled through the tempestuous water to land, but what they met was almost as deadly as the storm itself, for in many places every one of the strangers was put to the sword.

One ship, with a nobleman aboard, dragged into Tralee Bay with twenty-three survivors and surrendered to Lady Denny, thinking that, as one aristocrat to another, he might find mercy. But Lady Denny disliked invaders of whatever class, and ordered the entire company executed.

The company of the Gran Grifon fetched up on Fair Isle in the Shetlands, where the crew and Captain Lopez lived on sea birds' eggs for six weeks and then, unable to bear the diet any longer, gave up to the Scots. This group, however, fared better; the Fair Isle people were of a gentler disposition and allowed them to settle down, where they taught the natives the art of designing and weaving fabrics in gay bright colors which has stood the isle's weavers in good stead ever since. Some others managed to incorporate themselves in the life of various communities, and to this day not a few Scottish Robinsons and Frasers have borne a wild dark look and the improbable first name of Diego or Rodriguez.

The most memorable of the castaways, however, was a ship that escaped the storm, a high proud galleon, long and slim in the Portuguese fashion and designed for quick, hard fighting. She weighed 960 tons, carried seventy guns, over four hundred men, and was sunk in Tobermory Bay off the coast of Scotland in September 1588. These are the bare facts.

The rest of her story, assembled by many a researcher and documented by court records, photostats of letters, paintings, maps, lists, and miscellaneous papers in that closet off the Duke's library, is more intriguing. It details the spectacular death of the ship and the acquisition of her remains by the lofty house of Argyll, which is the beginning of her long association with the Dukes.

The first time she appeared in the English records was on September 23, 1588, when the English Ambassador to Edinburgh, Sir William Asheby, wrote to Sir Francis Walsingham (that same Walsingham who had furthered Drake's schemes so admirably) that ten days before, on September 13, a great Spanish ship had been driven ashore off the Isle of Mull on Tobermory Bay.

A month and a half later he reported the gossip coming to Edinburgh from Mull: that the ship was one of great and especial interest, that she was said to be very rich, with men aboard who ate off solid silver dishes, and that the local Scots would fain have taken her by force but that she was too well guarded by soldiers and guns.

Then, a week later, news came that the ship had been deliberately sunk, by treachery apparently, and lay in thirty feet of water a hundred feet offshore. Walsingham, who had told Asheby to see that this rich ship by no means got back to Spain, now dismissed the sunken wreck from his mind.

The "treachery" which was the cause of the galleon's death was a story fairly typical of the time and place.

After the debacle in the Channel, the great ship had wandered about the inhospitable shores of the North of Scotland, her supplies vanishing, her soldiers and sailors slowly starving, and by the middle of September, when she reached the bay of Tobermory on the west coast, all on board were desperate.

The waters hereabouts were controlled by the local chieftain, Sir Lauchlan MacLean, who was fighting an independent clan war with a neighboring chieftain, Clanranald, and when the Spanish ship drifted in, full of soldiers clamoring for food, Sir Lauchlan made a proposition: let the captain of the great ship lend him a hundred fighting men for his forthcoming attack on Clanranald and he should have his supplies for the voyage home. The Spaniard agreed, and during the next two months MacLean and the hundred men laid waste the islands of Rhum and Eigg, after which the Spaniard demanded his payment.

MacLean, with his eye on still another territory, Ardnamurchan, proposed an extension of the bargain. The Spaniard, anxious to be off home, demanded instead his promised supplies. MacLean refused irritably. The Spaniard insisted; there were hot words, an insulting exchange of accusations, a violent quarrel, which was continued with MacLean's son aboard the ship, and suddenly the Spaniard, losing his temper completely, pulled up anchor and started off home with his enemy's son as hostage.

At this young MacLean rushed below, seized a flint, and before the ship had gained more than a few yards, struck it in the powder magazine and blasted the ship, the crew, and himself to kingdom come.

Scotland's west coast, where the galleon ended her days, was under the general command of the Admiral of the Western Isles, who was also the Earl of Argyll, but though the ship had gone down near to his native Argyllshire, he took no notice of the event for a little while to come.

However, the Spanish court lost no time in announcing that while a ship called the *Juan Bautista* had admittedly been lost off the Scottish coast, the flagship of the Duke of Tuscany, which had been carrying the wages of the Armada soldiers, had returned safely home. The Armada payroll was fifteen thousand pounds a day, and the Dukes of Parma and Medina, waiting in Flanders, were expecting to receive a daily thirty thousand pounds from Spain as well, which made the safety or loss of this certain large galleon very important indeed.

The Earl of Argyll, with other things on his mind, gave the wreck no more thought, and for some twenty-three years the ship was left to work her way down inch by inch into the loose sand at the bottom of the Bay. Then in 1611 this seventh Earl, who had previously been married to a Protestant, married the Catholic daughter of Cornwallis, and their homeland being cold towards those of that faith, she persuaded him to move to the more congenial atmosphere of Spain. There he became extremely friendly with the King, even commanding his armies in the Netherlands—a real traitor in the eyes of Englishmen, though Argyll was a good Scotsman and never claimed to have anything to do with England's quarrels.

Through the Earl's friendship with the King of Spain he became privy to confidential documents in the Castle of Simancas, and there saw a letter from the Duke of Medina to Philip II dated September 3, 1588—shortly after the defeat of the Armada. In it Medina begged for money to pay his soldiers in Flanders, complaining that he had received not a penny and that they were starving. This was interesting, for Spain had certainly *sent* the money, and had announced long ago that the ship that carried it had returned to Spain unharmed. Why, then, were the troops starving? Could it be that their payroll had not after all reached them, as announced?

His curiosity thus aroused, the Earl made it his business to talk to people who might enlighten him, and managed to meet one Captain Andres Pereira. This Andres Pereira, a Portuguese, had been captain of the infantry on board the flagship sometimes known as the *Florencia*, which was the private contribution of the Duke of Tuscany to the Armada and had been in Admiral Rodrigo de Valdez's squadron. Pereira and Argyll became great friends. The captain told the Earl that his ship had been sunk while he was ashore, thus enabling him to escape capture and finally return to Spain. And then he gave him a piece of advice:

"Buy that sunken ship lying in Tobermory Bay. Obtain her at whatever cost." His meaning was plain.

Pereira, reasoned the Earl, was one who should know, for he had been on the flagship himself. He recalled that there had been gossip when she first appeared about her imposing appearance, and, mulling over the Spanish Government's hasty announcement that the payship had returned intact, realized that this could have been merely an effort to divert attention until such time as Spanish divers, who were after all not at war with the Scots, could come back and retrieve the treasure. He tucked the advice away against the time when he would return to Scotland.

When he did go back his welcome was cold, for by now England and Scotland were united under the new King, James I of England, VI of Scotland, and James declared that by going off to Spain he had become a rebel. He was therefore in such disfavor that this was no time to ask for royal grants. He did, however, tell his son what he knew, and some years later, when both he and James I had died, the eighth Earl made a deal with Charles I which provided that in return for the crown said to be in the wreck, and one per cent of all profits derived therefrom, the Earl, with his heirs and assigns, was accorded by royal grant "the said wreck and other vessels, with the whole ornaments, munitions and other goods and gear which will happen to be found and apprehended there in." But before the Earl could do much with his grant he and the King quarreled and he lost his head, the first but not the last of the Argylls to be beheaded. (The present Duke denies that any of his ancestors was beheaded *because* of the quarrels over the galleon, but certainly the kings who executed them stood to benefit by their extinction.)

In the century after she went down, the ship had been steadily settling into the sand, and when in 1683 one Archibald Millar went down in a diving bell he found nothing but the upper decks visible. Through the window in the bell he reported seeing a number of dishes of a blue-white color, either silver or pewter, he could not tell which, and a crown, which he was unable to reach, but he did bring up several cannon and a silver ship's bell weighing four pounds. Millar also reported that he had seen somewhere a page from the Spanish records listing the galleon's cargo as "thirty millions of money"—presumably Spanish ducats.

Charles I had granted ownership of the galleon to the eighth Earl without fully realizing her potential value, but when word of the fortune within reached his sons, Charles and James, both kings in turn, they instituted a series of lawsuits to confiscate the property. The successive earls fought back grimly for many years, even despite the execution of another of their number, but the litigation was finally settled in their favor and they became the owners forever.

Curiously enough, the earls promptly seemed to lose all interest. For fifty or sixty years the ship was allowed to sink lower and lower and almost everyone forgot her or, if they remembered at all, half disbelieved what they had heard. Then in 1740 the incumbent Argyll, whose title had by now been elevated to Duke, sent down a diving bell and received up one of the greatest prizes of the entire hunt, the eleven-foot Glied Gun. Not only was this bronze cannon beautiful to look at, but certain workings on it proved, to the satisfaction of all Argylls, that the ship from which it was taken was indeed the flagship of the Duke of Tuscany known as the *Florencia*, for it bore the coat of arms of François I of France. This gun was known to have been cast for the French King himself, and to have been captured in battle by the Florentines. It also bore the initials of its maker, the inimitable Benvenuto Cellini, and none but the ship of someone very important would be graced by such a gun, the Dukes were convinced. Some gold and silver coins also came up during this try, a gold chain, some teeth, beads, and pins, but after this burst of activity the Dukes let the ship lie for nearly another hundred years.

The ninth Duke, a dynamic personage who had won the hand of Queen Victoria's daughter in marriage and served as Governor General of Canada for five years, brought things to life again with a bang. Several different syndicates were given contracts to work the wreck, in 1903, 1912, and again after World War I. A diver named Gush had also gone down in a full diving suit supplied with compressed air, but he had found the galleon sanded over altogether, and he also had the misfortune of nearly drowning when his air hose broke.

Each time the expeditions failed, and each time the Scots living nearby chuckled, for skepticism was growing with each generation. Some called the whole business an old wives' tale that had blown up bigger with each telling. Some revived the original Spanish story that the sunken ship was only the *Juan Bautista*. Some even doubted the existence of a ship there at all, none having seen her with their own eyes. The stock of the great galleon of the Duke of Tuscany, flagship of Admiral de Valdez, whose troops were commanded by Andres Pereira, had sunk very low indeed. The Duke still believed in her, but he was about the only one.

Then, like a shot in the arm, the pewter platter came up, the shape and size of a soup plate, covered with mud and thickly encrusted with salt. The Duke sent it to the British Museum to be cleaned, and when it came back great was the jubilation, for engraved on the rim was a coat of arms, and on either side an initial. "A." "P." Andres Pereira, surely, the important personage mentioned in the Ambassador's letter to Walsingham, who ate off "silver" plates, who met the Earl in Spain and first advised him to acquire the ship. This plate, the present Duke's "amusing bit," is the Argylls' trump card.

The ninth Duke was succeeded by an engaging individualist who for fifty years fought the twentieth century off, keeping railroads, cinemas, fish-and-chip shops and automobiles firmly out of his domain. He was not interested in nonsense like treasure ships, and died at eighty, a bachelor, without accomplishing anything memorable.

Then, in 1949, came Ian Douglas Campbell, first cousin once removed; also, eleventh Duke of Argyll; Marquis of Lorne and Kintyre; Earl Campbell and Cowall; Viscount of Lochow and Glenisla, Baron Inveraray, Mull, Morvern, and Tirye, in Scotland; Duke of Argyll in the United Kingdom; Earl of Argyll; Baron of Lorne; Baron Kintyre in Scotland; and Baron Sundridge of Coomb Bank, Kent, and Baron Hamilton of Hameldon County, Leicester, both in Great Britain; and a Baronet of Scotland; Chief of the Clan Campbell; Hereditary Master of the Royal Household in Scotland; Admiral of the Western Coasts and Isles; Keeper of Dunstaffnage, Carrick, Tarbert, and Dunoon Castles, and Hereditary Sheriff of Argyll; F.R.S.A. (1953), D.L. co, Argyll, Captain 8th Battalion, Argyll and Sutherland Highlanders (T.A.), T.D. (1953); served in World War II, 1939–45 (prisoner 1940–45); K.St.J.

This man is different from any of his ancestors, for although his line reaches far back into Scottish conservatism, the influence of America is strong upon him. Born in Paris of an American mother,

Aimée Lawrence of New York, he was educated at Milton Academy in Massachusetts and then at Oxford. Married first to the daughter of Lord Beaverbrook, of London newspaper fame, and then to an American woman, Mrs. Vanneck, in 1951 he married a famous beauty of London society, Margaret Whigham Sweeney, who also was brought up in America and whose press clippings fill five or six large red leather scrap books. For many years he spent a good part of his time in America, and it was therefore not surprising that when he came into the title he should lose no time in modernizing the ducal plant.

Three telephones were installed on his library desk to connect with the world at large and the office below of Peach the butler. He threw Inveraray Castle open to the public for two shillings and sixpence a look; he went into the Argyll sock business, his lean face and blue eyes smiling from the best men's magazines; and he made three stalwart efforts to bring the Tobermory galleon into line.

The first assault began four months after he inherited the estates. The bay of Tobermory is a quiet landlocked harbor, the town of Tobermory on the Island of Mull no more than a single row of small buildings, neatly painted, along the water front. The island has many villages, Pennygowan with its fine old ruined chapel, and Calgary, from whence restless Highlanders went forth to settle the wilds of Canada and name their new home for their old, but Tobermory is the metropolis—700.

The galleon is part of the town's tradition, and though some of the inhabitants smile wearily and say "Hoots, there's more good money been poured into the waters of Tobermory than will ever be taken out of it," in March 1950, when two small Navy boats anchored offshore, Mishnish Hotel and the local citizenry welcomed the newspapermen, sailors, and nobles according to their individual convictions, some with bright anticipation, some with amused skepticism, but all with good Scots appreciation of the trade to come.

At the inauguration of proceedings the Duke of Argyll greeted the descendant of the Chief of the Clan MacLean, whose son blew up the ship in the first place and started all the fun, and then all sat down to a banquet whose menu was appropriately printed in Spanish. Afterwards Lieutenant Commander R. N. Parkinson,

Royal Navy, took over, and the Duke and his young heir, the Marquis of Lorne, became mere spectators.

The Navy had no direct interest in the treasure hunt other than the flat fee of four thousand pounds of the Duke's money and fourteen per cent of the proceeds if and when, but it did feel that here was a good chance to give its deep-sea salvage crews some practice, so it sent a motor launch and a fishing vessel and a crew of divers. The vessels moored three hundred feet apart over the spot eighty-four feet from the end of the Tobermory pier where the ship went down. Lines were drawn from ship to ship along the bottom of the bay, forming half a dozen ten-foot lanes and casting a grid over an area three hundred by three hundred. The divers, wearing suits with certain new and secret Navy features and with cylinders on their backs containing enough oxygen for forty minutes' work at the bottom, carried pointed lances twenty-eight feet long with which to probe through the silt.

Working sixty feet down in the twilight of the clearest water in all Britain, one man would operate a high-pressure hose while another followed with his probe. Water at a pressure of 150 pounds per square inch gushed down and literally blasted holes out of the hard-packed silt, throwing up a mushroom five or six feet across composed of milky-white sand and yellow and green sea shells. As he cleared away the silt and mud the other went down into the hole he had made with his probe.

One day a man's lance touched something hard. Soon another three feet away did the same. Eventually the lances were bringing up on their sharp points slivers of wood—a wood grown only in North Africa.

After a few days the probers had outlined the shape of the thing below. It was the stern of a ship, lying upright on the rock beneath the loose silt. She had been blown apart amidship, and the bow was not found. But that did not matter, for the stern would be the part containing the cell of the gun room.

Diving continued, but the weather was cruel, out of fifty-seven days only seventeen providing good working conditions. Often after a turbulent spell the clearing at the bottom would be found completely refilled by the wash of the currents, and the divers would have to start all over. But finally enough of the hull was laid bare to begin yielding up its contents, and then suction pumps were brought into play, by which the water and everything in it were drawn up and sprayed across a net.

Now pleasant things began to happen. A sword sheath came hurtling through the air; then another sheath; then a broken dagger. Finally, greeted by shouts of joy from those on board, two small medallions came up. They were of silver, about the size of a quarter and very thin. On one side, exquisitely modeled in fine aristocratic lines, was the reclining figure of a nude woman, on the other a hook to clip it to some other object. Everyone handled these delicate things reverently, and all agreed that they were unmistakably the decoration of a very aristocratic ship, and unmistakably Spanish.

Thus the ship below was identified to everyone's satisfaction and the Navy, its work done, sailed away. The Duke sat down to plan his next move.

These forays into the past were not to be undertaken lightly, for they cost a great deal, and though the Duke is the second-largest landowner in Scotland, taxes are commensurately large. But he had two small encounters to spur him on to his next effort.

During the 1950 diving operations, when he was in London for a few days, he received a telephone call. A Mrs. Duff of Deptford would be pleased if he would come to see her. A charming elderly lady, she told him that she and her sister were the last remaining descendants of Rodrigo de Valdez, the Admiral de Valdez who had commanded the squadron in which the great galleon of the Duke of Tuscany had sailed.

For centuries, she told him, certain facts had been known in her family. "That ship of yours—the treasure is in it. You go down under the captain's cell and directly in front of you there is a cabinet with a four-petaled rose on the door. The treasure is inside." The Duke thanked her and made a note of the four-petaled rose, but he did not publish the interview.

Later a call came from another old lady, the descendant of another of the Armada's officers. The ninety-year-old Marquise de la Rochethurlon looked at the Duke earnestly, her eyes boring into his.

"I will tell you something that my family has always known.

There is a treasure inside your galleon. It will be found in a cabinet with a four-petaled rose on the door."

The Marquise had never heard of Mrs. Duff of Deptford nor of her four-petaled rose. The astonished Duke felt much bucked up.

(Later, still a third old lady gave him something to make him blink. A Mrs. Eliza Sale of Hove bequeathed him fifty thousand pounds as head of the Clan Campbell. He had never heard of her before.)

As riches attract riches, so spectacular personalities attract their like. In 1950, Argyll had drawn into his orbit a man who, famous enough while he lived, by his death became a figure of world-wide controversy. Lieutenant Commander Lionel Kenneth Crabb was one of the divers sent by the Royal Navy to Tobermory. A comic figure, short, with a long curving nose, he had been one of the outstanding underwater men of the war. In November 1942 he went to Gibraltar as a mine- and bomb-disposal officer, but when he got there he found that the mines were under water, so he went under too, wearing improvised gear of swimming trunks, a pair of badly fitting goggles, and a breathing apparatus designed for escape from submarines. For the rest of the war Crabb did astonishing things in the way of removing mines and unexploded bombs from the waters of Gibraltar, Venice, Leghorn (where he worked with some of the Americans from the *Normandie*), Florence, and Haifa. Then when the war was over and he was released as over age he drifted about trying to get work as a civilian diver, trying one job, trying another. For a while he was technical adviser and script-writer for the film *Wonders of the Deep*. Then, in 1949, he went to work for the Admiralty Research Laboratory, experimenting on new underwater methods and equipments. Much of this work was known to be secret and important.

After that came more odd jobs, until in early April 1956, Crabb wrote to his mother that he was going on a "little job," a simple affair, and that while she was not to worry she was to tear up his letter.

A few days later, about the middle of April, the Russian cruiser *Ordzhonikidze* brought Marshal Bulganin and Mr. N. Khrushchev to Portsmouth for a visit, accompanied by two Russian destroyers.

On April 17, Crabb checked in at a Portsmouth hotel.

A week later Crabb's mother was informed by the Admiralty that Crabb had disappeared on underwater tests in the Portsmouth area.

Shortly thereafter an official statement given to the press said that Commander Crabb was presumed to have died during a test dive near Portsmouth.

Quite a hue and cry went up in the House of Commons, and many people asked the question, What was the frogman doing near the Russian ships? The Prime Minister said:

"It would not be in the public interest to disclose the circumstances in which Commander Crabb is presumed to have met his death . . . However, what was done was done without the authority of Her Majesty's Ministers."

Two days later the Soviet Government announced that a frogman had been observed floating between the Soviet destroyers at 7:30 A.M. on April 19.

The British Government replied that the diver seen to be swimming between the Soviet destroyers was, to all appearances, Commander Crabb, and that his presence in the vicinity of the destroyers occurred without any permission whatever. After expressions of regret the incident was considered closed.

But the furor was not over, and questions continued to be asked: What was Crabb trying to find out? Had he been recovered, dead or alive, by either the Russians or his own friends? Where was the body? No one answered, and a year later no one had answered yet.

Then, on June 9, 1957, a badly decomposed body clothed in frogman's equipment was found on a sandbank on Pilsea Island, a few miles from where Commander Crabb had disappeared. On June 26 the coroner at nearby Chichester announced that, by measurements and a malformation of the big toes, the body had been identified as that of Crabb. But this clarification of one mystery only produced a new one, for the body was now lacking both hands and the head, and whether the mutilation was due to accident, the action of predatory fish, or to more sinister causes was impossible to determine.

This was the man, so mysterious in his death, who in 1950 had been overseer of the diving team at Tobermory. And in 1954, when the Duke decided to go all out and make an independent try, the Admiralty released Crabb (he had gone back into service) to lead the divers on this privately financed job. The Duke, putting the entire project under the direction of Rear Admiral Patrick McLaughlin, R. N. Ret., bought a coaster, *Ardchattan*, for use as a depot ship, and a Glasgow firm of ship brokers chartered for him several small craft and a dredger equipped with suction hoses.

"Twenty thousand tons of mud will have to be removed before any of us can really enjoy ourselves," the Duke said, "and we may bring up nothing but guns and skulls and timber. But even guns will have historic value, and that's really why I'm going down."

But he hoped also to have a television show if things got hot ("Can't you see the excitement each day as the people watch and wonder what's going to come up next?"), and considering the crowds that stopped traffic when the sword was exhibited, he probably had something there.

The middle of August 1954 saw the start of the privately financed venture, equipped with underwater television cameras to guide the men and suction pumps of unusual power. Crabb headed the crew of five frogmen, which included an old colleague, now retired, with whom he had done much of his Mediterranean war work, leading stoker Sydney James Knowles, B.E.M.

For over a month the air lift sucked away at the silt, and by the first of October had made a deep hole. The plan was to work all through the winter, but a new difficulty arose when stones, in sizes anywhere from six inches to three feet across, kept sliding to the mouth of the suction pipe. Suddenly everything would stop dead and the men would have to halt work to dislodge the stone. Some boulders were too heavy to handle without a mechanical grab, and none was available in the neighborhood. Things became very sticky.

But they hated to give up, for all of them had an affection for the Duke and his gallant effort—all Englishmen like a sportsman willing to gamble. Moreover, they knew they were in the right place, for a few pieces of broken timber had been retrieved, some fragments of bone, a part of a five-foot spear. So they kept on, pushing the mouth of the air lift down into the mud, working ever deeper into the pit they were creating.

On a day halfway through October when Argyll was in England, Crabb was on the depot ship directing operations, Knowles' wife

Joan was in the galley, and Knowles himself was working seventy-eight feet down surrounded by a wall of loose mud studded with stones. Suddenly, as he bent over his air lift like a woman operating a vacuum cleaner, there was a terrific thud on his back and he was thrown flat on his face, pinioned by a huge boulder.

Like all frogmen who, having no telephone lines to the surface, never work alone, Knowles had his stand-by diver. Terry Yettan saw the boulder flatten him into the mud, and then saw the loosened wall dissolve and slip down on top of man and stone, burying them both.

For half an hour Joan Knowles, cooking lunch in the galley, noticed no undue excitement on the ship. True, everything was extremely quiet; what conversation could be heard was in very low voices, but mostly there was only a sort of urgent silence as the men moved about with the quick contained efficiency typical of Commander Crabb's operations.

When her husband finally strolled into the galley she looked up to smile greeting, and then took another wifely look.

"Sydney, you're looking awfully peaked. You're working too hard."

"Oh, I've just got a cold coming on," said Knowles.

"He *is* working too hard," Crabb said, his hand on his shoulder. "We must give him a rest."

When the Duke received news of this near squeak he called everything off. Realizing that without heavy grabs further work would be dangerous and futile, he dismissed Commander Crabb and his team, and on October 19 he chalked up another failure.

"But I haven't given up," he said. "I'll probably be back next spring."

And back he was, with a giant dredge. Because dukes and sunken treasure are both good for a headline or two, the newspapermen gathered again, but this time so little happened that they were driven to sending out dispatches about a swan that appeared mysteriously and was reported by the local grandfathers to be a Spanish princess who always returned in some form or other every time the wreck was molested. Timber came up, a seven-foot piece, a little earthenware, a small cannon, but at the daily rate of diving teams and ships they were too expensive, and when the deadline, September 23, came and passed, operations ceased.

Whether this was the end for all time cannot be even conjectured. Long periods have elapsed in the past when the galleon was left undisturbed. But chances are that the words of the Duke will be as true twenty or fifty years from now as they were when he spoke them recently:

"I still think the gamble is worth taking. The world is too drab these days. We could all do with a little romance."

This, perhaps, is how the world feels too, that it could do with a little romance. And perhaps that is what leads it on to its search for treasure at the bottom of the sea. Certainly there are surer ways of getting rich, certainly there are safer ways. But the gamble, the uncertainty, must be part of the charm, and, moreover, the bringing back to life of things of the past long dead.

Then, too, there is something about gold and silver not duplicated by a check written on a bank—this is the raw stuff of adventure itself, the "silver penny" of the child's first fairy tales, the "piece of gold" the pirate stories center on.

There is, besides, the daily battle with a powerful foe. Like the mountaineer who must try to climb Mount Everest simply "because it is there," perhaps as long as that all but invincible adversary, the ocean, closes implacably over four fifths of the world's surface, men will continue to seek adventure in its depths.

LATROBE HIGH SCHOOL LIBRARY

BIBLIOGRAPHY

CHAPTER I

American Neptune, "2000 Years Undersea," October 1947.

Bancroft, H. H. *The New Pacific*. New York: Bancroft Co., 1900.

Bankers Magazine, "Sunken Treasure Ships," July 1916, Vol. 19.

Bridges, T. C. *Romance of Buried Treasure*. London: Nisbet & Co., 1931.

British Association for Advancement of Science, Report of Meeting, 1911, by Leonard Hill, "Physiology and Submarine Work," Vol. 81.

Campbell, John. *Lives of the Admirals*. London: 1742. Vol. II.

Cooper, Gordon. *Treasure-Trove, Pirates' Gold*. New York: W. Funk, 1951.

Cornwall, Ernest. *Story of Money*. London: Tuck, 1938.

Craig, John. *Danger Is My Business*. New York: Simon & Schuster, 1938.

Crile, Jane and Barney. *Treasure-Diving Holidays*. New York: Viking Press, 1954.

Dominican Republic Magazine, October 1938.

Driscoll, Charles. *Doubloons*. New York: Farrar & Rinehart, 1930.

Ellsberg, Commander Edward. *Men under the Sea*. New York: Dodd Mead, 1939.

Encyclopaedia Britannica, Eleventh Edition, "Money."

Encyclopaedia Britannica, Eleventh Edition, "Peru."

Ffoulkes, Charles. *The Armourer and His Craft, 11th–16th Centuries*. London: Methuen Co., 1912.

Great Britain. Public Record Office. Calendar of State Papers. Colonial Series: America and West Indies. 1681–1685.

Great Britain. Public Record Office. Calendar of State Papers. Colonial Series: America and West Indies. 1685–1688.

Great Britain. Public Record Office. Calendar of Treasury Books in Public Record Office. Vol. 8.

Hill, G. F. *Treasure Trove in Law and Practise of Antiquity*. London: British Academy. Vol. IX.

Jacob, W. *Historical Inquiry into Production of Metals*. London:1831.

Japan Institute for Science of Labor, Tokyo, Report #5. "The Ama and Her Work."

Justice, A. *General Treatise on Money and Exchanges*. London: 1707.

Karraker, Cyrus. *Hispaniola Treasure*. Philadelphia: University of Pennsylvania, 1934.
Lounsberry, Alice. *Sir William Phips*. New York: Scribner, 1941.
Maine Historical Society. *Collections of the Maine Historical Society*. Portland, Maine, 1887, First Series. Vol. 9.
Maine Historical Society, Portland Collections. First Serial, Vol. 9 (1887).
Masters, David. *When Ships Go Down*. London: Eyre & Spottiswoode, 1932.
Mather, Cotton. *Life of Sir William Phips*. Preface, Mark Van Doren. Roanoke Series of Americana Classics, 1929.
Millar, George. *Crossbowman's Story*. New York: Knopf, 1955.
Morgan, E. Victor. *Study of Prices and the Value of Money*. London: Historical Association, 1950.
Natural History Magazine, "Modern Treasure Isle," March 1939.
New England Quarterly, "New Light on Phips," Vol. 6 (1933).
New England Quarterly, "Rise of William Phips," Vol. 1 (1928).
New England Quarterly, "Treasure Expedition of William Phips," Vol. 5 (1932).
Prescott, William. *Conquest of Mexico*. New York: 1843.
———*Conquest of Peru*. New York: 1847.
Quarterly Journal of Economics, Vol. 29 (1915).
Rawlinson mss. A 71 (or 171), "Information from Mr. Smith on Wreck." Boston: Gay Transcripts, Massachusetts Historical Society.
Rieseberg, H. E. *I Dive for Treasure*. New York: McBride, 1942.
———*Treasure Hunter*. New York: McBride, 1945.
Scientific American Supplement, Vol. 70 (1910).
Shaw, W. A. *History of Currency* 1252–1894. London: 1896.
Sloane mss. (50 or 1070), "Log of the *James and Mary*." London: British Museum.
Snow, Edward Rowe. *True Tales of Buried Treasure*. New York: Dodd Mead, 1951.
Sparks, Jared. *Life of Phips*. Library of American Biography, Vol. 7.
Twentieth-Century Fund, "World Population and Production," 1953.
U. S. Department of Labor, Bureau of Statistics, Bulletin 604 and Supplement, 1934.
Verrill, A. H. *They Found Gold*. New York: Putnam, 1936.
White, Benjamin. *Silver*. London: Waterlow & Sons, 1920.

CHAPTER II

Agricola, Georgius. *De Re Metallica*. Translated from the Latin edition of 1556 by Herbert Clark Hoover and Lou Henry Hoover. New York: Dover, 1950.
Bancroft, H. H. *The New Pacific*. New York: Bancroft Co., 1900.

Barrows, John. *Life of Sir Francis Drake*. London: 1843.

Benson, E. F. *Sir Francis Drake*. London: John Lane, the Bodley Head, 1927.

Burney, James. *History of the Buccaneers*. London: 1816.

———— *Voyages and Discoveries in the South Seas*. London: 1803.

Crouch, Nathaniel. *The English Hero: Or, Sir Francis Drake Reviv'd*. London: 1692.

Devonshire Association for Advancement of Science, Literature and Art: Report and Transactions. Plymouth, 1912. Vol. 44 (Series 3. Vol. 4).

Drake, Sir Francis. *The World Encompassed*. Annotated by G. E. Hollingworth. London: University Tutorial Press, 1933.

Driscoll, Charles. *Doubloons*. New York: Farrar & Rinehart, 1930.

An English Garner . . . Vols. 10–11. *Voyages and Travels mainly in the Sixteenth and Seventeenth Centuries*. Westminster: A. Constable & Co., Ltd. 1903.

Exquemelin, A. O. *Buccaneers of America*. "Narratives of Sharp and Ringrose." Vol. II, Second Edition. London: 1685.

Fieldiana, "Archaeological Investigations on Island of La Plata, Ecuador," Anthropological Series, Vol. 2, #5 (Publication 56).

Hacke, William. *Collection of Original Voyages*. London: 1699.

Hakluyt Society. Works . . . #16, "The World Encompassed."

Hakluyt Society. Works . . . (Second Series) #34 (1914). Nuttall, Zelie. *New Light on Drake*.

Handy & Harman Silversmiths. *Handy Book for Manufacturers*. New York: Handy & Harman, 1955.

Kelly, F. M., & Schwabe, R. *Short History of Costume and Armor*. London: B. T. Batsford, Ltd., 1931.

Laking, Sir Guy Francis. *Record of European Arms and Armor*. London: C. Ball & Sons, 1920.

Masefield, John. *On the Spanish Main*. London: Methuen & Co., 1906.

Newton, A. P. *Colonizing Activities of the English Puritans*. New Haven: Yale University Press, 1914.

————*European Nations in the West Indies*. London: A. & C. Black, 1933.

Roberts, W. A. *The Caribbean*. New York: Bobbs-Merrill, 1940.

Verrill, A. H. *Lost Treasure*. New York: Appleton, 1930.

———— *They Found Gold*. New York: Putnam, 1936.

Wafer, Lionel. *A New Voyage and Description of the Isthmus of America*. London: 1699.

Williamson, James A. *The Age of Drake*. London: A. & C. Black, 1938.

———— *Sir Francis Drake*. London: William Collins Sons & Co., Ltd., 1951.

———— *Sir John Hawkins*. Oxford: Clarendon Press, 1927.

CHAPTER III

Ashdown, Mrs. C. H. *British Costume*. London: T. C. & E. C. Jack, 1910.

Ayres, Philip. *Voyages and Adventures of Captain Barth. Sharp*. 1684.

Burney, James. *History of Buccaneers of America*. London: 1816.

Cruikshank, Brigadier General E. A. *Life of Sir Henry Morgan*. Toronto: Macmillan Co., 1935.

Delaware Notes, Series 26 (1953).

Dickens, Charles. *Child's History of England*. Vol. II.

Encyclopaedia Britannica, Eleventh Edition, "Buccaneers."

Exquemelin, A. O. *Buccaneers of America*. First Edition. London: 1684.

Gosse, Philip. *History of Piracy*. New York: Tudor Publishing Co., 1934.

Great Britain Colonial State Papers, American and West Indies, 1213, 1826, 1827.

Great Britain Historical Mss. Commission, Report on Mss. of A. G. Finch, Vol. I.

Great Britain Statutes, Ordinance of Lords and Commons.

Hispanic American Historical Review, "The Earl of Warwick," #10 (1930).

Historical Society of Trinidad and Tobago, Public Lectures, 1938.

Hubach, Enrique. *Aspectos Geograficos & Geologicos, Y Recursos de Las Islas de San Andres Y Providencia*. Republica de Colombia Ministerio de Minas Y Petroleos, Instituto Geologico Nacional.

Innes, A. D. *Maritime and Colonial Expansion of England Under the Stuarts*. London: Sampson Low, Marston & Co., 1931.

Leslie, Charles. *A New History of Jamaica*. London: 1740.

Lindsay, Philip. *Great Buccaneer*. New York: W. Funk Co., 1951.

Masefield, John. *On the Spanish Main*. London: Methuen & Co., 1906.

Newton, A. P. *Colonizing Activities of the English Puritans*. New Haven: Yale University Press, 1914.

—— *European Nations in the West Indies*. London: A. & C. Black, 1933.

Roberts, W. A. *The Caribbean*. New York: Bobbs-Merrill, 1940.

Sir Edward Seaward's Narrative of his Shipwreck. London: 1832.

Snow, E. R. *True Tales of Pirates and Their Gold*. New York: Dodd Mead, 1953.

Southey, Thomas. *Chronological History of West Indies*. Vol. I. London: 1827.

Verrill, A. H. *In the Wake of the Buccaneers*. New York: Century Co., 1923.

—— *Lost Treasure*. New York: Appleton, 1930.

Wanguemert Y Poggio, J. *El Almirante Don Francisco*. Madrid: 1905.

West India Pamphlets. #10. *Memoires de Louis XVIII*. Art. VIII. "Sir Edward Seaward's Narrative of His Shipwreck."

Woods, Dee. *Blaze of Gold*. San Antonio: Naylor Co., 1942.

CHAPTER IV

Billings, Henry. *Man under Water*. New York: Viking Press, 1954.

Davis, Sir Robert. *Deep Diving and Submarine Operations*. London: St. Catherine Press, 1951.

Ellsberg, Commander Edward. *Men under the Sea*. New York: Dodd Mead, 1939.

Illustrated London News, October 3, 1931.

The Listener, London, July 14, 1932.

Scott, David. *The Egypt's Gold*. London: Faber & Faber, 1932.

——— *Seventy Fathoms Deep*. London: Faber & Faber, 1931.

Whyte and Hadfield. *Deep-Sea Salvage*. London: Sampson Low, Marston, 1933.

Wilkins, H. T. *Treasure Hunting*. London: Ivor Nicholson, 1932.

CHAPTER V

Braly, William C. *The Hard Way Home*. Washington: Infantry Journal Press, 1947.

Clark, Allan. "We Found the Lost Millions," *The Saturday Evening Post*, September 13, 1952.

Cross, E. R. "Navy Brings 'Em Back," *Water World*, March 1956.

Guerrero, Leon Ma. *Philippine Review*, May 1943. Manila.

Hersey, John. *Men on Bataan*. New York: Knopf, 1942.

Lee, Clark. *They Call It Pacific*. New York: Viking Press, 1943.

Life magazine, October 15, 1945.

Masters, David. *Epics of Salvage*. Boston: Little, Brown, 1954.

Morton, Major Louis. "Glory and Tragedy of Bataan," *Army Combat Forces Journal*, December 1955.

The Quan (Publication of American Defenders of Bataan and Corregidor), November 1955.

Romulo, Brigadier General Carlos. *I Saw the Fall of the Philippines*. New York: Doubleday & Co., Inc., 1943.

Triumph in the Philippines. Vol. II. "Corregidor: Of Eternal Memory." (Manuscript.) On file in Office of Chief of Military History, Washington.

U. S. Army. Brigadier General Hugh J. Casey. *Forces in the Pacific*. "Engineers of the Southwest Pacific, 1941–1945."

U. S. Army in World War II. Washington: Office of Chief of Military History. *The War in the Pacific*. Morton, Louis. "The Fall of the Philippines."

U. S. High Commissioner to the Philippine Islands. Sixth Annual Report, 1941–1942. (Also published as: Seventy-eighth Congress, First Session, House Document 111. Serial set #10828.)

————Seventh and Final Report, 1945–1946. (Also published as: Eightieth Congress, First Session, House Document 389. Serial set #11144.)

Van Landingham, Charles. "I Saw Manila Die," *The Saturday Evening Post*, September 26, 1942.

Wainwright, General Jonathan. *General Wainwright's Story*. New York: Doubleday & Co., Inc., 1946.

Willoughby, Amea. *I Was on Corregidor*. New York: Harper, 1943.

CHAPTER VI, PART I

Africana News and Notes, June, September 1945.

Birkby, Carel. *Zulu Journey*. London: F. Muller, Ltd., 1937.

Chambers Journal, December 1933.

Chilvers, Hedley. *Seven Lost Trails of Africa*. London: Cassell & Co., 1932.

Dawson, E. B. "The Treasure of the Grosvenor," *Wide World Magazine*, Vol. 50 (1923).

Rowe, J. O. "South Africa's Fabulous Treasure Hunt," *The Outspan*, August 17, 1956.

Whyte and Hadfield. *Deep-Sea Salvage*. London: Sampson Low, Marston, 1933.

CHAPTER VI, PART II*

Daily Telegraph, London, August 14, 1954.

Gunn, Neil M. "The Clans of Scotland," *Holiday*, September 1954.

Larsen, Egon, *Men under the Sea*. London: Phoenix House, 1955.

Masters, David, *When Ships Go Down*. London: Eyre & Spottiswoode, 1932.

Paine, R. D. *Book of Buried Treasure*. New York: Sturgis & Walton Co., 1911.

Pugh, Marshall, *Frogman*. New York: Scribner, 1956.

* "A few of the incidents in this section appeared in an article in the New York *Times Magazine* of August 15, 1954, "A Scotsman and His Galleon," by Nora Stirling and Ruth Adams Knight.

US R29.16b